PRINCIPLES OF
BEHAVIOR THERAPY

PRINCIPLES OF BEHAVIOR THERAPY

G. TERENCE WILSON
Rutgers University

K. DANIEL O'LEARY
State University of New York, Stony Brook

Prentice-Hall, Inc. *Englewood Cliffs, New Jersey 07632*

Library of Congress Cataloging in Publication Data

WILSON, G TERENCE (date)
   Principles of behavior therapy.

   Bibliography: p. 306
   Includes index
   1. Behavior therapy.   2. Conditioned response.
I. O'Leary, K. Daniel, joint author.
II. Title.
RC489.B4W56   616.8'914   79-21444
ISBN 0-13-701102-4

36,610

*Editorial/production supervision and interior
  design by Penny Linskey and Linda Schuman
Cover design by Miriam Recio
Manufacturing buyer: Edmund W. Leone
Photo of Dr. O'Leary by Sydney Stafford,
  Stony Brook, New York*

**Prentice-Hall Series in Social Learning Theory
Albert Bandura, Editor**

Printed in the United States of America

10 9 8 7 6 5 4 3 2

PRENTICE-HALL INTERNATIONAL, INC., *London*
PRENTICE-HALL OF AUSTRALIA PTY. LIMITED, *Sydney*
PRENTICE-HALL OF CANADA, LTD., *Toronto*
PRENTICE-HALL OF INDIA PRIVATE LIMITED, *New Delhi*
PRENTICE-HALL OF JAPAN, INC., *Tokyo*
PRENTICE-HALL OF SOUTHEAST ASIA PTE. LTD., *Singapore*
WHITEHALL BOOKS LIMITED, *Wellington, New Zealand*

To Iris Wilson and Susan O'Leary

Contents

About the Authors

G. TERENCE WILSON

G. Terence Wilson, Ph.D., State University of New York at Stony Brook, is Professor of Psychology at the Graduate School of Applied and Professional Psychology, Rutgers University. He is President-Elect of the Association for Advancement of Behavior Therapy and was a Fellow at the Center for Advanced Study in the Behavioral Sciences, Stanford, California (1976–1977). He is Editor (with Cyril Franks) of the *Annual Review of Behavior Therapy: Theory and Practice* and has coauthored several books, including *Behavior Therapy: Application and Outcome* (with K. D. O'Leary), *Evaluation of Behavior Therapy: Issues, Evidence, and Research Strategies* (with Alan Kazdin), *Behavior Therapy: Toward an Applied Clinical Science* (with Stewart Agras and Alan Kazdin), and *Effects of Psychotherapy* (with Stanley Rachman). He is Associate Editor of *Journal of Applied Behavior Analysis* and *Cognitive Therapy and Research* and a member of the editorial board of several journals, including *Journal of Consulting and Clinical Psychology* and *Contemporary Psychology.* He is also a practicing therapist and a consultant to industry on behavioral health programs.

K. Daniel O'Leary, Ph.D., University of Illinois, Urbana, is Professor and Chairman of Psychology at the State University of New York at Stony Brook. He is Editor of the *Journal of Applied Behavior Analysis,* Associate Editor of the *Journal of Abnormal Child Psychology,* and he is on the editorial board of *Journal of Consulting and Clinical Psychology.* He was President of the Experimental-Clinical Section of Clinical Psychology, A.P.A. and is a Fellow of Clinical, Developmental, and Experimental Analysis of Behavior Divisions of A.P.A. He coauthored *Classroom Management: The Successful Use of Behavior Modification* with Susan O'Leary and *Behavior Therapy: Application and Outcome* with G. Terence Wilson. Finally, he is also a practicing clinical psychologist.

K. DANIEL O'LEARY

Preface

There are several reasons why reading this book is of direct relevance to you. In teaching psychology to college undergraduates we have consistently heard the complaint that there was too much emphasis on experimental psychology in the laboratory setting, on methodology and statistics, and too little attention given to real life human behavior. Often neglected has been an analysis of the different psychological problems most of us have experienced in one form or another. Almost always absent has been a presentation of practical and effective methods for helping those of our fellow human beings who are in distress. This book also concentrates on scientific research and experimental psychology. But there is a difference. The content of the research studies concerns treatment of problems you have heard about or witnessed, such as a mentally retarded child, the juvenile delinquent, unrealistic fears or phobias, sexual inadequacy, and the inability to diet, drink less, or stop smoking. More importantly, this is a book about how psychologists and psychiatrists have made use of the findings of experimental research in attempting to cope with these human difficulties. We think that this will show the relevance of at least that part of experimental psychology that previously might have seemed to have only a remote or abstract connection to life in the real world. We hope that our enthusiasm for the potential that scientific psychology has for improving our human condition will similarly inspire students who read this text.

Behavior therapy is the application of the principles of scientific psychology to human problems. In just under 20 years of existence it has shown phenomenal growth and currently ranks as one of the major approaches in the treatment of psychological problems. Psychiatrists, clinical and school psychologists, social workers, and nursing personnel have all increasingly adopted the principles of behavior therapy. The American Psychiatric Association has endorsed behavior therapy, declaring that it has "much to offer informed clinicians in the service of modern clinical and social psychiatry." In addition to the U.S.A. and Canada, Western Europe, Australia, New Zealand, and parts of Latin America such as Brazil and Mexico are active centers of behavior research and therapy. Behavior therapy now accounts for a significant part of the psychological and psychiatric literature. Aside from the ever burgeoning publication of new books, no fewer than eight major English-speaking journals are devoted exclusively to behavior therapy. So diverse and large is the behavioral literature that there is a need for a special series—the *Annual Review of Behavior Therapy: Theory and Practice*[1]—that summarizes and reviews the field on a yearly basis.

An important emphasis of this book is on the scientific evaluation of behavior change methods. Are they effective? Do they help people? Of course, these questions apply not only to behavior therapy but to all forms of therapy from psychoanalysis to encounter groups. This is the age of public and professional accountability, of greater consumer awareness than ever before. As a prospective client requiring therapy, as a heavily burdened taxpayer supporting massive federal funding of diverse treatment facilities, or simply as a concerned citizen, you will want to know the answer to these questions. But how do you evaluate such a complex matter as therapeutic outcome? In this book we try to do more than help you evaluate behavior therapy; we describe evaluation strategies that can—and *should,* we feel—be applied to various treatment programs that purport to deal with psychological disturbances and abnormal behavior.

Related to the issue of accountability is that of ethics. Mental health services in general and behavior modification in particular have sometimes been attacked as unethical and even illegal. *Who* decides *what* behavior should be changed and in *whom?* Although abuses have undoubtedly occurred, behavior therapy has addressed the ethical issue more directly perhaps than any other therapeutic approach. Procedures have been identified that can be followed to enhance personal freedom and growth and to minimize the risk of future abuses of psychiatric patients. Again, while we discuss these procedures in the specific context of behavior therapy, they have broad applicability to all other treatment approaches.

Last but not least, this book might help you to understand better your own behavior and the influences that regulate it. *Self*-control is a key focus of behavior therapy. Many behavioral methods have been delineated well enough that simply reading about them occasionally enables you to help yourself—and others—change. Although this is not a practical manual on behavior change, the principles described are those on which many popular self-help methods are based. Two examples of how a book of this nature might promote behavior change and personal understanding can be drawn from reactions to our previous text, *Behavior Therapy: Application and Outcome.*[2]

One of the editors of the book learned how to toilet train her child successfully after reading our description of the relevant behavioral procedure.

[1]Franks, C. M., and Wilson, G.T. *Annual review of behavior therapy: Theory and practice,* Vols. 1–7. New York: Brunner/Mazel, 1973–1979.
[2]O'Leary, K.D., and Wilson, G.T. *Behavior therapy: Application and outcome.* Englewood Cliffs, N.J.: Prentice-Hall, 1975.

Then there was the college junior who had confided to his parents that he was homosexual and came under severe pressure to enter into therapy designed to change him into a heterosexual. On reading our book he discovered that homosexuality is not a form of mental illness, that homosexuals can lead happy, fulfilling lives, and that most behavior therapists assist clients to choose their preferred life style rather than arbitrarily coercing adoption of the therapist's personal prejudices. A couple of sessions with such a therapist resolved the family crisis, alleviated the student's severe guilt, and helped the parents accept the mature decision that it was their son's prerogative to decide his sexual orientation.

Acknowledgments

Many individuals contributed to this book. Hillary Turkewitz extensively edited many of the chapters and participated in substantive conversations regarding principles and issues. Etienne Perold and Carol Treanor read several chapters and made helpful suggestions about style and presentation. Bea Porter and Susan Geiss (both State University at Stony Brook) and the following reviewers—Peter D. Balsam (Barnard College), C. Peter Bankart (Wabash College), James Couch (James Madison University), D. Balfour Jeffrey (University of Montana), Jeffrey C. Levy (Seton Hall University), Richard J. Morris (University of Arizona), Grover C. Richards (Georgia Southern College), Gary A. Szakmary (Case Western Reserve University), and Sherman Yan (Essex Community College)—provided useful comments on the entire manuscript. Ruth Shepard and Barbara Honig provided invaluable assistance in editing and typing the manuscript and in soliciting permissions to reprint material. Dr. Raymond C. Rosen of the Department of Psychiatry, Rutgers Medical School, was the co-therapist in the case of Mr. B, the exhibitionist, whose treatment is described in Chapter 1, and we thank him for permission to use this clinical illustration. We are particularly indebted to Albert Bandura, the general editor of the Prentice-Hall series on social learning theory who provided critical, detailed substantive feedback on each chapter.

One of us (GTW) completed several chapters while a Fellow at the Center for Advanced Study in the Behavioral Sciences, Stanford, California, an opportunity made possible through the financial support of the Foundations Fund for Research in Psychiatry, the National Institute for Mental Health (Grant Number 1T32 NH14581), and Rutgers University. Special thanks are due the staff and director of the Center, Gardner Lindzey, for providing a congenial social and intellectual environment in which to work. Numerous discussions with members of the "behavior therapy group" at the Center (Stewart Agras, Nate Azrin, Alex George, Alan Kazdin, Walter Mischel, and Jack Rachman) contributed directly and indirectly to this volume, although the ultimate responsibility for the views expressed here is ours.

Last, but hardly least, we express our gratitude to our wives, Elaine and Susan, for their constant support and encouragement in the writing of this book.

G. TERENCE WILSON
Rutgers University

K. DANIEL O'LEARY
State University of New York
at Stony Brook

PRINCIPLES OF
BEHAVIOR THERAPY

1

Behavior Therapy: Description and Definition

The Case of Mr. B

Mr. B was a thirty-five-year-old man, married, with two sons aged eight and five years, from a successful, middle-class family. He was a persistent exhibitionist whose pattern over the past twenty years had been to expose his genitals to unsuspecting adult women as often as five or six times a week. Fifteen years of intermittent psychoanalytic treatment, several hospitalizations at psychiatric institutions in the U.S.A., and a six-year prison sentence for his deviant sexual behavior had failed to help Mr. B change his unwanted, but apparently uncontrollable, behavior. He was currently under grand jury indictment for exposing himself to an adult woman in the presence of a group of young children. There was every prospect that he would receive a life sentence in view of his repeated offenses and his numerous failures to show improvement as a result of lengthy and costly psychiatric treatment. At least one psychiatrist had diagnosed him as untreatable and had advocated his removal from free society. Shortly before coming to trial, Mr. B's psychoanalyst referred him to one of the current authors as a last resort to see if behavior therapy might succeed where traditional forms of treatment had failed.

Mr. B was hospitalized and treated on a daily basis for six weeks, a total of about 50 hours of direct therapist contact. After spending some time to develop a trusting personal relationship so that Mr. B would feel comfortable in disclosing intimate details about his problems, the therapist conducted a series of intensive interviews to ferret out the *specific* environmental circumstances and psychological factors that were currently maintaining Mr. B's deviant behavior. With his permission, his parents and wife were also interviewed to obtain more information and to corroborate aspects of his own description of the development and present status of the problem. In order to obtain a sample of his actual exhibitionist behavior, a situation was arranged in a hospital office that closely resembled the conditions under which Mr. B would normally expose himself in real life. Two attractive female professional colleagues of the therapist were seated in a simulated doctor's waiting room, reading magazines, and Mr. B was instructed to enter, sit across from them, and expose himself. Despite the artificial setting, Mr. B proceeded to expose himself, became highly aroused, and nearly masturbated to orgasm. This entire sequence was videotaped, and objective measures of Mr. B's response to this scene as well as to various other adult sexual stimuli were obtained by recording the degree of penile erection he showed while observing the videotape and selected other erotic filmed material.

On the basis of this behavioral assessment, a detailed picture was developed of the chain, or sequence, of internal and external stimuli and responses that preceded his acts of exposure. For example, a woman standing alone at a bus-stop as he drove past in his car often triggered a pattern of thoughts and images that caused him to circle the block and eventually expose himself.

2

Alternatively, the anger he experienced after a heated argument with his father, which he could not handle, could also elicit the urge to expose himself. The more Mr. B thought about exposing himself, the more obsessed he became with a particular woman and her anticipated reactions. Since he tuned out everything except his immediate feelings and intentions, he became oblivious to the consequences of his actions. His behavior was out of control. Mr. B hoped that his victim would express some form of approval, either by smiling or making some sexually toned comment. Although this did happen periodically, most women ignored him, and some called the police.

Not atypically, Mr. B's idea about behavior therapy was that he would be passively "conditioned" so that his problem would disappear. The therapist systematically disabused him of this notion by explaining that success could be achieved only with his active cooperation in all phases of the treatment program. He was told that there was no automatic "cure" for his problem, but he could learn new behavioral self-control strategies, which, if practiced conscientiously and applied at the right time, would enable him to avoid further deviant behavior.

As in most complex clinical cases, treatment was multifaceted, meaning that a number of different techniques were employed to modify different components of the disorder. His own beliefs about his problem were that he was suddenly seized by a desire, which he could not consciously control, and that his subsequent actions were "involuntary." Analysis of the sequence of events that always preceded exposure altered Mr. B's expectation that he was unable to control his behavior. He was shown how he himself was instrumental in transforming a relatively weak initial urge into an overpowering compulsion to expose because he attended to inappropriate thoughts and feelings and engaged in behaviors that increased, rather than decreased, the temptation. It was explained that the time to break this behavioral chain, to implement the self-control strategies he would acquire as a result of treatment, was at the beginning when the urge was weakest. In order to do this, he would have to learn to be aware of his thoughts, feelings, and behavior, and to recognize the early warning danger signals.

Specific tension states had often precipitated exposure. Accordingly, Mr. B was trained to reduce this tension through the procedure of progressive relaxation. Instead of exposing himself, he learned to relax, an activity incompatible with exposure behavior. Assertion training was used to help Mr. B cope constructively with feelings of anger and to express them appropriately, rather than to seek relief through deviant behavior. Using role-playing, the therapist modeled an appropriate reaction and then provided Mr. B with reinforcing feedback as he rehearsed progressively more effective ways of responding to anger-inducing events. In covert modeling Mr. B was taught to imagine himself in a range of situations that customarily had resulted in exposure, and to see himself engaging in alternative responses to exposure, for example, relaxing away tension, expressing anger appropriately, reminding himself of the consequences of being caught, or simply walking away from a tempting situation.

Aversion conditioning was used to decrease the positive appeal exposure had for him. During repeated presentations of the videotape of his exposure scene, a loud, subjectively aversive police siren was piped over earphones he was wearing on an unpredictable schedule. In addition to this classical conditioning procedure in which Mr. B had no control over the presentation of the aversive stimulus, an avoidance and/or escape contingency was introduced at some sessions. By shouting "stop!" as soon as he heard the siren begin, Mr. B could terminate it. Whereas Mr. B initially found watching the videotape pleasurable and sexually arousing, he progressively lost all sexual interest in it. He reported that he experienced marked difficulty in concentrating on the scene because he began to anticipate the disruptive—and given his personal social learning history, an understandably frightening—police siren in connection with thoughts of exposure. The siren was also paired systematically with a range of fantasies of different situations in which he would expose himself. In addition to the siren, Mr. B learned how to associate self-administered aversive cognitive events with deviant thoughts or images. For example, imagery of an aversive event, such as being apprehended by the police, was coupled with thoughts of exposure. Periodically, Mr. B's sexual arousal to the videotape was assessed directly by measuring penile erection in order to provide an evaluation of his progress.

Mr. B had exposed himself only to women he did not know personally. The final treatment method consisted of asking Mr. B to expose his penis in front of a panel of three male and three female therapists. This procedure was extremely aversive to him and was designed to associate the act of exposure with unpleasant consequences.

Following every session with the therapist, Mr. B was given specific homework assignments to complete. These included self-monitoring and recording any urges to expose himself, so as to ensure awareness about any signs of reverting back to old habits. Other assignments involved practicing relaxation exercises and recording the degree to which the relaxation was associated with reduced tension; rehearsing the association of aversive imagery with fantasies of exposure, recording the intensity of the aversive imagery and the clarity of the exposure fantasies on ten-point rating scales; and engaging in assertive behavior where appropriate during interactions with other patients and staff on his assigned ward. Direct observation of his interpersonal behavior on the hospital ward provided an index of his utilization of assertive behavior.

Finally, after speaking with the therapist about cooperation and apparent progress in the treatment program, Mr. B's wife agreed to several joint therapy sessions which used behavioral methods for improving marital communication and interaction. Although the behavioral assessment had indicated that Mr. B's exhibitionist behavior was not directly caused by an unhappy marriage or lack of sexual satisfaction from his wife, the rationale was that improvement in these spheres of functioning would help consolidate and support his self-control over deviant sexual behavior acquired through the rest of the treatment program.

On leaving the hospital at the end of treatment, Mr. B continued to self-monitor any thoughts or feelings about exposing himself, to relax systematically, to assert himself, and to rehearse the pairing of aversive imagery with thoughts of exposure. Every week he mailed these records to the therapist for analysis, a procedure designed to generalize treatment-produced improvement to the real world and to maintain self-control over time. Another facet of this maintenance strategy was a series of booster sessions that were scheduled approximately four months after therapy in which he returned to the hospital for a week of intensive treatment along the same lines as described above.

In large part owing to the therapist's strong recommendation, the court gave him a suspended sentence. A two-year follow-up showed that Mr. B had refrained from any exhibitionism, had experienced very few such desires, and felt confident in his newly found ability to control any urges that might arise.

The Case of Diane T

Diane T was a nineteen-year-old college junior who had sought therapy at the psychological clinic of the university on the advice of a professor in whom she had confided. Struggling to keep back her tears, Diane slowly began to tell her therapist of her unhappiness—of her sense of loneliness, social insecurity, anxiety, and depression. The strain of her personal problems was beginning to interfere with her sleep and with her school work. An otherwise excellent student, Diane was finding it increasingly difficult to concentrate or study because of persistent anxiety and overpowering negative feelings about herself. A shy person, she had become almost completely withdrawn socially. This accentuated her sense of loneliness and depression.

The therapist spent the first session or two getting to know Diane and creating a climate of trust and cooperation, two indispensable elements of all effective therapy. Gradually the therapist began to pinpoint the specific conditions that were currently responsible for Diane's distress. Much of this information was obtained during a detailed, structured clinical interview. In addition, the therapist asked Diane to become an active participant in the therapeutic process by keeping a daily diary in which she was to record events relevant to her problem and her reactions to them. Diane's self-monitoring provided the therapist with the sort of specific information he needed to assess the variables influencing her behavior. It also helped Diane to become aware of the reasons for her unhappiness.

A focal point in Diane's problems was her shyness in social interactions. She was overly self-conscious, unable to express her feelings publicly, and afraid to try to get close to people, especially men she considered attractive. She had few friends at college and hardly ever dated. Her negative opinion of herself and her depression were closely related to this interpersonal problem. Diane's continual worries about her perceived inadequacies and her constant tendency to put herself down were interfering with other aspects of her life.

As a start, the therapist had Diane participate in a program of relaxation training to reduce her overall level of anxiety, overcome her insomnia, and improve her mental concentration. Then, using the technique of systematic desensitization, the therapist asked Diane to imagine anxiety-eliciting interpersonal situations while she was deeply relaxed. This pairing of relaxation with increasingly threatening scenes led to a decrease in her anxiety over several sessions. At this point Diane undertook an extensive program of assertion training in which she learned to be more expressive and relate more positively to members of both sexes. She was given specific "homework" assignments in which she engaged in carefully planned and rehearsed assertive actions between therapy sessions. As Diane became more assertive, her self-esteem increased and she became more self-confident. In order to counteract remaining feelings of personal inadequacy and the negative interpretation she often placed on various life experiences, Diane was given self-instructional training. In this method she was taught to identify negative thoughts involving a put down of herself and to substitute more constructive thoughts about her coping successfully with difficult situations.

Approximately three months after entering into therapy, Diane was able to report a dramatic reduction in anxiety and depression. Her insomnia had disappeared, and she was able to concentrate on her studies once more. Most importantly, she had gained in personal confidence and was less anxious and more active in social interactions. She had begun to date frequently and had established a satisfying relationship with a boyfriend. Although she still had an occasional tendency to lapse into overly negative assessments of herself, she was able to catch herself in the act and reinstate more constructive and balanced self-appraisals of her behavior.

The Case of Johnny K

Johnny was a fourth-grader who was having problems with school. He was inattentive in class; he often left his seat, interfering with other children and interrupting the teacher; he was often involved in fights; he seemed to lack any motivation for schoolwork and had begun to fall far behind in subjects like reading and math. In short, Johnny displayed all the academic and behavioral difficulties of what has traditionally been labeled a conduct disorder child.

Accordingly, Johnny's teacher referred him to a behavioral treatment program that was offered by a nearby university psychological treatment center. In making a behavioral assessment, the therapist assigned to the case first contacted Johnny's parents to obtain detailed information on present and background problems, as well as any other family conflicts. Subsequently, the therapist met with Johnny to establish rapport and to explain the nature of the program. This was followed by several visits to Johnny's school, where the therapist discussed the problem with the teacher, obtained standardized ratings by the teacher of different aspects of Johnny's behavior, and observed Johnny's behavior as well as the teacher's management of Johnny and the other children during an actual class. Prior to this visit to the school, an undergraduate student, who had been trained to do behavioral observation as part of the university treatment program, had gathered standardized recordings of Johnny's behavior in the classroom. In addition, Johnny's performance on the reading and math sections of the California Achievement Test (CAT) was assessed. Lastly, with the teacher's help, the therapist devised a daily report card that listed four key problem behaviors (for example, bringing in homework, completing assignments) that would be evaluated daily by the teacher.

Since Johnny's difficulties occurred in the school setting, treatment emphasized the modification of his problem behavior in the classroom itself. Under the therapist's direction, the teacher used positive reinforcement to increase improved work habits and appropriate social behavior. For example, completion of assignments was consistently rewarded with teacher praise and special attention. Undesired behavior was largely ignored. However, if Johnny's behavior was too disruptive, the teacher made sure to reprimand Johnny softly, so that it did not draw the attention of other children. Moreover, if Johnny showed clearly specified and objectively defined improvement on the two social and two academic target behaviors that were evaluated by the teacher on his daily report card, his parents were taught to praise him and allow him a special privilege at home that day after school. Extra television viewing and longer play periods with his friend next door were the privileges or rewards Johnny chose most frequently.

The therapist also devoted time consulting with Johnny's mother in order to coordinate the report card system and instruct her in how best to assist Johnny with his homework and special tutorial sessions. Specifically, the therapist modeled how to interact with Johnny while his mother watched. Thereafter the therapist provided feedback to Johnny's mother as she helped him with his homework for the next day. As the behavioral assessment had indicated that Johnny's parents predominantly used loud, angry scolding or corporal punishment to control him, the therapist explained and demonstrated the value of praising and rewarding appropriate behavior and ignoring bad behavior. If punishment were necessary, Johnny's mother was shown how to use restricted television or less play time with friends as a negative consequence. At most treatment sessions, the therapist met with Johnny alone for some time. These meetings were devoted to monitoring Johnny's feelings about the program and maximizing his cooperation by making him feel part of a mutual effort to help him improve at school.

A part of the therapist's time with Johnny's mother consisted of providing emotional support and help in overcoming increasing marital conflict with her husband. Unhappy with his job, he had been drinking heavily, which led to frequent arguments. In the course of these arguments Mr. K blamed his wife for Johnny's psychological problems. Worried over her husband's excessive drinking and feeling guilty because of his criticism of her as a mother, Mrs. K had begun to feel that she was unable to cope with a deteriorating situation. As a result, she had initially expressed doubt whether she could successfully implement the various procedures the therapist was asking her to follow with Johnny. At several joint sessions arranged by the therapist, the importance of the parents working together to remedy their son's difficulties was emphasized. Although Johnny's parents' problems were never the primary focus of the treatment program, strategies for improving marital communication and arriving at a more constructive, sharing relationship were discussed, together with specific suggestions on how Mr. K might cope with problems on his job and reduce his drinking.

Assured of her husband's support of her efforts with Johnny, Mrs. K conscientiously followed the treatment program. In all, the therapist spent approximately 20 hours of direct contact with the teacher and the parents from March to June. During the summer recess, a certified teacher from the treatment program met with Mrs. K on three occasions to encourage her tutorial efforts, to monitor Johnny's progress, and to provide motivating material for the tutorial sessions.

An evaluation of Johnny's progress midway through the following year showed that his disruptive classroom behavior had decreased significantly to the point where he was on a par with other children in the class. He had gained 1.4 years in reading comprehension and six months in math, as measured by the CAT, and his grades were satisfactory. Johnny seemed to have a new positive attitude toward school, and his teacher felt that the situation was well in hand.

The case studies of Mr. B, Diane T, and Johnny K illustrate some of the clinical applications of behavioral principles to psychological disorders, and they will be referred to repeatedly throughout this book to illustrate distinguishing features and principles of behavior therapy. Of course, a full description and analysis of the clinical practice of behavior therapy is beyond the scope of this book. (The student is referred to more directly clinical material in the list of *Suggested Readings* at the end of this chapter.) The main concern here is with the scientific foundations and principles of behavior therapy. However, in the chapters that follow we continually try to illustrate the applied or human relevance of the research on the mechanisms and methods of behavior change by using appropriate examples from clinical practice.

The clinical examples described above are broadly representative of how a behavior therapist would attempt to modify complex behavioral problems today. But before we discuss in detail the defining characteristics of contemporary behavior therapy, it is necessary to review the relatively brief but controversial history of behavior therapy as an applied science of clinical behavior change. A full understanding of the various principles and procedures that comprise the field can best be obtained by placing them in their historical context.

A Brief History of Behavior Therapy[1]

JOSEPH WOLPE IN SOUTH AFRICA

The contemporary origins of behavior therapy can be traced to separate but related developments in the 1950s in three countries. In 1958 Wolpe's book *Psychotherapy by Reciprocal Inhibition* presented the procedural details and results of his application of learning principles of adult neurotic disorders. Wolpe (1958) introduced several therapeutic techniques based on Pavlov's (1927) conditioning principles, Hull's (1943) stimulus-response (S–R) learning theory, and his own experimental research on fear reduction in laboratory animals. *Neurotic anxiety* was regarded as the causal agent in phobias and all neurotic reactions; it was defined as a persistent response of the autonomic nervous system that was acquired through the process of classical conditioning. (The emotions, such as fear and anger, are in large part a function of autonomic nervous system arousal.) According to Wolpe, phobic reactions are unusually resistant to extinction. In order to extinguish neurotic anxiety, special methods are required, whose theoretical mechanisms are called *reciprocal inhibition*. He hypothesized that anxiety could be neutralized if "a response antagonistic to anxiety can be made to occur in the presence of the anxiety-evoking stimuli so that it is accompanied by the complete or partial suppression of the anxiety response" (Wolpe 1958, p. 71). In a now famous sequel to Watson and Rayner's (1920) demonstration of the acquisition of a phobic reaction by a healthy eleven-month-old child, Mary Cover Jones (1924) used learning principles to eliminate fear in a young child. Peter was a thirty-four-month-old child with an irrational fear of rabbits. Peter was placed in the relaxing surrounds of his playroom, with other nonfearful children present, and given something to eat that he enjoyed. The idea was that the response of eating in a comfortable setting would suppress the conditioned fear re-

---

[1]The term "behavior therapy" is used synonymously with "behavior modification" in the present book. Although some writers have distinguished between these two terms, there has been no consistent use, and little has been gained in the process (Wilson, 1978e).

sponse. The rabbit, or feared stimulus, was then introduced into the room and gradually brought closer and closer to Peter until he would touch it without showing any signs of discomfort. Wolpe (1958) used this learning principle to develop the treatment technique of *systematic desensitization* that subsequently became one of the best known methods of behavior therapy. Systematic desensitization was one of the means used to treat Diane T in the case study described above.

The most dramatic aspect of Wolpe's (1958) book was his claim that 90 percent of his patients were either "cured" or "markedly improved." Moreover, this unprecedented success rate was apparently accomplished, not after years and years of therapy as necessitated by psychoanalysis, but within a few months, or even weeks. Significantly, in his work in South Africa, Wolpe also influenced A. Lazarus and S. Rachman, both of whom became leading figures in the development of behavior therapy.

HANS EYSENCK IN ENGLAND

A second landmark in the development of behavior therapy as an alternative approach to the traditional psychoanalytic model was the research and writings of Eysenck and his students at the Institute of Psychiatry of London University in England. In a seminal paper published in 1959, Eysenck defined behavior therapy as the application of modern learning theory to the treatment of behavioral and emotional disorders. In particular, Eysenck emphasized the principles and procedures of Pavlov and Hull, as well as learning theorists such as Mowrer (1947) and Miller (1948). *Behavior* therapy was said to be a scientific approach based on experimentally demonstrated methods that were more effective than traditional *psycho*therapy. The latter was characterized as unscientific in nature, based on purely speculative theories and procedures, and lacking any acceptable evidence of its efficacy. In sum, according to Eysenck, behavior therapy was an applied science, the defining feature of which was that it is testable and falsifiable. A *testable* theory is one that can be specified with sufficient precision so that it can be subjected to experimental investigation. A theory that is *falsifiable* is one that specifies experimental conditions that could result in the theory being disproved or falsified. Eysenck argued that in contrast to learning theory, psychoanalysis was too vaguely formulated to be really testable and that it was impossible to identify conditions under which it could be falsified.

In 1963 Eysenck and Rachman established the first scientific journal devoted exclusively to developments in behavior therapy—*Behaviour Research and Therapy.* As a result of the continuing research and writings of Eysenck and Rachman and their colleagues at the Institute of Psychiatry of London, this has remained one of the foremost centers of behavior therapy in the world.

B.F. SKINNER IN THE U.S.A.

The third major development in the emergence of behavior therapy in the 1950s was the growth of operant conditioning in the U.S.A. and the extension of operant principles to human problems. Particularly significant in this respect was Skinner's (1953) book *Science and Human Behavior*. In this book Skinner criticized the psychoanalytic approach and presented a conceptualization of psychotherapy in behavioral terms. The following excerpt captures the essence of Skinner's position:

> The field of psychotherapy is rich in explanatory fictions. Behavior itself has not been accepted as subject matter in its own right, but only as an indication of *something wrong somewhere else.* The task of therapy is said to be to remedy an inner illness of which the behavioral manifestations are merely "symptoms" . . . the condition to be corrected is called "neurotic," and the thing to be attacked by psychotherapy is then identified as a "neurosis." The term no longer carries its original implication of a derangement of the nervous system, but it is nevertheless an unfortunate example of an explanatory fiction. It has encouraged the therapist to avoid specifying the behavior to be corrected or showing why it is disadvantageous or dangerous. By suggesting a single cause for multiple disorders it has implied a uniformity which is not to be found in the data. Above all, it has encouraged the belief that psychotherapy consists of removing inner causes of mental illness, as the surgeon removes an inflamed appendix or cancerous growth or as indigestible food is purged from the body . . . It is not an inner cause of behavior but the behavior itself which—in the medical analogy of catharsis —must be "got out of the system." (Skinner, 1953)

This emphasis on accepting observable *behavior* as the critical subject matter of therapeutic change was an important milestone in the growth of behavior therapy. Philosophically, Skinner's operant conditioning position was one of *radical behaviorism,* in which overt behavior is regarded as the only acceptable subject of scientific investigation. The extent to which Skinner takes account of subjective experience in his formulation of behavior has generated considerable controversy. The problem does not lie in whether Skinner recognizes the existence of private, subjective events, such as images, thoughts, and feelings. He does. The important question is not whether subjective experience exists but what role it plays in the regulation of human behavior. Skinner (1963) himself has stated that private events should be included in an experimental analysis of behavior. For example, consider the following statement: "It is particularly important that a science of behavior face the problem of privacy . . . An adequate science of behavior must consider events taking place within the skin of the organism . . . as part of the behavior itself" (Skinner 1963, p. 953). However, it is clear that this recognition of the role of private events in behavior has always been carefully limited in Skinner's behaviorism. The Skinnerian or operant conditioning interpretation of private events is discussed at several points throughout the rest of this book. Suffice it to state here that in terms of the Skinnerian view, subjective processes such as thoughts or images can never exert a causal effect on behavior. Rather, they are events which are correlated with behavior that is a function of external consequences. In its strict form, the operant conditioning viewpoint assumes that apart from genetic influences, human behavior is controlled exclusively by environmental events that are ultimately beyond personal control.

Another defining characteristic of the operant approach has been its methodology, with its emphasis on the study of the individual organism. Repeated objective measurement of a single subject under highly controlled conditions has been the hallmark of operant conditioning methodology. Skinner rejected statistical comparisons between groups of subjects, arguing that group averages do not adequately reflect the actual behavior of individual subjects. His approach became known as the *experimental analysis of behavior,* a term used to distinguish it from the traditional scientific strategy of the statistical analysis of group data. In a derivation from this term, the extension of operant methodology to the modification of human problems subsequently was referred to as *applied behavior analysis.*

In addition to a set of philosophical assumptions about behavior and a methodology for studying it, the operant approach provided a number of learning principles that have had a decisive impact on the field. In terms of the operant approach, behavior is a function of its environmental consequences. Behavior is strengthened by positive and negative reinforcement; it is weakened by punishment. *Positive reinforcement* refers to an increase in the frequency of a response that is followed by a favorable event. For example, in the case of Johnny K, described earlier in this chapter, the teacher's use of praise whenever Johnny behaved well and the parents' rewards of playing time or T.V. when Johnny received a satisfactory report card were both instances of positive reinforcement. Notice that reinforcement involves a contingency between behavior and the reinforcing event. *If* Johnny behaved well, *then* he received the reward. Or put differently, no behavior, then no reward. *Negative reinforcement* refers to an increase in behavior as a result of avoiding or escaping from an aversive event that would have occurred had the behavior not been emitted. For example, Mr. B's shouting "stop!" in order to terminate the aversive police siren was an instance of negative reinforcement. *Punishment* is the presentation of an aversive event or the removal of a positive event contingent on a response that results in a decrease in the frequency of that response. In the case of Johnny K, the teacher's soft reprimand and the parents' denial of his favorite T.V. program were instances of punishment. These and related operant conditioning principles are discussed in greater detail in Chaps. 4 and 5.

Behavior Therapy: A Scientific Revolution?

There are several reasons why behavior therapy developed as it did in the 1950s. Up to that time psychoanalysis and derivative psychodynamic approaches had totally dominated clinical psychology and psychiatry. There had been previous applications of learning principles to behavioral problems, including Watson and Rayner's (1920) and Mary Cover Jones' (1924) pioneering investigations of the acquisition and extinction of phobic responses in young children. However, these were isolated events that had no impact on psychotherapy, partly because conditioning principles, derived as they were from animal laboratory research, were rejected as too simplistic and irrelevant to the treatment of human problems.

In the post World War II era the position began to change, and dissatisfaction with psychodynamic psychotherapy began to be expressed. In one of the most controversial articles in the history of clinical psychology, Eysenck (1952) concluded that no scientific evidence existed to support the widely accepted position that psychotherapy was effective. The onus, he suggested, was on psychotherapists to justify their continued practice. Eysenck's criticism sparked a bitter and continuing controversy. Yet Levitt (1957) echoed Eysenck's conclusion (based on adult patients) in his similarly negative evaluation of psychoanalytic treatment of children.

But criticism is not enough. The history of science has shown convincingly that a theory is abandoned only if there is a superior alternative. One alternative was an attempt to integrate psychoanalytic theory with learning theory. Dollard and Miller (1950), for example, translated psychoanalytic theory and therapy into the language of S–R learning theory. This only helped to perpetuate psychodynamic therapy since they were merely reinterpreting the psychotherapeutic status quo, rather than advancing different concepts and new procedures.

The other alternative was embodied in the beginnings of behavior therapy in the late 1950s. Behavior therapy was based on innovative conceptions of the determinants of behavior that shifted the focus to different causes and methods of treatment. This alternative model of the causes and treatment of clinical disorders was based on the findings and methods of scientific psychology and represented an explicit attempt to bridge the gap between the experimental laboratory and the clinic. Krasner (1971) has likened this switch from the prescientific psychodynamic model to an applied science position as a scientific revolution, or what the philosopher Kuhn (1962) has called a paradigm clash, that is, the confrontation of one model of abnormal behavior and its treatment with another radically different and competing model. According to Kuhn, the decision to change paradigms is determined not only by professional insecurity deriving from the failure of existing rules and procedures, but

13

also by the availability of an alternative paradigm to take its place. The emergence of behavior therapy during the late 1950s was the product of the convergence of these two forces.

These early developments in behavior therapy in the late 1950s represented an accommodation of interests rather than an identity of views. The dominant psychoanalytic establishment was the common foe, and its shortcomings were emphasized. Aside from the natural bond that derives from concerted opposition to a common enemy, the different approaches of Wolpe, Eysenck, and Skinner had some common fundamental assumptions, such as the commitment to an applied science. Although it received little attention at the time, there were also important differences in the type of problems they treated, the methods they used, and most importantly, in the assumptions about human behavior under which they operated.

As behavior therapy developed and matured throughout the 1960s and 1970s, these theoretical differences became more evident. Behavior therapy today is considerably more sophisticated and complex than it was in its earlier stages. A simple definition of behavior therapy in terms of conditioning principles is now outdated. As the clinical case illustrations in the beginning of this chapter make clear, the current practice of behavior therapy goes well beyond the application of classical and operant conditioning principles that were derived from laboratory research with rats and pigeons.

Current Conceptual Approaches Within Behavior Therapy

There are different conceptual approaches within contemporary behavior therapy. These approaches are summarized next. It is important to remember that while these approaches can be separated, they are not necessarily in opposition to each other and may be seen as different emphases, rather than distinctly different approaches. After these different approaches are described we shall indicate how they share important common assumptions.

APPLIED BEHAVIOR ANALYSIS

This approach is philosophically consistent with Skinner's (1953) radical behaviorism and relies upon the principles and procedures of operant conditioning. It has been used primarily on client populations with limited cognitive capacities and where considerable environmental control can be brought to bear on the problem behavior. Thus these operant techniques have been used extensively with young children, retarded persons, and institutionalized psychotic patients.

THE NEOBEHAVIORISTIC STIMULUS-RESPONSE APPROACH

This approach derives from the pioneering contributions of Wolpe and Eysenck and is an attempt to apply the S–R learning theories of Pavlov, Guthrie, Hull, Mowrer, and Miller to the treatment of clinical problems. Unlike the nonmediational nature of applied behavior analysis or operant conditioning in which the focus is exclusively on observable behavior, it includes an emphasis on *mediational* variables in the explanation and modification of human behavior. For example, neurotic disorders are assumed to be caused by an underlying fear or anxiety drive. Anxiety is a hypothetical construct that cannot be observed directly. Systematic desensitization (see the case of Diane T above) is a technique that has been closely associated with this approach and is directed towards extinguishing the anxiety that is believed to be maintaining phobic behaviors.

Although treatment techniques include private or symbolic processes, such as asking the client to imagine an anxiety-eliciting situation, as in systematic desensitization, these methods have always been defined in terms of stimulus and response events. Cognitive formulations of these mediational processes have been consistently rejected. This emphasis on conditioning as opposed to cognitions can be traced to the early emphasis on principles from the animal conditioning laboratory and the initial reaction of behaviorism and behavior therapy against the mentalistic concepts of traditional psychodynamic approaches.

COGNITIVE BEHAVIOR MODIFICATION

This is the most recent approach within behavior therapy. It rests on the fundamental assumption of the importance of cognitive or symbolic processes in the development, maintenance, and modification of abnormal behavior (see Mahoney, 1974). Important concepts in this approach include a person's subjective perceptions of events, interpretations and attributions of one's own behavior, thought patterns, self-statements, and cognitive strategies. The treatment techniques that best characterize it are known collectively as *cognitive restructuring*. The common denominator among these methods is the importance attributed to faulty or irrational thought patterns. The faulty thought patterns or self-defeating self-verbalizations are said to derive from inaccurate or distorted interpretations clients make about the world and the life situations they experience. Therapy is directed towards identifying these self-defeating interpretations and replacing them with more adaptive interpretations. The methods used to accomplish this goal vary considerably from purely cognitive means, such as rational argument and logical analysis, to explicit behavioral strategies.

15

SOCIAL LEARNING THEORY

In his now classic text *Principles of Behavior Modification,* published in 1969, Bandura presented the most comprehensive and sophisticated account of behavior therapy to date within the conceptual framework of social learning theory. Each of the conceptual approaches summarized above places primary emphasis on one dimension of psychological functioning to the relative neglect of the others. Thus applied behavior analysis is concerned with observable, overt behavior. The Wolpean, neobehavioristic approach emphasizes classical conditioning of responses of the autonomic nervous system. Cognitive behavior modification has focused preeminently on the role of faulty thought patterns in clinical disorders. One of the advantages of the social learning approach is that it integrates these three separate regulatory systems in a theoretically consistent framework (Bandura, 1977b). In terms of social learning analysis, some response patterns are regulated primarily by external stimulus events and are affected largely by paired experiences. The influence of environmental consequences, which is the main focus of operant conditioning, constitutes a second form of behavioral regulation. The third and most important system of regulatory influence is assumed to operate through cognitive mediational processes.

According to social learning theory, the influence of environmental events on the acquisition and regulation of behavior is largely determined by cognitive processes. These cognitive processes are based on prior experience and determine what environmental influences are attended to, how they are perceived, whether they will be remembered, and how they might affect future action.[2] Symbolic modeling is one of the best known and most widely used methods derived from the social learning approach. In modeling, learning is assumed to occur through coding of representational processes based upon exposure to instructional, observational, or imagined material. Learning occurs through observation alone without the need for direct reinforcement of the specific behavior that is acquired.

Psychodynamic theories assume that behavior is a product of largely autonomous unconscious forces within the individual. From an operant conditioning perspective, behavior is a function of the environment. As Skinner (1971) put it, "a person does not act upon the world, the world acts upon him" (p. 211). Both of these views are one-sided or unidirectional causal models of

[2]An operant conditioner would explain "what events are attended to, how they are perceived, whether they will be remembered, and how they might affect future action" as a function of the person's past reinforcement history in different situations. The relative merits of focusing on current cognitive events as opposed to past reinforcement history in behavioral treatment are discussed in Chapter 9. For the present, note that the concept of past reinforcement history introduces explanatory events that cannot be currently observed. In short, in invoking the role of past reinforcement history (an unobserved class of events), operant conditioning becomes *inferential* in nature.

16

behavior. They can be shown schematically as follows: $B=f(P,E)$, where B = behavior; f = function; P = cognitive and other internal events, and E = the external environment. The problems with this position have been summed up by Bandura (1978) as follows:

> Personal and environmental factors do not function as independent determinants; rather they determine each other. Nor can "persons" be considered causes independent of their behavior. It is largely through their actions that people produce the environmental conditions that affect their behavior in a reciprocal fashion. The experiences generated by behavior also partly determine what individuals think, expect, and can do, which in turn, affect their subsequent behavior. (p. 345)

A second distinguishing feature of social learning theory is that psychological functioning involves a reciprocal interaction among three interlocking sets of factors: behavior, cognitive factors, and environmental influences. This view can be shown schematically as follows:

In this conceptual scheme a person is neither driven by internal forces nor is he a passive reactor to external pressure. Rather, a person is both the agent and the object of environmental influence. Consider the case of Johnny K by way of illustration. The completion of academic requirements and the reduction of disruptive behavior resulted in his parents arranging reinforcing consequences for him. Were Johnny's parents controlling him, or was he controlling them? Descriptively it can be seen that a two-way regulatory situation was involved in which the behavior of both Johnny and his parents changed. They influenced each other.

A third characteristic of social learning theory related to the notion that the person is an agent of change is that it emphasizes the human capacity for self-directed behavior change. Operant conditioning accounts of behavioral self-control ultimately reduce to analyses of external situational control and fundamentally deny the notion of self-control. In addition to the acquisition and maintenance of behavior, activation and persistence of behavior is based mainly on cognitive mechanisms. The importance assigned to cognitive processes that explain how learning experiences have lasting effects and serve to activate future actions enables social learning theory to explain the fact that humans initiate behavior that at least in part shapes their own destinies. Mr. B, for example, acquired self-control skills that enabled him to neutralize potentially dangerous, environmentally triggered thoughts about exposing himself. Moreover, by altering his own behavior, such as replacing hostile actions towards his father with more constructive assertive responses, he evoked less hostility from his family. This in turn reduced some of the stressful events that had previously precipitated deviant behavior.

In addition to these conceptual advantages of social learning theory, it also offers practical benefits to the therapist. As a broad-based framework that emphasizes the multidimensional nature of psychological functioning, the social learning approach is especially useful in the treatment of diverse and complex clinical problems. Accordingly, the social learning approach to behavior therapy is emphasized throughout the remainder of this book.

MULTIMODAL BEHAVIOR THERAPY

Another approach to behavior therapy that goes beyond the primary emphasis on one dimension of psychological functioning is Lazarus' (1976) multimodal behavior therapy. In this approach clinical problems are analyzed in terms of seven separate but interactive modalities: *B*ehavior, *A*ffect, *S*ensation, *I*magery, *C*ognition, *I*nterpersonal behavior, and *D*rugs. This approach is known by the acronym of BASIC ID. Therapy then focuses on specific problems within each modality. The difficulty with this approach is that it is unclear what the criteria are for the choice of different treatment techniques under specific conditions. In the absence of the necessary guiding principles, techniques are likely to be chosen arbitrarily on the basis of the therapist's personal preference. Lazarus (1976) states that these seven modalities are "interdependent and interactive" and "not every case requires attention to each modality." However, the critical questions are what the nature of the interactive process among different modalities is and what the ramifications for maximally efficient therapeutic intervention are. These answers are most likely to be developed within the context of a consistent theoretical framework that yields precise predictions amenable to operational measurement and evaluation. Social learning theory provides such a framework.

Common Characteristics of the Different Approaches Within Behavior Therapy

It should be clear from the preceding discussion that there is no simple, universally agreed upon definition of behavior therapy. Instead of searching for a single definition of behavior therapy, it is more useful to think of it in terms of a number of basic common characteristics. Although the preceding approaches to behavior therapy often involve conceptual differences, there remains a common core of fundamental assumptions that all behavior therapists hold. In the ultimate analysis, behavior therapy is characterized in terms of two basic assumptions: (1) a psychological model of human behavior that differs fundamentally from the traditional intrapsychic, psychodynamic, or quasi-disease model of mental illness; and (2) a commitment to scientific method, measurement, and evaluation. Each of these two characteristics has several specific implications for assessment, modification, and evaluation.

A MODEL OF ABNORMAL BEHAVIOR

In order to understand fully the significance of the behavioral model of abnormal behavior upon which behavior therapy is based, it is important to indicate briefly how it differs from the traditional quasi-disease or psychodynamic model. According to the latter model, abnormal behavior is symptomatic of an underlying illness. However, this illness is not a physical one, such as a brain tumor or a viral infection; it is a mental illness, a psychic disturbance or personality conflict that functions *like* a medical disease. Hence the term *quasi-disease,* that is, it seems like, but is not really, a disease. This analogy with the medical model is responsible for the widespread use of such medical-sounding terms as *patient, etiology, psychodiagnosis, mental illness, psychopathology, cure,* and *relapse* in the clinical psychology literature. A person who has an emotional disorder is said to be "sick" and can be restored to "health" only by treating the underlying, unconscious motivational conflicts of which abnormal behavior is a function. These unconscious conflicts are traced back to early childhood development and intrapsychic processes that interfered with normal or "healthy" personality development. The focus of treatment is on these historical causes of personality malfunction, not the present behavior. As the earlier quotation from Skinner indicates, abnormal behavior is not merely symptomatic of "something wrong somewhere else." It is important in its own right and can be treated directly. There is no qualitative distinction between "healthy" and "sick" people; these are labels that do not reflect differences intrinsic in behavior as much as they represent the social value judgments made by mental health professionals about whether the behavior of any given person is appropriate at that given time and place. Adoption of this model has major consequences for one's interpretation of the development of clinical disorders, their classification or assessment, and their treatment. An example of this model applied to the case of Mr. B, the exhibitionist, is presented in Table 1–1. This case illustration is based on the psychodynamic therapy Mr. B had received prior to entering into behavior therapy and from Bak and Stewart's (1974) treatment of exhibitionism in the authoritative *American Handbook of Psychiatry.*

TABLE 1–1

The Quasi-Disease (Psychodynamic) versus the Behavioral Model of Abnormal Behavior: Contrasting Implications for Assessment and Treatment in the Case of an Exhibitionist (Mr. B).

Model	Psychodynamic	Behavioral
Etiology (Development)	A symptom of dramatized denial of an underlying castration anxiety. Reassurance of not being castrated is obtained from the observer's reaction to the sight of his penis. At a deeper level exposure symbolizes a fixation at the phallic stage of psychosexual development. There was a failure in resolution of the Oedipus complex, a phase involving an aggressive relationship with his father. An unresolved sense of sexual identity or bisexuality resulted with associated castration anxiety. In seeking reassurance he insists on the existence of the phallic female. Unconsciously what he is saying in exposing himself is "I show you what I wish you could show me (the female phallus)."	Initially an attention-seeking behavior that was positively reinforced by the concern it elicited. (He had a history of disruptive, attention-seeking behavior as a child). Endowed with sexual arousal properties through masturbatory *classical conditioning,* i.e., imagining the deviant behavior during masturbation. Imagery of exposure became a conditioned stimulus paired with the powerful unconditioned stimulus of orgasm. Endowed with pleasurable properties, exposure became *self-reinforcing* through its tension-reducing functions. First, the pleasure or excitement of exposure helped neutralize the negative feelings of anger, frustration, or apprehension directly. Secondly, by directing all his attention to the thought and act of exposing himself in a particular situation, Mr. B took his mind off tension-producing events such as an argument with his father. In addition, his behavior periodically met with *positive reinforcement* when some of the women he exposed himself to smiled or made some sort of sexually toned comment (possibly frightened that he might attack them and thus trying to humor him). Intermittent positive reinforcement leads to behavior that is usually resistant to extinction. The fact that he masturbated less and less during or immediately after exposing himself as the years passed is explained by the fact that his behavior was initially maintained primarily through classically conditioned sexual arousal but subsequently was maintained more as a function of its negative reinforcing (tension-reducing) and positive reinforcing (periodic apparent approval from the woman) effects.

20

TABLE 1–1 (*cont.*)

Model	Psychodynamic	Behavioral
Psychodiagnosis (Assessment)	A sexual perversion, one of the personality disorders The methods used to assess the case included the psychoanalytic interview, focusing on childhood experiences in general and his relationship with his mother and father in particular; free association; and projective tests such as the Rorschach Inkblot test, designed to uncover indirect signs of the underlying psychopathological personality structure.	Functional analysis of *specific* antecedant, mediational, and consequent variables that were currently maintaining his behavior, and which could be directly modified. No diagnostic labels applied, and results of traditional psychodiagnostic tests (e.g., Rorschach) ignored. Methods used in making behavioral assessment included intensive interviewing focusing on what he thought, felt, and did in specific situations; imaginal and behavioral rehearsal to assess his ability to cope with emotions like anger; direct observation of his interpersonal behavior on the ward; questionnaires about specific sexual preferences and behavior; and objective psychophysiological measurement of sexual arousal in response to specific deviant erotic stimuli.
Treatment	Long-term psychodynamic therapy aimed at remedying his sexual perversion by giving him insight into the causes of his behavior and allowing him to "work through" his castration anxiety and hostility towards his father. Mr. B's relationship with his therapist—the transference relationship—was the crucial vehicle for facilitating this therapeutic process. Once he had gained insight and worked through his psychosexual conflicts, he would be cured and his perverted behavior would cease.	Time-limited therapy including his expectancies of self-efficacy and probable outcome through direct verbal persuasion and logical analysis; aversion conditioning; assertion training; covert modeling; self-control techniques, e.g., relaxation training, aversive imagery, self-monitoring evaluation, and instruction; behavioral marital counseling. Explicit strategies designed to facilitate *generalization* and *maintenance* of treatment-induced improvement and to ensure utilization of newly acquired self-control skills, i.e., mailing therapist records of daily self-monitoring; booster session four months following treatment.

In terms of the behavioral model, abnormal behavior that is not a function of specific brain dysfunction or biochemical disturbance is assumed to be governed by the same principles that regulate normal behavior. Many types of abnormal behavior that are often regarded as illnesses or as symptoms of illness are viewed as nonpathological problems of living. Exhibitionism and childhood conduct disorder, described in the cases of Mr. B and Johnny K respectively, are examples of the sort of abnormal behavior that is inaccurately interpreted as "sick" or "psychopathological"

21

by traditional psychodynamic approaches. Table 1–1 summarizes how the behavioral model can explain an extremely deviant form of abnormal behavior, like persistent exhibitionism, in terms of the same social learning principles responsible for the development of normal social and/or sexual behavior.

Not all forms of abnormal behavior are considered to be the result of social learning experiences. Among others, psychotic disorders such as autism, schizophrenic reactions, and certain types of depression (for example, manic-depression), and mental retardation almost certainly have important organic determinants. While these disturbances might not be "cured" by behavior therapy, they are none the less subject to the effects of social learning influences within limits. In fact, behavioral principles have been uniquely useful in helping individuals afflicted with these disorders to lead more fulfilling lives.

Whereas psychodynamic therapies focus on the historical determinants of clinical disorders, behavior therapy emphasizes their current determinants. Treatment directed towards these current determinants is the most powerful and efficient means of eliminating the client's problems. The social learning analysis of the development of Mr. B's strange behavior presented in Table 1–1 is speculative. It makes theoretical sense, and it is consistent with the known facts about his social learning history, but it was not crucial in the design of the treatment program. The latter was determined by what factors were currently responsible for Mr. B's behavior. Moreover, the fact that his deviant behavior was successfully modified does not necessarily show that the social learning account outlined in Table 1–1 is correct. Success in changing behavior is not tantamount to knowledge about how it developed. To identify the origins of behavior would require the study of antecedent conditions and their effects on behavior as it develops.

Specificity is the hallmark of behavioral assessment, treatment, and measurement. There is little concern for diagnosing what type of personality the client has or what category of psychopathology described by the official Diagnostic and Statistical Manual of the American Psychiatric Association he would fit. To label a client like Mr. B a sexual pervert, a character disorder, or a psychopath is largely a futile semantic exercise. The reason is that diagnostic labels such as these have no real consequence for treatment. Calling a client a psychopath does not tell you how to treat him. Behavioral assessment is action-oriented. By asking questions beginning with interrogatives like *what, when, where, how* often, and with *whom,* the behavior therapist gathers specific information about the variables that have to be modified if the behavior is to change.

Behavioral assessment is a continuous process in which the client's progress and the therapeutic strategies used to effect change are progressively reanalyzed as treatment proceeds. In the case of Mr. B, for example, his penile erection response to sexual stimuli was monitored periodically through therapy in order to assess whether treatment was having the desired effect. Diane T self-monitored her daily progress while the daily report card provided a continuous index of the extent to which Johnny K was improving academically and behaviorally. In the event that no progress was demonstrated, the treatment strategy would have been reevaluated.

Just as the purpose and nature of the information required by a behavioral assessment differ from that of traditional psychodiagnosis, so do the methods used to complete the assessment. Instead of *projective tests* like the Rorschach inkblot test or standardized psychometric tests like the Minnesota Multiphasic Personality Inventory (MMPI), behavior therapy focuses on the specific interactions between a client's behavior and the conditions in which it occurs. *Personality tests,* based as they are on personality trait theory, attempt to uncover generalized traits that will predict behavior in widely differing real life situations. Unfortunately, personality trait theory has been shown to be extremely ineffective in predicting behavior across different situations (Mischel, 1968). The cases of Mr. B, Diane T, and Johnny K provide good examples of the sorts of techniques used in behavioral assessment. The nature and means of behavioral assessment are discussed in detail in the following chapter.

Since behavior therapy emphasizes the continuing interaction between client cognitions and behaviors and the particular life situations in which they occur, explicit strategies are employed to ensure that treatment-produced change generalizes to the client's natural environment, and that it is maintained over time. The cessation of a problem behavior in one situation (for example, a hospital ward or classroom) does not necessarily mean that the client will show similar improvement in other situations (for example, the home). The quasi-disease model makes no provision for this. The problem is assumed to be a psychic disturbance or personality disorder *in* the patient. "Curing" this disorder should lead automatically to improved behavior across different situations. The inappropriate analogy is to medicine. If cancerous cells cause illness, their successful surgical removal should cause the symptoms (for example, pain) to disappear. The process is unaffected by the specific social situation to which the patient returns. If Mr. B had exposed himself after a period of improvement, this would have been called a "relapse." In terms of the behavioral model, however, this would mean that the strategies designed to facilitate generalization and maintenance of initial change were incomplete or inadequate. With respect to generalization, notice that in the case of Mr. B, the therapist arranged for him to practice the self-control strategies he learned in the therapist's office on the ward where he resided and then at home, when he left the hospital. In the case of Johnny K the therapist intervened both in the classroom and in the home, instructing both teacher and parents in more effective child management skills. In terms of maintenance, remember that Mr. B was required not only to self-monitor behavior related to his former problem and mail these records to the therapist, but also to return for a booster session treatment. Johnny K's therapist arranged for a certified teacher to monitor his progress during the summer following the treatment program.

The case of Johnny K shows how in behavior therapy, problem behaviors are treated in the environment in which they typically occur wherever this is possible. The therapist visited the school to observe Johnny's behavior directly and instructed his mother how to help him by actively modeling the appropriate behavior in the home setting. In traditional psychodynamic therapy, Johnny K would be brought to the therapist's office for weekly sessions of approximately 60 minutes. The therapist would try to relate to him and understand his conflicts, often by using play therapy. Play therapy involves having children play with toys whereby they reveal their problems in a symbolic fashion. These problems are then interpreted to the child in an accepting manner. Under no circumstances would the therapist have trained the mother to relate more effectively to her son and to modify his behavior directly.

AN APPLIED SCIENCE

Behavior therapy is defined by a commitment to an applied science of clinical treatment. As a result there is a heavy emphasis on the precise specification of therapeutic methods. Methods are precisely specified so that they are replicable across different therapists and can be objectively evaluated. The experimental evaluation of treatment methods and concepts is essential. The techniques used to treat Mr. B and Diane T all had some empirical support from previous research studies. The program that Johnny K participated in consisted of behavioral methods that had been individually demonstrated to be effective. This is not to say that all behavior therapy treatment is based on solid scientific evidence; some methods have this support, but the evidence for others is still tenuous, as discussed in the following chapters. However, the attempt is constantly made to relate treatment methods to the available experimental evidence. Behavior therapy has radically changed the nature of research on psychological treatment methods. Both the quantity and quality of studies on therapy outcomes have increased dramatically. Innovative research strategies have been developed that allow rigorous evaluation of specific techniques applied to particular problems, in contrast to inadequate global assessments of poorly defined procedures applied to heterogeneous problems.

Behavioral treatment methods are either derived from or at least consistent with the content and method of experimental-clinical psychology. Behavior therapy should not be confused with the somatic or medical methods of behavior change such as psychosurgery or electroconvulsive therapy (ECT).

These latter methods may modify behavior, not on the basis of psychological principles and procedures, but through direct physical intervention.

Box 1–1 summarizes the core characteristics of behavior therapy.

Box 1–1   *Core Characteristics of Behavior Therapy*

1. Most abnormal behavior is acquired and maintained according to the same principles as normal behavior.
2. Most abnormal behavior can be modified through the application of social learning principles.
3. Assessment is continuous and focuses on the current determinants of behavior.
4. A person is best described by what he or she thinks, feels, and does in specific life situations.
5. Treatment is derived from the theory and experimental findings of scientific psychology, particularly social learning principles.
6. Treatment methods are precisely specified, replicable, and objectively evaluated.
7. Innovative research strategies have been developed to evaluate the effects of specific therapeutic techniques on particular problems.
8. Treatment outcome is evaluated in terms of the initial induction of behavior change, its generalization to the real life setting, and its maintenance over time.
9. Treatment strategies are individually tailored to different problems in different individuals.
10. Extensive use is made of psychological assistants such as parents and teachers to modify problem behavior in the real life settings where it occurs.
11. Behavior therapy is broadly applicable to a full range of clinical disorders and educational problems.
12. Behavior therapy is a humanistic approach in which treatment goals and methods are mutually contracted, rather than arbitrarily imposed.

Some Commonly Asked Questions About Behavior Therapy

1. DOES BEHAVIOR THERAPY IGNORE SUBJECTIVE EXPERIENCE?

As the cases of Mr. B and Diane T make clear, contemporary behavior therapy does not ignore private mental events. Expectations, imagery, symbolic self-regulatory processes, self-monitoring, and self-evaluation were all fundamental features of the analysis and treatment of these clinical problems. The social learning approach to behavior therapy that is emphasized in this book stresses the importance of the cognitive mediation of human behavior.

Behavior therapy should not be equated with behaviorism. *Philosophical behaviorism* is the discredited doctrine of J. B. Watson who, in the second decade of this century, attempted to reduce all experience to glandular secretions and muscular movements. He denied the existence of mental events or the mind. Although Skinner has labeled himself a radical behaviorist, he has stated that the study of subjective events (that is, images and thoughts) should not be rejected simply because they are private events. Nonetheless, operant conditioners have consistently deemphasized or ignored cognitive processes because they are not directly observable. They have tried to explain all behavior in terms of observable effects of the external environment on overt behavior. In our discussion of different approaches to behavior therapy earlier in this chapter, we noted that this operant conditioning approach has proved extremely valuable in the study and treatment of clinical disorders. However, most behavior therapists today adopt a broader approach that emphasizes the importance of cognitive factors in the treatment of complex clinical disorders.

It has been proposed that behavior therapy involves a commitment to methodological, rather than philosophical, behaviorism. Mahoney, Kazdin, and Lesswing (1974) define *methodological behaviorism* as the application of scientific methodology to the study of human behavior. Clearly one of the unifying assumptions among the different conceptual approaches within behavior therapy is the emphasis on an experimental-scientific approach, as we have shown earlier in this chapter. However, it should be noted that defining behavior therapy in terms of its commitment to methodological behaviorism does not always provide us with a clear distinction between alternative treatment approaches. Accepting Mahoney and others' (1974) definition of methodological behaviorism, for example, would mean that every experimental psychologist, including cognitive psychologists, could be considered methodological behaviorists. Aside from behavior therapy, any other form of therapy that relied upon scientific findings could be regarded as a form of methodological behaviorism.

2. DOES THE INCLUSION OF COGNITIVE FACTORS IN BEHAVIOR THERAPY MAKE IT SIMILAR TO PSYCHODYNAMIC THERAPY?

Although cognitive processes in social learning theory are not directly observable, there is a fundamental difference between the way they are conceptualized and the nature of unobservable psychodynamic constructs. Psychodynamic constructs like castration anxiety and the Oedipus complex are never tied directly to observable antecedent and consequent events; they function largely as autonomous psychic forces, divorced from the immediate influence of external contingencies. They are not easily amenable to experimental testing and cannot be falsified. By contrast, cognitive concepts in social learning theory are firmly anchored to observable events; they are directly activated and influenced by specifiable behavioral procedures; and they can be unambiguously tested because they are defined in a precise manner.

The way in which cognitive processes are tied to observable antecedent and consequent events that are objectively measurable in behavior therapy can be illustrated by reference to the case of Mr. B, the exhibitionist. The therapist asked him to imagine himself in a tempting situation in which he felt like exposing himself. Mr. B's verbal self-report that as he imagined this scene he felt himself becoming sexually excited was correlated with an increase in penile erection that was being objectively measured at the time. The therapist then asked him to transform the scene symbolically and imagine that the woman was talking to him, telling him how his behavior offended and frightened her. Since the victim's anonymity was known to have been a precondition for Mr. B's exposing himself, the prediction was that this transformation of the imaginal scene would result in a loss of sexual excitement. This is exactly what he reported, and once again it was correlated with decreased penile erection. This simple example demonstrates how an internal covert process can be objectively measured and indicates that introspective reports can be valid under certain conditions.

Cognitive activities can be directly linked to behavior change. In carefully controlled studies, covert modeling, a technique used with Mr. B, has been shown to be effective in reducing phobic behavior and in increasing assertive behavior (Kazdin, 1975). Moreover, cognitive processes (for example, associating information in the form of a verbal stimulus with specific, relevant imagery) facilitate learning and remembering beyond what is established by repeated reinforced performance (Bandura, 1971).

As the foregoing reveals, cognitive processes can be scientifically studied. They have a demonstrable causal influence on behavior. It follows that they must be studied and incorporated into behavior therapy if comprehensive understanding and treatment is the goal. The ultimate justification for including cognitive activities in a theory of behavior change is the utility of this strategy in generating more effective treatment methods.

3. IS BEHAVIOR THERAPY A SUPERFICIAL FORM OF TREATMENT?

Behavior therapy is *not* a superficial treatment that ignores the causes of behavior. Both behavioral and psychodynamic treatments attempt to deal with the causes of behavior. The difference is in what these respective approaches regard the causes of behavior to be. Psychodynamic theories focus on historical, unconscious determinants of behavior; behavior therapy emphasizes the current causes of behavior—the antecedent, mediational, and consequent variables that are presently regulating the client's problems.

Consider the treatment of Mr. B. Had therapy been limited to aversion conditioning only (that is, pairing deviant fantasies with an aversive stimulus), important variables that were important in maintaining the behavior would have been overlooked. He would not have been equipped with self-control skills to cope with the anger and tension that frequently elicited the deviant behavior. His self-defeating expectancies would have been left untouched. Had this happened, it would have been an example of incomplete treatment that might have produced only temporary results, at best. An adequate behavioral assessment of the problem results in multifaceted treatment that deals with the full range of maintaining variables (causes).

4. DOES BEHAVIOR THERAPY RESULT IN "SYMPTOM SUBSTITUTION"?

Behavior therapy was once widely criticized as a superficial form of treatment that only treats the "symptoms" while leaving the real causes of the problem untouched. As a result it was alleged that behavioral treatment would lead to *symptom substitution;* that is, the replacement of the symptom which was treated with another because the underlying problem had not been resolved. This was a misguided criticism since behavior therapy is *not* a superficial form of treatment. As we have already indicated, behavioral treatment does focus on the current causes of the client's problems. Moreover, treatment outcome research has convincingly shown that symptom substitution does not occur. It did not happen with either Mr. B, or Diane T, or Johnny K, and it has not happened in numerous well-controlled studies that were explicitly designed to look for it (Bandura, 1969; Kazdin and Wilson, 1978; Sloane and others, 1975). Typical of the evidence in this regard are the results from Sloane and others', (1975) widely quoted study of the behavioral treatment of neurotic disorders. These investigators summarize their findings as follows: "Not a single patient whose original problems had substantially improved reported new symptoms cropping up. On the contrary, assessors had the informal impression that when a patient's primary symptoms improved, he often spontaneously reported improvement of other minor difficulties" (p. 100).

5. WHAT IS THE RELATIONSHIP BETWEEN PSYCHOLOGICAL THEORY AND CLINICAL PRACTICE IN BEHAVIOR THERAPY?

Behavior therapy incorporates a wide range of innovative and distinctive therapeutic techniques. More fundamental to a definition of behavior therapy, however, is the fact that it derives from a particular conceptual model of human behavior that has direct implications for the assessment and modification of clinical disorders. Behavior therapy is a way of thinking about clinical disorders, a problem-solving orientation in which different principles and procedures are flexibly tailored to each individual client's specific problem. In this problem-solving approach, theoretical considerations help determine what techniques the therapist selects, guide general treatment strategies, and direct clinical research. It has been said that there is nothing so practical as a good theory. The advantages of social learning theory as an approach to behavior therapy include the following: (a) it integrates the known facts on behavior change; (b) it is testable using experimental methods; (c) it is heuristic in stimulating novel research and prompting therapeutic innovations; and (d) it compares favorably with existing theoretical alternatives.

Behavior therapists are professionals well-versed in the scientific foundations of behavior therapy *and* are possessed of the clinical and/or interpersonal skills required to design and implement effective behavior change methods. The variables that determine the therapist-client relationship are important for behavior change and can be fruitfully integrated with more formal behavioral techniques within the conceptual framework of social learning theory (Wilson and Evans, 1977).

6. IS BEHAVIOR THERAPY MECHANISTIC OR IMPERSONAL?

To some extent the details of the treatment of Mr. B, Diane T, and Johnny K allow readers to decide for themselves whether behavior therapy is mechanistic and manipulative. There are several important reasons why behavior therapy is not only a humane approach, but also shows more promise of facilitating personal freedom and self-determined emotional growth than traditional approaches.

The first is its greater efficacy with a larger number of behavior problems. Mr. B would have been deprived of his freedom and sent to a prison for sex criminals had he not learned to control his formerly ungovernable, deviant behavior. Effectively enhancing academic skills and appropriate social behavior in children like Johnny K can mean the difference between a productive educational experience and constant friction in the school and home, culminating in the high school drop-out who finds it difficult to find a job and who ultimately ends up on the welfare rolls as a disillusioned casualty of society.

Another reason why behavior therapy is a humane approach is the manner in which it is carried out. Although it has not always been emphasized, and although the scientific jargon in which behavior therapy is typically described often creates the impression of an impersonal and indifferent approach, the therapist-client relationship is of considerable significance in behavior therapy (Wilson and Evans, 1977). The fact that Mr. B and Diane

T trusted and believed in their therapist was a vital factor in their successful treatment. The therapists in the program Johnny K participated in were described by teachers and parents alike as warm, understanding, and empathic—personal qualities important in any form of therapy. The evidence shows beyond doubt that behavior therapists are as humanly committed to their clients as other therapists (O'Leary, Turkewitz, and Taffel, 1973; Sloane and others, 1975).

All forms of therapy involve social influence. The important ethical question is whether the therapist is aware of this influence and the behaviors it is being used either deliberately or unwittingly to develop. Chapter 10 shows how behavior therapy explicitly recognizes this influence process, and how it emphasizes specific, client-defined behavioral objectives. Behavior therapy is not a one-sided influence process that can be easily used by the therapist to effect changes in a client's beliefs and behavior. As social learning theory makes clear, therapeutic behavior change usually requires the active, conscious cooperation of the client in the treatment process.

7. HOW BROADLY APPLICABLE IS BEHAVIOR THERAPY?

Behavior therapy is applicable to a wide range of problems. The clinical case illustrations of the treatment of persistent exhibitionism and conduct disorder above demonstrate the use of behavior therapy with complex problems that are widely regarded to be resistant to therapeutic intervention. In addition to clinical psychology and psychiatry, areas of successful application include education, rehabilitation, and even medicine (see Brigham and Catania, 1979; Franks and Wilson, 1973–1978; Leitenberg, 1976; Kazdin and Wilson, 1978; Rachman, 1977a) Examples of applications of behavioral methods to these diverse problems across different areas are introduced throughout the remainder of the book. The evidence shows that behavior therapy is not only generally useful across a wide range of different disorders, it also indicates that behavior therapy might be the treatment of choice the more complex and more resistant to treatment the problem is (Kazdin and Wilson, 1978).

Summary

Behavior therapy has developed out of the systematic application of experimentally derived principles of learning to the modification of problem behaviors. Although several prominent examples of therapeutic behavior change through the use of methods based on conditioning principles were described during the first half of this century, the contemporary history of behavior therapy dates from the 1950s. During this decade, the pioneering work of Wolpe in South Africa, of Eysenck and his group in England, and the extension of operant conditioning principles to human disorders by Skinner and his students in the United States resulted in the emergence of behavior therapy as a distinctive alternative model of etiology and therapy to the prevailing psychodynamic approach.

Behavior therapy matured and became more complex during the 1960s and 1970s. The initial definition of behavior therapy as the application of conditioning principles is now outdated. Current conceptual approaches within behavior therapy include applied behavior analysis in which the emphasis is on operant conditioning; the neobehavioristic or Wolpean approach; cognitive behavior modification; and social learning theory.

Bandura's social learning formulation is the most comprehensive and sophisticated conceptualization of behavior therapy. It stresses the influential role of cognitive mediating variables regulating behavior in addition to external events. By emphasizing the constant reciprocity between personal actions and the environmental consequences they affect and in turn are affected by, it provides an analysis of and generates procedures for self-directed behavior change.

The distinguishing characteristics of contemporary behavior therapy include the rejection of the quasi-disease model and personality trait theory and a recognition that much abnormal behavior is developed and maintained in the same manner as normal behavior, that abnormal behavior can be treated directly, and that treatment is derived from the theory and experimental findings of scientific psychology. Contemporary behavior therapy focuses on specificity in assessment, treatment, and measurement; the precise specification of treatment conditions and the objective evaluation of therapeutic outcome.

Behavior therapy is not synonymous with behaviorism. Symbolic events are included in causal analyses since they are closely tied to observable antecedent and consequent events. Behavior therapy is not superficial or symptomatic treatment. A thorough behavioral assessment indicates all the current determinants of the person's problem, and several different techniques are then selectively included within a multifaceted treatment program aimed at modifying all aspects of the problem. Behavior therapy is a humanitarian approach in which the client has the major say in setting the goals of treatment. The therapist-client relationship is important to successful treatment. Behavior therapy is more than a technology; it has specific conceptual bases and entails a particular way of thinking about assessment and treatment. It is a generally useful approach that has broad applicability to diverse behavior problems in clinical psychology, psychiatry, education, rehabilitation, and medicine.

Suggested Readings

The clinical practice of behavior therapy:

GOLDFRIED, M.R., and DAVISON, G.C. 1976. *Clinical behavior therapy.* New York: Holt, Rinehart and Winston.

The operant or applied behavior analysis approach:

LEITENBERG, H. 1966. *Handbook of behavior modification and behavior therapy.* Englewood Cliffs: Prentice-Hall.

The cognitive approach:

MEICHENBAUM, D. 1977. *Cognitive behavior modification.* New York: Plenum Press.

The social learning approach:

BANDURA, A. 1969. *Principles of behavior modification,* pp. 1–80. New York: Holt, Rinehart and Winston.

BANDURA, A. 1977. *Social learning theory.* Englewood Cliffs: Prentice-Hall.

The treatment of sexual deviation:

MARKS, I.M. 1976. Management of sexual disorders. *Handbook of behavior modification and behavior therapy,* ed. H. Leitenberg. Englewood Cliffs: Prentice-Hall.

O'LEARY, K.D., and WILSON, G.T. 1975. *Behavior therapy: Application and outcome.* chap. 11. Englewood Cliffs: Prentice-Hall.

The modification of classroom behavior:

O'LEARY, K.D., and O'LEARY, S.G. 1977. *Classroom management: The successful use of behavior modification.* New York: Pergamon Press.

2

Assessment

Anyone in clinical practice regularly assesses clients and their problems. When a client comes to a clinic, a therapist has to make a judgment about whether emergency measures are necessary (for example, hospitalization), whether the case should be assigned a high, low, or moderate priority for treatment, or whether the problem presented by the client is serious enough to warrant any treatment. The latter issue is often of import with child cases where the parents want to know whether the child's problems (for example, bedwetting in young children) will change as a simple function of maturation. In making these judgments, a therapist relies on prior experience with clients who have had similar problems, psychological test data, comparisons with normative populations, and the client's distress. If the therapist and the client conclude that therapy is warranted, the therapist then must decide whether the treatment should be directed at the problem presented by the client (for example, behavior problems of a child) or at other issues (for example, marital discord). He or she must also determine what treatment procedures should be used, whether the treatment would have any undesirable side effects, and what regular assessments are necessary to ascertain whether the treatment procedures are having the intended effect. All of these decisions require a thorough initial assessment.

In this chapter we will discuss the behavioral model for assessment, a survey of the types of clinical assessment currently used by behavior therapists, and an evaluation of these assessment practices.

Model for Assessment

INTERPRETATION OF PRESENTING PROBLEMS

During the intake interview a client almost always identifies certain problems that he or she wants help with or wants to change. These problems are called *presenting problems.* A therapist must first decide whether the presenting problems are the problems to be addressed directly. Generally, presenting problems are important, and behavior therapists, in particular, have viewed presenting problems as legitimate targets for direct intervention. However, on occasion certain presenting problems may not be the problems to which the therapist should direct his or her primary attention. For example, sometimes alcohol abuse may be best treated by a focus on a client's interpersonal relationships, rather than on a reduction or elimination of drinking per se. In a case where drinking occurs each time the client is depressed and the depression reliably follows fights with the spouse, the marital relationship would be a focus of the therapy. Drinking, of course, can be addressed as an issue in therapy, but depending on its severity and frequency, it may not be the primary treatment focus. With a hyperactive child, a focus on increasing academic and social skill may be preferable to an emphasis on decreasing fidgeting and gross motor movements. In either case, the choice of treatment targets is based on a thorough knowledge of the natural history of the problem, how various treatments affect presenting and related problems, and what appears to be the central or critical cause of the presenting problems.

A related issue in the interpretation of presenting problems is the decision about whether there is a central or *higher order* problem. For example, an individual may report that his problem is that he gets very angry when his eight-year-old son does not obey him. Upon further questioning, it is learned that the father frequently fights with his wife and receives negative evaluations from his boss because he is overly critical of fellow employees. In such a case, a therapist may conceptualize all of the presenting problems within the context of the common themes—inability to accept other individuals' faults and to cope with anger. Sharing this interpretation with the client and structuring the therapy to address the higher order problems enables the client to deal simultaneously with many problems. In contrast, focusing solely on his interactions with his son would leave several related issues untouched and would reduce the likelihood of maintaining treatment gains and of having changes in treatment generalize to other areas.

ANTECEDENT, CONCURRENT AND CONSEQUENT EVENTS

A general strategy for analyzing presenting problems in a learning theory framework is to assess the antecedent, concurrent, and consequent events relevant to the presenting problem. To assess these events, three general questions should be kept in mind.

1. **What events usually precede the client's problem behavior?** The events may be overt or covert, so that it is often necessary to assess both the thoughts the client has and the events that occur in the client's environment prior to the occurrence of problem behavior. Precipitants of behavior are usually sought in occurrences of the past few weeks, months, or recent years, but on occasion, it is necessary to assess early developmental history. For example, in elementary school children with certain problems, such as hyperactivity associated with motor and neurological dysfunction, complications at birth may be the original determinant of the problem. With couples in marital distress, it is often important to discover what each of the spouses expected when the marriage began (Sager, 1976), as discord often emanates from changing or unfulfilled expectations that are not

clearly communicated. In every case assessment of what occurs just prior to the presenting problem is essential. For example, if excessive drinking is the problem, it is important to find out whether the drinking is preceded by feelings or thoughts of anger or depression or whether the drinking occurs in a jovial social atmosphere.

2. **What thoughts and feelings usually occur simultaneously with the problem behavior?** When a person is anxious in social situations, it is important to know what he or she is thinking about when the anxiety occurs, since those thoughts can either exacerbate or ameliorate the anxiety. For example, it is known that if a subject is instructed to attend to external cues in a room rather than to his or her physiological state, fear will be reduced (Borkovec and O'Brien, 1977).

   The import of tracing a client's thought patterns during the development of a problem behavior was illustrated in the case of Mr. B, the exhibitionist discussed in Chap. 1. As was noted there, before treatment Mr. B's feelings could change from an initially weak sexual urge into an overwhelming compulsion to exhibit himself if, once he had an urge, he attended to a particular woman and her anticipated reactions. Treatment consisted, in part, of teaching Mr. B to attend to nonsexual thoughts and feelings as soon as he felt a temptation to expose himself.

   In a series of interesting studies, Mischel and his colleagues (for example, Mischel, Ebbesen, and Zeiss, 1972) showed that what a preschool child thinks about while tempted has very important consequences. More specifically, children were placed in an experimental situation where they were asked to wait alone in a room for the experimenter who had to go "do an errand." During the waiting period there were two food treats accessible to the children, a very desirable one and one which was not as preferred. The children were told that to obtain the more desirable treat, they had to wait until the experimenter returned. Children who were taught to think about something else, other than the desired food object, were much more effective in delaying gratification (waiting for the experimenter) than children who were not given this suggestion.

3. **What events follow the client's problem behavior?** The therapist must look for a pattern of particular events that might follow the problem behavior because the client may not be aware that some of these events play a significant role in the maintenance of the problem. Consider the example of a woman who is debilitated by a hysterical paralysis in her leg (that is, a paralysis which is psychological rather than physical in origin). Such a paralysis may allow her to avoid

addressing a sexual problem with her husband, while her husband dutifully attends to her by preparing meals and doing housework. Psychodynamically oriented therapists call this set of circumstances "secondary gain" (Cameron, 1963). In this case, the secondary function of the paralysis is to keep the husband serving as a caretaker to his wife. A behavioral analysis of the wife's paralysis might lead to the interpretation that the hysterical paralysis is reinforced by two events, the attending and caretaking behaviors of the husband and the absence of sexual intercourse.

Another reason skillful interpretation of the client's report of the consequences of certain behaviors is critical is that a client may report a series of events as negative, yet those very events may actually serve as reinforcers of the problem behavior. For example, a mother may repeatedly yell "Stop it!" or "Cut it out!" when her child cries or clings to her skirt. Such attention, even though negative in form, may unwittingly reinforce the undesired dependent behavior. Similarly, it has been found that elementary school teachers can inadvertently encourage or reinforce overly active behavior by simply telling the child repeatedly to sit down (Madsen and others, 1968).

BROAD-SCALE ENVIRONMENTAL ASSESSMENT AND PREVENTION

In addition to the classic assessment of antecedent, concurrent, and consequent events that occur in an individual's immediate environment, ecological and broad-scale environmental assessment has become increasingly popular during the past decade. This assessment involves analysis of the influence of social and physical factors on the behavior of individuals and groups. More specifically, a broad-scale assessment could include factors such as economic or occupational opportunities, architectural design, public transportation systems, nutrition, environmental pollutants, and recreation facilities.

The general trend toward assessing environmental factors was prompted by the social action programs of the 1960s, the increasing interest in community programs, and the belief that many physical diseases, such as cancer, are environmentally influenced. The latter is particularly interesting in that only ten years ago the warning of the famous biologist, Barry Steele Commoner, that cancers were environmentally caused was deemed frivolous. However, in support of some of Commoner's hypotheses, investigators have indeed found that lung, liver, and bladder cancer frequently occur in areas near chemical industries. Melanoma, a skin cancer, is more prevalent in the South than in the North (*Time,* 1975a) because of the more intense sun rays in the South.

In fact, Dr. Upton, the head of the National Cancer Institute, believes that 90 percent of all cancers are environmentally determined (Greenberg, 1977).

In brief, evidence for the role of environmental factors in physical disease is increasing. Similarly, evidence for the impact of environmental factors on human behavior is also increasing. Heller and Monahan (1977), in a review of the psychology of social settings, cited very interesting data concerning this issue. For example, a positive correlation of 0.74 was found between the rate of suicide among white males and a yearly index of change of the price of common stocks. The distance between houses and the direction the houses faced were the two major factors influencing the development of friendships in a housing project. The type of outdoor designs of urban high-rise housing projects influenced the amount of socializing in the projects (Holahan, 1976). Children's behavior problems such as hyperactivity and attentional disorders have been associated with the ingestion of lead in paint (Walker, 1977), eating foods high in artificial salycylates (Feingold, 1975; Conners and Goyette, 1977), and classroom environments with little choice of tasks or the order in which the tasks were to be completed (Jacob, O'Leary, and Rosenblad, 1978). Children's disruptive behavior has also been associated with seating arrangements in which preschool children sat very close to one another while listening to stories (Krantz and Risley, 1977).

The implications of the data being collected by psychologists operating within an ecological, environmental, and community assessment framework are providing an impetus for behavior therapists to focus on prevention. Psychologists have implemented preventive approaches in which large numbers of specific groups of individuals (for example, parents, teachers) selected at random were surveyed for the specific types of problems they felt were most important to address. Following such an assessment with a normative group, intervention programs were designed to aid individuals in coping with such problems. While these assessment projects and the associated types of intervention programs do not emanate directly from broad-scale environmental assessment, they have resulted in part from the growing concern of community psychologists to assess and ameliorate problems before they are of clinical significance.

An example of such a preventive approach is a program devised by Anesko and O'Leary (1978), who taught parents how to aid their own children in completing homework assignments. Normative data regarding specific problems related to homework completion that parents found most difficult were obtained from a random sample of 340 parents. Twelve parents recruited by a school newsletter announcement were randomly assigned to a parent training group or a wait-list control group. Even though some of the children had behavioral problems, they were not attending a clinic for such difficulties. A manual and a three-session course were employed to teach parents how to cope with the most frequent homework-related problems, for example, to encourage their child's efforts, to minimize criticism, to communicate with their child's teachers. A homework problem checklist completed by the parents at the end of the program indicated that both the number and frequency of occurrence of problems decreased significantly from pre- to postintervention.

Another preventive approach was taken by Greene, Clark, and Risley (1977) in which the focus was on helping parents deal with troublesome everyday shopping problems. Initially, the approach involved identifying difficulties which frequently caused normal stresses in households (Risley, Clark, and Cataldo, 1976). Among these problems were arguments between family members during rush hour in the morning, disruptive behavior in stores, and troubles with the bedtime routine. A specific example of the Greene and others' program is provided by this description of their approach to shopping trip problems. After field testing a number of solutions, they found the following advice most helpful:

1. Talk to the child about shopping; include discussions of what items are desired and where they might be found and comparisons of prices and quality.
2. Specify rules of shopping behavior.
3. Give each child a small amount of money to spend at the end of the shopping trip.
4. If there are rule infractions, subtract money from the original amount given to the child.

Observations of twelve families in stores revealed that this preventive approach with nonclinic families led to decreases in parental coerciveness and increases in children's courteous behavior. Mothers' questionnaire data indicated that the use of the approach made shopping more pleasurable and led to learning experiences for the children.

Cohen and Flipczak (1971) underscored the need for a stress on prevention in their evaluation of a behavior therapy program for delinquents.

> . . . The only effective approach to juvenile delinquency is the development of effective academic and interpersonal programs within our nation's public schools. We must stop building prisons for youth and begin investing our funds and energy to establish preventive systems within our present ongoing schools and community centers. (p. 143)

Stumphauzer, Aiken, and Veloz (1977) echoed the Cohen and Flipczak plea. "Psychotherapy and individual behavior therapy are no answers to minimize the gang behavior. . . . behaviors such as gang stealing and drug addiction may only be successfully treated for most individuals by large scale intervention programs at the community level" (p. 83). Factors that those authors felt warrant assessment, in addition to individual deficits and competencies, are presence of jobs; perceived immunity from prosecution due to intimidation, beating, and killing of community residents who inform authorities about gang activities; peer groups' rewards for illegal activities and antisocial behavior; and juvenile courts where the adjudication for repeated offenders is merely probation.

HALLMARKS OF BEHAVIORAL ASSESSMENT

Behavioral assessment is noted for an emphasis on *observable* events, on *current* behaviors of interpersonal import, and on situational *determinants* of the problematic behavior. As will become apparent in this chapter, a behavior therapist has a decided focus on what a person *does* in particular situations rather than on inferences about general personality attributes (for example, introversion, defensiveness). It is assumed that people exhibit different behaviors in different situations, and if a therapist wishes to know whether a person is unassertive, dependent, or depressed, the therapist must carefully ascertain in what situations the problematic behavior occurs. (Does the client cower in his supervisor's presence? Is the client afraid to criticize his wife?) This emphasis on observing behavior and its situational determinants may be contrasted with an approach in which a behavior is almost always interpreted as a sign of some underlying personality characteristic or unconscious conflicts (that is, a psychodynamic approach to personality assessment).

While a behavior therapist focuses on the assessment of the current problems reported by the client as well as on current determinants of those problems, nonetheless, as will be illustrated, a behavior therapist certainly obtains some history about the development of the problems. In contrast to much traditional assessment, however, with most adult problems there is little detailed discussion of very early childhood experiences. Assessment is conducted to describe precisely current problem behaviors and to analyze their determinants. The assessment is conducted for the purpose of deciding which treatment procedure should be used. Finally, it is important to note that assessment is a continuing process in behavior therapy. It does not occur simply when the client initially comes to the therapist's office; instead, progress throughout therapy is monitored.

Types of Assessment Data in Behavior Therapy

Swan and MacDonald (1978) conducted a survey of the assessment practices of 353 behavior therapists. The ten most frequently noted assessment practices and the percent of clients with whom the procedures were used are presented on the following page.

Assessment Procedures:	% Usage
1. Interview with identified client	89%
2. Client self-monitoring	51%
3. Interview with identified client's significant others	49%
4. Direct observation of target behaviors *in situ*	40%
5. Information from consulting professionals	40%
6. Role-play	34%
7. Behavioral self-report measures	27%
8. Demographic questionnaires	20%
9. Personality inventories (tests)	20%
10. Projective tests	10%

As is very clear from this survey, an interview with the identified client is almost universally employed. A probable reason why the interview was not used 100 percent of the time is that with young children, a therapist may sometimes choose to interview the parents instead of the child and begin treatment without having talked with the child. With adolescents, however, the interview is almost always used. On occasion, when an adolescent is unwilling to attend therapy sessions, his or her parents may be aided by consultation about how to approach their teenager (for example, in regard to drugs and alcohol, sex, and matters of personal hygiene).

After obtaining demographic information and conducting the initial interviews with the client or significant others (for example, parents, teachers, physicians), a therapist will often collect data that is more amenable to quantification than that obtained from the interview per se. Specifically, other than interviews and demographic questionnaires, the assessment practices most frequently used by behavior therapists can be subsumed under four rubrics: (1) self-recording, (2) observation of the problem *in situ,* (3) personality inventories and self-report measures, and (4) role-playing. We will consider the advantages and disadvantages of the assessment interview as well as these four assessment practices. Additionally, because of the theoretical import of physiological data, we will briefly note the role of physiological assessment.

THE ASSESSMENT INTERVIEW

During assessment interviews a clinician moves from general descriptions of a client's problem to specific areas that should become the focus of treatment. To allow a client to feel free to divulge information that may be stressful and embarrassing, emphasis should be placed on building a relationship of trust and mutual understanding, that is, a relationship with mutual rapport. Rapport is desired throughout assessment and treatment, and because of its crucial nature, some guidelines for establishing rapport will be briefly discussed. Then the natural progression through intake interviews will be examined in order to illustrate how a therapist obtains critical assessment data and establishes the groundwork for treatment. Finally, methodological issues regarding reliability and validity of interviews will be explored.

Rapport building. Bernstein, Bernstein, and Dana (1974) provided some useful guidelines for establishing rapport.

1. *Be Especially Attentive:* Try to follow the client's description of the problem, encourage his or her talking, and don't talk too much yourself.

2. *Be Emotionally Objective:* While remaining attentive and interested, a therapist should try to keep his or her values from influencing the client—especially in the initial interview. The therapist should also be nonjudgmental, for if the client believes that the therapist dislikes what he or she has to say, the client may not speak openly.

3. *Be an Empathic Listener:* Try to understand the problem from the client's point of view and let the client know you understand by accurately reflecting or restating the feelings or thoughts the client is expressing.

4. *Make Clear That the Therapeutic Relationship is Confidential:* A client should know that information conveyed to a therapist will not be shared with anyone else.

Progression through intake interviews. Upon meeting the client for the first time, a therapist eases the client's anxiety by asking simple questions regarding demographic matters, for example, name of spouse, place of work, and educational background. Asking the client to talk about fairly simple matters very early in the interview not only relieves the client's anxiety, but also allows the therapist to compare the client's behavior in problematic and nonproblematic discussions.

A behavior therapist then focuses more directly on the presenting problem:

a. When did the problem begin?

b. How frequently does it occur?

c. When and in what situations does it occur?

d. Generally, what occurs before and after the problem behavior?

e. What does the client think about while the problem is occurring?

f. What has been done to change the problem thus far?

After obtaining detailed information about the parameters of the presenting problem, the therapist should ascertain the strengths or assets the client feels he or she has. A focus on the client's assets is an excellent way to proceed toward the end of the first interview since the client may leave the session feeling more optimistic. Clients often do not pay sufficient attention to their assets, and having clients discuss their strengths is a first step toward the frequent therapeutic goal of enhancing confidence in themselves.

Methodological issues. Interview data are often unreliable and subject to distortion, particularly if information is being obtained about past events. However, when the behavior of interest is about current events and is easily quantified (for example, child wet bed; spouse cried), and where global and inferential judgments are minimal, interview data can be quite reliable (Rutter, in press). Clinic and nonclinic children can be distinguished on the basis of structured interviews, and Herjanic, Herjanic, Brown, and Wheatt (1975) found 80 percent agreement between mothers and their children when they answered comparably structured interview questions.

Further, a client's self-report in an interview is often highly predictive of critical future behavior. For example, asking a young engaged couple how well they will succeed in marriage was more predictive of marital stability two years later than a number of personality or marriage tests (Markman, 1977). Similarly, it has been found that asking college students to predict their grade point average was as predictive of that average as were complex personality and interest inventories (Mischel and Bentler, 1960). Finally, in predicting adjustment to living in Alaskan military army posts, asking a soldier if he liked cold weather was more predictive than a number of psychological tests (Gottman, 1978*). In brief, clients may be much more aware of their own ability to do things than psychologists have assumed. If the right questions are asked in an interview, the client can provide information that may allow the therapist to skillfully integrate assessment and treatment.

SELF-RECORDING

Self-recording is one of the oldest methods of obtaining information used by psychologists, and its use by well-known individuals to monitor the change or maintenance of behavior is quite interesting. For example, in Skinner's (1967) autobiographical account, he wrote:

> In general I write very slowly and in long hand. It took me two minutes to write each word of my thesis and that is still about my rate. From three or four hours of writing each day I eventually salvage about one hundred publishable words. . . . I induce myself to write by making production as conspicuous as possible (by keeping a chart on the wall showing number of words written). (pp. 403, 408)

Skinner spends a certain amount of time per day in his office and, as noted above, he makes daily recordings of the number of pages he has written.

Irving Wallace, noted author of *The Prize* and *The Man,* depicted his

*Personal Communication, August 3, 1978

own self-recording as well as that of other novelists in an especially intriguing article written with a behavioral psychologist (Wallace, 1977):

> With my fifth book, I started keeping a more detailed chart which also showed me how many pages I had written by the end of every working day. I am not sure why I started keeping such records. I suspect that it was because, as a free lance writer, entirely on my own, without employer or deadline, I wanted to create disciplines for myself, ones that were guilt-making when ignored. A chart on the wall served as such a discipline, its figures scolding me or encouraging me.

The use of self-recording in behavior therapy has become increasingly prevalent in the past few years for a number of reasons. (1) Self-control procedures have been developed which incorporate self-monitoring as an integral part of the therapeutic strategy (for example, weight reduction programs which involve daily recording of caloric values of food consumed, times and places eating occurs, and feelings associated with eating). (2) Using observers in the natural environments of many clients, particularly adults, can be an invasion of privacy, is often extremely expensive and impractical, and sometimes may produce changes in the behaviors observed. (3) Self-monitoring permits the assessment of extremely infrequent but important behaviors (for example, seizures) that an independent observer could not record unless the observer followed the individual throughout the day. (4) The only way to assess the frequency of thoughts, urges, and fantasies is to have the client monitor and record such events. (See Box 2-1, Daily Log of Depressed Feelings.)

Current methods of self-recording vary from simple checks on a note pad to electronic devices that the client simply turns on to record his or her behavior. There have been a number of studies in which a simple golf-stroke counter is used to record the frequency of discrete events, such as number of cigarettes smoked, number of urges to hit someone, and number of supportive comments made to one's child. To avoid the conspicuousness of the golf-stroke counters, decorative wrist bands designed as miniature abacuses have been used to record several events at one time. The bands are designed with leather and a series of small decorative beads which can be moved from one side to another as the events in question occur. Azrin and Powell (1968) developed a cigarette case that automatically records the number of times it is opened. Gravity-sensitive watches have been worn by hyperactive children to obtain a measure of their activity level (Schulmann and Reisman, 1959). Finally, as a result of the space-age technology, very sophisticated telemetry devices have been developed. The client can wear a sensor that sends a signal to a recording device at home so that physiological measurements such as heart rate can be obtained in the natural environment.

Reliability. *Reliability* here refers to the percent of time that two individuals, usually a client and another observer, agree that a particular event

Box 2-1 *Daily Log of Depressed Feelings*		
Preceding Events	Feelings	Consequent Events
Monday		
Got a 65 on chemistry exam.	Had no energy. Didn't want to talk to anyone.	My boyfriend said I was a bore.
Tuesday Had a good night's sleep.	Good Day!	Caught up on Bio homework.
Wednesday Saw my boyfriend eating lunch with another girl.	Felt angry and jealous.	Cut class and took a nap.
Thursday Couldn't do chem lab assignment.	Just can't learn chemistry.	Called teaching assistant to ask about tutoring.
Friday Roommate got a permanent—looked great.	I'm ugly! (cried a lot)	She said she would cut my hair tomorrow.
Saturday My parents called.	Lonely—nothing to do here.	Listened to records and went to bed early.

has occurred. The reliability rates of self-recording have varied from approximately 50 to 100 percent. Lipinski and Nelson (1974) found that the reliability of the self-recording of face touching was 52 percent. McFall (1970) found that the self-recordings of smokers agreed with the observations of nonsmoking peers 61 percent of the time over a seventy-day period. Azrin and Powell (1969) obtained an agreement rate of 98 percent between hospital employees' records and self-recorded pill taking.

When the reliability of self-recording is low, procedures can be implemented to increase the agreement between self- and others' records. First, telling the client that his or her recording will be intermittently checked almost always leads to increased accuracy (Ciminero, Nelson, and Lipinski, 1977). Second, the reliability of self-recording rates can be improved if clients are reinforced for accurate self-recording (Ciminero and others, 1977). Even with elementary school children, the reliability of self-recordings of social and academic behavior in a classroom has been as high as 75 to 85 percent across a two-month period if the children are reinforced for accurate recordings (K. D. O'Leary, 1978).

Reactivity. If a client is simply asked to record minutes spent studying and then finds that there is an increase in study time, the self-recording is said to be *reactive,* in that the use of this procedure prompts a behavior change. Reactivity is a double-edged sword. If the therapist wishes to obtain a stable baseline of certain behaviors before instituting treatment so that the therapy can be evaluated, then reactivity is a clear disadvantage. On the other hand, since the therapist's goal is to help the client change, the reactivity of self-recording can be beneficial. Whether self-monitoring is reactive or not depends upon the specific behavior or factor being monitored. For example, monitoring calories is reliably associated with weight reduction, whereas monitoring of eating habits is not (Green, 1978). Similarly, self-monitoring of nicotine content is more reactive than self-monitoring of number of cigarettes.

OBSERVATION IN VIVO

Observing problem behaviors in natural environments has been a hallmark of behavioral psychologists. Bijou (1965) emphasized the need for precise recordings of children's behavior in their home and school environments, and he urged psychologists to use the frequencies of observable behaviors as their major dependent measures. This orientation is widespread. In fact, one of the major psychological journals, the *Journal of Applied Behavior Analysis* (JABA), often requires authors to provide some *in vivo* observational measure of the behavior in question. Such *in vivo* observations have generally proven reliable, valid, and sensitive to treatment changes in a wide variety of settings, including homes, schools, and hospital wards (see Kent and Foster, 1977; Paul and Lentz, 1977). See Box 2-2 for example.

While assessment devices such as self-reports and psychological tests have long been known to suffer from a lack of reliability and the inability to predict the occurrence of behavior in the natural environment, the methodological problems of *in vivo* observation of behavior have become apparent only in the past few years. Problems of interest have been observer bias (the likelihood that an observer will be influenced by his or her expectations about what should occur), the effects of feedback on observational data, and the reactivity of the subjects to the observational process itself.

Observer biases. Rosenthal was one of the first investigators to document the problem of observer biases (summarized by Rosenthal, 1969). He and his associates showed that when observers were told to expect certain events to occur in an experiment (for example, one group of animals should learn faster), they reported the events even though unbiased measures indicated that the events did not occur. These findings, as well as studies by Azrin, Holz, Ulrich, and Goldiamond (1961) and Scott, Burton, and Yarrow (1967) led investigators to question the objectivity of observational recordings. We now know that the expectation effect or knowledge of experimenters' hypotheses is critical only when the behavior being observed is evaluated in a global fashion. In contrast, if an observer is asked to record the presence or absence of a behavior in small time units (for example, every 30 sec or every 2 min), no observer biases are found (Kent and Foster, 1977).

Feedback effects on observational data. In many clinical situations, investigators may be very enthusiastic and indicate sincere relief and delight when an observer reports to the investigator that the problem behavior (for example, severe self-destructive behavior or intense tantrums) has decreased. O'Leary, Kent, and Kanowitz (1975) assessed whether this kind of experimenter feedback could artificially alter or bias an observer's recordings. They trained observers to record reliably the disruptive behavior of children in a classroom and then showed them videotapes that were purportedly of baseline and treatment phases of a recently completed study. The experimenter told the observers that certain of the behaviors were expected to decrease with the onset of treatment and other behaviors were not expected to change. In fact, as you might guess, the videotapes showed almost identical rates of behavior during the purported "baseline" and "treatment" phases. When an observer gave the experimenter data that indicated the "expected" decrease, the experimenter made comments such as "The treatment really seems to be working," or "Dr. Kent will really be glad to see the changes you are finding!" The expectations and feedback led the observers to report decreases in the "manipulated" behaviors, and no decreases in the behaviors which were "expected" to remain stable. The implication of this study is that investigators must be careful not to give feedback to observers that might artificially bias the data collection.

Reactivity of observation. The potential effect of an observer's presence on the behavior being observed has been a concern for over twenty-five years (for a review, see Kent and Foster, 1977). One of the first systematic investigations of reactivity was conducted by Roberts and Renzaglia (1965), who found that counselors made more interpretative statements when they knew that their sessions were obviously recorded than when the sessions were surreptitiously recorded. (The counselors knew that there was always some chance that sessions would be recorded.)

White (1977) evaluated the effects of observer presence on the interactions and activity level of family members in a simulated living room setting by having observers both in the room and behind a one-way mirror. He found lower rates of disruptive behavior for older children and less movement for all family members during the times when an observer was in the room. His study is limited by the brevity of observation periods (four consecutive half-hour intervals), but it points to the need for an adaptation period in which the effects of observers would diminish. For example, when the effects of observers were evaluated in studies lasting at least ten days in institutions for retarded (Mercatoris and Craighead, 1974), psychiatric hospitals (Hagen, Craighead, and Paul, 1975), or in elementary schools (Dubey and others, 1977) and junior high schools (Nelson, Kapust, and Dorsey, 1978), very few effects of observers have been found. While there is no systematic research evaluating the factors that increase reactivity, the present authors feel that the reactivity effect will be strongest when brief observations are made of normal adolescents and adults and of children with conduct disorders.

SELF-REPORT AND PERSONALITY INVENTORIES

Role of personality tests in behavior therapy. Psychologists have used personality tests or inventories for decades, but behavioral psychologists have often been reluctant to use them. In fact, as noted earlier in the Swan and MacDonald (in press) survey, behavior therapists use personality tests with only 20 percent of their clients. One of the personality tests most widely used by psychologists, the *Minnesota Multiphasic Personality Inventory* (MMPI), is used largely to classify patients into diagnostic categories, such as schizophrenic, depressive reaction, or psychopathic personality. See Box 2-3. A second example of a frequently used personality test is the *Taylor Manifest Anxiety Scale* (MAS) which is used to determine the level of anxiety of adults. Tests such as the MMPI and MAS were developed to describe individuals in terms of personality traits, that is, enduring psychic structures or stylistic consistencies in social behavior. Thus, individuals are asked to make statements about themselves that would apply to them in diverse situations (for example, I generally perspire; I feel uneasy in the presence of others). While there have been many legitimate criticisms of the utility of personality tests in the measurement of traits and in the assignment of individuals to diagnostic categories (see Mischel, 1968; 1977), the tests have been useful in predicting how people will behave in certain situations and in estimating the severity of an individual's problems. It is compatible with a behavioral approach to use personality tests for this latter purpose and to do so does not necessitate adopting a trait theory of personality (Hogan, Desoto, and Solanto, 1977). For example, on the basis of a *Hyperactivity Index* (Conners, 1969) completed by a parent or teacher, the therapist can compare the referred child with large normative populations and say, "Your child scores in the upper 5 percent of the school population with regard to his activity level." Similarly, normative profiles are available for college men and women on a 122-item *Fear Survey Schedule* used to assess diverse fears of a client (Tasto, Hickson, and Rubin, 1971). The score a client receives can be compared to those of a nonclinical population, and as noted above, this comparison can aid the therapist in determining the severity of the problem.

Behavioral psychologists such as Eysenck recommended personality inventories as a means of placing an individual on a particular dimension (Eysenck and Eysenck, 1976). For example, Peterson and Quay (Quay, 1979) developed a children's assessment device which involves having a parent complete a 55-item checklist on which he or she indicates whether the child exhibits certain behaviors. On the basis of the parent's responses, a child can be described on four basic dimensions: namely, conduct disorder, personality disorder, subcultural delinquency, and inadequacy-immaturity. This assessment device is sensitive to change from both psychological and pharmacological treatments and has been validated in scores of studies using both laboratory measures and observations *in vivo.*

Specific self-report questionnaires. While traditional personality tests were designed to measure modes of responding which were characteristic of an individual in diverse situations (for example, anxiety and fear), behavior therapists have placed a strong emphasis on assessing responses to specific situations (for example, fear of public speaking). Some examples of self-report questionnaires are fear surveys to assess fear of small animals, pain, death, and aggression (for example, Geer, 1965; Wolpe and Lang, 1964); social anxiety tests (for example, Watson and Friend, 1969); and assertiveness inventories (for example, Rathus, 1973). These self-report devices are designed to measure relatively focal areas of clients' problems and, as such, may be used more and more frequently by behavior therapists. The specificity of the assertiveness assessment is seen in the *Rathus Assertiveness Schedule* (see Insert Box 2–4).

Methodological issues. *Validity.* In general, *validity* refers to the relationship or correlation between a test score and some criterion measure. Personality tests and specific self-report inventories have long been plagued by low validity. More specifically, the correlations between individuals' scores on personality tests and outcome criteria are seldom greater than 0.40 (Wiggins, 1973). Further, even individuals' scores on self-report inventories such as a fear survey like that mentioned earlier (Geer, 1965) often correlate only slightly

The Rathus Assertiveness Schedule (RAS) is a 30-item self-report schedule developed for the purpose of assessing assertive behavior. Using a 6-point scale, subjects rate the degree to which each statement is characteristic or descriptive of them. Sample items from the schedule appear below:

When the food served at a restaurant is not done to my satisfaction, I complain about it to the waiter or waitress.

If a salesman has gone to considerable trouble to show me merchandise which is not quite suitable, I have a difficult time in saying "No."

If a close and respected relative were annoying me, I would smother my feelings rather than express my annoyance.

If a famed and respected lecturer makes a statement which I think is incorrect, I will have the audience hear my point of view as well.

If someone has been spreading false and bad stories about me, I see him or her as soon as possible to "have a talk" about it.

If a couple near me in a theatre or at a lecture were conversing rather loudly, I would ask them to be quiet or to take their conversation elsewhere.

higher with outcome criteria than more general personality tests' measures. For example, Geer (1965) reported correlations of 0.39 and 0.55 between Fear Survey Schedule scores and the Manifest Anxiety Scale (MAS) for men and women, respectively.

Client distortion. A client can easily consciously overdramatize or deny his or her problems and complete a personality test or self-report inventory accordingly. Certain personality tests such as the MMPI contain scales to measure client distortions such as "faking good," and such distortion is used to make corrections on separate subtests of the MMPI. However, these correction indices are often difficult to devise, and they do not always lead to increases in the validity of the test.

Lack of specification of problems for treatment. Even a specific self-report inventory, such as one which requires that a parent or teacher complete a questionnaire regarding hyperactivity of a child, does not necessarily give a therapist clear notions of problems that are to be treated. For example, a child may receive a score on a rating scale of hyperactivity which places him or her in the upper 5 percent of the population of elementary school children. However, such knowledge does not provide the therapist with enough information to delineate problem behaviors that should be treated or to make various decisions regarding a treatment program, such as: (1) Completion of math assignments should receive first priority; (2) Cooperation with other children on in-class projects is of secondary importance; and (3) An increase in frustration tolerance regarding siblings' late bedtime should not be addressed until some progress is made in school. Such treatment goals generally come only from detailed clinical interviews and/or *in vivo* observation.

ROLE-PLAYING

Role-playing, as the name implies, consists of having a client enact various interpersonal encounters, for example, asking a friend for a date, questioning a supervisor's judgment, complimenting a family member, responding to a job interviewer in a confident manner, or communicating without hostility with spouse. Role-playing has long been used by therapists of varying persuasions. In fact, role-playing has been made popular by Moreno, a psychodynamically oriented psychiatrist, who introduced psychodrama in the United States in 1925. Psychodrama involves the enactment of interpersonal experiences in a group therapy context. The therapist serves as a director of the role-plays; the fellow group members assume various roles; and the clients are prompted to express feelings associated with critical interpersonal experiences—often related to early childhood interactions (Moreno, 1946). Similarly Gestalt therapists use role-playing games or exercises (Levitsky and Perls, 1970) to help clients in groups experience feelings in the "here and now." In assessing a client's problem, a behavior therapist uses role-playing in an individual therapy context as a series of mini-experiments in which he or she tries to systematically expose the client to relevant, largely current, interpersonal encounters, likely to be associated with the client's problems. Behavior therapists use role-playing both to assess interpersonal problems and as a treatment procedure, but we will restrict our discussion primarily to role-playing as an assessment procedure.

Functions in assessment. As noted by Swan and MacDonald (1978), role-playing is used with 34 percent of the clients seen by behavior therapists. The assessment of a client's behavior is facilitated by the therapist taking the role of the person with whom the client has difficulty, for example, the supervisor, child, or employer. Using role-playing, a therapist can quickly assess a client's skills in a wide variety of interpersonal situations. As noted earlier in this chapter, while direct *in vivo* observation of a client's interpersonal skills is often desirable, such observations may be impractical with an employer, a grandparent, or a girlfriend or boyfriend. The role-playing encounter allows a therapist to discover how a client reacts and feels when presented with situations that resemble a client's most anxiety-provoking or threatening real-life encounters.

Factors influencing role-playing. The enactment of roles by client and therapist provides for a direct and very specific assessment of the client's behavior. The validity of this approach is partly a function of the client's ability to assume roles and to do so in a manner that captures some of the emotional tenor of encounters with critical persons in his or her life. Fortunately, after some practice and guidance, most clients are able to overcome uneasiness they have about the "acting" role and can simulate their significant encounters quite well. Where such is not the case, the therapist can ask the client to give detailed verbal descriptions of what he or she would say in situations which cause interpersonal difficulty.

The therapist's ability to effectively utilize role-playing is dependent upon his or her knowledge of typical problems presented by the significant other individuals in the client's life. For example, if a therapist has a mother role-play her interactions with her teenager, the therapist should know both characteristic problems presented by the teenager as well as the verbal style and idiomatic expressions which are likely to elicit emotional responses in the mother. Similarly, if a therapist has a client assume the role of a job applicant, the therapist should have some clear knowledge of the types of questions asked by an employment interviewer and the interpersonal styles of such interviewers.

Role-playing as an assessment procedure has not received as much research attention as have the previous assessment methods. As Goldfried and Linehan (1977) noted, there is a trend towards assuming that role-playing itself serves as an adequate assessment of the actual encounters of the client. The assessment of assertive behavior is one of the few areas in which the validity of role-playing has been examined empirically, and there is evidence that it is useful in the assessment of assertion of adolescents and college students (Freedman, 1974; MacDonald, 1978; McFall and Lillesand, 1971). Since role-playing is a widely used procedure, research on its reliability and validity is clearly needed.

PHYSIOLOGICAL MEASUREMENT

Physiological measures have been increasingly used in behavioral assessment research in recent years, but they are infrequently used by clinicians. Temperature, respiration rate, penile erection measures, and vaginal blood flow have been used to measure sexual arousal. Measurements of heart rate, blood pressure, and skin resistance responses have been used extensively in studies assessing fear. While certain physiological measures, such as blood pressure and heart rate, could easily be obtained in any behavior therapist's office, most physiological measures require expensive instrumentation not usually found in psychological or psychiatric clinics. In addition to cost factors, many physiological measures do not correlate highly with self-report and observational measures. This does not mean that physiological measures are less valid than self-report or observational measures, but a client's self-report is the report clinicians generally choose to attend to most seriously, since self-report of problems is almost always the criterion for entry into and termination of therapy (Barlow, 1977). Despite the infrequent use of physiological measures by clinicians, several examples of their role in clinical research and/or treatment follow.

The type and duration of women's sexual responses have long been the subject of debate largely because there were no devices that allowed a clinician to assess women's genital responses. Fortunately, Geer, Morokoff, and Greenwood (1974) developed a device which measures blood flow in the vaginal wall. A clear, light-sensitive probe (½ in. diameter by 1¾ in.) allows a clinician to measure the amount of light reflected by vaginal wall tissue (see picture below). As arousal and blood flow increase, less light is transmitted through the probe. For some women, change in vaginal blood volume is a reliable indicator of orgasm (Geer, 1977), and this technological development has clearly enabled researchers to assess sexual arousal in females.

The role of physiological measurement is highlighted in the treatment of certain enuretic children (bedwetters) with night terror. Such children have frightening dreams; they awaken abruptly, sometimes screaming (for example, "I won't do it!"); and then they wet their beds (Sperling, 1971). Dreams usually occur during a period of sleep in which there is a great deal of electrical discharge in the brain, and the eyes move rapidly (REM sleep). It is possible to detect REM sleep by placing a small sensing device near the corner of the eye (electro-oculogram). When the clinician has a suspicion that night terror and REM sleep are precursors to bedwetting, a physiological assessment can be made to confirm or disconfirm the clinician's hunches. If night terror and REM sleep are precipitants of the enuresis, the therapist can address the child's fears and dreams rather than focus on toileting habits and exercises designed to increase bladder size.

A CALL FOR MULTIMETHOD ASSESSMENT

It should now be clear that no assessment method is uniquely superior. Each has its particular advantages and disadvantages, and sometimes there is only moderate agreement between the various assessment methods. For example, with regard to the measurement of sexual behavior of women by the probe mentioned earlier in this chapter, it has been shown that alcohol decreases sexual arousal as measured by the probe but increases women's self-report of sexual arousal (Wilson and Lawson, 1976). In the assessment of anxiety, Lang (1977) has shown that behavioral, physiological, and subjective reports are not always significantly correlated and sometimes change differentially in response to different treatment methods. Given this lack of correspondence between various assessment measures and the advantages and disadvantages of each assessment domain, numerous behavioral clinicians, such as Lazarus (1976),

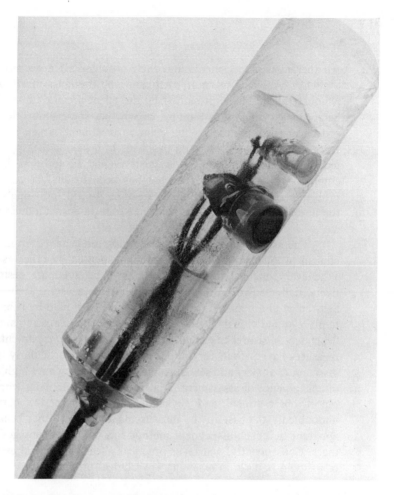

Vaginal probe containing light source (light circular area) and photocell (dark circular area) that is used to measure vaginal blood volume changes. Reflected light passes through the vaginal wall tissue and is reflected to the photocell surface. When viewing erotic films, the blood volume increases markedly over a resting period. (Geer, Morokoff, & Greenwood, 1974).

O'Leary and Johnson (1979), Patterson (1974), and Lobitz and Johnson (1975), and have argued for a multimodal or multimethod assessment approach using a combination of demographic questionnaires, interviews, personality inventories, and where possible, naturalistic observations of the problem behavior.

Summary

All therapists assess clients and their problems. If a decision is made that a client's problems warrant treatment, the therapist must carefully decide whether the problems presented by the client are the problems that should be addressed directly in therapy, or whether some unmentioned or "higher order" problem should be the primary treatment target. A general framework for analyzing presenting problems in behavior therapy is to assess antecedent, concurrent, and consequent events. In addition, however, recent emphasis in behavioral assessment has been to analyze common everyday problems and their determinants in order to aid individuals in preventing the development of problems which require intensive individual therapeutic aid.

The assessment interview is the most important step in analyzing any clinical problem, but it should be supplemented by other assessment data. Whenever possible, direct observations of behavior are desirable. Alternatively, daily self-recordings often can provide a useful account of behavior. Self-report and personality inventories have been used by behavior therapists to place an individual with regard to some normative group and sometimes as dependent measures to evaluate the effectiveness of a treatment. Physiological measures have proven very informative in that—particularly through the assessment of anxiety and sexual responsiveness—they have highlighted the lack of convergence of assessment data from different domains (for example, self-report, observational, and physiological). Such imperfect correspondence is undoubtedly the case in the measurement of most other behavior, and it is apparent that each assessment method has unique advantages and disadvantages. Consequently, whenever practically feasible, several assessment methods should be used in assessing any clinical problem.

Suggested Readings

Interviewing:

EGAN, G. 1975. *The skilled helper.* Monterey, CA: Brooks/Cole Publishing Co.

SULLIVAN, H. S. 1954. *The psychiatric interview.* New York: W. W. Norton & Co., Inc.

Self-recording, Observation *in Vivo,* and Physiological Measurement:

CIMINERO, A. R., CALHOUN, K. S., and ADAMS, H. E., eds. 1977. *Handbook of behavioral assessment.* New York: Wiley.

CONE, J. D., and HAWKINS, R. P., eds. 1977. *Behavioral assessment: New directions in clinical psychology.* New York: Brunner/Mazel.

Self-report, Personality Inventories, and Role-Playing:

CRONBACH, L. J. 1970. *Essentials of psychological testing.* 3rd ed. New York: Harper and Row.

KORCHIN, S. J. 1976. *Modern clinical psychology.* New York: Basic Books.

MISCHEL, W. 1968. *Personality and assessment.* New York: Wiley.

3

Methodology and the Evaluation of Treatment Outcome

A defining characteristic of behavior therapy is its commitment to scientific method, measurement, and evaluation. This emphasis on careful specification of treatment methods and their objective evaluation is the cornerstone of an applied clinical science. As a result of the development of behavior therapy, the quantity and quality of research studies on treatment outcome have increased dramatically. Never before have psychological treatment methods been subject to such intense experimental evaluation. The importance of applied research of this kind is obvious. For the potential consumer (client), the taxpayer who is likely to have to support some sort of national health scheme, and the professional providing the treatment service, the most important question is, Does behavior therapy work? Is it more effective than alternative treatments? Is it a genuine therapeutic breakthrough or is it merely another of the many therapeutic fads that have come and gone so often in the history of psychotherapy? Answering this ostensibly simple question is far from easy. Evaluation of the results of behavior therapy—and all other psychological treatments—is one of the major challenges that face behavioral scientists.

A major contribution of behavior therapy has been the development of several innovative research strategies for the analysis and evaluation of treatment outcome. These research strategies range from single-case experimental designs to a variety of different group designs including tightly controlled laboratory-based methods and more applied evaluations of complex therapeutic programs in the actual clinical setting. These different research strategies go far beyond traditional treatment research methods and allow more refined empirical analyses of specific treatment techniques under different conditions. Scientific progress in the behavioral sciences is usually characterized by increasing specificity in the types of questions that are asked and the ways in which they are investigated. It should also be emphasized that these methodological advances in the evaluation of treatment outcome are not restricted to behavior therapy techniques. They are applicable to all psychological treatment methods that are specified in a testable fashion. This chapter summarizes the methodological issues involved in treatment outcome research and analyzes the adequacy of the different research strategies that have been employed in the evaluation of behavior therapy.

The Clinical Case Study

Clinical case studies such as those of Mr. B, Diane T, and Johnny K presented in Chap. 1 cannot be used to demonstrate the efficacy of a treatment method. The reason is that these case studies were uncontrolled. Among other factors, successful outcome could be due to changes in the client's life that are unrelated to treatment; to the mere passage of time; or to the unusual persuasiveness of the therapist, and not the treatment method itself. There is no way of excluding (controlling for) these factors in a case study; hence a cause-effect relationship between treatment method and therapeutic improvement cannot be established. However, this does not mean that a clinical case study is without value.

The advantages of the case study have been summarized by Lazarus and Davison (1971, p. 200) as follows:

a) A case study may cast doubt upon a general theory.

b) A case study may provide a valuable heuristic to subsequent and better-controlled research.

c) A case study may permit the investigation, although poorly controlled, of rare but important phenomena.

d) A case study can provide the opportunity to apply principles in entirely new ways.

e) A case study can, under certain circumstances, provide enough experimenter control over a phenomenon to furnish "scientifically acceptable" information.

f) A case study can assist in placing meat on the theoretical skeleton.

Single-Case Experimental Methodology

It is possible to study the individual case without sacrificing experimental control. An important contribution of the operant conditioning approach has been the development of *single-case* experimental methodology with which to conduct controlled research and treatment in individual clients. The clinical adaptation of operant own-control designs in which therapeutic change is evaluated relative to the individual's own performance demonstrates that behavior change in an individual client is the result of specific treatment interventions and not simply due to the passage of time, placebo reaction, or some other uncontrolled event.

THE ABAB OR REVERSAL DESIGN

The *ABAB, or reversal design,* is a prototype of single-case experimental designs. In this design, following a period of baseline observation (A) during which no treatment of any kind is attempted, a treatment phase (B) is introduced while the behavior in question is continuously observed. Usually the behavior will show change in the desired direction, after which the treatment is withdrawn in a return to the baseline procedure (A). If the treatment per se was responsible for the observed change then the behavior should generally return almost to its former level during the original (A) period.

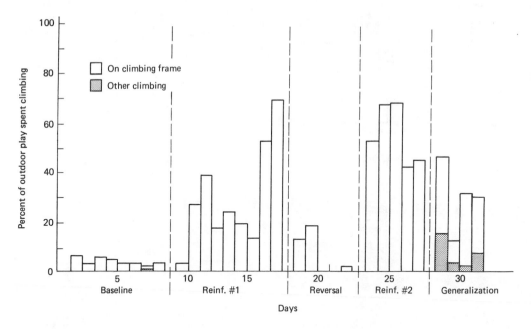

FIGURE 3.1
Percentages of each morning spent by a nursery school boy in using
a climbing-frame apparatus. (Johnson and others, *Child Development,*
37, 379–387.)

A classic example of the reversal design is a study by Johnston, Kelley, Harris, and Wolf (1966). Don was an excessively passive preschool boy who consistently stood quietly in the play yard while other children ran around, rode tricycles, and climbed on various playthings. Attempts to encourage him to engage in vigorous play through suggestion and invitation failed. In fact, it appeared that some of the teachers' efforts to encourage the boy may have inadvertently rewarded his passivity. A treatment procedure was then devised that focused on increasing Don's social responsiveness by systematically reinforcing him for such behavior. A climbing frame was selected as the first place in which to apply this behavioral treatment. Initially, the teachers attended to any approximation of their final goal. Accordingly, they attended only to touching the climbing frame. Later they attended to a minimal amount of climbing and finally only to extensive climbing. Figure 3–1 shows that during baseline (Phase A), Don was spending less than 10 percent of his time climbing, but that within the nine-day reinforcement period (Phase B), he markedly increased the time spent climbing.

The teachers then withdrew their attention for climbing (extinction, Phase A), and within three days the climbing rate dropped precipitously.

61

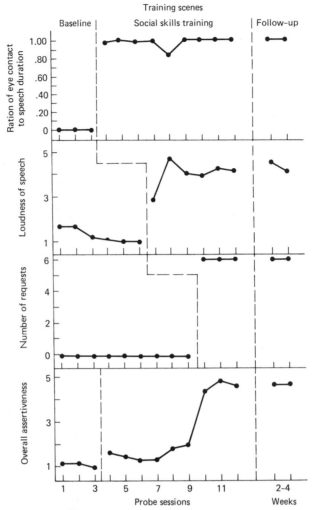

FIGURE 3.2
Probe sessions during baseline, social-skills treatment, and followup
for training scenes for Jane. A multiple-baseline analysis of: ratio of eye
contact while speaking to speech duration, loudness of speech, number of requests, and overall assertiveness. (Bornstein, Bellack, and
Hersen, *Journal of Applied Behavior Analysis,* 1977, 10: 183–196.
Copyright 1977 by the Society for the Experimental Analysis of Behavior, Inc.)

However, when the teachers again attended to climbing in the second reinforcement phase (Phase B), the climbing rate increased immediately. Following this increase the teachers attended to climbing other than on the climbing
frame (for example, on trees, playhouse, and fences), and during a final phase,
called the generalization period, it was found that Don engaged in various

climbing activities. In brief, there was clear evidence that changing the teachers' behavior altered Don's behavior.

MULTIPLE BASELINE DESIGNS

Two variations of the multiple baseline design will be presented here: (a) the multiple baseline design across behaviors; and (b) the multiple baseline design across subjects.

Multiple Baseline Design Across Behaviors. In this design, different responses are identified and measured over time so as to provide a baseline against which changes can be evaluated. Each response is then successively modified in turn; if each behavior changes maximally only when specifically treated, then a cause-effect relationship can be reliably inferred. This procedure is illustrated in Fig. 3–2. In this study, social skills training, consisting of instructions, feedback, modeling, and behavior rehearsal, was used to increase assertive behavior in an eight-year-old third grade girl who was referred for treatment because of her difficulty in relating to other children. Following baseline, the social skills training was applied successively to specific components of assertive behavior measured during role-playing that required the subject to respond to a series of interpersonal situations. The components chosen were eye contact, loudness of speech, and verbal requests for the other child to change his or her behavior. An overall index of assertion was also obtained. All measures were based on behavioral observations of the interpersonal situations. As can be seen from Fig. 3–2, the specific responses increased only when made the target of social skills training, indicating that the specific treatment technique was responsible for the behavioral change.

Multiple Baseline Design Across Individuals. In this design, baseline data are recorded for at least one behavior across several individuals in the same situation. Once the behavior is stable for all individuals, the treatment is applied to one individual while baseline conditions are continued for the others. A cause-effect relationship between the treatment technique and behavioral change can be drawn if the behavior of each individual changes only when the technique is applied to him or her. Figure 3–3 illustrates this design.

GENERAL CHARACTERISTICS OF SINGLE-CASE EXPERIMENTAL DESIGNS

The single-case experimental designs shown above are only some of the different types of single subject methodology that have been used to study a wide

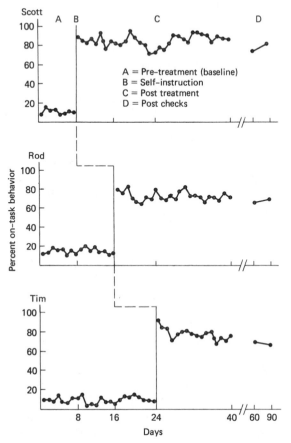

FIGURE 3.3
Daily percent on-task behaviors for Scott, Rod, and Tim across experimental conditions. (Bornstein, P. H., and Quevillon, R. P. The effects of a self-instructional package on overactive preschool boys. *Journal of Applied Behavior Analysis,* 1976, 9, 179–188. Copyright 1976 by the Society for the Experimental Analysis of Behavior, Inc.)

variety of different problems in different individuals. (For a detailed discussion of the full range of single-case experimental designs see Hersen and Barlow [1976]). The most important characteristics that are common to all single-case experimental designs are as follows:

1. **The objective study of overt behavior.** *Objective measures* of behavior refer to direct observation of what the individual does. Independent observers can be trained to record overt behavior reliably. For example, the dependent variable in each of Figs. 3–1, 3–2, and 3–3 above

was measured by behavioral observations. Such observations are not totally free from bias, as the previous chapter indicated, but they are less vulnerable to artifact or distortion than the impressionistic and global therapist ratings that were once the main source of outcome data. Objective physiological measures such as penile tumescence are frequently used in single-case experimental studies (see Fig. 6–5, Chap. 6).

2. **The continual measurement of behavior.** The target behavior is assessed regularly before, during, and after treatment intervention, often on a daily basis. An advantage of continual measurement is that it provides immediate information on treatment progress and makes possible data-based decisions about whether to continue or modify treatment.

3. **Experimental and therapeutic criteria for evaluating treatment.** *Experimental criteria* refer to demonstrating that reliable changes have been produced that are the result of the specific treatment technique. In brief, the investigator must be satisfied that the pattern of results that are obtained could not plausibly be explained by variables unrelated to the specific treatment intervention. The *therapeutic criterion* refers to assessing the clinical importance of the treatment-produced change.

ADVANTAGES OF SINGLE-CASE EXPERIMENTAL DESIGNS

There are several distinct advantages to using single-case experimental designs in treatment evaluation. These are as follows:

1. The treatment of individual clients can be evaluated objectively. The personalistic quality of the clinical case study is largely preserved without sacrificing experimental rigor.

2. Clinical problems can be studied that otherwise would be rejected as unsuitable for group methodology. Some problems are relatively rare and insufficient numbers of subjects are available for group comparisons.

3. Effective treatment strategies can be developed by adding different therapeutic components to facilitate behavior change in a cumulative manner. This process is aided greatly by the continual, ongoing assessment of treatment outcome.

4. Different techniques can be compared in the treatment of the individual client.

5. Single-case experimental designs occupy an important place in the overall research strategy for evaluating psychological treatment methods. Innovative therapeutic techniques are often derived from basic psychological principles of uncontrolled clinical practice. Instead of making the jump from a clinical case study to an expensive, large-scale between-group study, small-scale testing of the technique with the appropriate single-case experimental design is recommended as an intermediate step. In this sense, single-case experimental designs are useful in the development of effective behavior change methods when it is too costly or impractical to use a full-scale between-groups design. Once the efficacy of a treatment has been established its broader value can be evaluated in a large-scale comparative outcome study.

LIMITATIONS OF SINGLE-CASE EXPERIMENTAL DESIGNS

No one form of methodology is appropriate for all evaluation purposes. Each design has its advantages and disadvantages, and single-case experimental designs are no exception to this general rule. The limitations of these designs can be summarized as follows:

1. The possible interaction of subject variables with the specific treatment technique cannot be easily studied. In other words, since only a single subject is studied, the effect of different subject characteristics (for example, high versus low anxiety) on the treatment procedure cannot be directly assessed. This requires group designs.

2. The generality of the findings with a single-case design is difficult to determine. It may be that the results obtained with one person do not generalize to other cases. One answer to this problem is the replication of single-case experiments (Hersen and Barlow, 1976). The *direct replication* strategy tests the efficacy of a single technique applied by the same therapist to a particular problem under the same conditions to more than one client. If this technique is consistently successful with all cases, interpretation of the results is clearcut. If the results are mixed or inconsistent, as is often the case in clinical research, problems in interpretation arise. Proponents of single-case experimental designs emphasize that the failure to replicate results with all subjects does not detract from the successes achieved in some subjects. However, there is a danger in attributing the successes to the

treatment method and dismissing replicative failures as due to the inadequate use of otherwise effective reinforcers. In these instances it is possible that the observed changes in behavior are due to the influence of unobserved or uncontrolled factors that happened to covary with the treatment procedure in the successful cases (Bandura, 1976).

Hersen and Barlow (1976) summarize the problem of mixed replicative results as follows:

> If one success is followed by two or three failures, then neither the reliability of the procedure nor the generality of the finding across clients has been established, and it is probably time to find out why. If two or three successes are mixed in with one or two failures, then the reliability of the procedure will be established to some extent, but the investigator must decide when to begin investigating reasons for lack of client generality. (p. 335)

Direct replication strategies require homogeneous clients, that is, clients who have the same problems. However, this rarely occurs in applied research. If the treatment is effective with all clients despite the heterogeneity that is usually found with clinical cases, interpretation of the data is easy. If the results are mixed, however, the investigator cannot know whether the method is of limited utility or whether outcome is attributable to simple variations in the problems shown by clients.

Even if the data from direct replications can be unambiguously interpreted, the problem of generalizing the results from the individual case to a more general population of clients remains. The solution proposed by operant conditioning is *systematic replication.* Systematic replication is defined as the attempt to replicate the findings from direct replication studies, varying the therapists who administer the procedures, the type of clients, the nature of the behavior being modified, the setting in which treatment occurs, or any combination thereof. But there are difficulties with this strategy. The question is, When is a systematic replication series finished? Or put differently, when can the investigator decide that the generality of a finding has been scientifically established? This question is part of the more general concern in experimental psychology with external validity (see Campbell and Stanley, 1963). Hersen and Barlow (1976) suggest that a systematic replication series is never over, that knowledge gained in this fashion is cumulative, and that investigators and treatment methods vary in terms of the relative amount of confidence therapists can place in them. But this involves subjective judgment, and it is clear that there are disagreements even among therapists about what constitutes "relatively effective" treatment methods in this sense.

3. Interpretation of the findings of single-case experimental designs is straightforward when the target behavior is stable during baseline and when treatment effects are clearly different from baseline. However, these ideal conditions are not always obtained in clinical research. Most treatments are not that effective when administered individually since clinical problems are usually the product of several interacting determinants. As a result, not every determinant is controlled for. Marked variability in the target behavior over different phases of a single-case experimental design makes it difficult to evaluate whether significant change has occurred. There is evidence that researchers asked to judge change in the target behavior of an individual across successive phases of a single-case design do not always agree as to whether the treatment produced a significant effect on that behavior.

4. It has also been demonstrated that results from a single-subject design that are judged to be significant by visual inspection can be shown to be statistically nonsignificant when appropriate statistical analyses are conducted. Consider Fig. 3–4 which illustrates the results from an ABAB reversal design. "Eyeballing" this graph indicates that the reinforcement of social interaction produced a significant change in observed behavior. However, Gottman (1973) conducted a statistical analysis of these data and found that there were no statistically significant changes either in amount of social interaction or in the slope of the data across successive phases of the experiment. One of the more interesting developments in single-subject methodology has been the recent attention given to methods for the statistical analysis of these data (Kazdin, 1976b).

5. Specific limitations attach to different designs. In the ABAB reversal design, for example, demonstrating the efficacy of the treatment requires that the treatment effect is reversible and that the target behavior returns to baseline level once the treatment is withdrawn. However, it is often ill-advised or unethical to return to a baseline condition after a treatment has been shown to be effective. For example, when a self-destructive child has responded to a particular intervention, such as praise from attendants for positive interactions with other children on the ward, it may be very detrimental to the child's physical and mental health to ask the attendants to withdraw their praise. In short, a reversal design can only be used when a return to a baseline phase will not seriously harm the client or patient.

A second problem with the reversal design is that it is limited to treatment conditions which can be readily reversed. There are certain treatments which lead to changes in behavior which are relatively permanent and which do not change even when the treatment is withdrawn; for example, if enuretic

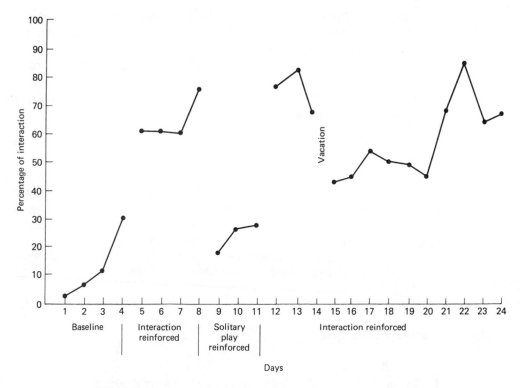

FIGURE 3.4
Percentage of time a withdrawn boy spent in social interaction before treatment began, during periods when social behavior toward peers was positively reinforced, and during periods when teachers gave attention for solitary play. (From Harris, F. R., Wolf, M. M., and Baer, D. M. Effects of adult social reinforcement on child behavior. *Young Children*, 1964, 20, 8–17. Copyright 1964, National Association for the Education of Young Children, 1834 Connecticut Avenue, N. W., Washington, D. C. 20009. Reproduced by permission.)

children (bedwetters) are given certain toilet training, their bladder size increases. They no longer wet the bed, and the withdrawal of the treatment does not lead to a return to a baseline condition. This limitation applies especially to the learning of new skills. Once a child has learned to read, for example, removal of external incentives to read will not make the child illiterate. In cases like this, the original baseline can never be reinstated. If the behavior of interest shows no reversal, little of significance can be concluded. Another important consideration is that the goal of clinical treatment is to produce long-term changes in desired behaviors. Accordingly, one would hope that treatment effects would *not* reverse easily. As a result the ABAB design cannot be used to study lasting therapeutic changes.

The multiple baseline design across behaviors requires that the different responses be independent of one another. If more than one behavior changes when a single behavior is treated, it is impossible to draw cause-effect relationships. Yet another goal of clinical treatment is to produce generalized behavior change. Accordingly, one would hope that treatment effects generalize broadly. As a result the multiple baseline design cannot be used effectively to study generalization processes.

To summarize, the single-case experimental designs discussed above are invaluable in determining functional relationships between treatment and behavior change in the individual case. However, they are of limited value when it comes to assessing the interaction between subject variables and specific treatment procedures, in studying the generalization and maintenance of behavior change, and in establishing the overall generality of a particular finding. Between-group designs are required for these purposes. In addition, determining the comparative efficacy of different treatment procedures necessitates the use of between-group methodology. Some of the more important variations of between-group methodology for evaluating treatment outcome are discussed next.

Between-Group Designs

When a number of subjects are assigned to a treatment group or a control group and their outcome then compared, the design is called a *between-group design.* A variety of between-group designs have been used to evaluate treatment outcome. As with other research strategies, each between-group design has its particular advantages and disadvantages.

LABORATORY-BASED EVALUATION
OF TREATMENT METHODS

At first glance it might seem as though the best way to evaluate treatment outcome would be to study the effects of therapy carried out by experienced practitioners with actual clients under clinical conditions. This is extraordinarily difficult to do for several reasons. From a methodological point of view it is hard and often impossible to conduct highly controlled research in such service-delivery settings. From a practical point of view it is difficult to recruit experienced therapists who have the time or desire to participate in such research. Similarly, finding sufficiently large numbers of similar clients with common problems is a formidable task. Finally, from an ethical point of view it is difficult to assign clients to control groups that do not receive the most effective form of treatment (see O'Leary and Borkovec, 1978).

An alternative research strategy to studying the clinical situation directly is to evaluate specific treatment methods applied to well-defined, circumscribed problems under controlled laboratory conditions. Among the problems treated under these controlled conditions have been fears of harmless animals and snakes, social and interpersonal anxieties (for example, fear of public speaking), and test anxiety. This research strategy is recommended for several reasons.

Advantages of Laboratory-Based Research Strategies.

1. The treatment method can be carefully specified and standardized. Different parameters of the treatment technique can be systematically varied and different components selectively analyzed. This makes it possible to determine what the necessary and sufficient conditions of treatment success are.

2. The selection of a homogeneous subject population with the same problem behavior permits evaluation of the particular type of problem for which the specific treatment is best suited.

3. Experimental variance can be further reduced by selecting homogenous therapists with similar training and experience.

4. Multiple measures of the treatment process and outcome can be frequently obtained. Most importantly, specific behavioral and psycho-physiological measures of treatment effects are made possible.

5. Subjects can be randomly assigned to different treatment and control conditions. Unlike the actual clinical situation where the therapist is ethically and professionally obliged to offer the client the most effective treatment in the most efficient manner possible, specific elements of therapy or even therapy itself can be selectively withheld in the laboratory setting.

The advantages of this laboratory-based strategy are illustrated in the research on the development and evaluation of treatment techniques for phobic disorders. A common strategy has been to use individuals with highly specific phobias about harmless snakes. (Examples of this strategy are described later in Chaps. 6 and 9.) Sufficient numbers of such subjects can be found to use several different treatment and control conditions. Advances in assessment strategies have enabled investigators to measure actual avoidance behavior and physiological fear arousal directly in the phobic situation (see Lang, 1969). The former is measured by seeing how close a subject approaches an actual snake before and after treatment. The latter is assessed by monitoring physiological measures, such as heart rate and muscle tension. In addition to the measurement of these two response systems, the experimental control afforded by this type of laboratory study enables the investigator to make precise measures of subjects' self-report of fear as they approach the phobic object. This opportunity to assess subjective fear reactions specifically in relation to the phobic object has facilitated the evaluation of different theories of successful therapy outcome. For example, Bandura's (1977a) theory that all fear reduction techniques are effective because they increase the person's sense of self-efficacy was tested and developed using the precise subjective measures that are possible in the laboratory study of fear reduction. (This is discussed in greater detail in Chap. 9.) Therapists have been trained to administer well-defined treatments that not only have demonstrated the efficacy of techniques like systematic desensitization but also have contributed to our understanding of the theoretical mechanisms responsible for therapeutic success (see Bandura, 1977a).

The Limitations of Laboratory-Based Research Strategies.

1. Concern is often expressed about whether the results from these laboratory studies can be generalized to the clinical treatment of clients. A target of such criticism has been a large number of studies on fear reduction methods using only mildly fearful college students as subjects. These subjects participate mainly because they are offered course credit or money and do not seek treatment because of a pressing personal problem. The problems presented by these subjects differ considerably from the more severe phobias of clients, and they are more easily influenced by placebo factors than more intense fear reactions. As such, these studies are of little value in evaluating treatment outcome (Bernstein and Paul, 1971).

   However, not all laboratory-based studies have been limited in importance because of the inclusion of only mildly fearful, relatively unmotivated subjects. Studies such as those of Bandura and his associates of individuals with genuine phobias about snakes that interfere with their daily lives, cause personal distress, and lead them to seek treatment are most appropriate for the evaluation of treatment outcome (for example, Bandura, 1977a; Bandura, Blanchard, and Ritter, 1969). These studies incorporate methodological rigor while still focusing on significant personal problems. Of course, findings with subjects with simple phobias, such as a fear of snakes or heights, are not necessarily generalizable to other more complex neurotic disorders like agoraphobia (the terror of leaving home alone and of crowded public places). There is suggestive evidence that agoraphobics respond differently from other phobics to the same treatment (Hallam, 1978; Mathews, 1978).

   A common tactic in outcome research in behavior therapy has been to recruit subjects by advertising treatment programs in the media. Some critics have charged that subjects recruited in this way are intrinsically different from individuals who on their own accord seek therapy in the clinical setting (e.g., Gurman, Knudson, and Kniskern, 1978; Marks, 1978). However, if care is taken to demonstrate that subjects recruited for clinical research are as severely distressed and motivated to change as their counterparts in the natural clinical setting, this objection ceases to be a problem. Consistent with this view, Grey, Sartory, and Rachman (1979) found that they were unable to distinguish between phobic subjects recruited for research and phobics who had already sought therapy either in terms of their reactions to fearful stimuli or their response to treatment.

2. The question of whether the findings of a research study are generalizable to therapeutic situations applies to *all* clinical research, including studies conducted with clients in actual clinical settings. In evaluating therapy outcome research, the critical question is to what degree do the conditions of the study approximate the clinical situation to which the investigator wishes to general-

ize. The generalizability of a study has to be evaluated along several different dimensions. These dimensions include the target problem; the type of subject; the subjects' motivation for treatment; therapist characteristics and training; the nature of the treatment method and how it might vary from the way it is usually administered in clinical practice; the assessment of treatment effects, and so on (see Kazdin and Wilson, 1978). It is assumed that the closer the similarity of a study along a particular dimension, the greater will be the generalizability of the results.

As Kazdin and Wilson (1978) have pointed out, the generality of findings based on "real" clients seen in clinical settings is not intrinsically greater than data derived from laboratory investigations. It is often the case that the way in which subjects are selected in these clinical outcome studies results in the admission of only highly select clients with particularly favorable chances of improvement. In addition, the motivation of clients seen in clinical practice and the severity of their behavior disorders may vary as widely as they do in laboratory-based studies.

3. It is often alleged that treatment effects are easier to achieve in laboratory-based studies than in the clinical setting. This is not necessarily the case. Once again, the various dimensions listed above must be considered. In some cases of mild or transient fears, this may be true. In other cases, however, treatment effects may be *more* difficult to achieve in the laboratory setting than in clinical practice. The laboratory-based evaluation of a treatment method may be more stringent because it minimizes parameters of therapy that are likely to facilitate successful outcome, for example, tailoring the content and duration of therapy to individual clients. Typically in laboratory-based studies, the length and nature of the treatment is decided upon in advance and applied routinely to all subjects.

To summarize, laboratory-based research plays an important role in the overall evaluation of therapy outcome. It allows the unambiguous demonstration of the efficacy of treatment methods, specification of the procedural parameters that contribute to their efficacy, and the analysis of the theoretical mechanisms that account for behavior change. It is difficult, if not impossible, to address these issues in a controlled manner in the clinical situation. Once these findings have been established, they can be extended to and evaluated in less controlled clinical settings where the questions of comparative efficacy and cost-effectiveness among different treatment methods are of paramount importance.

THE TREATMENT PROGRAM RESEARCH STRATEGY

Evaluation of the efficacy of a single treatment method applied to a circumscribed problem is an example of *technique-oriented* research. The relatively restricted conditions of controlled research along these lines require that all subjects are treated in the same way with the same procedure. Yet clinical experience indicates that such homogeneity among a large number of clients is questionable. It is usually the case that different variables maintain problem behavior in different individuals. Moreover, clinical disorders are typically determined by multiple factors rather than a single maintaining variable, and a multifaceted therapy program is required to change behavior. This means that clinical practice emphasizes a *problem-oriented* approach in which several treatment methods are tailored to the individual client's particular problem. The treatment program, or what has also been called the package research strategy, takes this into account by evaluating therapy programs that "include as many component procedures as seem necessary to obtain, ideally, a total treatment success" (Azrin, 1977). If the multi-component treatment program proves to be successful, subsequent research can be directed towards identifying the effective components of the overall package.

Alcoholism, for example, is a complex disorder that has been extremely difficult to treat successfully. Accordingly, Azrin (1976) devised a multifaceted treatment program consisting of numerous techniques that could be expected to counteract alcoholism. The program included methods to improve the alcoholic's marriage and family relationships, find him a satisfying job, develop social activities and friends unrelated to drinking, prevent impulsive drinking by the use of the drug Antabuse, institute special motivational procedures to ensure that the alcoholic took his Antabuse, and other techniques. Compared to routine hospital care, this treatment package proved to be very effective in reducing alcoholism over a two-year follow-up. Future research can determine which of these many treatment components contribute to successful outcome and which do not. In this way the treatment package can be refined and made more efficient.

Advantages of the Multi-Component Treatment Program Research Strategy.

1. It is a problem-oriented research strategy that allows for an evaluation of multiple treatment methods that are typically used in clinical practice. The primary emphasis is on producing clinically significant change and thus it is close to the nature and purpose of clinical practice.

2. It is logically one of the first approaches to evaluate a given treatment approach. If it is successful, it indicates the need for continued research. If it fails to produce therapeutic improvement, it makes little sense to try to analyze the component parts of the program. In other words, it serves as a useful screening procedure in determining whether further component analysis research is warranted.

Limitations of the Multi-Component Treatment Program Research Strategy.

1. From the standpoint of treatment evaluation and analysis it is important to ensure that the program is not so complex and wide-ranging that it is difficult to identify the specific techniques in complex programs. Every component of the program must be operationally defined and replicable.

2. The treatment program should not be so multifaceted that it becomes difficult to identify it as a distinctive program that is procedurally different from alternative treatments to which it might be compared.

To summarize, the treatment program strategy focuses on treatment outcome, that is, Is treatment effective? Understanding the reasons for the efficacy of treatment requires analytic research that involves component analysis of the treatment program. Two such analytic research strategies are discussed next.

THE CONSTRUCTIVE RESEARCH STRATEGY

In this approach the effect of a single, basic treatment component is established, and additional components are sequentially added to determine if they increase the treatment effect. The effective components are retained and a multi-component treatment program is constructed.

An example of the constructive strategy in outcome research in which the incremental value of adding successive treatment components was assessed is a study by Romancyzk, Tracey, Wilson, and Thorpe (1973). The following were the different treatment groups they used in the treatment of obese clients:

1) No treatment control (waiting list).
2) Self-monitoring control (weight only).
3) Self-monitoring control (weight and calorie intake).
4) Self-monitoring and symbolic aversion.
5) Self-monitoring, symbolic aversion, and relaxation.
6) Self-monitoring, symbolic aversion, relaxation, and behavioral management (stimulus control) instructions.
7) Self-monitoring, symbolic aversion, relaxation, behavioral management, and contingency contracting.

Briefly, the results showed that self-monitoring of daily caloric intake was about as effective as any of the more complex packages in producing weight loss in the short term. If this study had merely involved group 7 (the full multi-component program) and group 1 (no-treatment control), then it would have demonstrated the efficacy of the behavioral package. What it would not have shown is that the total program is not significantly better than the simple calorie monitoring component. Unfortunately, such designs are often impractical because they require a large number of subjects with the same problem.

THE DISMANTLING RESEARCH STRATEGY

In the *dismantling strategy,* specific components of the treatment package are systematically eliminated, and the associated decrement in treatment effects is measured. The relative contributions of each component to the total treatment program can then be assessed. Both the separate and combined effects of components can be analyzed. It can also be determined whether these effects are interactive or additive.

Research on the technique of systematic desensitization provides an example of the dismantling strategy. As Wolpe (1958) originally described the technique, three fundamental procedures were essential for effective treatment: (a) progressive relaxation training as a response that was incompatible with anxiety; (b) a graded hierarchy of anxiety-eliciting situations; and (c) pairing each anxiety-eliciting situation with the incompatible response by instructing the client to imagine each hierarchy item while deeply relaxed. Studies using the dismantling strategy have analyzed the role of each of these components in influencing outcome. Thus variations of the desensitization procedure, without relaxation or with tension instead of relaxation, and desensitization, without a graded hierarchy or with only intensely fearful items, have been contrasted with the full technique (including all three components). As a whole the findings from this research have shown that neither the relaxation training nor the graded hierarchy is essential for treatment success. The critical component is repeated exposure in imagination or real life to the anxiety-eliciting situations (Kazdin and Wilcoxon, 1976; Wilson and Davison, 1971). These findings have had important practical consequences for the treatment of anxiety disorders as well as implications for our understanding of the theoretical mechanisms responsible for treatment outcome (see Chap. 6).

THE COMPARATIVE RESEARCH STRAGEGY

Comparative treatment outcome studies are directed towards answering the question whether one therapy method is superior to another. Ideally, alternative treatment methods are evaluated in comparative studies after their efficacy has been established in single-case experimental designs or controlled laboratory-based research. Unfortunately, this has not always been the case. Conventional comparative outcome research has been preoccupied with determining whether "psychotherapy" is more effective than "behavior therapy." This is the wrong question to ask and has led to a large number of mostly uninterpretable studies that compare ill-defined treatment programs with heterogeneous clinical disorders using global and unsatisfactory outcome measures (see Kazdin and Wilson, 1978).

Inadequacies of Conventional Comparative Outcome Research. The conventional comparative outcome research stragegy is illustrated in a much publicized study by Sloane, Staples, Cristol, Yorkston, and Whipple (1975). Briefly, ninety-four adult clients with neurotic or personality problems were randomly assigned to one of three treatment groups, after being matched for sex and severity of disturbance. The three treatment groups consisted of (a) psychoanalytically oriented psychotherapy, conducted by experienced therapists of this theoretical persuasion; (b) behavior therapy, conducted by equally experienced therapists, including Wolpe and Lazarus; and (c) a waiting-list control group. Clients in the latter group received identical pretreatment assessment procedures, were promised therapy after four months, and were contacted periodically to determine their status. Therapy lasted for four months followed by a post-treatment evaluation and an eight-month follow-up. The outcome measures consisted of ratings of three primary symptoms, subjective estimates of work, social, and sexual adjustment derived from a structured interview, and an overall rating of improvement. These ratings were made by therapist, client, a psychiatrist who did not know the nature of the study, and an "informant" who was a relative or close friend of the client.

The results? On the primary symptoms roughly 50 percent of the control group and 80 percent of the behavior therapy and psychotherapy groups were considered improved. Behavior therapy produced significant improvement in both work and social adjustment whereas psychotherapy resulted in marginal improvement in work. Behavior therapy was significantly superior to the other groups on the overall rating of improvement. On this global measure of outcome 93 percent of the group receiving behavior therapy were rated as significantly improved, whereas 77 percent of the psychotherapy and waiting-list patients were rated as significantly improved. There were no differences among the three groups at follow-up.

In many ways the Sloane and others (1975) study is the best conventional comparative outcome study yet conducted. The overwhelming majority of conventional comparable outcome studies entail fundamental methodological problems that make meaningful interpretation of the results virtually impossible (see Kazdin and Wilson, 1975). However, even in the Sloane and others (1975) study, a number of conceptual and methodological problems make it difficult to draw unambiguous conclusions from the findings. One of the major problems which is typical of traditional outcome studies is inadequate assessment of outcome.

Inadequate Assessment of Outcome. The failure to obtain any objective behavioral measure of treatment effects is a major shortcoming. Assessing outcome by means of subjective global ratings derived from a single clinical interview is scientifically unacceptable. The therapist's own ratings are obviously open to bias, just as the client's self-rating is. In an improvement on these measures, which have often been the only measures used to evaluate treatment outcome, Sloane and others (1975) obtained an independent assessor's ratings of outcome. The problem with these ratings is that they were based on the client's self-report during the clinical interview and not on observations of the client's behavior in real-life problem situations.

Ideally, outcome measures should reflect the clients' functioning in the naturalistic environment. These clinical ratings must be distinguished from systematic observations of actual behavior. The therapist's or, by extension, an independent assessor's ratings of client functioning on the basis of a clinical interview has long been uncritically accepted as an appropriate means of measurement. As such, it is consistent with the traditional psychotherapy model that is predicated on the assumption that the relationship between therapist and client is the primary vehicle through which change takes place and is to be evaluated. The behavioral approach, based upon the rejection of internalized personality traits and on the recognition of situation-specific effects of behavior (Mischel, 1968), has emphasized that clients' behavior in the clinical interview (a relatively contrived situation) does not necessarily provide a satisfactory sample of their behavior in the natural environment. Nor do changes that occur in the therapist-patient relationship necessarily generalize to other situations (Wilson and Evans, 1977). From a behavioral viewpoint, the assessor's ratings would have been more informative had they been based on samples of clinically relevant behavior.

Sloane and others (1975) also attempted to obtain ratings of outcome from friends or family of the clients in their study. Unfortunately, practical difficulties resulted in sketchy and incomplete information from these "informants." Moreover, it might be noted that ratings by "informants" may be inconsistent and unreliable unless they are specially trained to be observers. In view of these difficulties with subjective ratings, it is not surprising that the correlations among the four types of raters in the Sloane and others study were extremely low. As Bandura (1969) has noted, "conflicting data of this sort are not at all surprising as long as they are not erroneously considered as measures of behavior outcome but are understood instead as differences between therapists' judgmental responses (which rarely correlate perfectly with clients' actual behavior functioning)" (p. 458).

Another problem common to many conventional comparative outcome studies has been the inadequate specification of treatment methods.

Ill-Defined Global Treatment Approaches. Attempts to compare something called "psychotherapy" with something labeled "behavior therapy" assume that these are uniform, homogeneous approaches. However, there is no "behavior therapy" to which other approaches can be compared in any general sense. There are several different procedures that collectively can be referred to as behavior therapy. Similarly, there are different methods of psychotherapy. Sloane and others (1975) tried to define psychotherapy and behavior therapy respectively by drawing up a list of defining characteristics of each approach. However, both approaches still encompassed a wide range of different procedures.

Some behavioral techniques are clearly more effective than others, as the remainder of this book indicates. As a result, evaluations of behavior therapy are likely to be distorted if it is assumed that all behavioral methods are uniformly effective. Behavior therapy consists of numerous techniques that are constantly being developed and refined. Two of the behavioral techniques in the Sloane and others (1975) study, for example, were systematic desensitization and electrical aversion conditioning. These were two of the most important methods in behavior therapy in its early stages. However, alternative methods to systematic desensitization have now been developed that appear to be even more effective. Electrical aversion conditioning, once widely used with problems like alcoholism and sexual deviance, has been shown to be largely ineffective and is rarely used.

Comparative outcome studies also require clearly defined alternative treatments. If procedural differences between contrasting techniques are blurred, it is difficult to interpret results. Replication also depends on precise specification of treatment methods. Specification is essential in order to determine if the treatments were implemented correctly and were procedurally distinct from each other. A well-designed study should include independent measures of whether alternative treatments were distinct from one another and whether they conformed to specifications. Data can be collected either through video- or audio-tapes, transcripts, or direct observation to ensure that treatments were implemented properly. For example, Sloane and others (1975) analyzed audio-tape recordings of the fifth session of therapy to determine whether their psychoanalytically oriented psychotherapy was perceived as procedurally distinct from their behavior therapy condition.

To summarize this section, methodological flaws in conventional comparative outcome research have obscured potential differences among alternative treatment methods. Claims made on the basis of studies such as the Sloane and others (1975) investigation (and other even more inadequate studies) that there are no differences between behavior therapy and psychotherapy can be seriously questioned (see Kazdin and Wilson, 1978). More relevant data on the differences between alternative treatment methods are presented in later sections of this book. Meaningful comparisons among different treatment methods require careful specification of treatment procedures and objective assessment of outcome. Specificity is a *sine qua non* of adequate evaluation of treatment outcome.

Comparative Outcome Research Revisited. Rather than asking whether "behavior therapy" is more effective than "psychotherapy," the appropriate outcome question is *what* treatment method applied by *whom* is most effective for *what* problem in *which* individual. This question cannot be answered by a single study, but it provides the framework in which outcome research can be conducted constructively. Well-designed comparative outcome studies play a vital role in answering this question.

An excellent example of well-controlled comparative outcome research is Paul and Lentz's (1977) evaluation of the psychosocial treatment of chronic mental hospital patients. The subjects were all diagnosed as schizophrenic, were of low socioeconomic status, had been confined to a mental hospital for an average of seventeen years, and had been treated previously with drugs and other methods, without success. As Paul and Lentz state, they were "the most severely debilitated chronically institutionalized adults ever subjected to systematic study." Twenty-eight of these subjects were assigned to each of three treatment groups so that the groups were "identical on level and nature of functioning and on every characteristic of potential importance to treatment responsiveness." The three treatment groups were alternatively given:

(a) *Social Learning Therapy*. This consisted of the direct application of the experimentally established principles of learning, including modeling, classical conditioning, reinforcement procedures, such as shaping and prompting, and the token economy; (b) *Milieu Therapy*. This consisted of creating a therapeutic community structure in the institution. Within this therapeutic community, the focus was on the communication of positive expectations, group cohesiveness and group pressure directed towards normal functioning, and group problem solving in which the "residents" (as the subjects in this study were called) were treated as responsible people rather than as custodial cases; (c) *Routine Hospital Therapy*. This consisted of typical state hospital treatment of the chronic schizophrenic patient, emphasizing chemotherapy, custodial care with practically no psychological treatment, and little positive expectation of patient improvement.

Two identical adjacent units were established at a mental health center to house the social learning and milieu therapy programs. Both were staffed by the same professional personnel at a level equal to that existing in a comparison state hospital where the routine hospital treatment was administered. The remarkable degree of experimental control that Paul and Lentz built into this study can be highlighted by the following excerpt from their book:

> The milieu and social-learning programs were not only equated on all potentially relevant characteristics of the patient population, but were equally high prestige programs in identical physical settings with exact equation in the degree of operationalization, clarity, specificity, explicitness, and order provided for both staff and residents. Both programs also provided identical activity structure and focus upon specific classes of behavior, with the same staff not only conducting both programs, but equating time and focus within programs, with both running concurrently over the same time periods, subject to the same extraneous events. (p. 423)

As a result of this unprecedented experimental control in the treatment of such a severely disturbed, chronic mental population, definitive conclusions could be drawn about the comparative efficacy of the different treatments.

As subjects were discharged from the hospital, they were replaced by other subjects so that the equivalence among the groups was maintained. Subjects released into the community were provided a special twenty-six-week intensive aftercare program designed to help them readjust to life outside of the institution.

Detailed, multiple measures of subjects' functioning were obtained prior to treatment and at every six-month interval during the four-and-a-half years the programs were in effect. Most importantly, specific behavioral observations of subjects' behavior across different situations were recorded continuously throughout the treatment programs. Similar observational measures were used to assess the performance of the staff who administered the treatment programs and the interactions between the subjects and the treatment staff. All raters were professionally trained, and the consistently high reliability of their ratings was checked constantly. Subjects who were released from the hospital were assessed in their community settings. The treatment phase of the study lasted for four and a half years with a one-and-a-half-year follow-up.

The results? The social learning therapy was clearly the most effective, although both psychosocial programs produced significantly greater improvement than the routine hospital treatment. Compared to the milieu therapy and routine hospital programs, the social learning treatment produced significantly superior improvement in the residents' functioning while they were hospitalized, greater release rates, and more successful adjustment in the community. Patients in the routine hospital treatment failed to reflect a significant change in functioning. These differences at posttreatment were essentially maintained during the one-and-a-half-year follow-up evaluation. In addition to being most effective in improving personal functioning, achieving the highest release rate from the hospital, and maintaining subjects longer in the community, the social learning therapy program was the most cost-effective, amounting to roughly 30 percent less than the less effective state hospital treatment program. As a whole, these are the best results ever reported in the treatment of the chronic institutionalized patient.

There are several features of this landmark study by Paul and Lentz that illustrate important methodological points that must be observed in conducting comparative outcome research. (It is instructive to compare the methodological sophistication of this study with the Sloane and others [1975] study.)

1. The components of the social learning program used in this study had already been shown to be effective in previous single-case experimental designs and other controlled studies (see Ayllon and Azrin, 1968). Accordingly, it was timely to compare their efficacy and cost-effectiveness with other widely used treatment programs. Aside from the social learning approach, the literature indicates that the milieu treatment approach is the most effective. Thus Paul and Lentz compared the two most effective methods with the most common treatment of the chronic psychotic patient, that is, state hospital care.

2. Assessment of treatment outcome included multiple specific measures of a wide range of patient functioning both in the hospital and in the community. Objective measures that were shown to be highly reliable were used.

3. The treatment programs were operationally defined and specified precisely through the use of standardized therapy manuals. This makes it possible to replicate the procedures in other settings. It also enables one to draw cause-effect relationships between the specific treatment procedures employed and the therapeutic outcomes.

4. In addition to multiple objective measures of treatment effects on subjects' functioning, the assessment criteria included estimates of cost-effectiveness, the hospital staff's perception of the treatment programs and their effects, and other factors relevant to the consumer evaluation of alternative treatment methods. A full evaluation of treatment outcome must include information on efficiency and consumer satisfaction as well as therapeutic efficacy (see Kazdin and Wilson, 1978).

5. Continuous assessment of the behavior of the staff of the treatment programs indicated that the social learning therapy and milieu therapy approaches were being faithfully implemented, consistent with their original specifications. There were clear procedural differences between these two programs making it possible to attribute the superior outcome of the social learning program to the specific learning procedures employed by that program. The interpretation of many conventional comparative outcome studies is obscured because it is not clear whether the treatments being compared were in fact procedurally different from one another (see Kazdin and Wilson, 1978).

CONTROL GROUPS FOR THERAPY OUTCOME RESEARCH

Control groups are important in treatment evaluation in order to rule out alternative explanations of therapeutic change. Several different control conditions are possible. The choice of a particular control group depends on the research question that is being addressed and the nature of the treatment being evaluated. Some of the more common control conditions are described below.

No-Treatment and Waiting-List Control Groups. A basic question in evaluating therapy outcome is whether therapy produces greater change than would be the case without any intervening therapy. In order to answer this question a control group is required that does not receive treatment but is evaluated in the same manner as the group(s) receiving actual treatment. Such a group controls for factors like the reactive effects of assessment procedures; maturation over time; concurrent changes in the client's life; and so on. In the psychotherapy literature, changes that occur independently of formal treatment are called *spontaneous remission* (see Rachman, 1971). Spontaneous remission cannot be predicted accurately and is a function of a complex set of variables including the target problem, the client's age and socioeconomic circumstances, the criteria used to evaluate improvement, and others. A no-treatment control group is important to control for these variable influences.

There are both practical and ethical problems associated with the use of no-treatment control groups. From a practical viewpoint, if treatment is withheld the client is likely to go elsewhere for therapy. Ethically, it is difficult to justify withholding treatment for individuals in distress. Accordingly, clients are often promised treatment after a certain waiting period. This period corresponds to the time taken to administer therapy to the other treatment groups in the study. This control procedure is known as a *waiting-list* control group and is illustrated by the Sloane and others (1975) study, described above. One of the limitations of the waiting-list control group is that treatment can be compared to no treatment only during the period in which treatment is administered. Any follow-up comparison between the treatment and no-treatment groups is impossible because the latter eventually receives treatment. However, it is often important to know whether treatment effects that are initially greater than no treatment immediately after therapy are maintained over time.

The different implications that no-treatment and waiting-list control groups may have for the evaluation of treatment outcome may be illustrated by the findings of a study by Kent and O'Leary (1976). In this study, a behavioral program for conduct problem children greatly improved behavior both in the home and at school relative to a no-treatment control group. Interestingly, the highly favorable effects of treatment were no longer significant on a number of dependent variables at a nine-month follow-up. The no-treatment group improved over the follow-up interval across diverse measures, with some exceptions. In this study, the conclusions drawn would have differed if a waiting-list rather than a no-treatment control group had been used.

Placebo Treatment Control Groups. All forms of therapy share certain elements in common. Among these are providing the client with a rationale about the therapeutic technique, the building of a therapeutic relationship between the therapist and client, the client's expectations of therapeutic improvement, the therapist's supportive attitude, and similar factors. These potential therapeutic influences which are not necessarily specific to any particular method of treatment have been referred to as *nonspecific* therapeutic factors. The term "nonspecific" is unfortunate. The many therapeutic factors lumped together under this rubric are quite specific. It is more realistic to propose that, although many "nonspecific" influences still remain to be specified, they are neither intrinsically unspecifiable nor qualitatively very different from other independent variables involved in planned behavior change (see Wilson and Evans, 1976).

Once one has determined that a particular treatment program is superior to no treatment, the next question is to what extent the treatment effects are due to the specific technique (for example, systematic desensitization), as opposed to the therapeutic influences common to virtually all treatment interventions. To answer this question a procedure that controls for these common or "nonspecific" treatment influences is required. In the behavioral literature such a control group has been referred to as an *attention-placebo* control group. This group is designed to equate for placebo (nonspecific) influences without presenting the specific treatment technique. The attention-placebo control group is modeled on the placebo in drug research in which subjects receive a "drug" that is actually a chemically inert substance. If the treatment group produces greater improvement than the attention-placebo group, the conclusion is that specific active elements of the treatment technique caused the difference.

An example of an attention-placebo control group can be drawn from a study by Gelder, Bancroft, Gath, Johnston, Mathews, and Shaw (1973) that is discussed in greater detail in Chap. 6. The purpose of this study was to demonstrate that specific behavioral treatment techniques—systematic desensitization and flooding respectively—produced greater improvement than could be attributed to placebo factors or common therapeutic influences such as the therapist-client relationship. The therapist asked clients to report images that were relevant to their phobias. This served as a starting point for free association by each client who then described the thoughts and feelings elicited by the image and any new images that occurred. The therapist expressed interest in whatever the client reported and did not attempt to regulate and repeat specific imaginal scenes, as in the technique of systematic desensitization. Nor did the therapist train the client in progressive relaxation or deliberately construct an anxiety hierarchy as in systematic desensitization proper. The therapist was nondirective and let the clients lead the discussion where they wanted, unlike the more structured nature of systematic desensitization. This control procedure was described as *associative psychotherapy,* and the clients were informed that exploration of their feelings in this manner could result in a better understanding of themselves and hence lead to a reduction in their phobias. This control procedure was successful in generating expectations of therapeutic success in subjects. The fact that flooding and systematic proved to be more effective than the control group then allowed Gelder and others (1973) to conclude that the success of these two behavioral techniques could not be accounted for solely in terms of a placebo effect.

The use of attention-placebo control groups has proven invaluable in enabling investigators to pin down the effective ingredients of behavioral treatment techniques. However, these control groups are not without their limitations. The first problem is an ethical one—depriving subjects of what is thought to be the more effective treatment. However, one has to weigh the human necessity of developing effective treatment methods against this reservation. Unless carefully controlled research is undertaken, we will never be able to develop maximally effective methods for the benefit of future clients. The use of *any* control group in treatment outcome research should be monitored[1] carefully and provision made for coping with any untoward consequence. More specifically, if the treatment method proves to be significantly more effective than the control group, it can be made available to control subjects following the study.

A second limitation of some attention-placebo control groups that have been reported in the literature is that they have not always been successful in controlling for the potential therapeutic factors the investigator is trying to rule out. For example, one of the influences that an attention-placebo group is designed to control for is the subject's expectation of being helped by the treatment procedure. Accordingly, it is important that the therapeutic expectations created by the attention-placebo condition be as positive and as plausible as those created by the specific treatment technique itself. This was the case in the Gelder and others (1973) study described above. However, in other studies on systematic desensitization, it has been found that the attention-placebo condition has been perceived as less positive and plausible than desensitization. In this instance it would be difficult to interpret superior treatment effects obtained with desensitization as evidence for the specific technique. It might simply mean that the more convincing the method, the more effective it will be (see Kazdin and Wilcoxon, 1976).

Follow-Up Evaluation and the Maintenance of Therapeutic Change

A major shortcoming in therapeutic research has been the lack of long-term follow-up studies and the failure to analyze the factors that facilitate maintenance of initial treatment-produced improvement. One of the problems has been the reliance of traditional research strategies of treatment outcome evaluation on the quasi-disease model of abnormal behavior. The emphasis in this model is on the concepts of "cure" and "relapse." *Relapse* refers to the recurrence of previous problems and implies that the person has "lapsed back" into the disease for which (s)he was treated (Marlatt, 1977). The original treatment is regarded as insufficient or inappropriate and subsequent therapy is directed at the same psychodynamic processes initially assumed to cause the problem. No attempt is made to facilitate maintenance of improvement directly by the use of additional and possibly different procedures. Although the concepts of "cure" and "relapse" appropriately describe the treatment of some

[1]This is usually accomplished by requiring all research involving human subjects to be approved by Human Subjects Ethics committees at all universities and medical schools.

physical diseases, they are less useful in conceptualizing changes in behavior which are under the control of social-psychological variables. Unlike physical disease, deviant or disturbed behavior is, for the most part, a function of antecedent and consequent environmental events, and internal cognitive mediating processes which may vary in different situations, in different people, and often, at different times in the same person.

From a social learning perspective, when one asks if a treatment effect lasts, one has to consider the type of treatment, the problem being treated, and circumstances under which the person lives. Some newly acquired behaviors such as orgasmic responsiveness and urinary continence have their own immediate and powerful rewards, and such behaviors would likely generalize to new situations and would be maintained for long periods. Other newly acquired behaviors, such as eating less or not drinking, often have few powerful, positive, immediate consequences, and there are many immediate rewards inherent in eating and drinking more. The treatment of Mr. B, the exhibitionist, is a case in point. He had to learn to defer the immediate reinforcement obtained by exposing himself so as to avoid delayed punishment, that is, imprisonment. The explicit maintenance program he was placed on was designed to support his acquisition of self-control for which the immediate rewards were weak, compared to that obtained from exposure. As Mr. B developed more constructive ways of coping with emotional states and as he began to experience the rewards of a nondeviant life style, the maintenance program could be gradually faded out. Notice also that Johnny K's therapist arranged for a teacher to meet with his mother during the summer vacation to facilitate his progress in the tutorial program. *Outcome evaluation* of psychological treatments should distinguish among the initial induction *of therapeutic change, its generalization to the natural environment, and its maintenance over time.* It is important to distinguish among these processes since they might be governed by different variables. Generalized behavior change should not be expected unless specific steps are taken to produce generalization. The same consideration applies to maintenance.

The importance of differentiating between initial treatment-produced change and its maintenance over time is illustrated in a study by Kingsley and Wilson (1977). Both individual and group behavior therapy were compared to a stringent social pressure comparison program in the treatment of obese women. Following an eight-week treatment phase, half of each treatment condition received four additional booster sessions whereas the remaining half simply reported for regularly scheduled follow-up weigh-ins at three, six, nine, and twelve months respectively. The results are shown in Fig. 3–5. Both behavioral treatments were significantly superior to the social pressure treatment at posttreatment. However, whereas the two group treatments resulted in successful maintenance of treatment-produced weight reduction, subjects treated by individual behavior therapy showed substantial relapse at long-term follow-up. Importantly, the booster sessions produced continued weight loss

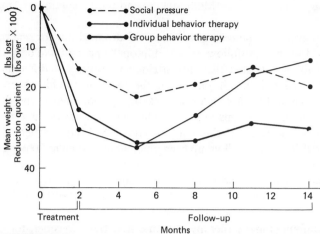

FIGURE 3.5
Mean weight reduction quotients of the three treatment groups across
therapy and follow-ups. (Kingsley, R. G., and Wilson, G. T. Behavior
therapy for obesity: A comparative investigation of long-term efficacy.
Reprinted with permission from *Journal of Consulting and Clinical
Psychology*, 1977, 45:228–289. Copyright 1977 by the American
Psychological Association.)

while they were in effect during the three months following treatment. This
facilitative effect of booster sessions was independent of the initial treatment
methods.

These results show that a specific treatment method and a specific maintenance method are *both* necessary in order to produce lasting therapeutic
change. In the treatment of obesity, for example, clients initially have to learn
effective self-control techniques for losing weight. Once these skills have been
acquired, weight becomes a function of how effectively these self-control
strategies are implemented in the real-life setting—the issues of commitment
and motivation to lose weight. Specific maintenance strategies, such as booster
sessions, that succeed in sustaining the implementation of self-control techniques will result in continued weight control. Without these maintenance
strategies, initial weight loss will rapidly dissipate. This phenomenon of temporary weight loss followed by "relapse" is typical of most treatment programs
that lack adequate maintenance strategies. This up-and-down pattern of
weight control has been called the "rhythm method of girth control!"

THE DROP-OUT PROBLEM

A number of factors must be considered in evaluating the scientific adequacy
of follow-up data. One such factor is that of subject attrition, that is, the
drop-out rate from the program. In the Kingsley and Wilson (1977) study, for
example, twenty-six clients were randomly assigned to each of three treatment
groups at the beginning of treatment. At the end of an eight-week treatment

program, 7.7 percent of subjects had dropped out for one reason or another. At the one year follow-up, an additional 3 percent had dropped out. Statistical analysis indicated that this attrition rate was not different across the three treatment groups. If it had been, the results would have been confounded. The reason is that there is evidence showing that clients who drop out of weight reduction programs are those who have not shown any improvement. Similarly, the value of this study would have been drastically reduced had the attrition rate at follow-up been much higher, such as 20 percent or more. Since those clients who prematurely terminate their participation in weight reduction programs tend to be failures, any study that focuses only on the results of the remaining clients probably presents an artificially inflated estimate of success because it is based on a biased sample. This type of sampling bias confounds many therapy outcome statistics. Consider, for example, Wolpe's (1958) claim of 90 percent success in his use of behavior therapy. Specifically, in the analysis of his results he states that he excluded some clients who had received less than fifteen sessions of therapy. Again, it is likely that those clients who dropped out were those who were least likely to improve.

Many outcome studies on behavior therapy have shown unusually small numbers of client attrition during treatment or over follow-up. With regard to obesity, attrition rates ranging from 20 to 80 percent were commonplace in traditional treatment approaches. The relatively minimal drop-out rate reported by Kingsley and Wilson (1977) is not inconsistent with findings from other behavioral studies. Similarly, follow-up studies of alcoholic clients have usually failed to report data on a large proportion of clients (for example, 20 to 50 percent treated). In one of the most impressive behavioral outcome studies yet conducted with alcoholics, Sobell and Sobell (1976) reported complete outcome data on 98.6 percent and 92.8 percent of their clients for the first and second years of follow-up, respectively.

One of the reasons for the lower client drop-out rate in many behavior therapy outcome studies is the use of contingency contracting. In brief, clients are asked to deposit a certain sum of money that is meaningful to them with the therapist at the onset of treatment. A contract is then agreed to by both therapist and client specifying that certain portions of this deposit will be progressively refunded to the client over the course of therapy and then follow-up provided the client attends a certain minimum number of therapy sessions and returns for follow-up evaluation. The contingency specified by the contract focuses on participation in the program, rather than the direct modification of the target problem itself. No method is equally applicable to all clients in clinical practice. Although contingency contracting is acceptable to most clients, some object, claiming it is coercive. In other rare instances, clients have demanded their deposits back before completion of the study.

Summary

Determining the efficacy of behavior therapy is of considerable importance for patient, therapist, and society alike. Clinical case studies do not constitute scientific evidence of treatment efficacy, although they are extremely useful in illustrating the application of techniques and suggesting what works. Judgments of therapeutic efficacy must depend on well-controlled scientific research.

Behavior therapy has been responsible for a dramatic increase in the quantity and quality of treatment outcome studies. A major contribution of behavior therapy has been the development of different research strategies for addressing different issues related to therapy outcome. Single-subject methodology, which is identified historically with the operant conditioning approach, enables cause-effect relationships to be drawn between treatments and outcome in the individual case. There are several single-case experimental designs. In the ABAB, or reversal design, a treatment is administered following an initial baseline period (A), withdrawn in a return to baseline conditions (A), and then reinstated (B). If the target behavior changes in the desired direction during treatment and returns to its original level during baseline, it can be concluded that the treatment caused the change. In the multiple baseline design, different responses are continuously measured. Treatment is then applied successively to each in turn. If the desired behavior changes maximally only when treated, then a cause-effect relationship can be inferred. The general characteristics of single-subject methodology include the objective study of overt behavior; the continual measurement of behavior; and experimental criteria for evaluating treatment.

Among the advantages of single-case experimental designs are that individual clinical problems can be studied that are unsuitable for group designs; different methods can be compared in treating the same person; and innovative treatments can be developed efficiently before being tested in group outcome studies. Limitations of single-subject methodology include the inability to examine the interaction of subject variables with specific treatment effects; difficulty in generalizing findings to other cases; problems of interpretation if the results are not clearcut and the treatment effects obviously different from baseline levels; the ethical objections to using a reversal design and the fact that some target behaviors do not reverse following treatment; and the possibility in multiple baseline designs that the different responses are not independent of each other. It is difficult to study the processes of generalization and maintenance with single-subject methodology.

Several different types of between-group designs are used in the evaluation of treatment outcome, each design having its particular advantages and limitations, depending on the question being asked. Laboratory-based studies make possible the evaluation of specific techniques applied to particular problems under tightly controlled conditions. Their advantages include the use of multiple objective measures of outcome, the selection of homogeneous subject samples and therapists, and the freedom to assign subjects to experimental and control groups. Limitations include the possibility that findings with only mildly disturbed subjects might not be generalizable to more severely disturbed clients. Generalizability has to be evaluated along several key dimensions such as the nature of the target problem, the type of subject, subjects' motivation for change, therapists' training, and the specific treatment technique used. The need to consider generalizability of findings along these dimensions applies to all clinical research.

The treatment package strategy evaluates the effect of a multifaceted treatment program. If the package proves to be successful, its effective components are analyzed in subsequent research. Two important strategies for identifying critical components of treatment packages are the constructive and dismantling research strategies. In the constructive strategy, the effect of a single, basic therapy procedure is established and additional components added sequentially to see if they increase the treatment effect. The effective components are used to construct a broader treatment package. In the dismantling strategy, components of the treatment package are systematically eliminated and the associated decrement in treatment outcome measured. The relative contributions of each component can then be evaluated.

The comparative research strategy is directed towards determining whether some therapeutic techniques are superior to others. Comparative studies are appropriate after specific techniques have been shown to be effective in single-subject or laboratory-based research, and the parameters that maximize their efficacy are known. Unfortunately, conventional comparative outcome research has prematurely investigated ill-defined treatment packages with heterogeneous clinical disorders, using inadequate global measures of outcome. This has obscured potential differences among different methods and has led to the faulty conclusion that there are no differences in outcome between different schools of therapy. Well-controlled comparative research requires operational definitions of all treatment procedures, independent evidence that rival treatment methods are procedurally distinct from each other, multiple specific measures of outcome, and cost-effectiveness analyses of alternative approaches.

Different group designs require different control groups depending on the research question that is addressed. The no-treatment control group controls for the possible therapeutic effects of assessment of outcome, maturation, and other changes in clients' behavior that occur independently of formal treatment. A waiting-list control group is one that receives treatment at the end of the time taken to administer therapy to other treatment groups in the study. Long-term comparative follow-up is not possible with a waiting-list control group. Attention-placebo control groups are used to parcel out the contribution to treatment effects of factors that are common to all forms of therapy. These factors include the relationship between therapist and client, expectations of therapeutic progress, suggestion, and others. Attention-placebo groups should be assessed to see how credible they are to subjects in generating expectations of therapeutic improvement.

Long-term follow-ups are rarely reported in treatment outcome studies, and behavior therapy has been no exception. The behavioral model distinguishes among the initial induction of therapeutic change, its generalization to other settings, and its maintenance over time. These treatment phases might be governed by different processes, and explicit maintenance strategies are necessary in order to facilitate maintenance of improvement in many cases. Follow-up evaluations must include a careful description of the number of clients contacted at follow-up. Drop-outs from therapy and during follow-up create a biased sample and tend to artificially inflate outcome statistics.

Suggested Readings

Single-subject methodology:

HERSEN, M., and BARLOW, D. H. 1976. *Single case experimental designs.* New York: Pergamon Press.

Between-groups research:

PAUL, G.L. 1969. Behavior modification research: Design and tactics. In *Behavior therapy: Appraisal and status,* ed. C.M. Franks. New York: McGraw-Hill.

Comparative outcome research and alternative research strategies:

KAZDIN, A.E., and WILSON, G. T. 1978. *Evaluation of behavior therapy: Issues, evidence and research strategies.* Cambridge, Mass: Ballinger.

An overview of the evaluation of the effects of psychotherapy and behavior therapy:

RACHMAN, S. and WILSON, G. T. *The effects of psychotherapy,* 2nd. ed. London: Pergamon Press, in press.

4

Operant Conditioning

Clinical Case Study

Billy, a third grade student, had been doing poorly in his academic subjects and was frequently in trouble in the classroom. He had a short attention span, was fidgety and restless, and often wandered around the room aimlessly. He was aggressive with peers in the neighborhood and seemed extremely overactive at home. Billy was diagnosed hyperactive by his pediatrician and had been receiving a psychostimulant medication, Ritalin, for a year. During the time he was receiving medication, his attention span and his handwriting improved markedly. Billy's parents were referred by his pediatrician to a behavior therapist because they were concerned about his behavior at home after school. (A child generally cannot be given psychostimulant medication late in the day because it may prevent him from sleeping.) Billy's parents reported that at home he was overaggressive and still had difficulty concentrating. They also felt that although he appeared more attentive in the classroom while taking medication, his academic skills were still deficient.

After an initial assessment, which included (1) interviews with Billy, his parents, and his teacher, (2) a classroom observation, and (3) completion of standardized behavior checklists by his parents and teacher, a behavior therapy program was begun, and his medication discontinued. Both Billy's teacher and his parents were anxious and skeptical about the plan to withdraw medication because on days when he forgot to take the medication, he was described as a "hellion" in school.

The therapy involved eleven consultations with Billy and his parents and ten consultations with Billy's teacher. The program stressed reinforcement of academic goals, such as three pages of reading assignment completed and cooperation with his neighbor on a science project. To systematize the reinforcement, Billy was evaluated by his teacher twice per day and if he had done well, he was given a check on a card indicating that he deserved a reward from his parents. The rewards given by his parents included special desserts, playing Monopoly, extra television, and reading stories.

In order to teach Billy to work appropriately in the absence of special rewards, the program was designed to "fade out" the extrinsic reinforcers. For example, after Billy successfully met his academic and interpersonal goals for two weeks, he started receiving rewards at home only after obtaining two good daily reports, rather than after each one. Subsequently, he was required to earn four out of five good reports per week to earn a special treat. Across a four-month period, Billy made continual school progress with this home-based reinforcement system.

Billy's parents were taught to encourage his cooperative behavior at home. They were given suggestions regarding games enjoyed by active boys, and his father was encouraged to play ball with Billy after supper several times a week. Both parents were asked to help Billy increase his attention span during sedentary tasks by reading stories to him and by having him read to them. Throughout the treatment program, there was continued emphasis on praise, encouragement, and physical attention for any of Billy's efforts that evidenced increased academic interest and cooperation with others. Although there were some initially trying periods shortly after Billy stopped taking medication, at the end of four months of behavioral treatment, neither his parents nor his pediatrician saw any need for medication for his hyperactivity (S. O'Leary and Pelham, 1978). On the basis of classroom observations, Billy was indistinguishable from randomly selected peers; his teacher rated him as markedly improved both academically and socially; and his parents rated him as more organized, attentive, and socially mature. Most importantly, both Billy and his parents felt confident that he could lead a happy life without being dependent upon medication.

The above case, like that of Johnny K discussed earlier in this book (Chap. 1), illustrates the efficacy of a positive reinforcement approach to ameliorating children's behavioral problems. Billy's success demonstrates that behavior therapy is a viable alternative to medication for children labeled hyperactive. Approximately 2 percent of elementary school children in the United States receive psychostimulant medication (Krager, Safer, and Earhardt, 1979). Given the recent serious concerns about the possible deleterious effects of implicitly teaching children that the only way to control their behavior is with a drug (Whalen and Henker, 1976), the success of behavioral treatment is being heralded as an important treatment breakthrough (Deactivating the Overactive Child, *Family Health,* 1977).

Let us now turn to a discussion of the conceptual and empirical foundation that provides the bases for such treatment.

Conceptual Foundations

Operant conditioning refers to a particular experimental approach to the study of behavior. The approach is most often associated with B. F. Skinner, who in 1938 broke with the psychological tradition of his time and created a new conceptual foundation for viewing behavior. Basically, he urged psychologists to begin focusing on the observable consequences of behavior. This focus may seem eminently reasonable now, but in Skinner's professional youth, psychologists spent the bulk of their time theorizing about mental events. Both verbal and nonverbal behaviors were seen as a window to the mind. Problem behaviors were regarded as symptomatic of an internal mental imbalance. In contrast, as noted in Chap. 1, Skinner (1953) argued that psychotherapists should accept behaviors described as problematic by clients as appropriate subject matter, not as an indication that something was necessarily wrong in the client's mind.

While some operant conditioners now argue for the utility of nonobservable factors such as memory and history of reinforcement in the understanding of behavior (for example, Shimp, 1976; Rachlin, 1977), Skinner's emphasis on the specification of observable behavior has become a hallmark of behavior therapy. As will become apparent, the present authors do accept nonobservable events (for example, anxiety) as legitimate determinants of behavior, but whenever possible, observable data that confirm the nonobservable events should be provided by the therapist or researcher. Furthermore, a survey of noted behavior therapists, specifically selected because they purportedly represented operant (noncognitive) and cognitive viewpoints, indicated that both groups felt that certain nonobservable events such as awareness and expectancy deserve serious attention (Mahoney, 1977). There were some clear differences of opinion between the two groups of respondents in which the cognitive group viewed the "power and promise of private events" as more important factors in adjustment than did the operant group. However, Skinner has had a decided impact on the continued emphasis by many psychologists on dealing with observable events, even if they are not the exclusive interest of the therapist or investigator.

In the understanding of the principles of behavior therapy, it is important to appreciate the development of a science of behavior that had a clear impact on the therapeutic interventions utilized by clinical, educational, and developmental psychologists. This evolution is of critical interest because there are many basic scientific enterprises involving experiments that yield results which are clearly replicable but do not have an impact on society. In contrast, basic operant conditioning research had an impact on society that began in the 1960s and continues unabated now. Before examining the principles of operant conditioning in any detail, let us look at some of the factors which led to the wide scale application of operant conditioning to human problems.

Skinner (1953) prophesied about what could be done at a·societal level if one systematically applied the principles of reinforcement. In brief, he provided a model of human behavior. A model is generally seen as a way of viewing something "as if" it operated in a certain fashion. Skinner viewed men and women as organisms who operated on their environment in a fashion that produced certain events. Moreover, he held that if one observes humans closely, one will notice that their behavior is consistently followed by certain events called *reinforcers* or rewards. Skinner held that many behavior problems of individuals are the result of poorly arranged reinforcers. For example, in some cases reinforcers are not prevalent enough and the operant behavior of an individual may decrease to the extent that he or she is not functioning well (for example, he or she is depressed). Alternately, the environment may be arranged so that ultimately self-destructive behavior, such as alcoholism, is reinforced. Skinner's conceptualization was that if society would rearrange its reinforcement contingencies, our lives could be immeasurably improved.

Skinner reasoned that educational institutions, government, and families could place their emphasis on *positive reinforcement,* or rewards, and minimize punishment.

Skinner is the best-known American psychologist, and his scientific research and his popular writing, especially his fictional account of a utopian society, *Walden Two* (1948), often become confused with the general field of behavior therapy. Skinner's *Walden Two* and a more recent book, *Beyond Freedom and Dignity* (1971) have generated public concern about a society based on behavioral principles in which a particular way of life may be advocated for all citizens. Consequently, the principles that can be used to change human behavior are sometimes repudiated by individuals seeking therapy because the particular life style described by Skinner in his books may be uninviting (Bandura, 1977b). As noted in Chap. 1, behavior therapists vary in their interpretation of the most important determinants of behavior, and they also vary in the types of societal practices they advocate. In brief, we need to separate principles of behavior therapy from specific behavior therapists and their particular political ideologies.

Illustrations of Positive Reinforcement

Case Studies in Behavior Modification, written by Ullmann and Krasner in 1965, was very influential in illustrating how Skinner's approach could be utilized to change socially significant behaviors of individuals. This book consists of an introductory chapter which explains the basic principles of behavior modification and fifty case studies about individuals treated by clinicians generally using an operant approach. In their excellent introductory chapter, Ullmann and Krasner argue that maladaptive behavior develops according to the same principles as normal or adaptive behavior. Many behavior therapists now consider such a position as extreme since they feel certain maladaptive behavior (for example, autistic behavior, various types of hyperactivity, eneuresis, schizophrenia) develops in a manner different from most social behavior (Davison and Neale, 1974; Nathan and Harris, 1975; O'Leary and Wilson, 1975). Nonetheless, this orientation spurred many investigators to begin behavioral treatment programs with diverse clinical populations.

An example from Ullmann and Krasner (1975) depicts the efficacy of using the behavioral approach. Allen, Hart, Buell, and Harris consulted with the nursery school teachers of a four-year-old child, Ann. Ann spent most of her time in isolate behavior; she spoke so slowly and softly that she was difficult to understand. Ann spent much of her time simply standing and looking or retiring to a make-believe bed to "sleep." She also used many techniques to gain adult attention, such as complaining about invisible bumps and abrasions.

After several weeks of observing such behavior and documenting that Ann spent only 10 percent of her time with peers, Allen and others suggested that the teachers positively attend to (reinforce) her immediately if she spent time interacting with children. In contrast, when Ann played alone, she was not given attention; and when she talked with an adult, she was given minimal attention. An example of the teachers' comments to Ann when she was with others was "You three girls have a cozy house! Here are some more cups, Ann, for your tea party." Within six days of the intervention, Ann spent 60 percent of her time interacting with her peers. To document the influence of the change in the teachers' behavior on Ann's behavior, the teachers were asked to return to their former mode of interacting with Ann, namely, attending to her bids for adult attention. Within five days, Ann was spending only 15 percent of her time with children. The experimenters were convinced that the change in the teachers' behavior resulted in changes in Ann's behavior, and thus they again asked the teachers to attend to Ann primarily when she was with peers. This redirected teacher attention was associated with an increase in peer interaction as well as salutory changes, such as increases in speech volume and tempo. Further, her complaints about abrasions and bumps stopped altogether. The teachers provided a classic example of how critical their behavior is in changing the maladaptive behavior patterns of children. Related case studies in the Ullmann and Krasner book described how persistent crying, temper tantrums, and attending could be altered simply by changing teacher and parent attention.

Behavior therapists now question assumptions upon which Skinner and Ullmann and Krasner based their arguments. More specifically, as noted earlier, most behavior therapists do not accept the exclusive emphasis on observable behavior (Mahoney, 1977). The theory that abnormal behavior is learned in the same way as any other behavior is considered inconsistent with certain genetic and biochemical data that document the hereditary and biochemical influences on abnormal behavior (O'Leary and Wilson, 1975). Finally, most practicing behavior therapists presently view modeling, instructions, and cognitive factors, which were long eschewed by Skinner, as important and critical ingredients of their therapeutic interventions.

Despite the questioning of the aforementioned assumptions, scores of successful examples of operant approaches with individuals and larger segments of the population which convey the efficacy of the method have been published. Illustrations of the applications of positive reinforcement for desired behavior with large groups have utilitarian consequences. Home fuel oil consumption in Pennsylvania has been reduced by a combination of informational feedback and small decals for households that reduced consumption (Seaver and Patterson, 1976). Large electrical energy reductions have been produced by providing direct payments to efficient consumers (Hayes and Cone, 1977). The U.S. Civil Service Commission in Washington, D.C. has given top priority parking only to those who use car pools.* McCalden and Davis (1972) found that when special uncongested lanes on the Oakland-San Francisco Bay Bridge were reserved for cars with several passengers, car pooling increased, and traffic flow was improved. Further, that practice remains in effect on the Oakland-San Francisco Bay Bridge.† Litter has been efficiently removed from state forest parks by children when they were intermittently reinforced for participating (Clarke, Burgess, and Hendee, 1972); such a system has been adopted by twenty-six national park services.‡ Finally, parents in rural areas have been effectively encouraged to seek dental care for their children through prompts and incentives (Reiss, Piotrowski, and Bailey, 1976). In summary, both government and industry have already begun to use the principles of positive incentives to improve the health of children and increase the ecological efforts of the citizenry. In the future, low taxes and rebates may be used as incentives to increase the purchase of low gas-consuming cars. To reduce car use and smog, free bus services to center city locations may be provided with a portion of the cost borne by center city businesses, and rebates may be given to individuals who use small amounts of electricity during peak usage hours (Nietzel and others, 1977).

ASSESSING REINFORCERS

Before one can attempt to modify behavior with positive reinforcement, it is necessary to identify effective reinforcers. The clearest way to know whether a given thing, event, or interpersonal interaction will reinforce a certain behavior is to conduct an empirical test. One observes the frequency of a behavior and then makes the event in question contingent upon the behavior. If the frequency of the behavior reliably increases when the event follows that behavior, the event is then called a reinforcer. Events are thus classified according to their function or effect.

As testing each event to assess its potential as a reinforcer is impractical, assessment surveys have been devised for children and adults to ascertain likely reinforcers for particular behaviors. Some items from a reinforcer survey for children (Tharp and Wetzel, 1969) are as follows:

The best reward anyone can give me is_____.

If I had $10, I'd_____.

My favorite relative is_____.

*Personal communication: Dr. Brian S. O'Leary, U.S. Civil Service Commission, Washington, D.C., February, 1977.
†Personal communication: M. Scott McCalden, Highway Operations Branch, Caltrans, San Francisco, CA, April, 1977.
‡Personal communication: Dr. Robert Burgess, Pennsylvania State University, November 1977.

Two things I like to do best are_____.
My two favorite TV programs are_____.
My favorite adult at school is_____.
I feel terrific when_____.

In the absence of a formal reinforcer survey, a therapist can obtain detailed information in an interview regarding potential reinforcers. The simplest way to do this is to ask the client what he or she would like to do (for example, spend more time with her husband dancing or taking walks; go fishing with his father). However, with careful interviewing a therapist can also assess potential reinforcers by finding out what a client does in his or her free time (for example, listens to records, reads the newspaper, builds models). Premack (1959) demonstrated that behaviors which occur frequently under free choice situations can be used to reinforce behaviors which have a low probability of occurrence. Thus, an interviewer can find out what an individual does when he or she is free to do many things and then suggest that the high probability behavior (for example, listening to rock music) be used to reinforce a low probability behavior (for example, studying). That is, if the client wishes to study more, the therapist may suggest that the client listen to rock music after an hour of studying is completed. By making listening to rock music contingent upon studying, the client can increase his or her academic output.

Primary or unconditioned reinforcers. There are certain events which are almost invariably reinforcing. These events are called *primary,* or *unconditioned, reinforcers* because they require no learning history to acquire reinforcing value. For example, food and water are unconditioned reinforcers to hungry and thirsty organisms. Primary reinforcers are often used by parents to alter the behavior of normal children. Children are taught to smile, vocalize, speak, walk, and even to engage in some social behavior through the use of primary reinforcers, for example, a parent prompting a child to say "please," before giving him or her a cookie.

Unconditioned reinforcers, such as food, have been used systematically to teach speech to retarded and autistic children. Such children are often unresponsive to social reinforcers such as adult attention, praise, and pats on the back. In a language training program, Baer, Peterson, and Sherman (1967) initially taught three nine- to twelve-year-old mute retarded girls to imitate simple responses, such as hand clapping and arm raising. The therapist-teacher always said, "Do this," before demonstrating the response to be imitated. Then, to encourage the correct motor response, the therapist would guide the child's arms through the correct response and say, "Good," while simultaneously placing a piece of food in the child's mouth. Gradually the physical assistance was faded out. After imitation of motor responses was taught, a more complex skill, imitation of speech, was taught, using unconditioned reinforcers (food) and social reinforcers (the words "good" and "great"). In similar experiments using slightly different methodologies, it has been shown that after many verbal responses are learned and continuously reinforced, some new imitative responses are learned even though they are not directly reinforced. Thus the children learn skills by means of a phenomenon variously described as *generalized imitation* (Baer, Peterson, and Sherman, 1967) or generalization of imitative responses (Bandura, 1972). That is, individuals gradually learn to imitate words that are never reinforced. The mechanisms accounting for the learning of nonreinforced imitation appear to result from complex factors including instructions, the particular discrimination teaching procedure employed, and presence of experimenters (Whitehurst, 1978; Steinman, 1977).

There are events, such as mastery of material, which may be primary reinforcers, but because of the complicated social history of humans, it is impossible to separate the social factors that might have led one to *learn* that mastery is a "good" thing. Nonetheless, pragmatically it is worthwhile to assume that mastery of material is generally a reinforcer for humans. In fact, from many points of view, it is useful to design therapeutic or educational environments so that an individual will be reinforced by the accomplishment of any variety of tasks. A general guideline in designing a reinforcing environment is to have an individual experience very frequent success. Careful observation in the beginning of any therapeutic program is crucial since an individual's self-confidence and attitudes toward particular tasks can be markedly enhanced by success. While mastery may be reinforcing for everyone, the criteria for mastery are clearly relative. Individuals in distress may have such high performance standards that a self-perception of mastery of tasks is very improbable. To aid clients in developing self-confidence and a sense of mastery, it is often necessary to teach them how to define realistic criteria for judging their own mastery.

Secondary reinforcers. Few human behaviors—especially those of adults—are directly supported by primary reinforcers, like food and water. Instead our behaviors are primarily influenced by secondary reinforcers. A *secondary reinforcer* is simply a reinforcer which acquires its value through association with a primary reinforcer or with other secondary reinforcers. One of the most important secondary reinforcers is praise. Words or phrases like, "good," "good job," "I like that," "great," and "lovely," acquire their value by being associated with primary reinforcers, such as food and tactile stimulation. For example, when a young girl does something a mother likes, the mother may praise the girl, smile, and hug and kiss her. Fortunately, frequent pairing of the words with primary reinforcers is unnecessary because the meaning of "good" becomes clear by its association with a wide variety of primary and secondary reinforcers. Social reinforcement in the form of adult attention and approval is probably the most powerful and versatile of all secondary reinforcers.

One example of the effective use of secondary reinforcers is provided by

Klotz and Shantz (1973), who randomly assigned twelve emotionally disturbed adolescent boys to experimental and control groups for the purpose of assessing the contingent application of social approval in group activity sessions. The investigators were interested in whether a male group leader's approval could be used to increase the degree to which the boys cooperated with each other during activity sessions. In each 40-minute activity session, the six boys in the experimental group sat at one table in the activity room, and the six boys in the control group sat at another table. All boys were given toy models to build during the sessions, but each table was given only one tube of glue. The group leader smiled and gave verbal approval to boys in the experimental group when they shared the glue with a tablemate. In contrast, the group leader smiled and gave verbal approval to boys in the control group for individual achievement (for example, working neatly and accurately); the boys in this group did not receive any leader approval for cooperative behavior. As indicated in Fig. 4–1, the frequency of cooperative behavior in the experimental group rose markedly across the twelve activity sessions whereas the cooperative behavior in the control group remained unchanged. Thus it was clear that attention or praise per se was not the critical factor. A special type of contingency, namely, approval for cooperative behavior, was necessary to increase the boys' cooperative behavior.

In marriage, the frequency of pleasing events (for example, a partner complimenting the other, smiling at the other, thanking the other, complying with a request, giving a gift, and participating in joint activities) relates positively to the couple's overall satisfaction with the relationship (Patterson, Weiss, and Hopps, 1976). Further, couples seeking marital therapy have significantly fewer positive interactions than do couples judged to be nondistressed. Most importantly, it appears that spouses can learn to be more socially reinforcing of one another, and as a consequence, their marriage improves. Although being socially reinforcing of a partner with whom one has become disenchanted is not easy, one can learn to attend to certain behaviors which are pleasing and indicate approval of them. As such behaviors occur more frequently and are responded to in a positive manner, the spouses feel a greater desire to be nicer and be more considerate of one another. For example, in marital therapy when a husband begins to display a behavior desired by his wife, and the wife indicates approval of this behavior, the husband's behavior will likely continue. When he continues to interact with her in a desired way, she will often respond by being more considerate of his needs. Thus, both the husband and the wife respond to mutual positive reinforcement in a way that enhances their satisfaction with the marriage.

TOKEN REINFORCEMENT PROGRAMS

A dull dime or an old dollar bill is not reinforcing to a two-year-old, but money becomes one of the most powerful secondary reinforcers for people in most societies. Money becomes reinforcing to most of us because it provides access

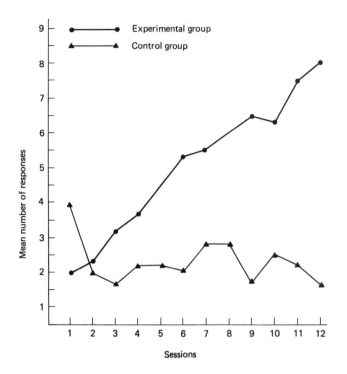

FIGURE 4.1
Mean number of cooperative responses as a function of treatment group and session. (Reprinted with permission from *Journal of Behavior Therapy and Experimental Psychiatry,* 4, 33–37. Klotz, J., & Shantz, D. W. Cooperative behavior of emotionally disturbed boys as a function of contingent application of social approval. Copyright 1973, Pergamon Press Ltd.)

to many desired things.[1] In fact, the versatility of money is one of the reasons why it is so powerful as a reinforcer. An employer who provides his employees with goods and privileges, such as insurance, lunches, and beer breaks, may feel that he is caring extremely well for them. However, an employer cannot adequately determine the needs of each individual employee. Thus, employees often prefer to receive the highest amount of monetary reinforcement possible in order that they, rather than their employer, can decide how additional moneys should be spent.

Before considering examples of *token reinforcement programs,* a definition of a token program is in order. The basic ingredients of a token program usually include: (1) a set of instructions about the behaviors that will be

[1]Token reinforcers are technically generalized conditioned reinforcers, that is, reinforcers which are paired with and/or provide access to many reinforcers.

reinforced, (2) means of making a token, such as a plastic chip or a numerical rating, contingent upon a behavior, and (3) a set of rules governing the exchange of tokens for back-up reinforcers, such as prizes or opportunities to engage in special activities. Let us now turn to several therapeutic examples of token programs.

Miss Duke was a friendly teacher with several years of teaching experience in regular classes. She was well liked by her peers and had gained a good reputation as a teacher. However, after four months with a class of seventeen emotionally disturbed children in an inner city school in Urbana, Illinois, Miss Duke told the principal that she was going to quit her job if he could not find some aid for her. These children frequently fought, cursed, and knocked things over on neighbors' desks as they passed them in the aisles. They were largely inattentive, and there was very little academic progress. Observations indicated that Miss Duke's praise often led to snickering, and her voice was usually hoarse by the end of the day because she had to talk over the noise in the class. As Miss Duke noted, "When I tried to compliment them or tell them they had done something well, they would look around the room and make faces at one another." Field trips, interesting curricular materials, and movies had only transient positive influence on the children.

The behavioral intervention in this class involved rating books that were placed on each child's desk. Every 30 minutes, using a one to ten scale, Miss Duke placed a rating in each child's book indicating how well he or she had behaved both academically and socially. At the end of the day the ratings were exchangeable for items such as pencils, erasers, candy, kites, and other small prizes. Before introducing the token program, to evaluate the effectiveness of the intervention, the disruptive classroom behavior was observed for five weeks. The baseline or pretreatment measure of disruptive behavior indicated that the children were disruptive 26 percent of the time. As can be seen from Fig. 4–2, as soon as the token program was initiated, the children's disruptive behavior dropped dramatically. More importantly, although at the beginning of the token program, the children were able to exchange their ratings for prizes at the end of every day, as the program continued, the children were encouraged to save their tokens for two days, then three days, and finally for four days (see Fig. 4–2 from O'Leary and Becker, 1967). Although the children had to work for longer and longer periods of time before receiving the back-up reinforcers, they maintained their low level of disruptive classroom behavior. Two children who had never previously completed academic assignments before the introduction of the token program completed assignments with near perfect accuracy during the token program (O'Leary and Becker, 1967). Thus, the comparison with the baseline indicated that the token program was a tremendous aid to Miss Duke, enabling her both to increase academic output and to gain control over disruptive antisocial behavior.

Ayllon and Azrin (1965) established a token reinforcement program for institutionalized female adult psychiatric patients in which the patients were

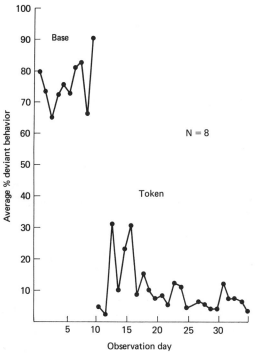

FIGURE 4.2
Average Percentages of Deviant Behavior during the Base and Token Periods. (O'Leary, K. D., & Becker, Wesley. Behavior modification of an adjustment class: A token reinforcement program. *Exceptional Children,* May 1967, 33, 637–642.) Reprinted from *Exceptional Children* by permission of The Council for Exceptional Children, copyright 1967.

taught to engage in a number of behaviors they had not displayed previously while in the hospital. The behaviors the staff chose to change were self-care activities, such as grooming and bathing, and job activities, such as washing dishes, working as a dietary assistant planning meals, or serving food. The conditioned reinforcers used in the study were special tokens that operated a TV and a turnstile that provided access to certain areas of the hospital.

Ayllon and Azrin showed that if tokens were made contingent upon a preferred job, patients spent the maximum time allotted (6 hours a day) on that job, but when the reinforcement was shifted to a nonpreferred job, the patients immediately spent 6 hours a day at the originally nonpreferred job. At first, the patients said that they had chosen their jobs on the basis of social contact and job satisfaction. However, after they received tokens for engaging in the originally nonpreferred job and were told they could go back to their originally preferred jobs but would not be reinforced for such work, they made statements about their initially preferred jobs such as: "No, honey, I can't work at the laundry [the originally preferred job] for nothing; I'll work at the laboratory [the nonpreferred job]. I just couldn't make it to pay my rent, if I didn't get paid."

The import of the Ayllon and Azrin work is not that patients can be taught to switch jobs if the reinforcement is switched from one job to another. Rather, a method for changing a host of social and vocational behaviors was documented with patients that heretofore were considered highly unlikely to change. The use of the token program demonstrated that patients could be taught to engage in behaviors that might ultimately enable them to function effectively outside the hospital, for example, housekeeping, following instructions, and interacting with fellow employees. In fact, to guide the investigators in their treatment plans, the following rule was used: Teach only those behaviors that will continue to be reinforced after training; that is, teach those behaviors that are necessary for a successful adjustment to daily living.

The utility of token reinforcement programs has been compared with standard hospital treatment programs. Fairweather and his associates (Fairweather and others, 1969) showed that when psychiatric patients were taught vocational and interpersonal skills using a program that included an emphasis on self-direction, social behavior, and the employment of a variety of incentives, they could ultimately function in the community better than patients in traditional hospital programs. They found that ex-patients who had been in a twenty-four-week token program were later able to live and work together in lodge environments that were operated under a token reinforcement paradigm. Further, the ex-patients spent approximately 80 percent of their time in the community after the lodge closed (the lodge was operative for thirty-three months), whereas the control group who received standard hospital treatment, that is, psychotherapy, medication, and vocational therapy, spent only 20 percent of their time in the community (see Fig. 4–3, p. 108). As can be seen in the figure, the patients who were in the token reinforcement program in the hospital and the lodge maintained themselves better in the community following the closing of the lodge than did the control group. Finally, after the lodge closed, nearly 40 percent of the lodge patients, as opposed to only 3 percent of the control patients, were employed full time.

A comprehensive evaluation of a behavioral program for hospitalized adult psychiatric patients was recently conducted by Paul and his associates (Paul and Lentz, 1977). In this program discussed in Chap. 3, they compared a standard hospital program (the control group) with two experimental hospital programs: (1) a *milieu-oriented* treatment program in which group social expectations and group decision making were emphasized, and (2) a social learning treatment program in which social reinforcement, token reinforcement, and modeling were emphasized. The patients in both experimental treatment programs did better than the patients in the control program in terms of their ward behavior, as assessed by independent observers, and the social learning patients fared better than the milieu patients on this observational measure. In sum, the social learning program which emphasized a token reinforcement program for patients acquiring basic social skills had therapeutic effects superior to the control and milieu program both while the patients were in the hospital and after they had been discharged to community aftercare facilities.

A detailed comparison of token and milieu programs is beyond the scope of this chapter. Here it is sufficient to simply point out that token programs have repeatedly proven their efficacy in treating adult psychotic hospitalized patients. In assessing behavioral maintenance following hospitalization and aftercare treatment, both the Fairweather and others (1969) and the Paul and Lentz (1977) studies documented that patients who had been in token reinforcement programs fared better than control patients treated with the standard hospital regimen.

Highly systematized reinforcement contingencies, such as those in token programs, are used by therapists, ward attendants, teachers, and parents to teach new skills, but after the skills are established, they can be brought under the influence of naturally occurring contingencies so that the behavior does not extinguish. For example, once language and social skills are taught to schizophrenic patients, they generally are reinforced by significant others who listen and talk to them (for example, family members, personnel in half-way houses and shelters, and other patients). Similarly, once children learn to become continent, they are reinforced enough by their own sense of mastery and occasional praise from others that they do not need to receive the reinforcement of a therapist. Consequently, a therapist initially can use special reinforcement contingencies and later help the client enter into natural environments when the usual reinforcement contingencies will maintain the newly acquired skill, even though the therapist's arbitrary reinforcers are discontinued.

REINFORCEMENT SCHEDULES

A *schedule of reinforcement* refers to the manner in which positive consequences follow behavior. In everyday interactions behavior is usually reinforced or rewarded irregularly, but in treatment programs a therapist or teacher may maximize his or her impact by systematically rewarding behavior. From numerous experiments it has been found that four basic schedules of reinforcement have particular effects which can be utilized in designing therapeutic programs. Those schedules are as follows: fixed interval, variable interval, fixed ratio, and variable ratio.

An interval schedule of reinforcement is one in which the first response made after a predetermined interval has elapsed is reinforced. The expression "A watched pot never boils" highlights the distinguishing feature of interval schedules. People often look at a pot of water and increase

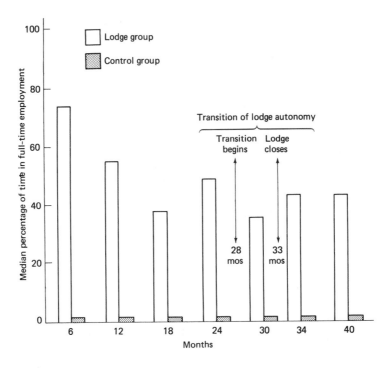

FIGURE 4.3
Percentage of time that patients in the lodge and hospital programs were employed full time for 40 months of follow-up. (Fairweather, G. W., Sanders, D. H., Maynard H., and Cressler, D. L. *Community life for the mentally ill: An alternative to institutional care.* Chicago: Aldine, 1969.)

their rate of looking as time passes, even though the behavior of looking at the pot clearly has no effect on the water. An excellent way to remember the critical feature of an interval schedule is to check to see if the responses during the time interval have an effect on the probability of reinforcement (Miller, 1975). A ratio schedule of reinforcement is simply one in which a certain number of responses are required before positive reinforcement is received.

Fixed interval schedules of reinforcement. A *fixed interval schedule* is one in which the first behavior that occurs after a constant predetermined time interval is reinforced. One example is the behavior of looking at a watch when attending a 50-minute class, if the reinforcing event is seeing that class is over. The looking at the watch during the interval does not make the time go faster, and thus only the response just after an interval elapses is reinforced. Fixed interval schedules of reinforcement are characterized by a rapid rate of responding before reinforcement and pauses after reinforcement. For example, the student in a 50-minute class will begin to look at the clock often near the end of the hour. Following the end of the class, the student is not likely to look at the clock often until the end of the next class nears.

Variable interval schedules of reinforcement. An individual who is reinforced variably for the first response after intervals of 3, 8, 1, 7, and 6 minutes each have elapsed is said to be on a *variable interval schedule of reinforcement.* The aforementioned schedule is called a Variable Interval 5' (VI 5') since the average interval between reinforcements is 5 minutes. For example, when a person dials a busy phone number, none of his or her responses are reinforced until the number is no longer busy. The first response of the dialer, however, when the line is free will be reinforced (providing, of course, that the receiving party did not run out the door just after talking with the other person). Thus, a variable period of time will pass before a response is reinforced when an individual dials a busy number.

Fixed ratio schedules of reinforcement. Very simply, a *fixed ratio schedule of reinforcement* refers to reinforcement after a fixed number of responses. For example, a field worker may be paid only after a certain number of bushels (for example fifteen) of sweet corn have been picked. Such a schedule is a Fixed Ratio 15 Schedule (FR 15). A factory worker may be given a coffee break only after a certain number of pieces of furniture have been inspected. Fixed ratio schedules of responding generate high rates of responding, but there is often a pause after reinforcement when such schedules are utilized. Fixed schedules of reinforcement (for example, piece-rate plans in industry) have such powerful effects on behavior that union members often oppose them (Hackman and Suttle, 1977).

Variable ratio schedules of reinforcement. In a *variable ratio schedule,* the number of responses required for reinforcement will vary every time the individual is reinforced. For example, if a teacher indicates approval and interest when a student talks about reading novels, and that approval is given after every second, fifth, first, and eighth time that the student does this, the behavior of talking about novels is said to be on a variable ratio schedule of reinforcement. In this case, the schedule is a Variable Ratio 4 (VR 4), because the average number of required responses is four. Variable ratio schedules of reinforcement generally produce high steady rates of responding.

In most human interactions, interval schedules of reinforcement have less import than ratio schedules, because it is difficult to arrange our environments so that behaviors between the intervals have no relevance to the reinforcers. That is, our environment is most often structured so that a certain work output is required for reinforcement.

Although Ferster and Skinner's book, *Schedules of Reinforcement* (1957) is held by some (Miller, 1975) to be the "Bible of operant psychology," attempts to produce behavior patterns that follow typical schedule control often have not succeeded. In part, these failures may be due to the lack of control one has in working with humans. However, it is also possible that factors other than schedules of reinforcement have a superordinate influence on human responding, such as the feelings of the student toward the person (teacher) who is attempting to help him or her, the awareness the child has about the desire of the therapist to reinforce certain responses (Dulany, 1974), or the feelings of industrial workers that they will lose their jobs if they are too productive (Porter, Lawler, and Hackman, 1975). Given the powerful nature of reinforcement schedules with lower animals, however, it may well be that we simply need to determine the complex interdependencies of many schedules of reinforcement that are operative at one time with humans.

EXTINCTION

Extinction refers to a procedure in which reinforcement of a behavior is discontinued. In most human endeavors, extinction refers to the withholding of rewards or attention for a particular behavior.

After interval and ratio reinforcement. As mentioned earlier, ratio schedules are more important for human behavior than interval schedules since they occur in many normal endeavors. Further, ratio schedules produce greater resistance to extinction (that is, greater responding in the absence of reinforcement) than interval schedules.

After fixed and variable reinforcement. Variable schedules produce greater resistance to extinction than fixed schedules. Of the four basic schedules of reinforcement, variable ratio schedules are known to produce the greatest resistance to extinction. Gamblers often become addicted to slot machines and continue to play them after very long periods of no payoff *(extinction)*.

After continuous reinforcement. When an individual is reinforced after each and every response, he or she is said to be on a continuous reinforcement schedule. If a behavior is continuously reinforced and then no longer reinforced (that is, placed on extinction), a burst of responding often occurs just after the extinction begins. This response burst is often seen when parents attempt to eliminate temper tantrums. Generally, it is held that temper tantrums are reinforced by parental attention. Thus, parents are often advised to stop attending to such tantruming. The modification of such tantrums is exemplified by the treatment of a twenty-one-month-old child by Williams (1959).

This 21-month-old child had been seriously ill during the beginning of his life. His health later improved, but throughout the first 18 months of his life, he demanded a great deal of attention and care. He received attention by exhibiting tantrum behavior—especially at bedtime. If the parent left the bedroom after putting the child to bed, the child would scream and fuss until the parent returned to the room. As a consequence, the parents were unable to leave the room until the child went to sleep; they had to spend from 1½–2 hours each evening, just waiting in the bedroom until the child went to sleep. Following a medical checkup which proved that the child no longer had physical problems, it was decided to remove the reinforcers or attention for his tantrum-like behavior. After bedtime the parent was asked to leave the bedroom and close the door; the door was not to be reopened even if the child screamed. The length of time the child screamed and cried was measured from the time the door was closed.

The results are presented in Figure 4–4. It can be seen that on the first day the parents began the extinction procedures the child continued to scream for 45 minutes from the time he was put to bed. The child did not cry at all the second time he was put to bed, and by the tenth occasion he no longer cried or whimpered when his parent left the room. Unfortunately, after the institution of this procedure, an aunt put the child to bed; the child cried, and the aunt reinforced the tantrum behavior by returning to his bedroom and remaining there until he went to sleep. It was then necessary to extinguish the child's behavior a second time. The second extinction series showed a curve that was almost identical to the first (Fig. 4–4), with the child's crying declining to a zero level by the ninth occasion. Following this second extinction of tantrum-like behavior, no further tantrums were reported during the next 2 years of the child's life. No unfortunate side effects were observed and according to the investigator, at 3¾ years of age the subject appeared to be a friendly, expressive, outgoing child. (O'Leary and Wilson 1975, pp. 45–46)

Williams' study demonstrated the application of extinction procedures as well as the strong reactions to the beginning of an extinction procedure as exemplified by the 45 minutes of crying that followed the initial withdrawal of reinforcement and the 53 minutes of crying on the first day of the second extinction.

After partial reinforcement. Common sense might dictate that the greater and more frequent the reinforcement for a response, the more difficult it would be to extinguish that behavior. In fact, this is not true. When a response has been rewarded only part of the time, the response will be harder to extinguish than if the behavior has been continuously reinforced. This result which does not fit with common sense or grandma's psychology is called the "Humphreys' Paradox," after L. G. Humphreys who first demonstrated the effect in 1939. The therapeutic implications of this paradoxical effect have not been explored seriously. One might surmise that parents who reinforced a response, such as a tantrum, continuously, just before beginning an extinction

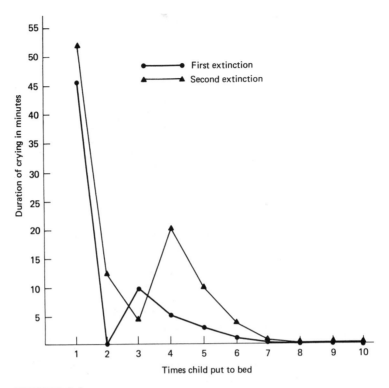

FIGURE 4.4
Length of crying in two extinction series as a function of successive occasions of being put to bed. (Williams, C., The elimination of tantrum behavior by extinction procedure. *Journal of Abnormal and Social Psychology*, 59, 1959, 269. Copyright 1959 by the American Psychological Assoc. Reprinted by permission).

series would be more effective in eliminating the tantrums than parents who intermittently reinforced their child before an extinction series. In fact, Glavin and Moyer (1975) found suggestive evidence for this notion when they had parents change from an intermittent to continuous schedule of attention to crying before they attempted to decrease crying by ignoring the child for unnecessary crying and by requiring that the child be quiet for one minute before being picked up. However, another factor of even greater import may be an instruction from the parent, such as, "I do not intend to come back to your room any more tonight. You are a brave boy, and you are big enough to go to bed without any more stories or back rubs." In brief, it appears that any factors which will enable a person to know that his or her behavior will definitely be ignored will facilitate extinction. On the other hand, if the very statement noted above is made to a child by a mother who conveys her guilt and ambivalence by her tone of voice and indecision, the child may well

tantrum for days. In summary, any factors that will unequivocably indicate
an extinction condition will facilitate that extinction. (See Box 4–3)

Box 4–3 *Delivering Reinforcement Effectively:*
General Guidelines

1. Reinforce immediately when possible, especially when a new skill is being
   taught.
2. Use a variety of reinforcers.
3. Try to pick reinforcers that will occur in the client's natural environment.
4. Make sure that the individual who is to receive the reinforcer knows what
   behaviors are being reinforced.
5. Don't reinforce more frequently than necessary or use reinforcers that are
   any more powerful than necessary.
6. Gradually reduce the frequency of reinforcement.
7. Pair social reinforcers with tangible reinforcers and gradually shift to social
   reinforcers alone.

Shaping

Shaping refers to the reinforcing of successive approximations to a terminal
behavior. Consider the following example of shaping in which Lovaas and
Newson (1976) described the teaching of verbal imitation by shaping and
prompting.

> In Step 1, the therapist increases the child's vocalizations by rewarding him
> (usually with food) contingent upon such behavior [any imitation]. . . . In Step
> 2, the child is trained to make a temporal discrimination: his vocalizations are
> reinforced only if they occur within about five seconds of the therapist's vocaliza-
> tions. In Step 3, finer discriminations of the therapist's vocal topography (form
> of vocal response) are reinforced. The child is rewarded for making successively
> closer approximations to the therapist's speech sound until he matches the
> particular sound given by the therapist (e.g., emits "a" when the therapist says
> "a"). In Step 4, the therapist repeats Step 3 with another sound very dissimilar
> to the first one (e.g., "m"), intersperses this sound with the previous one, and
> reinforces the child for correct production only. Increasingly, finer discrimina-
> tions are required as new sounds are added, then syllables, words, and sentences
> are taught as the child becomes able to master them. (pp. 325–26)

The shaping process is also evident in the interaction between two
roommates where one prompts and reinforces the tidiness of the other.
Consider the following example: One roommate, Sue, indicated her desire
to have the other, Kathy, be more careful about picking up her clothes

and spend more time cleaning the room. Kathy agreed that their living conditions would be more pleasant if she were to put more effort into keeping the room clean. Instead of waiting until Kathy picked up all of her clothes and cleaned the entire room, Sue thanked her for simply putting her coat on a hanger rather than throwing it on their sofa. Later, Sue indicated her appreciation for Kathy's cleaning the top of her desk and making her bed. Even later, Sue told Kathy how much she enjoyed having both of them work together to clean the room regularly. Sue felt good about any attempts Kathy made to respond to her requests, so she thanked Kathy for even the smallest efforts. Sue was shaping Kathy's behavior by reinforcing successive approximations to the desired goal.

The general approach of gradually building upon an individual's present skills while moving toward an educational goal is held desirable from many different theoretical orientations. J. McV. Hunt in his book, *Intelligence and Experience* (1961), wrote that if a child is to learn maximally from experience, there has to be a minimal amount of incongruity between his or her past experience and the present event. That is, the individual has to experience some challenge in the new material presented to him or her, but the challenge has to be clearly within his or her grasp. This concept of the optimal amount of incongruity was derived from the developmental child psychologist, Piaget, but the pragmatic recommendations that would be derived from this theoretical position are very similar to those derived from operant reinforcement principles.

In psychoanalysis, one therapeutic goal is to encourage the patient to recall traumatic past events, primarily through free associations and the interpretation of dreams. As evidenced in the recent book and movie *Sybil* (Schreiber, 1974), the therapist initially encouraged the patient with multiple personalities (sixteen in fact) to recall events which were only minimally painful. Later the therapist set the stage for recalling of events which were somewhat more painful by making interpretations and by encouraging discussions of events that would trigger certain memories. Finally, the recall of very traumatic events was encouraged through hypnosis and interpretation. In this manner, the therapist shaped the behavior of recalling and discussing deeply traumatic experiences.

In client-centered therapy, a major therapeutic goal is to have clients experience feelings which are congruent with their behavior. The clients are encouraged to become open to emotional experiences gradually and to become aware of what they have repressed. Presumably because their concept of themselves and their ideal selves becomes less incongruent, they can slowly experience their true feelings with a minimum of tension and anxiety. Relevant to the shaping principle, the client-centered therapist encourages clients to begin to accept themselves for what they are. Thus, the therapist *gradually* encourages clients to become trusting of him or her as a listener who cares and respects them as they are. The clients must learn to perceive the positive regard the therapist has for them. In a therapeutic relationship where clients perceive this, they will eventually develop a higher regard for themselves (Rogers, 1961).

These examples are presented to illustrate the commonality of procedural efforts made by therapists from disparate therapeutic orientations. In this sense, it is important to remember that shaping is a key to many—if not almost all—therapeutic endeavors. In fact, almost all complex behavior is developed through shaping of one sort or another, and we are well advised to remember that patience is necessary to shape behavior most effectively.

Prompting and Fading

A *prompt* in learning terms is very much like the prompt to a player in a drama; it is a hint or cue which makes the likelihood of the correct response more probable. Examples of prompts would be the following use of additional cues or stimuli to increase the likelihood that a child will know the correct answer or display the correct behavior:

Parent: What is the largest state in the union?

Child: I don't know.

Parent: The state begins with "A."

Child: Alaska!!

A child is learning the difference between a cat and a dog. The child often says "dog" when presented with a picture of a cat and vice versa. The parent thus makes the sounds, "meow" or "bow-wow," as the pictures of the cat and dog are presented, respectively. Later, as the child learns to label the pictures correctly and consistently, the parent will begin to whisper, then mouth, and finally intermittently eliminate all cues. In brief, the parent "fades" the prompts. Fading is a procedure in which the prompts are gradually withdrawn as the correct or desired response becomes more probable. Fading is the suggested way of withdrawing prompts because a gradual transition may increase the likelihood that the newly learned behavior will be maintained.

Chaining

Chaining is a process which occurs in behavioral sequences such as piano playing and typing such that responses serve as stimuli which both prompt and reinforce a behavior. For example, in practicing a piano lesson, when a correct note is played, the response serves to reinforce an individual for the previous notes and to prompt the next response (that is, playing the next note). Thus each behavior in a chain has two functions, namely, a reinforcing function and a prompting function. Interestingly, this conceptualization of chaining involves full recognition that an individual's behavior alters the environment which, in turn, influences behavior. In short, it recognizes the ability of an individual to influence his or her own behavior.

Chaining can be easily seen in the sequence of behaviors involved in the recitation of the Gettysburg Address. The links or subskills in the beginning of this chain are listed as follows:

1. Four score and seven years ago
2. our fathers brought forth on this continent
3. a new nation
4. conceived in liberty and dedicated to the proposition that all men are created equal.
5. Now we are engaged in a great civil war

As you know from learning to recite poetry or prose, if you forget any link in the chain, you often cannot proceed to the next critical link. In fact, the chain is only as strong as its weakest link, for the chain will be broken at the point of the weakest link.

Let us now consider several therapeutic ramifications of chaining. In certain chains of behavior, the whole sequence of behavior may be interrupted by preventing an individual from engaging in one component of the chain. For example, if you prevent an individual who has a ritualistic compulsion, such as hand washing in a particular bathroom, from engaging in one of the ritualistic behaviors, such as lathering his or her hands with a particular soap, the individual may be unable to complete the hand-washing sequence. Similarly, children with seizure disorders who are interrupted in the early stages of their preseizure behaviors have markedly fewer seizures than when they are not interrupted (Zlutnick, Mayville, and Moffat, 1975). For example, a mother was taught to shout, "No," and to shake a fourteen-year-old epileptic female whenever she raised her arm slowly to a position parallel to her head, as this arm raising was always followed by seizures. As can be seen in Fig. 4–5 the number of seizures dropped from approximately eleven per week to two per week during the interruption phase. When the interruptions were ceased, the seizure rate

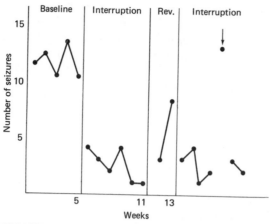

FIGURE 4.5

The number of minor motor seizures per week for Subject 4. (Zlutnick, Mayville, & Moffat, *Journal of Applied Behavior Analysis,* 1975; *8,* 1–12.) Copyright 1975 by the Society for the Experimental Analysis of Behavior, Inc.

increased, and thus the interruptions were reintroduced. The only week in which the interruptions were not effective (see arrow in figure) was when the fourteen-year-old began her menstrual cycle.

Operant Control of Autonomic Functioning

Before 1970, most physiologists and psychologists did not believe that *autonomic responses,* such as heart rate, blood pressure, and gastric secretions, could be influenced by environmental contingencies. In 1969, Miller documented the efficacy of operant control of heart rate, blood pressure, and intestinal contractions, and new treatment vistas were suddenly proffered.[2] For example, Shapiro (1973) taught subjects to raise and lower their systolic blood pressure within a single session if they were given feedback and a reward for such changes. In a typical experiment, subjects were provided with binary feedback (Yes or No) regarding whether their blood pressure was lowered or elevated coincident with each heart beat. After a fixed number of specified correct responses for raising or lowering blood pressure, the subject was rewarded with a token or a slide. The tokens or slides represented points exchangeable for monetary bonuses. Subjects in these studies learned to decrease their diastolic pressure by 15 percent and

---

[2]Although some of the initial Miller experiments were not replicated, his work served as a major impetus for others to use operant technology to treat individuals with autonomic disorders (Shapiro and Surwit, 1976).

their systolic pressure by as much as 10 percent. These results were deemed revolutionary for, if they could be replicated with patients with high blood pressure (hypertensives), they might provide the basis for the treatment of many individuals at risk for coronary disease. In fact, during the past few years it has become very clear that various learning proce- dures can be used to reduce blood pressure effectively in a laboratory situ- ation (Shapiro and Surwit, 1976; Tarler-Benlolo, 1978). The initial work of Miller and his colleagues was a seminal influence in the development of this treatment program.

The early reports of demonstrations of operant conditioning of auto- nomic functioning have been replicated many times, although the relative contribution of reinforcement and feedback in the control of autonomic re- sponding is not clear. Nonetheless, this work prompted major research efforts with tremendous implications for treatment of clinical problems. These efforts will be considered in more detail in the section on biofeed- back in Chap. 8. Most importantly, it renewed serious interest in self-con- trol of behavior, an area that had generally been neglected by behavioral psychologists.

The Individual in the Reinforcement Process

The role of external reinforcement in changing behavior has been illus- trated throughout this chapter. Given the power of external reinforcers in changing the behavior of both groups and individuals, one may question the role of the individual in the influence process. As we conclude this chapter, we must emphasize that most attempts to efficiently change the behavior of another person require that the individual be aware of the reinforcement contingencies (Dulany, 1968).[3] Second, an individual can re- sist the influence process by engaging in countercontrol activities as illus- trated by refusing to engage in certain activities, forgetting assignments, and discussing pseudo issues (Davison, 1973). Third, reinforcement need not be immediate; the individual remembers and cognitively acts upon his or her interpretation of past events, and these cognitive events in turn in- fluence overt behavior. In brief, while external reinforcers play a very pow- erful role in society, individuals are not mere automatons whose behavior is influenced by environmental events. They have a crucial role in deter- mining their own destiny.

[3]There has long been considerable debate on whether one can learn without awareness. While certain responses (e.g., muscle contractions) apparently can be changed without the sub- ject's awareness, in most behavior therapy endeavors, the client would have to know of the desired behavior to change his or her behavior.

Summary

The role of operant conditioning both as a paradigm for viewing human behavior and as a set of principles for changing behavior was examined. In brief, in 1953 Skinner argued that our behavior is largely determined by reinforcers or rewards and that if society would systematize those reinforcers, teaching, child care, work, and rehabilitation could be made more satisfying. Some systematic use of reinforcement contingencies has already begun in modifying fuel consumption, highway use, littering, and obedience to the law.

Unconditioned reinforcers, like food, influence the behavior of all of us, and secondary reinforcers, like the words "Good," "Great job," and "Splendid," are universal shapers of our behavior. Token reinforcers, like money, also acquire very potent force in determining the behavior of adults in all societies. Examples of the clinical use of primary and secondary reinforcers in modifying behavior were reviewed. Token reinforcement programs have been used extensively in schools and hospitals, and their success in changing behavior is well established. To ensure maintenance of behavior established in the token program, however, clients need to be helped as they move from systematized to natural reinforcement contingencies.

Four basic reinforcement schedules were reviewed, and the role of chaining and its therapeutic implications were examined. Extinction or cessation of reinforcement will usually lead to reduction of a behavior, but it is more difficult to extinguish behavior after partial reinforcement than after continuous reinforcement.

Shaping, or reinforcing successive approximations to a terminal behavior, is a concept deemed desirable in changing behavior from many theoretical orientations. Although the *processes* which purportedly underlie the procedure called shaping vary, all therapists should know the way in which shaping is accomplished. Prompting and fading are ways to present and withdraw stimuli in teaching new behaviors. Operant conditioning experiments of autonomic functioning were examined, and their implications for treatment of disorders, such as hypertension, were discussed. Finally, the crucial role of the individual's awareness of reinforcement contingencies, cooperation with the change agent, and interpretation of events were noted, and the role of individuals in shaping their own destiny emphasized.

Suggested Readings

Basic Principles:

HONIG, W. K., and STADDON, J. E. R., eds. 1977. *Handbook of operant behavior.* Englewood Cliffs, NJ: Prentice-Hall.

MILLER, L. K. 1975. *Principles of everyday behavior analysis.* unit 2. Monterey, CA: Brooks/Cole Publishing Co.

RACHLIN, H. 1976. *Introduction to modern behaviorism.* 2nd ed. chap. 3. San Francisco: W. H. Freeman and Company.

REYNOLDS, G. S. 1968. *A primer of operant conditioning.* chaps. 3, 5, 6, 7. Glenview, Ill: Scott, Foresman and Co.

Clinical Applications:

KAZDIN, A. E. 1977. *The token economy.* chaps. 3, 4, 5, 7, 8, 9. New York: Plenum Press.

O'LEARY, K. D., and O'LEARY, S. G. 1977. *Classroom management: The successful use of behavior modification.* 2nd ed. chaps. 2, 6. New York: Pergamon Press, Inc.

5

Aversive Conditioning

Classical Attitudes Regarding Aversive Influence

Professionals in the mental health field have long argued against the use of aversive control. Freud, in his psychodynamic model of mental illness, espoused the view that mental disorders result from repression of sexual urges and that this repression begins in the first few years of life. Victorian attitudes of the time which were essentially punitive toward expression of childhood sexuality contributed to the behavior patterns Freud observed.

The mental health profession was almost solely dominated by the psychodynamic model from the 1920s to the 1950s when Rogerian, or nondirective, therapy was accepted by many psychologists. The Rogerian model of psychotherapy was more a model of therapeutic change than a model of the etiology of mental illness, but aversive control—particularly punishment—was clearly eschewed. Rogers postulated that people are innately good and become hateful and self-centered only because of learning; a person develops behavioral disorders because of a fundamental conflict between what he or she feels is good and what others approve. Consequently, the individual denies or distorts the feeling. Thus a cornerstone of Rogerian therapy is that a therapist should be consistently warm, attentive, and nonevaluative so that the client will feel free to express feelings that have been denied or distorted (Rogers, 1951). While Rogerians espouse the view that therapists should be unconditionally positive, there is a discrepancy between theory and practice in that Rogerians may subtly indicate approval of clients' behaviors they themselves like and indicate disapproval of behaviors they dislike or feel are maladaptive (Murray, 1956). Nonetheless, the thrust of Roger's position, namely, that one should convey unconditional positive regard, is consistent with the explicitly negative attitude toward punishment.

With certain exceptions, to be described later, behaviorists have also been opposed to aversive control. Skinner was adamantly opposed to punishment because he held that it had only a temporary suppressive effect on behavior. In a now classic study on punishment (1938), Skinner trained two groups of four animals each to press a bar reliably on a fixed interval schedule of reinforcement. Later, both groups were placed on an extinction schedule (that is, food was no longer forthcoming when the bar was pressed). For one group, Skinner then arranged the bar so that it would instantly move upward against the rat's paws when the rat pressed the bar. Essentially, the bar slapped the rat's paw. When the punishment was applied, there was an almost complete suppression of the responses. However, two days after the aversive consequences were removed, the cumulative record of responding showed the same rate of bar pressing in each group.

Skinner concluded from this experiment, not only that the effects of punishment were temporary, but that after the punishment is eliminated, the suppressed behavior of punished subjects may become equal to or greater than that of unpunished subjects. Skinner's views on punishment have been influential, and he has argued against its use for almost four decades. The consistency of his attitude that punishment should be avoided is reflected in the following quotations which span a twenty-three-year period:

> We are gradually discovering—at an untold cost in human suffering—that in the long run punishment does not reduce the probability than an act will occur. (The character Frazier, in *Walden Two,* 1948, p. 244)
>
> In the long run, . . . punishment does not actually eliminate behavior from a repertoire, and its temporary achievement is obtained at tremendous cost in reducing the over-all efficiency and happiness of the group. (1953, p. 190)
>
> People still control each other more often through censure or blame than commendation or praise, the military and the police remain the most powerful arms of government, communicants are still occasionally reminded of hellfire, and teachers have abandoned the birch rod only to replace it with more subtle forms of punishment (p. 61). . . . yet there are better ways. (1971, p. 81)

The general thrust of the positions of influential psychodynamicists, Rogerians, and behaviorists was to discourage the use of punishment in human endeavors for almost three decades. This attitude led to a more permissive approach to child rearing (Spock, 1940; 1957), shorter prison sentences, probational therapy, rehabilitation programs for legal offenders (Cortes and Gatti, 1972), and an emphasis on positive reinforcement in the education process, such as programmed instruction which focused on providing immediate positive feedback to students (Skinner, 1963).

Many people feel uncomfortable about changing behavior by means of threats, spanking, reprimands, incarceration, and isolation, because of their own direct or indirect experience with these methods. However, despite this discomfort and despite the criticism of the use of punishment by psychologists and psychiatrists, parents and teachers almost universally use punishment in one form or another. Sears, Maccoby, and Levin (1957) found that 99 percent of the parents of 379 kindergarteners spanked their children. Lefkowitz, Walder, and Eron (1963) found that 57 percent of the parents of third graders used physical punishment. Madsen, Madsen, Saudargas, Hammond, and Edgar (1970) in an analysis of teacher-pupil interactions in thirty-two classrooms (kindergarten to grade six) found that only 23 percent of the teachers' interactions with children were positive.

A predominance of negative teacher-pupil interactions was also reported by White (1975), who collected observational data on 104 teachers in grades one through twelve. In grades one and two, approvals occurred more frequently than disapprovals, but in all other grades, disapproval predominated. A closer analysis of White's data revealed that all teachers tended to approve of academic behavior (presumably correct responses), but they did not evidence approval of social behavior. In essence, the teachers acted as if good social deportment was expected, and when it did not occur, the teachers reacted aversively. The above research makes it clear that punishment or the threat of punishment is all around us. Further, "normal" children present occasional problems which many parents, teachers, and even many professionals feel deserve punishment, for example, a three-year-old throws a rock at another child or runs into a busy street, a teenager misses a Saturday night curfew by two hours, someone throws a tray of food on the floor in the cafeteria, and a fight breaks out in the classroom.

While most behavior therapists would question the use of corporal punishment, some recent U.S. Supreme Court decisions reflect societal attitudes that corporal punishment in schools is viewed as proper under certain conditions. In October 1975, the U.S. Supreme Court in a hearing regarding spanking in the schools *(Baker* v. *Owens)* upheld state laws authorizing corporal punishment when administered with certain procedural safeguards. Only three states forbid all corporal punishment in the schools, and seventeen states now expressly permit it (Maurer, 1974).

In a related vein, there has been a very recent societal trend to be more encouraging of strong penalties for certain crimes. In New York State in 1974, it became a felony to kill an on-duty policeman, and there is mandatory execution or life imprisonment for such a crime (McCullough, 1975). Gallup polls in 1960 and 1976 showed that there has been a marked rise in the number of Americans favoring capital punishment. In 1960, 42 percent favored such punishment; in 1976, this figure rose to 66 percent (*NBC News,* January 17, 1977). In 1977, a number of states began to reinitiate capital punishment, as exemplified by the much publicized execution of Gary Gilmore in Utah on January 17, 1977.

While psychologists long espoused the view that aversive control, particularly punishment, was to be avoided, a catalyst for the resurgence of interest in punishment was an article by Solomon (1964), who argued that psychologists have helped build a "legend" that punishment is an extremely ineffective means of controlling behavior. Solomon noted that the scientific bases for that conclusion were shabby, and that even as early as 1938, there were experimental data which demonstrated the effectiveness of punishment in controlling behavior (Warden and Aylesworth, 1927). Animal experiments in the 1940s and 1950s which involved teaching organisms to avoid certain stimuli added impressive data that aversive stimuli can have long-lasting behavioral effects (Solomon and Brush, 1956). More recently, it has become apparent that punishment can be effective with humans under many circumstances and the negative side effects can be minimized when certain guidelines are followed (S. O'Leary, 1976).

Punishment: Definition and Parameters

Punishment refers to an operation in which an aversive stimulus is made contingent upon a response.[1] With humans, the *aversive stimuli* are those which we will generally be expected to avoid, and they thus vary tremendously. They include spanking, reprimands, disapproval, social isolation, monetary fines, withdrawal of privileges, detention, and even what is commonly referred to as the silent treatment, for example, glaring at someone without comment.

Let us now examine some of the factors which influence the effectiveness of punishment with humans.

TIMING

Should you punish a child who takes cookies from a cookie jar just as he or she approaches the cookie jar but before he or she touches it, or after a child has eaten the cookie? Is it more effective to mildly reprimand and correct an adult vocal student in individual instruction as he or she is beginning to sing off key or after he or she has sung several stanzas flat? Walters, Parke, and Cane (1965) and other investigators have found that punishment early in a behavioral sequence is more effective than punishment late in that sequence. In brief, when possible, it appears best to "nip the behavior in the bud" or to punish at the initiation of an act. Further, when punishment follows a behavior, the longer the delay between the forbidden act and the punishment, the less effective the punishment will be. Practically, however, ward attendants, parents, police officers, and teachers cannot always be surveillant, and there is often a delay between the commission of a forbidden behavior and the punishment of that behavior (for example, when father arrives home at 6:00 P.M., he is asked to punish a child for a transgression which occurred at 11:00 A.M.). Fortunately, a symbolic or verbal representation of the transgression increases the effectiveness of delayed punishment. For example, if individuals listen to a videotape recording or a verbal description of themselves committing the deviant act before receiving the delayed punishment, the effectiveness of the delayed punishment is enhanced (Walters and Andres, 1967; Verna, 1977).

INTENSITY

As one might expect, as intensity of punishment increases, response suppression increases. For example, working with alcoholics, Davidson (1972) showed

[1]Some investigators define punishment in a functional sense, that is, as any consequence which reduces the future probability of a behavior (see Honig and Staddon, 1977).

that as punishment intensity increased, patients' rate of pressing a lever to receive alcohol diluted with water decreased. Similarly, Powell and Azrin (1968) found that smoking rate decreased as the intensity of shock increased (a specially designed cigarette case delivered a shock when opened). We should not, however, infer from these findings that it is generally best to use intense punishment. In fact, when an external agent delivers the punishment and intense punishment is used, it appears that the punisher loses his or her effectiveness. Moreover, the punisher's positive reinforcing properties decrease with intense punishment, and the punitive person will be avoided (Redd, Morris, and Martin, 1975). In like fashion, when the intensity of the punishment delivered by the cigarette case in the Powell and Azrin (1968) study was increased, the case was carried less frequently.

CONSISTENCY

Parents are frequently admonished to be consistent and to present a united front when they punish their children. This ideal cannot always be upheld, but all experimental evidence suggests that it is certainly a well-advised goal. For example, six- to nine-year-old children were first taught to hit a life-size clown doll in the stomach. One-third of the children were always rewarded with marbles when they punched the doll; a second third of the children received rewards half the time and were punished half the time (heard a loud buzzer which informed them that they were "doing badly"); and the last third of the children were rewarded half the time with marbles, but nothing occurred on the other occasions (that is, they were placed on extinction). Following the training to hit the clown doll, all three groups of children were told they could then continue to play the game on their own. In the posttraining, as expected, the group which had half reward and half punishment (that is, the inconsistent group) hit the doll more than the other two groups (Deur and Parke, 1970).

Studies of parent-child interactions have shown that a combination of punitive and lax discipline is associated with the highest crime rates of any types of discipline studied, that is, greater than discipline that is strictly punitive or strictly lax (McCord, McCord, and Zola, 1959). Interestingly, it appears that consistent punitive parental discipline per se leads to conformity to parental rules. Unfortunately, however, the punitive parents provide models of aggression for their child. That is, they show the child that when they are angry, they often release their frustration by hitting, spanking, or slapping. In this regard, Lefkowitz, Walder, and Eron (1963) gathered parent disciplinary data from mothers and fathers through interviews and children's aggression scores through peer ratings. Generally, the children's aggression scores in school were found to be related to the number of physical punishments, such as slapping, spanking, and washing the mouth out with soap. Similarly, Hoffman (1960) showed that domineering punitive parents have children who cower in their presence but who are very aggressive with peers at school. We will return to the important negative side effects of punishment later.

REASONING AND PUNISHMENT

If a child is given a reason for engaging or not engaging in a behavior, the adults' proscriptions are more likely to be followed than if no reasons are given. For example, in one experiment some children were given the following reason for not playing with an attractive toy when the experimenter was away: "It's bad to play with that toy while I am away because it belongs to someone else." The other half of the children were not given any reason; they were simply told: "It's bad to play with this toy while I am away." The children given a reason played with the toy significantly less frequently and for less time in the experimenter's absence than did the children given no reason (Cheyne and Walters, 1970). Elliot and Vasta (1970) also found that if children were exposed to a model who shared and if an experimenter gave children reasons for sharing, they shared more than when simply exposed to the model who shared.

Although there is a paucity of applied research on reasoning coupled with punishment and reward, it appears that whenever reasons are used in combination with contingencies, they generally facilitate desired behavior (Tucker, 1976). When reasons are given to children, they learn why things should or should not be done (for example, why you don't touch a radiator; why you shouldn't eat too much candy), and the adult probably is viewed in a much more positive sense. In short, reasons seem both educative and humane.

TYPE OF RESPONSE PUNISHED

Therapists should be especially alert to naturally occurring aversive consequences in early parent-child interactions and in adolescent sexual development. This recommendation follows from laboratory research with animals in which eating and sexual behavior are greatly suppressed by moderate punishment (Lichtenstein, 1950; Masserman, 1943). For ethical reasons, studies of punishment cannot be performed on children's eating behavior or the sexual behaviors of teenagers and adults. However, the laboratory findings with animals have considerable import for child-rearing practices and sex therapy. It has been the authors' experience that clients who have problems with children refusing to eat have often rebuked their children for poor eating habits, for example, eating slowly, sloppily, and in a finicky manner. Interestingly, these rebukes may lead to stomach contractions which make the eating process even more unlikely. Our general advice in such circumstances is to have the parents give the child small portions of food, to have a highly desired dessert or snack available after dinner, and to tell the child that he or she will obtain a snack if the dinner is eaten. Usually after several days of testing the parents, children begin to eat without difficulty.

Sex therapists often find that impotence and lack of orgasmic functioning in women are associated with various types of aversive experiences related to critical early sexual experiences. For example, in commenting on the origins of orgasmic dysfunctions in women, Masters and Johnson (1970) noted that there are many women who "specifically resist the experience of orgasmic response, as they reject their sexual identity and the facility for its active expression" (p. 225). Often these women had been consistently admonished by their parents or by religious authorities against personal admission or overt expression of sexual feeling.

While even mild punishment apparently can have very serious consequences for certain behaviors, most obese adults do not stop eating when verbally rebuked, and sexual offenders do not readily stop their unlawful sexual activity when punished by fines and/or incarceration. Thus, it appears that certain developing behavioral repertoires in children (that is, eating) and adolescents (that is, sexual activity) are much more susceptible to punishment than are well established habits in adults.

Aversive Stimulation

ESCAPE AND AVOIDANCE

The term *escape conditioning* refers to an operation in which an aversive stimulus is presented to an individual and is terminated when a specified response by the individual occurs. *Avoidance* refers to a procedure which allows an individual to postpone or even completely avoid the aversive stimulus. Escape and avoidance have not been used frequently by behavior therapists, and even when they are purportedly effective, we caution against their use. Most importantly, we would ask whether positive reinforcement procedures have first been used to teach the behavior in question.

There have been illustrations of escape procedures with adults where the goal has been to increase talking in a therapy session. For example, Heckel, Wiggins, and Salzberg (1972) used an escape procedure to increase the amount of conversation in group therapy for chronic psychotic patients. If the patients were silent for too long a period (a predetermined time), a noxious noise was presented which could be terminated only by talking. More recently, Fichter,

Wallace, Liberman, and Davis (1976) successfully taught three chronic schizophrenics to increase their voice volume and duration of speech by using an
avoidance procedure. Staff members would prompt the patients to talk louder
and longer when engaged in conversation; if the patients did not talk louder
or longer, the staff members would ask them to repeat what they said so they
could be heard at a distance of ten feet. According to Fichter and others (1976)
the

> avoidance procedure proved successful after several attempts with positive rein-
> forcement techniques had failed. There seemed to be no objects or events that
> could be used as positive reinforcers; a reinforcer sampling procedure [where the
> patient is given free access to potentially reinforcing events to assess their value]
> proved ineffective in establishing such items, and [the patient] refused to con-
> sume objects that he had verbally indicated that he liked "very much" (p. 384).

As mentioned earlier, escape and avoidance procedures must be carefully
and very cautiously utilized, and Fichter and others (1976) reportedly used
avoidance procedures only after other treatment methods failed. They noted,
however, that avoidance procedures require patient cooperation. Without such
cooperation, a patient who simply refuses to talk can use counter-control and
place the staff member in a very awkward position where he or she is inces-
santly nagging. Fortunately, such was not the case in the Fichter and others'
study, and in fact, in one case staff members outside the experimental-ward
environment were instructed in the successful use of the avoidance procedure.
Furthermore, after its use, the patients' parents noted improved conversations
at home.

REPRIMANDS

Verbal reprimands, probably the most common aversive procedure, are used
daily by almost all parents and teachers, but little research exists on their use
in applied settings. Generally, when a teacher reprimands a child, almost the
entire class can hear the reprimand. Loud reprimands usually serve to maintain or intensify undesired behavior; however, as illustrated in Fig. 5–1, if a
teacher reprimands so that only the child being reprimanded hears the reprimand, the child's undesired behavior decreases (O'Leary and others, 1970;
Timm, 1975). Further, a teacher who gives loud reprimands is rated less
positively by his or her students than a teacher who gives softer, private
reprimands (Timm, 1975).

Thomas, Becker, and Armstrong (1968) found that when a teacher
showed high and intense disapproval of classroom behavior by yelling, be-
littling, grabbing, or spanking, there was three times more classroom disruption as when the teacher reinforced desired classroom behaviors. On

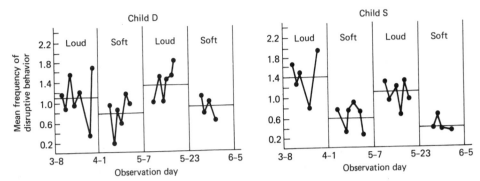

FIGURE 5.1
Disruptive behavior in children D and S in Class A. (O'Leary et al., *Exceptional Children,* 37, 1970, 149). Reprinted from *Exceptional Children* by permission of The Council for Exceptional Children. Copyright 1970 by The Council for Exceptional Children.

the other hand, Jones and Miller (1974) assessed the effects of a combination of brief negative attention to a child (usually in the form of reprimands audible to the class) when he or she was disruptive, combined with (1) praise of others who were behaving appropriately, and (2) reinforcement of the child who had been disruptive. Such a combination of praise and a brief reprimand audible to the class led to marked decreases in disruptive behavior. The implication of the studies is clear: If necessary, soft or brief reprimands can lead to reductions in disruptive behavior, but they should only be used in conjunction with praise and reinforcement for desired behavior.

THREATS

Threats are used frequently in our society as a means of influencing behavior. Usually, threats are invoked to decrease behavior (for example, "If you don't stop criticizing me, I'm going to file for divorce"), but they can also be used to increase behaviors (for example, "If you don't hang up your clothes before supper, you won't get dessert"). Basically, the threat is a signal that an aversive event will occur if behavior does not change in an appropriate manner, and the use of threats can be roughly conceptualized as avoidance conditioning. The signal or threat is followed by an aversive event if the appropriate avoidance response does not occur in a specified time period. Despite the almost ubiquitous use of threats in our culture, especially by parents and teachers, there are few studies of threats in applied settings where the effects of threats are observed across time. It is clear, however, that if a threat is made and no consequences occur for failure to behave in the specified way, the effect of the threat is decreased (S. O'Leary, 1974).

OVERCORRECTION

This procedure generally involves having a person correct the consequences of his or her behavior by restoring "the disturbed situation to a 'greater improved state'" (Foxx and Azrin, 1972, p. 16). For example, if a child writes on the walls, he is required not only to erase the writing on the wall, but to clean the entire wall or room. If an adult patient shrieks and screams, he or she may then have to remain exceptionally quiet for a fixed period. Overcorrection has been successfully used to reduce aggression (Foxx and Azrin, 1972), stealing (Azrin and Wesolowski, 1974), self-stimulation (Harris and Romanczyk, 1976), and spelling errors (Foxx and Jones, 1978).

According to Foxx and Azrin (1972), who have most frequently evaluated overcorrection, the restitutive action should be immediate and should be directly related to the misbehavior. For example, if the misbehavior is aggression, the aggressor will have to act cooperatively. In addition, while engaging in the restitutive action, the person should not be allowed to engage in other activities that are reinforcing; in this sense, the restitution serves as a removal from rewarding activities or a time-out from reinforcement. Finally, Foxx and Azrin (1972) suggested that the person very actively perform the restitution without pause. That is, the restitution should be monitored, and the client should not be allowed to spend time resting or dallying during the restitution.

Restitution is well exemplified in the study by Foxx and Azrin (1972) with a fifty-year-old profoundly retarded (IQ = 16) female named Ann who had been hospitalized for forty-six years. One of her frequent problems was the overturning of beds, chairs, and tables. The behavior was first recorded when this patient was thirteen, and it was mentioned throughout her hospital records. Time-out, verbal chastisement, physical restraint, and the requirement that Ann place overturned furniture in their correct positions had been unsuccessfully used in attempts to reduce Ann's disorderly behavior.

In this case, restitution included returning overturned beds to their correct position, remaking the beds neatly, and fluffing the pillows of all the other beds on the ward. If Ann turned over a dining room table containing food, she was required to clean the entire dining room after sweeping and mopping up the debris. Since she did not know how to make beds or rearrange furniture, she had to be guided physically in such efforts. The patient was also required to apologize to individuals whose furniture had been turned over (she was to nod "yes" when an attendant asked her if she were sorry for what she had done). The results of the restitution training are depicted in Fig. 5–2. As you can see, it was dramatically effective in reducing disruptive behavior.

As one might expect from the foregoing description of overcorrection, patients may strongly resist following the attendants' instructions, as was the case for this patient who remained passive and held her arms rigid during

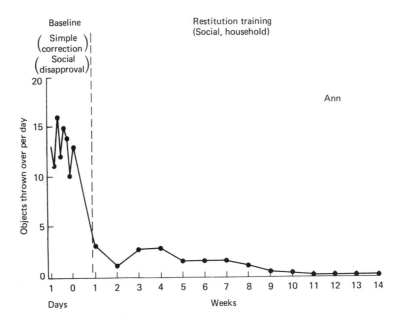

FIGURE 5.2

The effect of Restitution Training procedures on the number of objects thrown by an institutionalized retarded female. Each data point represents one day in the baseline period and one week in the Restitution Training period. During the baseline period, the resident was reprimanded, "social disapproval," and required to correct the position of each disturbed object "simple correction." The arrow indicates a period when training was conducted improperly by one of the trainers. [Reprinted with permission from (*Behavior Research and Therapy,* 10, Foxx, R. M., & Azrin, N. H., Restitution: A method of eliminating agressive-disruptive behavior of retarded and brain damaged patients.) Copyright 1972, Pergamon Press, Ltd.]

initial training efforts. Fortunately, Ann stopped resisting physical guidance as the program progressed, and it was rarely needed after the seventh week of training.

Overcorrection is a multifaceted intervention procedure which includes positive reinforcement, passive shaping (physical guidance), warnings, restraint, and punishment. Most importantly, however, overcorrection requires cooperation from the client or patient if it is to be implemented without a great deal of arguing. Where cooperation is expected to be minimal, other options such as reinforcing alternatives to the undesired behavior, restraint, and timeout should be implemented before overcorrection.

TIME-OUT FROM REINFORCEMENT

> *Time-out from reinforcement* refers to a procedure in which the means of access
> to the sources of various forms of reinforcement are removed for a particular time
> period contingent upon the emission of a response. . . . Either the behaving
> individual is contingently removed from the reinforcing environment or the
> reinforcing environment is contingently removed for some stipulated duration.
> (Sulzer-Azaroff and Mayer 1977, p. 524) For example, a young boy who likes
> to be with his brothers and sisters in the den may be asked to go to his bedroom
> contingent upon hitting one of his brothers; a woman may not allow herself to
> purchase clothes for a particular time period when she gains weight.

An example of time-out was provided by Drabman and Spitalnik (1973),
who were working in a psychiatric hospital school for male adolescents who
displayed very high rates of disruptive behavior—physical aggression, verbal
abuse, and little regard for classroom or hospital rules, in particular. Drabman
and Spitalnik selected three residents of the school who exhibited unusually
high rates of disruptive behavior. After a baseline period in which rates of
inappropriate vocalization, aggression, and being out of seat without permission were recorded, the time-out procedure was instituted. More specifically,
a student was placed in a small room for 10 minutes if he was aggressive and
or was out of his seat without permission. The other behavior, inappropriate
vocalizations, was not a target of the intervention. When the study began, the
students were aware that if they displayed aggression or were out of their seats
without permission, they would be escorted by the teaching assistant from the
classroom to the small room down the hall.

As predicted, the two punished behaviors, aggression and being out of
seat without permission, decreased significantly, whereas the unpunished behavior, vocalization, did not change when the other two behaviors were punished (see Fig. 5–3). Thus, the study indicated that time-out had a relatively
specific and clearly strong effect on undesired behaviors. When introducing a
time-out procedure in the form of social isolation in a classroom, however,
caution should be taken to insure that the classroom is reinforcing for the
children most likely to be punished. In brief, one needs to ascertain whether
the disruptive classroom behavior results from boredom, inappropriate academic instructions, or work beyond the child's capability. If any of these
applies, time-out is inappropriate.

Porterfield, Herbert-Jackson, and Risley (1976) demonstrated that social
isolation may not be necessary when the activity in the classroom is highly
reinforcing. Under such conditions, time-out from active participation can be
an effective means of reducing aggressive behavior. In the Porterfield and
others study of normal one- to two-year-old children in a day-care center,
having the child "sit and watch" the other children for less than one minute
contingent upon undesired behavior, such as aggression and destruction of
toys, was more effective than attempts to redirect the child to another activity.

133

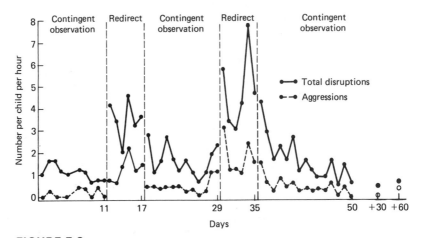

FIGURE 5.3
Number of disruptions and aggressions per child per hour in a Toddler Day Care Center for 50 days and follow-up days at one and two months. (Porterfield, Herbert-Jackson, Risley, Contingent observation: An effective and acceptable procedure for reducing disruptive behavior of young children in a group setting. *Journal of Applied Behavior Analysis,* 1976, 9, 55–64. Copyright 1976 by the Society for the Experimental Analysis of Behavior, Inc.)

Additionally, the day-care sessions were rated as "more pleasant" by independent observers and the staff when the "sit and watch" procedure was employed.

An interesting use of time-out with adults was reported by Murray and Hobbs (1977), who had a husband and wife impose a time-out from reinforcement procedure on themselves. Both spouses were approximately forty years old and had been referred to a Veterans Administration Hospital for excessive alcohol consumption. The husband had been an outpatient at the VA hospital four to five days a week but refused to accept the label "alcoholic." His wife reported that they both drank excessively, and that such drinking had resulted in her husband's job loss and the forced sale of their house. Almost all of this couple's drinking occurred at night when they were together. At these times, they reported drinking 4/5 quart of vodka a day.

Since the couple's drinking occurred almost exclusively at home, the treatment involved a self-imposed time-out from reinforcement contingent upon any drink with greater than one ounce of alcohol. The time-out consisted of 15 minutes in which all social reinforcement (for example, talking, playing cards) was to stop. If they drank, they were to do so in isolation; the therapists chose this restriction because they knew that the clients disliked solitary drinking. Later in the treatment, time-out was made contingent upon consumption of more than four drinks a day and/or consumption of any drink in less than 30 minutes.

The data from this case report are very impressive. When time-out was contingent upon mixing drinks with greater than one ounce of alcohol, overall alcohol consumption was reduced by 35 percent and 25 percent for the husband and wife, respectively. When time-out was later made contingent upon more than four drinks a day and/or consumption of drinks in less than 30 minutes, alcohol consumption dropped even further. At follow-up, the husband and wife were consuming 4.4 and 5.1 ounces of alcohol a day, whereas their baseline rates had each exceeded 13 ounces a day.

Time-out from reinforcement has been used to reduce thumb-sucking (Baer, 1962), improper eating habits (Barton, and others, 1970), and lunchroom disruptions (MacPherson, Candee, and Holman, 1974). It is beyond the scope of this text to elaborate on all the numerous factors that might influence the effectiveness of time-out, but Gelfand and Hartmann (1975) have reviewed time-out and presented useful guidelines for its use with children. (See Box 5–1)

Box 5–1   *Guidelines for Time-Out Use*
(Gelfand and Hartmann, 1975)

1. Carefully assess the actual and potential reinforcers for the individual as use of time-out implies that the therapist or change agent has isolated and is withholding the positive reinforcers that maintain the behavior.

2. Decide upon the time-out contingency and make it apparent to the child, for example, each time the child destroys a toy he or she will be placed in time-out.

3. Escort the individual to be placed in time-out to the time-out area or room in a calm but businesslike manner.

4. Use as brief a time-out period as possible.

5. The return from time-out should occur only when the individual has been cooperative. For example, if a child was placed in time-out because of tantrums, he or she should not be released because he or she remained there for a specific period. The individual should be released from time-out only after a period of no tantrums.

RESPONSE COST

Response cost refers to a penalty or fine that is contingent upon a specific behavior. The most common example of a response cost is the fine imposed on motorists who exceed speed limits, but because speeders can so often drive at very high speeds without negative consequences, this response cost system may be relatively ineffective. A more recent example of the use of a response cost or fine procedure is the penalty system imposed on individuals who use more than their allotted amount of telephone directory assistance services. Specifically, the response cost plan adopted was as follows: telephone subscribers were allowed three directory assistance calls and then charged for each additional call. The initiation of this charge (a response cost) dramatically reduced the use of directory assistance calls in a population of a million phone users (McSweeney, 1978), and a portion of the savings was passed on to the consumer.*

Although most of the initial token reinforcement programs (Ayllon and Azrin, 1968; Atthowe and Krasner, 1968; Birnbrauer and others, 1965; O'Leary and Becker, 1967) involved almost exclusive attention to instances of acceptable behavior, while unacceptable behavior was ignored entirely, this position has changed radically. Presently, most long-term token reinforcement programs include some means of consequating undesirable behavior. Usually, the individuals in the token program can both earn and lose tokens. That is, the individuals face the possibility of a response cost; they can lose tokens if they display undesirable behavior.

The initial experiments on response cost were conducted by Weiner (1962), who demonstrated that response cost functions as a punishment procedure, and Burchard (1967), who was one of the first researchers to incorporate response cost procedures in a token economy. Burchard introduced a token economy in an intensive training unit for twelve mildly retarded boys who had a long record of antisocial behavior, such as theft, breaking and entering, and aggression. Tokens which were exchangeable for candy, recreational activities, and trips downtown were earned for school work, cooperating with peers, and proper care of clothing. The boys would lose tokens for fighting, lying, and cheating. In addition to the loss of tokens, the boys were secluded in a room (time-out from reinforcement) for major offenses (for example, physical assaults). Burchard's study provided suggestive evidence for the effectiveness of response cost, and a series of experiments in a home-style rehabilitation center for predelinquent boys has provided conclusive evidence for its effectiveness (Phillips, 1968; Phillips and others 1971). For example, when boys made aggressive statements, such as "I'll kill you," or "I'm going to kick your butt," they lost 20 points. Similarly, when the boys were late in returning home either from school or after completing errands, they were fined 20 points for every minute they were late. The fines were effective in reducing both aggressive statements and tardiness. (See Box 5–2)

Response cost, like most punishment procedures, is not without problems. In some instances, the point loss may result in rebellious behavior as was the case in a study by Boren and Colman (1970), who found greater absentee-

*Personal Communication, Mr. Raymond Weitzel, Cincinnati-Bell Telephone Company, Cincinnati, Ohio, July, 1978.

ism and antagonism when fines were imposed for absenteeism at group meetings. Thus one must be very careful in choosing the behaviors that are to be followed by response cost. If people perceive that they are being unfairly fined, they may cause wanton destruction.

At a more general level, in most social systems ranging from marriages, communes, churches, to governments, individuals cannot engage in any behavior they choose without consequences. Failure to complete certain household tasks, adultery, stealing, and property destruction have their penalties (response costs) in almost all cultures. The desire to have both rewards and costs in a self-governing system was illustrated by predelinquents who preferred to have the opportunity to both award *and* take away tokens in a foster-style home, Achievement Place, in which an elected peer manager assigned chores and evaluated performance (Phillips and others, 1973).

Box 5–2 *Examples of Behaviors Leading to Reward and Cost at Achievement Place*	
Behavior	Points
Social	
Participation in Family Conference	+1,500
Fighting	−10,000
Stealing	−20,000
Elected or Candidate for School Office	+3,000
Maintenance	
Vacuuming Living Room	+400
Dusting Living Room	+300
Sweeping Front Proch	+300
Setting Table	+100/place setting
Leaving Items Outside (Carelessness)	−1,000
School	
Homework at Home (Small)	+500/Assignment
Homework at Home (Large)	+1,500/Assignment
Having to Stay After School	−1,000

Taken from Phillips, E. L. and others. *The Teaching Family Handbook.* Lawrence, KS: University of Kansas, 1974, Pgs. 94–99.

Response cost systems are often approximately as effective as reward or reinforcement systems alone (Kaufman and O'Leary, 1972; McLaughlin and Malaby, 1972; Iwata and Bailey, 1974). While it is often necessary to use some form of response cost in a token reinforcement system, it is important to emphasize strongly the positive reinforcing aspects of such a system since it is relatively easy to become sensitized to the undesired behavior.

Ethical Issues Surrounding Aversive Control

ARE ALTERNATIVE METHODS OF POSITIVE REINFORCEMENT AVAILABLE?

Most behavior therapists never use the aversive procedures that are severely criticized by both professionals and the consumers of services (for example, contingent electric shock and long time-out periods). Nonetheless, the criticism regarding aversive control has generally centered around the use of such aversive procedures since they cause the greatest social concern. Some of these criticisms have undoubtedly been legitimate, and some ethics panels composed of behavior therapists (May and others, 1975) have recommended that no punishment procedures be used unless positive reinforcement methods have first been systematically implemented. That is, procedures which are least intrusive, least restrictive, and most benign should always be tried before more punitive methods are used. For example, a mild reprimand should be used before overcorrection, and overcorrection should precede seclusion. The general principle used by May and others (1975) is consistent with a legal position called the "least restrictive conditions." May and others realized that the use of the least restrictive sequencing of interventions could undermine the effectiveness of some treatment programs. For example, a self-injurious individual who is a severe head banger may require strong punishment, such as electric shock contingent upon the self-destructive behavior. The present authors believe that the strategy of using positive reinforcement and least punitive procedures is an excellent overall strategy, and the risk of undermining some treatment programs is one we should take with prudence. On occasion, however, it may be necessary to violate the "least restrictive principle," and a clinician should violate it when there is compelling reason for the use of a punishment procedure. As will be discussed more in Chap. 10, Ethics, the more restrictive treatment procedures, however, should be used sparingly and only after a majority of a peer review group agree that such a course of action is advisable.

CAN THE SIDE EFFECTS OF PUNISHMENT BE AVOIDED?

As was mentioned earlier, Skinner has long argued that side effects of punishment are so negative that punishment should be avoided at all costs. There are clearly undesirable side effects of punishment, such as dislike of the punishment administrator, avoidance of the punisher, the punisher's providing an aggressive model for others, and sometimes the punishment producing severe

138

counterattack. However, these side effects do not always occur and can often, if not almost always, be avoided. To avoid undesirable side effects, the following procedures should generally be followed: (1) use punishment sparingly, (2) provide a reason for the punishment (for those who would understand it), (3) make available other means for the individual to obtain positive reinforcement, (4) avoid physical punishment whenever possible, (5) do not punish when in an unusually angry or highly emotional state, and (6) punish at the initiation of a behavior (S. O'Leary, 1976).

Summary

Research and clinical applications regarding aversive procedures of all sorts have generally been eschewed by psychologists. Psychologists have long argued that aversive procedures led to undesirable side effects and/or that such control was ineffective in the long run. However, in 1964, Solomon very effectively argued that there was a *legend* that punishment was ineffective and always associated with deleterious side effects. It is clear that parents, teachers, and probably foremen universally utilize aversive procedures of one sort or another and that their use should be systematically evaluated.

Punishment or aversive stimulation contingent upon a response has been used effectively in a wide variety of situations with children and adults. Punishment is most effective when it occurs early in a behavioral sequence, when it is generally consistent, and when it is coupled with reasons for the punishment. Escape and avoidance procedures have not been used frequently by behavior therapists, and even when effective, we caution against their use. Verbal reprimands, one of the most common aversive procedures, appear effective if combined with praise for desired behavior or if administered in a quiet manner. Threats should be used very sparingly and then only if they are generally followed through. Overcorrection refers to having a person correct the consequences of his or her behavior by restoring the disturbed situation to a greater improved state. Overcorrection, a multifaceted intervention, has been effective in reducing aggression, stealing, and self-stimulation, but client cooperation is necessary for effectiveness, and when cooperation is expected to be minimal, alternatives to overcorrection should be used. Time-out from reinforcement and response cost have been effectively used in a wide variety of situations, but like most aversive procedures, the individuals being punished should perceive the punishment as fair or the punishment may be ineffective.

Most behavior therapists can and should try varied forms of positive reinforcement before using aversive procedures, although there are instances where both can profitably be used in combination. There are a number of procedural guidelines which should be followed to minimize side effects of aversive control. Most importantly, when aversive procedures are used, they should be used sparingly, and there should be means for making positive reinforcement available for the individual being punished.

Suggested Readings

Basic Principles:

HONIG, W. K., and STADDON, J. E. R., eds. 1977. *Handbook of operant behavior.* Englewood Cliffs, NJ: Prentice-Hall,

MILLER, L. K. 1975. *Principles of everyday behavior analysis.* unit 4. Monterey, CA: Brooks/Cole Publishing Co.

REYNOLDS, G. S. 1968. *A primer of operant conditioning.* chap 9. Glenview, Ill: Scott, Foresman and Co.

SOLOMON, R. L. 1964. Punishment. *American Psychologist* 19:239–53.

Clinical Applications:

GELFAND, D. M., and HARTMANN, D. P. 1975. *Child behavior analysis and therapy.* chap. 6. New York: Pergamon Press, Inc.

O'LEARY, K. D., and O'LEARY, S. G. 1977. *Classroom management: The successful use of behavior modification.* 2nd ed. chap. 3. New York: Pergamon Press, Inc.

6

Classical Conditioning: Principles and Procedures

Albert B was a healthy, nine-month-old baby whose mother was a wet nurse in a children's hospital. At this age Albert's reactions to various stimuli were tested. The stimuli included a white rat, a rabbit, a dog, a monkey, masks with and without hair, cotton wool, and a burning newspaper. None of these stimuli evoked a fear response. However, a loud sound produced by suddenly striking a steel bar with a hammer did elicit fear as shown by trembling, startle reflexes, and crying. In other words, the sudden loud sound was an *unconditioned stimulus* (US) that reliably evoked the unconditioned response of fear.[1] It was this unconditioned stimulus that J.B. Watson, widely regarded as the founder of behaviorism, and his graduate student Rosalie Rayner, used to conduct the first formal experiment on conditioned fear reactions in 1919.

The experiment began when Albert was eleven months old. By repeatedly pairing the rat (the *conditioned stimulus*—CS) with the loud noise, a conditioned response was established in which the rat alone came to evoke a fear response in Albert. A test five days later showed that the conditioned fear response transferred to a rabbit, a dog, a sealskin coat, cotton wool, Watson's hair, and a bearded Santa Claus mask. This process whereby a fear that is conditioned to one stimulus spreads to other related stimuli is known as *stimulus generalization.* There was no transfer to Albert's building blocks, nor to the hair of two observers. Tests carried out after an additional five days showed the persistence of the fear response to the rat although it had become "much less marked." In the final session, a month later, Albert was presented with a Santa Claus mask, the sealskin coat, the rat, the rabbit and the dog, all of which still evoked a fear response. Albert was removed from the hospital by his mother the day these tests were made, so the authors had no opportunity to try to remove Albert's conditioned fear response. Watson and Rayner concluded that they had established conditioned fear which had generalized across time and objects.

Four years later, Mary Cover Jones (1924) described how she eliminated a phobia in another little boy named Peter. His fear of a rabbit was systematically reduced by the use of procedures that were the forerunners of current behavioral treatment methods. One procedure involved gradually moving the rabbit closer to him while he was happily involved in eating. Eventually, he was even able to tolerate the rabbit nibbling at his fingers. This procedure served as a basis for Wolpe's (1958) development of systematic desensitization, a treatment technique that is described later in this chapter. Another procedure that received less emphasis at the time involved the use of peer models who were unafraid of the rabbit. Modeling is widely used now as a treatment method (see Chap. 7).

The cases of Albert B and Peter were extremely influential in the early theoretical formulations of behavior therapy by Eysenck (1960) and Wolpe

----

[1]Any study of this nature with human subjects raises important ethical issues. These ethical considerations in contemporary behavior therapy are discussed in Chap. 10.

(1958). They served as a model of the development of phobias and other neurotic reactions and influenced the type of treatment that was used. Today, however, the inadequacies of a classical conditioning model of neurotic fear reactions are clearly apparent.

The Classical Conditioning Model of Phobias: A Critical Analysis

Rachman (1977b) has summarized several lines of evidence showing that the classical conditioning model fails to provide an adequate account of the development and maintenance of neurotic fear reactions.

1. Many people who are exposed to intense fear-provoking conditions do not develop phobias. For example, not all people involved in car or plane crashes develop phobias about cars or planes.

2. Watson and Rayner's (1920) findings with Albert B have not been replicated (see O'Leary and Wilson, 1975). At present there is no conclusive evidence that lasting conditioned fear reactions can be established in humans in the laboratory (Evans, 1976; Hallam and Rachman, 1976).

3. In clinical cases it is often difficult if not impossible to find any traumatic experience that might have produced a conditioned fear reaction (Marks, 1969).

4. The classical conditioning model does not explain the fact that only certain types of stimuli are usually associated with intense fear reactions (Seligman, 1971). Thus people commonly have phobias about heights, flying, driving automobiles, dentistry, germs, small animals, snakes, and so on. Inanimate objects like grass, hammers, wall-sockets for electricity, and typewriters are not the stuff of which phobias are made although they are frequently associated with trauma of one sort or another (for example, receiving an unpleasant electric shock from a power outlet).

5. Related to the previous point is the difficulty of explaining why phobias appear only at certain times. For example, why does an agoraphobic client report an acute onset of fear in situations (such as leaving her house, crowds, and driving an automobile, among others) that have not troubled her before? Common clinical examples like this indicate that the acquisition of neurotic fears may be associated with critical periods when the person is somehow vulnerable or at risk.

Clinical experience shows that these critical periods often involve general states of stress including physical illness and emotional upset.

6. Classically conditioned fear reactions typically extinguish very quickly if the conditioned stimulus is repeatedly presented without the unconditioned stimulus. People with phobias frequently come into contact with situations or objects they fear (the CS) without any adverse effects (the absence of an US) yet their phobias remain intact. For example, an agoraphobic client will often be exposed to what for her are anxiety-eliciting situations like crowds of people, supermarkets, and traffic, and others, but still remain fearful. The classical conditioning model cannot explain the well-known resistance to extinction of neurotic fear reactions.

Contemporary analyses of classical conditioning have moved away from the once popular notion that what was learned consisted of simple stimulus–response (S–R) bonds. In what is known as a molar account of classical conditioning, it is the learning of a correlational or contingent relationship between the CS and US that defines the conditioning process (Rachlin, 1976; Rescorla and Wagner, 1972). Classical conditioning is no longer seen as the simple pairing of a single CS with a single US on the basis of temporal contiguity. Instead, correlations between entire classes of stimulus events can be learned. Rachlin (1976) gives the following example of this molar or correlational view of classical conditioning:

> The reading on a thermometer in the window gains importance for us because its ups and downs signal corresponding feelings of hot and cold when we step outside. The thermometer reading (not a single value of it, but the whole range of values) serves as a conditioned stimulus. The temperature outside (again the whole range of values) serves as an unconditioned stimulus. The correlation between the two serves as a conditioning procedure. (p. 190)

The advantage of this correlational view of conditioning is that it more closely resembles complex behavior than the simple one-to-one pairings of single CS's and US's that have traditionally been studied in classical conditioning experiments. The molar view provides an explanation for the first of the six problems with the conditioning model of fear reactions presented above. People may be exposed to traumatic events (contiguity) but not develop phobic reactions unless a correlational or contingent relationship is formed between the situation and the traumatic event. However, the molar view still fares poorly in accounting for the remaining problems with a conditioning model. It fails to explain neurotic fears where no traumatic event (US) can be identified, the selectivity of neurotic fears, or why neurotic fears, unlike classical conditioning reactions in the laboratory, are so resistant to extinction.

In sum, classical conditioning may be a factor in the acquisition of some fear reactions, but it cannot account fully for neurotic reactions. Partly because of the problems with a straightforward classical conditioning model, behavior therapists next turned to a more elaborate conditioning explanation of neurotic fears—two-factor theory.

Two-Factor Theory of Neurotic Fear and Avoidance Behavior

Originally proposed by Mowrer (1939) in his attempt to translate Freud's psychoanalytic conception of anxiety into more scientifically acceptable terms, two-factor theory involves two key assumptions: (a) anxiety is an acquired drive that is established on the basis of a classical conditioning process in which a neutral stimulus is paired with an unconditioned stimulus; (b) this anxiety motivates instrumental or avoidance behavior which in turn is reinforced by the reduction of the underlying anxiety drive. For example, take the case of a compulsive handwasher with an obsession about dirt and cleanliness. It is assumed that his fear about dirt or contamination is a classically conditioned response that causes him to wash his hands repeatedly after touching anything he believes to be contaminated. Handwashing removes any dirt and reduces the fear of contamination. This fear reduction then reinforces the hand-washing behavior.

INADEQUACIES IN THE TWO-FACTOR THEORY OF NEUROTIC BEHAVIOR

Subsequent research has demonstrated several major problems with two-factor theory. These include the following:

1. The difficulty in explaining the resistance to extinction of neurotic behavior is still not resolved. The fact that an avoidance response removes the conditioned stimuli that elicit anxiety and thereby reduces the amount of nonreinforced exposure to the conditioned stimuli (that is, presentation of the CS in the absence of the US) does not change the fact that *some* nonreinforced exposure occurs. By definition, some classically conditioned anxiety must be elicited in order to motivate the avoidance behavior. Nonreinforced exposure to the conditioned stimulus is the necessary and sufficient condition for extinction. By this process, anxiety must inevitably extinguish with the result that the avoidance response will disappear. Yet as we have noted, this does not happen in neurotic fears like phobias.

2. Experimental and clinical evidence clearly shows that avoidance be-
    havior is *not* causally mediated by an underlying drive state of auto-
    nomic arousal (Herrnstein, 1969; Leitenberg, 1976a; Rescorla and
    Solomon, 1967). There is no consistent relationship between auto-
    nomic arousal and avoidance behavior. Surgical deactivation of auto-
    nomic functioning in animals has little effect on the acquisition of
    avoidance behavior and virtually no effect on the maintenance of
    avoidance behavior. Avoidance behavior often continues long after
    any classically conditioned anxiety (autonomic arousal) has been ex-
    tinguished. Moreover, avoidance behavior can be effectively elimi-
    nated without reducing conditioned anxiety. Leitenberg, Agras, Butz,
    and Wincze (1971), for example, have shown that in the treatment of
    phobias, avoidance behavior can be eliminated by directly altering its
    reinforcing consequences without first inhibiting physiologically
    defined anxiety. In fact, anxiety reduction is sometimes the conse-
    quence rather than the cause of behavioral change and in both labora-
    tory animals and clinical patients. A more accurate conceptualization
    is that both autonomic arousal and overt avoidance behavior are
    correlated coeffects of some as yet undetermined central mediating
    state (Bandura, 1969).

Contemporary Conditioning Models of Fear and Avoidance Behavior

Contemporary conditioning models provide different formulations of the development and maintenance of phobic reactions that have attempted to answer
the various criticisms outlined above.

THE INCUBATION HYPOTHESIS

Eysenck (1976) argues that the basic law of extinction of a conditioned response has to be revised. In his view, presentation of an anxiety-eliciting
conditioned stimulus without the unconditioned stimulus can result either in
extinction of the conditioned response of anxiety (the usual effect) *or* the
maintenance and enhancement of the conditioned response. The latter result
is referred to as the *incubation effect.* According to this hypothesis, the conditioned response of anxiety has drive properties in the same way as the unconditioned response. Under what conditions will the presentation of the conditioned stimulus alone lead to extinction and when will it result in enhancement
or incubation? Eysenck suggests that incubation is likely to occur under the

following circumstances: very short exposures to the conditioned stimulus; very potent unconditioned responses; and certain genetically determined personality characteristics that make the individual susceptible to fear arousal.

There is evidence that brief exposure to anxiety-eliciting conditioned stimuli alone can increase measures of autonomic arousal (McCutcheon and Adams, 1975; Stone and Borkovec, 1975). However, there is still insufficient evidence for Eysenck's position.

THE PREPAREDNESS HYPOTHESIS

Seligman (1971) has suggested animals and humans are biologically *prepared* to learn certain fears as a result of our evolutionary past. This would explain the nonrandom distribution of fears and phobias people suffer from. Phobias about heights, germs, or snakes are more common than phobias about hammers or electric outlets because the former, and not the latter, were associated with danger and threats to life in our evolutionary history. According to Seligman, "prepared" fears are often acquired on the basis of a single pairing with an aversive stimulus and are highly resistant to extinction.

There are conceptual and empirical objections to this hypothesis. Conceptually, Bandura (1977b) points out that fears and phobias about sexual activities are among the most common complaints therapists encounter for which there are obviously no evolutionary advantages. More people have drowned than died of snake bites, yet fear of snakes is more prevalent than fear of water. Laboratory studies of classical conditioning have shown that the specific nature of the CS can affect resistance to extinction. Hugdahl (1978) paired pictures of either snakes and spiders (a fear-relevant CS) or circles and triangles (the fear-irrelevant CS) with either electric shock or the threat of electric shock as the UCS. The dependent measure or CR was a change in skin conductance, a widely used measure of fear. All four groups of subjects showed equal evidence of conditioning. During extinction, when subjects were informed that no further shock would be given, the two groups who had been conditioned with the fear-irrelevant CS showed an immediate reduction in fear response. The two groups who had experienced the fear-relevant CS indicated resistance to extinction. Hygge and Ohman (1978) obtained similar results during extinction of a vicariously conditioned fear response. However, Seligman's "preparedness" hypothesis is only one possible explanation of these results. An alternative view would emphasize differential social learning experiences. In our culture we learn to react quite differently to salient, fear-relevant stimuli like snakes than we do to less salient stimuli like circles and triangles.

Particularly damaging to the notion of "prepared" fears is the fact that contrary to the hypothesis, they do not appear to be unusually resistant to extinction in actual treatment studies. As documented later in this chapter, phobias are readily extinguished in clients when the appropriate learning conditions are arranged. In a clinical test of the preparedness hypothesis, De Silva, Rachman, and Seligman (1977) rated sixty-nine phobic and eighty-two obsessional clients for the "preparedness," or evolutionary significance, of their fears and related these measures to therapeutic outcome. The results showed that the "preparedness" ratings failed to predict treatment outcome, stimulus generalization, severity of the problem, the suddenness of the onset of fear, or the age of onset.

THE MOLAR, CORRELATIONAL VIEW

The correlational view of the classical conditioning does not provide an adequate model of neurotic fear reactions, as mentioned earlier. However, an interpretation of avoidance behavior that is based on a correlational analysis of the relationship between behavior and its consequences overcomes several of the objections to the two-factor theory of avoidance behavior (see Herrnstein, 1969; Rachlin, 1976). In short, this correlational interpretation of avoidance behavior is an operant analysis that assumes that avoidance behavior is learned and maintained because it reduces or eliminates negative consequences. In contrast to two-factor theory, the concept of classically conditioned fear is said to be unnecessary. Avoidance behavior is more parsimoniously explained by analyzing the observable relationship (correlation or contingency) between the organism's responses and environmental outcome, without any reference to an internal mediating state, such as fear.

The advantages of this operant analysis of avoidance behavior are as follows. First, it is consistent with the evidence that clearly shows that fear is probably not a necessary condition for the learning of avoidance behavior and is definitely not necessary for the maintenance of avoidance behavior. Fear may affect avoidance behavior, but it is not critical for its explanation. Second, this operant analysis leads to the prediction that the most efficient way of extinguishing avoidance behavior would be to concentrate on the avoidance behavior directly, rather than on the presumed underlying state of fear as in two-factor theory. As we shall show later in this chapter, this prediction is borne out by the clinical evidence.

Finally, since a classically conditioned fear response is not the cause of avoidance behavior in this operant analysis, it is easier to explain that resistance to extinction would take place only if the correlation between avoidance behavior and outcome was broken. In order for this to happen, the organism has to recognize that the contingency has changed and that avoidance behavior is no longer necessary to reduce or eliminate negative consequences; that is, it is now safe to stop avoiding. While this correlation-based operant view is an improvement over two-factor theory, a problem still remains. Phobic clients are not always successful in avoiding their feared situations or objects but continue to be phobic. In other words, the correlational relationship between behavior and outcome appears to be broken, and nothing terrible happens to them (no US is experienced). Yet extinction does not occur. The problem seems to be that it is not the objective or observable relationship between behavior and its consequences that is often the decisive fact in maintaining neurotic reactions. It is the client's perception of that relationship, irrespective of whether it is real or not, that is often the critical factor. We turn next to the way in which social learning theory attempts to integrate this fact in a broader conception of neurotic fear and avoidance behavior.

Social Learning Theory and the Analysis of Neurotic Disorders

In the previous sections we have noted that classical conditioning today is viewed more accurately as the learning of correlations between stimuli rather than simple S–R bonds. In terms of social learning theory, these correlational relationships are seen as learned expectations. It is further assumed that this learning is cognitively mediated (see Bandura, 1977b; Bower, 1978; Brewer, 1974). The reason is that a person can be exposed to two stimuli that are related to each other objectively and still form no association. Conversely, a person can be told or believe that two events are associated, even if actual correlation does not exist. Learning does not take place automatically on the basis of temporal contiguity or objective correlation between events. Neither human or animal findings establish that the procedure known as classical conditioning has direct effects on a particular response, as opposed to influencing some central motivational or cognitive state that, in turn, affects the specific response observed (Black, 1971).

There are two major components to Bandura's social learning analysis of how a formerly neutral stimulus comes to elicit anxiety as a function of being paired with an aversive experience: (a) the development of a predictive relationship between the two stimuli; and (b) a self-arousal process in which the person consciously generates anticipatory feelings of anxiety in response to an antecedent event or a conditioned stimulus. For example, consider the agoraphobic client who, in the course of a conversation, hears the word "panic" and suddenly becomes anxious. The anxiety attack is not evoked merely by the word "panic" but by the client actively thinking about how terrifying it would be if she were to experience a panic attack. As in the case of operant conditioning, awareness is probably not a necessary precondition for classical conditioning in people. Nonetheless, awareness of the relationship between two stimuli greatly facilitates the acquisition of specific responses and hastens their extinction. The evidence seems to indicate that fear reactions and other emotional responses may be functions of two different stimulus sources. The first is the emotional arousal that is self-generated by distressing thoughts or images. The second is the emotional arousal that appears to be more directly elicited by the conditioned stimulus. Many phobics, for example, respond instantaneously to situations or objects they fear before they have time to think about the possible dangers involved. It is likely, however, that even in these cases the original learning was cognitively mediated. The fear reaction becomes so powerful and so frequently rehearsed that phobics begin to react fearfully at the first sign of what they fear. One of the advantages of viewing learned fear reactions in this manner is that two stimulus sources of emotional responses suggest different therapeutic interventions. In the first case of self-generated arousal through thoughts and images, treatment methods known as cognitive restructuring seem indicated. These methods and their rationale are described in Chap. 9. In the second case of the more direct elicitation of fear, behavioral procedures, such as flooding that extend prolonged nonreinforced exposure to the feared situation or object, are required. These methods are described later in this chapter.

Several of the problems noted in regard to the classical conditioning and two-factor theories are more easily understood in terms of the social learning perspective. In the discussion of two-factor theory it was pointed out that autonomic arousal does not directly motivate avoidance behavior. Autonomic arousal and avoidance behavior are correlated coeffects which, according to social learning theory, are both products of expectations of personal harm or threat.

A social learning analysis also provides a theoretically consistent framework for integrating what Rachman (1977b) called the "three pathways to fear." The first pathway is the acquisition of fear through direct experience with a traumatic event. In terms of social learning theory, such experiences create learned expectations that are either self-activated, as in the case of the panicky agoraphobic client, or elicited directly by the external fear stimulus without any intervening self-arousal process. An example of the latter would be a snake phobic individual who experiences an instantaneous fear reaction upon seeing a snake apparently before (s)he has the time to think of the dangers associated with snakes. Even in this type of fear reaction, however, it is possible to argue that the response is cognitively mediated (Bandura, 1977b). It might be that the fear reaction is so intense and so well learned that it is no longer subject to voluntary control by simply regulating one's thoughts. Fears that are mediated by a self-arousal process may be more easily modifiable through strictly cognitive methods than are fears that appear to be elicited directly. The latter will require exposure with the feared object or situation so that the learned expectations of threat can be disconfirmed as a result of direct behavioral contact.

The second pathway to fear is by observing some other person behaving fearfully or being harmed. This cognitive process of the social transmission of fear is known as *modeling* and is discussed in detail in Chap. 7. It helps explain how people can develop phobias even though they have never had any direct contact with the feared situation or object. Of course, as with direct experience with a traumatic event, not all observation of fearful behavior results in the acquisition of fear by the observer. Among the factors that would determine this are the extent to which the observer attends to the fearful model's behavior and personalizes the model's distress, that is, imagines that (s)he is in the model's place. Teaching neurotic clients to detach or "distance" themselves from emotionally distressing events is one of the cognitive treatment methods discussed in Chap. 9.

The third way in which fears are acquired is through instruction and information. Take the case of phobias about snakes and other animals. Our folklore is full of frightening stories depicting snakes as slimy, evil, and deadly adversaries of human beings. Hearing (and believing) these stories from childhood will understandably affect future behavior. Rachman (1977b) may be correct in suggesting that this informational mode of transmission is the basis for most commonly encountered fears. It may also be that fears created in this fashion are more susceptible to extinction by cognitive means, such as correcting misconceptions and providing accurate information.

How does social learning analysis account for the marked resistance to extinction of phobic reactions? Although it is not incompatible with the notion that some people may be biologically vulnerable to acquiring persistent fears, social learning theory emphasizes learned expectations about potentially dangerous events. Bandura (1977b) argues that in many instances phobic expectations are maintained because occasional mishaps occur. Take the person with a fear of flying. Planes do crash from time to time. The phobic focuses selectively on the highly improbable consequence of his or her flight being one of the statistically rare crashes. In addition, the exposure phobics have to their feared situations or objects, and which inevitably produces extinction of conditioned anxiety responses (unless Eysenck's incubation hypothesis is invoked), does not automatically alter fearful expectations. Whether these fearful expectations are disconfirmed and phobic behavior hence eliminated will depend on the nature of the information the person derives from exposure with the phobic situation. If the exposure to the phobic situation is such that the person concludes that (s)he can cope effectively with the situation without experiencing undue anxiety, then extinction will progress rapidly. If the exposure is such that the person concludes that (s)he cannot cope and will experience unnerving anxiety, no extinction will take place. Indeed, by strengthening the person's expectation that (s)he cannot cope, the exposure might enhance phobic sensitivity. This latter process might be viewed as a cognitive explanation of the same phenomena that Eysenck (1976) seeks to explain with his incubation hypothesis. The conditioning and the cognitive theories generate different predictions, however, about the most effective ways to modify phobic disorders. These differences are discussed later in this chapter and in Chap. 9.

Regardless of the validity of the classical conditioning and two-factor theories of neurotic disorders, they have been extremely influential in the development of therapeutic *procedures* for the treatment of these disorders. It is quite possible for treatment methods to be effective for reasons other than those put forward by their originators. From a practical point of view, what really counts is how successful treatment methods are in alleviating human suffering. It is to these treatment methods that we now turn.

Therapeutic Techniques and the Treatment of Neurotic Disorders

Procedures originally based upon classical conditioning and two-factor theory have been widely used to treat neurotic disorders in which anxiety is of central importance. The two most important techniques are systematic desensitization and flooding.

SYSTEMATIC DESENSITIZATION

Mary Cover Jones' (1924) treatment of a child's phobia has been mentioned earlier. Wolpe (1958) applied essentially the same principle in introducing the technique of systematic desensitization. In experimental research on neurotic fears in cats, Wolpe found that conditioned emotional responses could be eliminated by gradually feeding animals closer to the locus of the original fear conditioning. Accordingly, Wolpe formulated his reciprocal inhibition principle which stated that anxiety-eliciting stimuli could be permanently neutralized if "a response antagonistic to anxiety can be made to occur in the presence of the anxiety-evoking stimuli so that it is accompanied by the complete or partial suppression of the anxiety response" (1958, p. 71). This procedure has also been referred to as *counterconditioning* (Davison, 1968).

In applying these laboratory findings to the development of a practical clinical treatment technique, Wolpe adapted from Jacobson (1938) a technique called *progressive relaxation training* as a means of producing a response which is incompatible with anxiety. Briefly, this consists of training clients to concentrate on systematically relaxing the different muscle groups of the body, which results in lowered physiological arousal and a comfortable subjective feeling of calmness in the client. In another massive extrapolation from basic laboratory research findings to the therapeutic situation, Wolpe found that imaginal representation of stimulus conditions seemed to be as effective in eliciting anxiety as their actual occurrence. This development was of major importance in aiding the therapist to arrange conditions for the extinction of maladaptive anxiety reactions which are generally evoked by stimuli involving past or future events or social situations which could not be easily controlled or directly dealt with in the therapist's office.

In order to ensure that anxiety is inhibited by the antagonistic response of muscle relaxation, a major procedural element of systematic desensitization is that the client is instructed to imagine anxiety-producing scenes in a carefully graded fashion. Hierarchies of anxiety-eliciting situations are constructed, ranging from mildly stressful to very threatening items which clients are instructed to imagine while they are deeply relaxed. In the event that any item produces much anxiety, the client is instructed to cease visualizing the hierarchy item and to restore feelings of relaxation, since the technique is predicated on the rationale that anxiety be kept at a minimal level during exposure to previous anxiety-producing situations. The item is then repeated, or the hierarchy adjusted, until the client can visualize the scene without experiencing anxiety. Only then does the therapist present the next item of the hierarchy.

Progress during systematic desensitization treatment should be paralleled by improvement in the client's phobias outside the therapist's office. Imaginal desensitization may be deliberately supplemented by instructing the client to engage in graduated performances of previously inhibited behavior in the naturalistic situation. The term *in vivo desensitization* is used to describe the treatment that consists entirely of graded exposure to the anxiety-producing situation or object. The behavioral treatment of sexual dysfunction provides an excellent illustration of *in vivo* desensitization treatment (see Box 6–1).

Systematic desensitization is not applicable to all anxiety-related disorders. As a general rule, it is indicated only where conditioned negative emotional responses are the client's primary problem. Systematic desensitization would not be applicable, for instance, in the case of the young man with heterosexual anxiety as a secondary function of an absence of appropriate social skills, rather than a fear of women per se. Therapy would be more fruitfully directed towards teaching effective interpersonal skills, instead of focusing on the anxiety response directly.

A related caution concerning the appropriate clinical application of systematic desensitization—or any behavioral technique—is the necessity of isolating the relevant controlling cues in constructing the stimulus hierarchy. This is illustrated in an excerpt from a clinical interview by Lazarus (1971) (see Box 6–2).

How Effective Is Systematic Desensitization? Systematic desensitization is perhaps the most intensively researched psychological treatment technique on record. For example, in a review of controlled group outcome studies, Kazdin and Wilcoxon (1976) found over seventy such studies in only five of the journals they surveyed. A large majority of these studies has consisted of

Box 6–1 *Behavioral Sex Therapy*

The most dramatic demonstration of the efficacy of the direct behavioral treatment of male sexual inadequacy, in particular, and sexual problems, in general, has been Masters and Johnson's (1970) two-week rapid therapy program.

Sexual dysfunction is viewed as a fear reaction—a fear of failure, or "performance anxiety." The program is designed to extinguish this fear through an *in vivo* desensitization procedure. Typically, sexually dysfunctional individuals are so preoccupied with worrying about performing appropriately and satisfying their partner that they assume what is aptly referred to as the "spectator role" during sex which distracts them from the biological and psychosocial stimulation that produces sexual arousal. The first step in reducing this performance anxiety is to prohibit any sexual activity not specifically sanctioned by the therapists, and then to embark upon a carefully graduated program of mutually pleasurable sensual and sexual involvement between the partners which is termed sensate focus. The clients are instructed to learn to think and feel sensuously by giving and getting bodily pleasure, first by nongenital contact and then by specific genital stimulation. The fundamental significance of the sensate focus exercises is in increasing verbal and nonverbal communication between the partners and in teaching them that sexual gratification does not necessarily depend on coitus. As sexual arousal spontaneously occurs in these "homework" assignments, the treatment is oriented towards the specific form of sexual inadequacy in question.

Several distinctive concepts define the Masters and Johnson program. A strict rule is that both marital partners participate in the treatment since Masters and Johnson consider that the "relationship between the partners is the patient," even if one is clearly dysfunctional and the other is not. Emphasis on treating the patient dyad reflects the importance attributed to shaping up effective interpersonal communication and precludes the possibility of the partner not being seen in therapy accidentally or purposefully interfering with therapy because of mutual emotional involvement in the sexual problem. The use of a dual-sex therapy team eliminates the "feeling of being ganged up on" by the client, who is in the minority in the two-to-one sex ratio occasioned by a single therapist, and reduces the possibility of getting biased information from the clients since with both sexes present, the "games people play" to impress the other sex are minimized. Masters and Johnson assert that it requires a cotherapist of the same sex to understand the sexual problem of a male or female client and in turn to communicate the uniquely sex-appropriate knowledge of sexual functioning to that client.

Finally, they emphasize the importance of cotherapists in obviating the development of any "transference" or special relationship between a client and a therapist of the opposite sex. They regard "transference" as disastrous insofar as their entire therapy is predicated on establishing intimate emotional communication between the clients themselves—which would be interfered with should either client form an emotional attachment to one of the therapists. This dictate again highlights the fundamental differences between the behavioral and psychodynamic approaches to therapy, since in the latter, the development of the transference relationship is held to be the primary vehicle through which therapeutic change occurs.

The Treatment of Impotence

The treatment of impotence illustrates the rapid therapy program. In primary impotence the man has never been able to have intercourse of any description. In secondary impotence a man has successfully engaged in intercourse on at least one occasion previous to losing the capacity. Treatment initially focuses on the interpersonal relationship between the two partners which is often strained. To reduce goal-oriented performance, the couple are instructed to continue with sensate focus exercises until erection spontaneously occurs. Thereafter the woman uses a "teasing technique" in which she manipulates the penis to erection and then relaxes with her partner until the erection disappears. She then repeats the procedure several times, thereby effectively extinguishing the man's fear of losing an erection and not getting it back during sexual interaction. The therapy continues with the woman facilitating nondemanding intromission followed by progressively more vigorous thrusting until orgasm occurs involuntarily.

How Effective Is Behavioral Sex Therapy?

The overall outcome results of the Masters and Johnson program for different types of sexual disorders are summarized in Table 6–1. The success rates of 81 percent at the end of treatment and 75 percent at a five-year follow-up are unprecedented. Only twenty years ago sexual problems such as these were without reliably effective treatment of *any* kind. Although the lack of any control group suggests that caution must be had in interpreting these results, they are strengthened by the fact that over 50 percent of the clients treated by Masters and Johnson had tried previous psychotherapy without success. Other uncontrolled clinical reports and controlled outcome studies have consistently indicated the efficacy of behavioral methods in the treatment of male and female sexual disorders (Franks and Wilson, 1978; Mathews and others, 1976; Munjack and others, 1976; Nemetz, Craig, and Reith, 1978). Consistent with evidence from other clinical disorders reviewed in this and later chapters, an *in vivo* treatment approach appears to be superior to methods that rely upon imaginal or symbolic procedures. For example, Mathews and others (1976) found that a Masters and Johnson-type program that was based on directed behavioral practice was approximately twice as effective as imaginal systematic desensitizations in the treatment of couples complaining of sexual dysfunction.

TABLE 6–1.
Overall Results of the Masters and Johnson Treatment Program (1970)

Type of Sexual Problem	Numbers of Couples Treated	Percentage Success at the End of Therapy	Percentage Success at Two-Year Follow-up
Primary impotence	32	59.4	59.4
Secondary impotence	213	73.8	69.1
Premature ejaculation	186	97.8	97.3
Ejaculatory incompetence	17	82.4	82.4
Male totals	448	83.1	80.6
Primary orgasmic dysfunction	193	83.4	82.4
Situational orgasmic dysfunction	149	77.2	75.2
Female totals	342	80.7	79.2
Male and female totals	790	81.1	80.0

laboratory-based investigations with subjects who were only mildly fearful. Consequently, the generalizability of the findings to severely phobic clients is questionable (Mathews, 1978). Nonetheless, the net result of all these studies in which systematic desensitization has been employed by different therapists with different client populations has shown that it is an effective technique for treating neurotic anxiety.

The attraction systematic desensitization has had for experimentally minded clinical researchers is in large part attributable to the procedural precision with which Wolpe (1958) described it—a relatively rare occurrence in the history of psychotherapy. A landmark study by Paul (1966) illustrates both the efficacy of systematic desensitization as well as the sort of research strategy that is required in conducting a well-controlled outcome study. College students who experienced debilitating anxiety in public-speaking situations were administered a comprehensive, pretreatment assessment procedure, encompassing personality questionnaires of both general emotional responsiveness and specific public-speaking anxiety and physiological and overt behavioral measures of anxiety. The latter consisted of highly reliable observations of subjects' behavior under stress during a four-minute speech to an

The successful use of systematic desensitization requires that the current determinants of a client's phobia be correctly identified. The following excerpt from a case reported by Lazarus (1971) indicates how such an assessment is arrived at. (From Lazarus, A. A. *Behavior Therapy and Beyond.* New York: McGraw-Hill, 1971, pp. 33–35.)

Patient: I have a fear of crossing bridges.

Therapist: Do you have any other fears or difficulties?

Patient: Only the complications arising from my fear of bridges.

Therapist: Well, in what way has it affected your life?

Patient: I had to quit an excellent job in Berkeley.

Therapist: Where do you live?

Patient: San Francisco.

Therapist: So why didn't you move to Berkeley?

Patient: I prefer living in the city.

Therapist: To get to this institute, you had to cross the Golden Gate.

Patient: Yes, I was seeing a doctor in San Francisco. He tried to desensitize me but it didn't help so he said I should see you because you know more about this kind of treatment. It's not so bad when I have my wife and kids with me. But even then, the Golden Gate, which is about one mile long, is my upper limit. I was wondering whether you ever consult in the city?

Therapist: No. But tell me, how long have you had this problem?

Patient: Oh, about four years, I'd say. It just happened suddenly. I was coming home from work and the Bay Bridge was awfully slow. I just suddenly panicked for no reason at all. I mean, nothing like this had ever happened to me before. I felt that I would crash into the other cars. Once I even had a feeling that the bridge would cave in.

Therapist: Let's get back to that first panic experience about four years ago. You said that you were coming home from work. Had anything happened at work?

Patient: Nothing unusual.

Therapist: Were you happy at work?

Patient: Sure! Huh! I was even due for promotion.

Therapist: What would that have entailed?

Patient: An extra $3,000 a year.

Therapist: I mean in the way of having to do different work.

Patient: Well, I would have been a supervisor. I would have had more than fifty men working under me.

Therapist: How did you feel about that?

Patient: What do you mean?

Therapist: I mean how did you feel about the added responsibility? Did you feel that you were up to it, that you could cope with it?

Patient: Gee! My wife was expecting our first kid. We both welcomed the extra money.

Therapist: So round about the time that you were about to become a father, you were to be promoted to supervisor. So you would face two new and challenging roles. You'd be a daddy at home and also big daddy at work. And this was when you began to panic on the bridge, and I guess you never did wind up as a supervisor.

Patient: No. I had to ask for a transfer to the city.

Therapist: Now, please think very carefully about this question. Have you ever been involved in any accident on or near a bridge, or have you ever witnessed any serious accident on or near a bridge?

Patient: Not that I can think of.

Therapist: Do you still work for the same company?

Patient: No. I got a better offer, more money, from another company in the city. I've been with them for almost 1½ years now.

Therapist: Are you earning more money or less money than you would have gotten in Berkeley?

Patient: About the same. But prices have gone up so it adds up to less.

Therapist: If you hadn't developed the bridge phobia and had become foreman in Berkeley at $3,000 more, where do you think you would be today?

Patient: Still in Berkeley.

Therapist: Still supervisor? More money?

> **Patient:** Oh hell! Who knows" (laughs) Maybe I would have been vice-president.
>
> **Therapist:** And what would that have entailed?
>
> **Patient:** I'm only kidding. But actually it could have happened.
>
> Systematic desensitization was used successfully to treat this case. However, instead of desensitizing the client to bridges, the therapist desensitized the client to his fears of increased responsibility and vulnerability to criticism.

unfamiliar audience. Using within-sample matching, subjects were then randomly assigned to the following four groups: (1) systematic desensitization; (2) insight-oriented psychotherapy; (3) attention-placebo; and (4) no-treatment control. Five paid, experienced psychotherapists whose orientation was "dynamic and insight-oriented" individually treated subjects in all groups for five hours over a six-week period following which all subjects were readministered the anxiety-assessment measures. This procedure controlled for any possible therapist bias in favor of systematic desensitization; if anything, it favored the psychotherapy condition. The psychotherapy involved an interview approach, stressing insight and self-understanding of the psychological nature of the subjects' anxiety. The therapists routinely used this approach in their daily work, and they confidently expected it to be successful. The therapists were unfamiliar with systematic desensitization and had to be specifically coached in its use.

Subjects in the attention-placebo group were given what they believed to be a "fast-acting tranquilizer" which supposedly helped them to learn how to respond nonanxiously while working at a bogus "stressful task." They were given the rationale that this training would immunize them against stress reactions in outside social situations. This group controlled for any improvement which could be attributed to nonspecific therapy factors such as suggestion, expectation of relief, and the therapist-patient relationship. Subjects in the no-treatment condition were administered the pre- and posttreatment assessment procedures but received no therapy.

The results, which are summarized in Fig. 6–1, showed that systematic desensitization produced consistently greater improvement on all dependent measures than either the no-treatment control or the insight-oriented and attention-placebo treatment groups. In terms of the behavioral measure of anxiety, for example, 100 percent of the systematic desensitization group improved as against 60 percent of the insight group, 73 percent of the attention-placebo group, and 24 percent of the control group. The psychotherapy and placebo treatments were superior to no treatment in terms of self-report and behavioral measures, but only the desensitization group showed a significant decrease in physiological arousal, relative to the control group. There were no significant effects due to the different therapists, the improvement being directly attributable to the treatment procedures. Follow-up evaluation based upon subjects' self-report of anxiety, six weeks and two years after therapy, demonstrated essentially the same pattern of results; 85 percent of the systematic desensitization subjects showed a decrement in subjective anxiety from pretreatment estimates, as compared to 50 percent of both the psychotherapy and placebo groups, and 22 percent of the nontreated controls. Moreover, subjects treated with systematic desensitization not only maintained their therapeutic gains, but also showed no sign of any form of symptom substitution. This study does not demonstrate that psychotherapy, in general, is no more effective than an attention-placebo treatment. It may be, for example, that psychotherapy of longer duration might have proved more effective. However, the onus is on proponents of traditional psychotherapy methods to demonstrate their efficacy. Even if a lengthier form of psychotherapy were to be shown to be as effective as systematic desensitization, the behavioral method is clearly superior on grounds of efficiency.

The efficiency of systematic desensitization is further demonstrated by its consistently successful use as a form of group treatment. This is illustrated in a study by Lazarus (1961) of phobic clients who were more representative of the typical client commonly encountered in clinical practice. Thirty-five severely phobic patients, including acrophobics (fear of heights), claustrophobics (fear of enclosed places), impotent men (fear of sexual intercourse), and a group of mixed phobias were matched with respect to age, sex, severity, and type of phobia and randomly assigned to either group desensitization or interpretive psychotherapy treatment conditions. The latter was devoted to self-exploration and developing insight into the underlying origins of the phobic disorders. In the systematic desensitization procedure, common stimulus hierarchies were constructed and presented in small, homogeneous subgroups. Alternatively, in the mixed phobia subgroup, clients read hierarchy items from index cards so that different phobias could be concurrently desensitized in the same group. The rate and duration of each stimulus presentation were determined by the progress of the most anxious group member. Lazarus himself treated subjects in both the desensitization and interpretive psychotherapy conditions for roughly twenty-two sessions. This fact leaves the study open to the criticism that therapist bias might have influenced the results.

Treatment outcomes for the acrophobic and claustrophobic patients were objectively assessed one month after therapy by requiring them to engage publicly in their previously feared behaviors. For example, accompanied by the therapist, the acrophobics had to climb a fire escape to the third story of a building (about 50 feet), proceed to an eight-story roof garden, and then count the cars below for two minutes. An independent observer was present at these behavioral assessments to provide reliability in judging the patients' performance. Only the impotent men and members of the mixed phobic group were not objectively tested. Patients were considered to be treatment successes only if they displayed "total neutrality or indifference to the formerly anxiety-

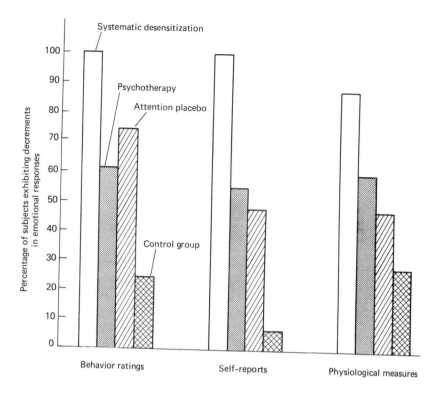

FIGURE 6.1
Percent of subjects in each of the four conditions who displayed decreases in anxiety as measured by behavior ratings, self-reports of emotional disturbance, and measures of physiological arousal. (Adopted from Bandura, *Principles of Behavior Modification,* 1969. Copyright © 1969 by Holt, Rinehart and Winston Publishers. Reprinted by permission of Holt, Rinehart, and Winston).

generating stimulus constellation"; moderate or slight improvements were classified as failures. The phobic behavior of thirteen of the eighteen patients who were desensitized was completely extinguished whereas only two of the seventeen psychotherapy subjects responded favorably. Confidence in the superior efficacy of systematic desensitization revealed in these findings is still further increased by the fact that ten of the fifteen phobics who showed no improvement as a result of the interpretive psychotherapy treatment subsequently were successfully treated in an average of ten systematic desensitization sessions. Follow-up inquiries after a mean period of nine months established that 77 to 80 percent of the desensitization treatment successes had maintained their improvement and evidenced no symptom substitution, despite the most stringent evaluation criteria in terms of which even the slightest phobic recurrence was considered a relapse.

Still more efficient is the use of self-administered systematic desensitization. In self-administered desensitization, clients use written instructional materials to teach themselves procedural details and conduct their own treatment without direct supervision by a therapist. Thus Rosen, Glasgow and Barrera (1976) have shown that totally self-administered desensitization was as effective as therapist-administered desensitization in the treatment of phobic clients. These impressive results were maintained at a two-year follow-up. Another variation of systematic desensitization that has proved successful is self-control desensitization (Goldfried, 1971). This method and the use of relaxation training as an effective treatment technique in its own right are described in Chap. 9.

Other controlled outcome studies demonstrating the efficacy of systematic desensitization are described in succeeding sections of this chapter (that is, Gelder and others, 1973) and in other chapters (that is, Bandura, Blanchard, and Ritter, 1969; Meichenbaum, Gilmore, and Fedoravicius, 1971).

Theoretical Mechanisms in Systematic Desensitization. The preceding section has shown that systematic desensitization is effective in reducing neurotic anxiety. In order to explain *why* the technique is effective, the necessary and sufficient procedural conditions for successful treatment must be identified. Typically, this kind of research has been conducted in the laboratory where it is possible to ensure the tight experimental controls and to obtain objective measures of outcome that are required to evaluate different theoretical positions. For example, the effects of desensitization on snake phobias have been evaluated by the administration of a behavioral avoidance test both before and after treatment. This is an objective measure of how close snake phobic subjects will approach a snake in a glass cage and whether they will then place their hands in the cage, touch, or hold the snake. In addition to this behavioral test, subjects' self-report of fear and physiological measures, such as heart rate, are also assessed so as to obtain multidimensional response measurement.

Some investigators have suggested that it is not possible to conclude that systematic desensitization is any more effective than a persuasive placebo treatment (see Kazdin and Wilcoxon, 1976). Although the technique has not always been shown to be superior to a highly persuasive attention-placebo control treatment, other studies indicate that the effects of systematic desensitization cannot be explained solely on the basis of placebo influences (Gelder and others, 1973; Paul, 1966; Rachman and Wilson, in press; Steinmark and Borkovec, 1974). Consider the Paul (1966) experiment that was described earlier. Critics of that study have argued that the attention-placebo group may not have been as credible or convincing to the subjects as was the desensitization treatment. This would mean that the placebo group did not control satisfactorily for variables like subjects' expectations of therapeutic improvement across groups. However, it must be remembered that systematic desensitization was also significantly more effective than the *psychotherapy* treatment in the Paul (1966) study. There is no evidence to suggest that subjects in this psychotherapy condition were less enthusiastic about treatment or expected less improvement. Factors such as subjects' confidence in an impressive sounding therapeutic technique and consequent expectations of success undoubtedly contribute to the overall efficacy of systematic desensitization. However, the specific procedures used have an effect over and above these general placebo influences.

Another explanation that has been advanced to explain the success of systematic desensitization is that the interpersonal relationship between the therapist and client is the critical agent of change. However, the efficacy of the technique itself is established by studies in which the influence of the therapist is intentionally minimized; for example, Lang and others (1970) have shown that desensitization administered by a computer known as the Device for Automated Desensitization (DAD), was as effective in reducing snake phobias as therapist-conducted desensitization. Moreover, totally self-directed desensitization has proved as effective as therapist-administered treatment in some studies (Rosen and others, 1976).

Studies on the influence of specific elements within the desensitization treatment method have employed a *dismantling* research strategy (Lang, 1969). In this strategy different components of the systematic desensitization technique such as relaxation training or hierarchy construction are selectively omitted and the remaining procedure compared to the full therapeutic package. These various studies can be summarized by concluding that neither graded exposure to aversive stimuli nor the presence of anxiety-competing responses are necessary in order to extinguish phobic behaviors effectively (Bandura, 1969; Lang, 1969). The decisive factor governing the extinction of phobias is the systematic nonreinforced exposure to the anxiety-arousing stimulus conditions; that is, arranging for phobic clients to confront the source of their anxieties without experiencing the catastrophic consequences neurotics typically anticipate. *In vivo* exposure is more effective than imaginal exposure. These findings contradict Wolpe's hypothesis of reciprocal inhibition, which clearly states that phobic responses cannot be eliminated unless graded anxiety-eliciting stimuli are paired with a physiologically incompatible response, such as relaxation.

Although they are not necessary ingredients for effective desensitization treatment, relaxation training and graded stimulus presentation may often be useful in facilitating nonreinforced exposure to feared events, especially in severely phobic clients. Using relaxation training and a graded series of hierarchy items helps to buffer the client against emotional distress and facilitates the necessary nonreinforced exposure in a manner that is most acceptable to the client (Wilson and Davison, 1971).

Given that nonreinforced exposure to the feared object or situation is the necessary and sufficient condition for the reduction of neurotic fears by systematic desensitization, it still remains to provide a theoretical mechanism explaining how nonreinforced exposure produces this outcome. The reciprocal inhibition hypothesis is inadequate as is two-factor theory. According to the latter, nonreinforced exposure results in the extinction of the classically conditioned anxiety state that mediates phobic avoidance behavior. Some of the problems with two-factor theory are discussed earlier in this chapter, including the fact that conditioned fear does not always mediate avoidance behavior.

In terms of social learning theory, nonreinforced exposure leads, not to the extinction of any underlying anxiety drive state, but the modification of the client's expectations of self-efficacy. *Self-efficacy* refers to clients' beliefs that they can cope with formerly feared situations. Systematic desensitization is seen to produce changes in efficacy expectations in a number of ways. A major source of information about self-efficacy provided by systematic desensitization is the reduction in the client's level of physiological arousal to the feared stimulus. Increased levels of self-efficacy are derived from this information that (s)he is responding less fearfully. Additional sources of information about self-efficacy derive from systematic desensitization. Thus clients are usually taught to manage tension through the use of relaxation procedures. Learning this relaxation coping skill boosts the client's sense of efficacy. Moreover, the fact that clients repeatedly visualize successful coping experiences strengthens efficacy expectations (Bandura, 1978a). In sum, as a result of treatment with systematic desensitization, clients (a) perceive that they are no longer upset by previously feared situations; (b) they acquire a coping skill for managing anxiety; and (c) they rehearse in imagination the successful performance of previously feared actions.

FLOODING AND IN VIVO EXPOSURE

Unlike systematic desensitization which relies on client-controlled, graduated exposure to anxiety-eliciting stimulus conditions, *flooding* involves therapist-controlled, prolonged exposure to high intensity aversive stimulation with the soothing effects of relaxation training.[2] Flooding may be conducted in imagination, but it is more usually done *in vivo*. The rationale behind this technique was originally based on two-factor theory and the principle of extinction. As we have already discussed, this principle states that a conditioned fear response can be extinguished by repeatedly presenting the stimuli that elicit the conditioned fear response, in the absence of actual aversive stimulation (for example, physical pain or injury). The presentation of feared stimuli is expected to elicit

---

[2]Flooding should not be confused with *implosion therapy*, a technique developed by Thomas Stampfl (Stampfl and Levis, 1967). A major difference is that implosion therapy involves an emphasis on psychodynamic themes (e.g., aggressive and sexual impulses; Oedipal conflict) that are assumed to play a role in the etiology and maintenance of neurotic disorders. The evidence shows that these psychodynamic themes are irrelevant to the extinction of phobic reactions (Leitenberg, 1976a). Furthermore, whereas implosion therapy relies exclusively on the use of imagery, the current trend is to conduct flooding *in vivo*.

a strong emotional response initially; however, continued exposure to these stimuli should result in a rapid decrease in fearful response. In order to ensure full exposure to the stimuli that elicit anxiety, the client is prevented from making an avoidance or escape response. Whether the exposure is presented in imagination or in real life, the client is strongly encouraged to continue to attend to the anxiety-eliciting stimuli despite the initial stressful effects this usually entails. Moreover, the way flooding has traditionally been conducted, every effort is made to elicit as intense anxiety response as possible in the client so that total extinction to the full range of anxiety-eliciting stimuli will ensue. For example, an agoraphobic client would typically be asked to imagine experiencing a sudden panic in a crowded supermarket, surrounded by an uncaring group of people, developing uncontrollable palpitations of the heart, being bathed in a nervous sweat, feeling intense shame and public embarrassment, fainting, and being taken by ambulance to a mental hospital. Such a scene would be presented continuously in imagination until the client's initial anxiety shows a definite decrease and the formerly frightening stimuli no longer elicit much distress.

In vivo exposure is similar to flooding *in vivo* except that it may be conducted on a graduated or hierarchical basis. The purpose is to have clients confront their feared situations or objects without avoiding. This graduated version of *in vivo* exposure is not designed to elicit maximum levels of anxiety, as in flooding (Boersma and others, 1976).

The Efficacy of Flooding and In Vivo Exposure. Several well-controlled studies have demonstrated that flooding can be an extremely effective therapeutic technique in the treatment of different neurotic disorders. Some of these studies have involved comparisons between flooding and systematic desensitization. The overall pattern of results indicates that flooding appears to be the more widely applicable and more effective method (Leitenberg, 1976a; Marks, 1978).

Outcome studies on behavior therapy have been criticized on the grounds that the subjects were not severely phobic and hence not necessarily representative of more seriously disturbed clients that many clinicians are called upon to treat. A controlled outcome study on flooding that meets the requirements of both methodological rigor and clinical relevance is provided by Gelder and others (1973). Briefly, flooding was compared to both systematic desensitization and an attention-placebo control condition in the treatment of phobic clients. Treatments were carried out by experienced therapists explicitly trained in the administration of the different methods. An attempt was made to induce a high expectancy of success in half of the subjects by describing the treatment and therapist chosen in very favorable terms and showing them a videotape of a patient who had benefitted from the treatment they were to receive.

Half of the clients were agoraphobics; the other half, a mixed group of specific social or animal phobias. Agoraphobics, who exhibit generalized anxiety reactions, are regarded as more difficult to treat than simple phobics. Clients were assigned to treatments and therapists in an experimental design that permitted an analysis of the possible interactions among treatment effects, therapist differences, type of phobia, and levels of expectancy.

Therapy consisted of fifteen weekly sessions that included both imaginal and real life exposure. Treatment effects were evaluated in terms of multiple measures of behavioral avoidance, blind psychiatric ratings, client self-ratings, physiological responsiveness, and standardized psychological tests at the end of treatment and at a six month follow-up. The adequacy of the control group in eliciting expectancies of treatment success comparable to those evoked by the two behavioral methods was assessed directly, thereby avoiding the problem with the attention-placebo group in Paul's (1966) study. Expectations of improvement were similar across all three groups.

The results of this study are shown in Fig. 6–2. Both behavioral treatments, particularly flooding, produced greater improvement than the control condition on the behavioral avoidance tests, physiological arousal measures, and psychiatric ratings of the main phobia and patients' self-rating of improvement, although only the flooding as opposed to the control condition comparison reached acceptable levels of statistical significance. These treatment gains were maintained successfully at follow-up. Simply put, flooding was roughly twice as effective as the powerful attention-placebo treatment. An important finding in this study was that the placebo control treatment was markedly less effective than both flooding and systematic desensitization with agoraphobics than with the other subjects. This result provides additional evidence that the success of behavioural methods such as flooding and systematic desensitization cannot be attributed solely to the role of placebo factors or expectations of favorable therapeutic outcome.

It is sometimes alleged that behavior therapy is appropriate for simple phobias but is inapplicable to the more complex and severe forms of neurotic disorders. However, the evidence—much of it the product of recent and ongoing research programs—shows that this view is incorrect. Thus complex agoraphobic disorders have been successfully treated with behavioral methods, as documented by controlled studies by different groups of clinical investigators working in different countries (for example Emmelkamp and Wessels, 1975; Leitenberg, 1976a; Marks, 1978; Mathews and others, 1976).

Still another excellent example of the broad applicability and clinical relevance of behavior therapy is the treatment of obsessive-compulsive disorders. There is wide agreement among clinicians of different theoretical orientations that obsessive-compulsive disorders are among the most severe and disabling psychiatric problems there are. They have remained notoriously resistant to successful treatment of any kind, and they provide a searching and decisive testing ground for potentially effective therapies. As in other areas, the behavioral treatment literature shows a definite progression towards the devel-

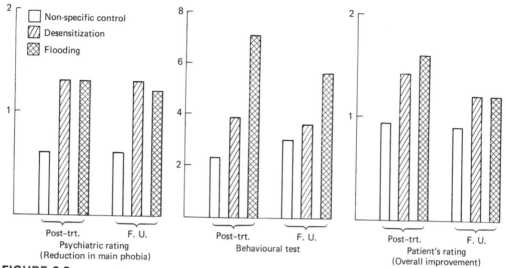

FIGURE 6.2

Results at posttreatment and follow-up of the three treatments on different measures of outcome. (*From:* Gelder and others, *British Journal of Psychiatry,* 1973, 123, 445–462.)

opment of increasingly refined and more effective therapeutic techniques. After methods like imaginal systematic desensitization proved to be largely ineffective, more effective alternative techniques, such as *in vivo* flooding, were developed (Rachman and Hodgson, 1980).

The evidence of behavioral treatment of obsessive-compulsive disorders may be illustrated by reference to a clinical outcome study by Hodgson, Rachman, and Marks (1972). They compared the efficacy of three treatments: (a) flooding *in vivo;* (b) modeling *in vivo;* and (c) flooding combined with modeling *in vivo.* The severity of the subjects' compulsions is indicated by the fact that six were unable to work while the others were severely hampered in their work. Family relationships were often completely imperiled, as in the case of an affectionate mother who was unable to touch her three children for fear of contamination. The clients were hospitalized for a seven-week period. After an initial week's evaluation, all subjects received fifteen one-hour sessions of relaxation training over the next three weeks. This extended period of relaxation therapy was designed to serve as an attention-placebo control. Thereafter the subjects were randomly assigned to the three treatment conditions for an additional fifteen sessions of therapy during the final three weeks.

Flooding consisted of encouraging subjects to engage in their most feared activities. The *in vivo* modeling treatment was similar to what is described as participant modeling in Chap. 7 of this book. The therapist modeled a series of increasingly threatening behaviors which the patient then imitated under the therapist's supportive supervision. All the subjects were asked to refrain

167

from carrying out their rituals between treatment sessions, but there was no nursing supervision to ensure that this instruction was followed. Subjects were assessed before treatment, after the three weeks of relaxation therapy, at the end of flooding or modeling, and at a six-month follow-up. The measurements taken included self- and psychiatric rating scales, attitudinal responses, behavioral avoidance tests which were tailor-made to individuals' specific problems, and direct measures of compulsive acts.

The results are summarized in Fig. 6–3. Both flooding and modeling were significantly more effective than the relaxation control treatment on all measures but did not differ from each other. The combined treatment did not increase the success of either method alone. A subsequent two-year follow-up (Marks, Hodgson, and Rachman, 1975) revealed that of the twenty clients who had been treated, fourteen were judged to be much improved, one improved, and five unchanged. Subjects who had improved at the six-month follow-up maintained their progress. This outcome is very encouraging especially since it is consistent with the results of uncontrolled clinical findings and experimental research reported by different investigators in different countries (see Rachman and Hodgson [1980] for a detailed review of this research).

The following factors suggest caution in interpreting the results. First, it is not clear that relaxation training is a powerful control treatment against which to assess the effects of other behavioral techniques. Second, the experimental design that was used confounded order effects with different treatments. In other words, since each subject received flooding or modeling only after relaxation training, it could be argued that the subsequent success was due in part to the cumulative effects of all treatment. It would have been preferable to compare different groups of subjects who received different treatments as Gelder and others (1973) and Paul (1966) did. Third, the efficacy of the specific behavioral methods at the two-year follow-up is difficult to determine because many subjects received additional treatment during this period. Eleven subjects had to be treated in their home settings after being discharged from hospital. Long-lasting treatment effects with complex problems is achieved largely to the degree that explicit steps are taken to ensure the generalization of behavior change to the client's natural environment and its maintenance over time. In the case of many disorders, including obsessive-compulsive problems, family members often have to be taught how to reinforce alternative activities and to cease inadvertently sustaining maladaptive behavior.

A more extensive evaluation of in vivo flooding in the treatment of obsessive-compulsive disorders, using a larger number of subjects, has been recently reported by Rachman and his colleagues (in press). The effects of behavioral treatment alone, and in combination with an anti-depressant drug (clomipramine), were investigated with 40 chronic obsessive-compulsive patients. Consistent with previous findings, the behavioral method produced significantly greater reductions in compulsive rituals than a relaxation training

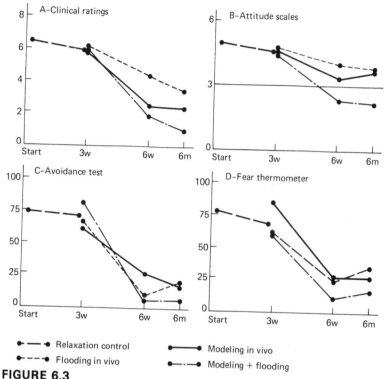

FIGURE 6.3

Summary changes of 15 patients' obsessions at posttreatment and at six months follow-up. Lower scores indicate improvement. (From: Hodgson, Rachman, and Marks, "The treatment of chronic obsessive-compulsive neurosis; followup and further findings," *Behaviour Research and Therapy,* vol. 10: 181–89, 1972. Elmsford, N. Y.: Pergamon Publishing Co. Copyright 1972, Pergamon Press, Ltd. Reprinted with permission.)

control treatment. The flooding treatment did not, however, result in an improvement in the patients' depressed mood. The use of the clomipramine did produce a general improvement in patients' mood states as well as some change in compulsive behavior. Somewhat surprisingly, there was no interaction between the behavioral and the drug treatments. These data indicate that the total clinical management of chronic obsessive-compulsive disorders may require a multifaceted treatment program that includes pharmacotherapy in addition to behavior therapy, a conclusion that is consistent with other research findings (Turner, Hersen, Bellack, & Wells, 1979).

Response prevention is an important part of the technique of flooding. In the case of a client who is a compulsive hand washer, for instance, response prevention means blocking the compulsive ritual of hand washing. The thera-

169

peutic value of response prevention was demonstrated by Mills, Agras, Barlow, and Mills (1973) in an experimental study of five hospitalized compulsive clients. A reversal design was used where each client served as his own control in evaluating the effect of sequentially introducing then removing a therapeutic procedure. Evaluations were made in terms of individual compulsive behavior which was reliably recorded on a continuous twenty-four hour basis. The results of the treatment of one of the clients, a compulsive hand washer, are shown in Fig. 6–4.

Recordings of the frequency of hand washing and urges to engage in this behavior were made over the first eight days of the baseline period. During the last eight days of baseline the client was exposed to objects that typically elicited hand washing. Predictably, hand washing increased at this point. Next, a placebo condition was introduced in which the client was given two "drugs" —actually a glucose capsule, four times a day and an injection of saline, once daily—that she was told would enable her to control her hand-washing compulsion. As can be seen from Fig. 6–4, hand washing increased slightly during this phase to an average of sixty episodes a day. With the introduction of response prevention during the third phase of this experiment, no hand washing was possible. The handles were removed from the sink and shower in the client's room. During phase four the client was once more able to wash if she so desired. However, episodes of hand washing were minimal, and this improvement was maintained during the final baseline phase of the study, when no treatment intervention was in effect. Note, however, that the client still reported urges to wash. The difference was that now, as a result of treatment, she could control her behavior. Additional exposure treatment in her home setting, following release from the hospital, resulted in a reduction in the urge to wash her hands compulsively. Similar substantial and lasting improvements were achieved with all four of the other subjects. These findings show that response prevention is significantly more effective than either placebo factors or simple exposure to the threatening situation alone.

Factors Affecting the Outcome of Flooding Therapy. Several critical procedural parameters of flooding have been identified. These can be outlined briefly as follows:

1. Exposure to the actual feared situation or object is more effective in reducing phobic and compulsive behavior than exposure to the imagined situation (for example, Emmelkamp and Wessels, 1975);

2. Exposure to the feared situation should be as long as possible. For example, Stern and Marks (1973) found that two hours of continuous flooding *in vivo* was significantly more effective than four separate hours in one afternoon in the treatment of agoraphobic patients. Too short a duration of exposure may be ineffective or even result in a temporary increase in fear (for example, McCutcheon and Adams, 1975);

3. It is not necessary to elicit intense feelings of anxiety during exposure in order for flooding to be effective (for example, Mills and others, 1973);

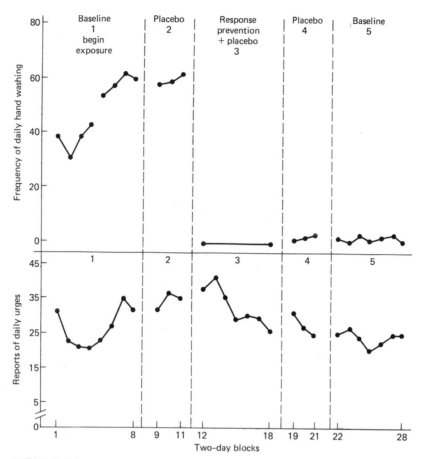

FIGURE 6.4
Top, Frequency of hand washing across treatment phases; each point represents average for two days. Bottom, Total urges reported by patient. (Mills et al., *Archives of General Psychiatry*, 28, 1973, 52. Copyright 1973, American Medical Association.)

4. *In vivo* exposure appears to be as effective as *in vivo* flooding in which the client is exposed to the most fearful situation from the onset (for example, Boersma and others, 1976);

5. Flooding conducted by a live therapist produces better results than tape recordings of therapeutic instructions (for example, Marks, 1978);

6. Flooding conducted within a group setting is as effective as individual treatment (for example, Hand, Lamontagne, and Marks, 1974);

7. *In vivo* exposure treatment in which the exposure is client-controlled may be as effective as therapist-controlled exposure and is more cost-effective (for example, Emmelkamp and Kraanen, 1977);

8. Flooding conducted by nursing personnel under the supervision of a professional behavior therapist appears to be comparable to treatment carried

out by clinical psychologists or psychiatrists. This increases the cost-benefit ratio for efficient delivery of treatment services (for example, Marks and others, 1977).

Flooding versus Systematic Desensitization. Several studies have compared the relative efficacy of flooding versus systematic desensitization. Some of the early studies, using as subjects college students who were only mildly fearful and not highly motivated to change their behavior, found that systematic desensitization seemed to be superior to flooding (Levis and Hare, 1977). Subsequent studies with more fearful or clinically distressed subjects who were highly motivated to overcome their problems have shown a different pattern. Consistently, flooding has been as effective or more effective than systematic desensitization with phobias and clearly more effective than desensitization in the treatment of obsessive-compulsive disorders (Leitenberg, 1976a; Marks, 1978; Rachman and Hodgson, 1980). The Gelder and others (1973) investigation, which is described above, found that flooding and systematic desensitization were equally effective. However, it is important to remember that both treatments involved *in vivo* as well as imaginal exposure to the feared situations. It is this *in vivo* exposure that appears to be the critical component of all fear-reduction techniques (Mathews, 1978).

Theoretical Mechanisms in Flooding and In Vivo Exposure. The now well established fact that prolonged exposure to situations that elicit high levels of anxiety can produce considerable therapeutic benefit directly contradicts Wolpe's (1958) reciprocal inhibition hypothesis, which predicts that extinction will occur only if anxiety is minimized during treatment. As was the case with the systematic desensitization literature, it is clear that nonreinforced exposure to the feared situation is essential for improvement to occur. However, this is only a description of what effective treatment involves. The reason why exposure works still has to be explained. The original conditioning explanation of this finding—two-factor theory—does not fare well in the light of available evidence. Contrary to the firm prediction from the learning theory from which it was derived (Levis and Hare, 1977), there does not appear to be a consistent relationship between level of anxiety during exposure and treatment success. For example, in the Mills and others (1973) study, anxiety in their subjects was highest before and after response prevention, rather than during prolonged exposure.

The operant analysis which stresses the contingent, or correlational relationship, between avoidance behavior and its consequences fares much better in accounting for the results. Flooding, *in vivo* exposure, and response prevention are all effective methods breaking the existing relationship between phobic behavior and its consequences. By bringing the person into contact with a different contingency (that is, it is safe to stop avoiding or engaging in compulsive rituals), the phobic avoidance or compulsive behavior is extinguished.

However, even this operant analysis falls short of explaining some of the clinical and experimental findings on flooding and *in vivo* exposure. For example, an adequate theory of flooding will have to explain the variability in treatment outcome. Why does the same amount of exposure result in improvement for one client, no effect for a second client, and perhaps increased fear in still a third client? There is also evidence indicating that the objective condition of exposure to the feared situation alone is insufficient for explaining treatment effects. An important consideration seems to be what it is that the person does during exposure (Marshall, Gauthier, and Christie, 1976). Thus, in imaginal flooding for example, treatment outcome may be enhanced by the person imagining realistically coping with the feared situation, instead of passively being exposed to it. In other words, how the subject perceives the external situation will be a determinant of behavior. This point, which is elaborated upon in Chap. 9, emphasizes the role of cognitive mediating processes in explaining the effects of behavioral procedures. Hand and others (1974) put it thus: "With the 'right' cognitive set a situation can be therapeutic, which with a different attitude could be disastrous. Exposure to a certain event can be 'traumatic' and induce a phobia, or it may lead a person to gird his loins and emerge strengthened" (p. 599).

According to social learning theory, the effects of flooding and *in vivo* exposure are explained in terms of the modification of the client's sense of personal efficacy. Self-efficacy theory is discussed in greater detail in Chap. 9. From this perspective, all forms of treatment influence the client's expectations about whether (s)he can cope successfully with a previously feared situation. Exposure treatment may or may not increase the strength and generality of efficacy expectations, depending on a number of associated factors like discrimination learning and attributional processes. Inevitably, it will require a sophisticated and complex analysis of this sort in order to account for the highly variable patterns of therapeutic outcome that are obtained. Self-efficacy theory also suggests why it is not necessary to evoke maximally intense anxiety during flooding in order to produce improvement (see Wilson, 1978e). It is not the intensity of the anxiety drive but the informative function of the situation that the client is exposed to that determines the effects of prolonged exposure. The latter are not correlated highly with the former as two-factor theory has long supposed. Marshall and others (1977) have proposed an analysis of flooding that is similar to self-efficacy theory. They suggest that phobic behavior is reduced to the extent that the flooding treatment increases clients' confidence about coping with previously feared situations.

METHODS FOR INCREASING SEXUAL RESPONSIVENESS

Evidence from numerous sources shows that human sexual behavior, whether it is heterosexual, homosexual, or some form of deviant expression, is mainly determined by learning and cultural influences. This was the view of the famous sex researcher, Alfred Kinsey, who stated that "Even the most extremely variant types of human sexual behavior may need no more explanation than is provided by our understanding of the processes of learning and conditioning. Behavior which may appear bizarre, perverse, or unthinkably unacceptable to some persons, and even to most persons, may have significance for other individuals because of the way in which they have been conditioned." (Kinsey and others, 1953, p. 645). Classical conditioning is an important part of a more comprehensive social learning analysis of the development and maintenance of sexual behavior, the details of which are discussed elsewhere (see Bandura, 1969; O'Leary and Wilson, 1975). For example, repeatedly pairing sexual arousal with a formerly neutral stimulus can result in the experimental induction of a mild fetish.[3] Rachman and Hodgson (1968) showed that penile erection evoked by pornographic stimuli could be classically conditioned to a previously neutral stimulus, for example, a boot. Moreover, clinical evidence suggests that the repeated association of specific fantasies with orgasm produced by masturbation endows these fantasies with erotic qualities that then function as powerful instigators of actual sexual behavior (McGuire, Carlisle, and Young, 1965). Given this likely role of classical conditioning in the development of sexual behavior, it is not surprising that behavior therapists have used methods based on classical conditioning to alter unwanted or undesirable forms of sexuality.

One application of this principle involves pairing sexual arousal elicited by pictures of deviant sexual activity with conventional sexual stimuli. Although adequate experimental controls have been lacking, several clinical successes have been reported with this method (Freeman and Meyer, 1975; Barlow, Reynolds, and Agras, 1973). A more widely used method is known as orgasmic reconditioning.

Orgasmic Reconditioning. This technique is used to overcome deficits in sexual arousal or to alter deviant arousal (for example, to young children) to acceptable forms of adult sexuality. Its use is illustrated by the treatment of a thirty-one-year-old policeman with a long history of *public transvestism,* achieving sexual arousal by dressing as a woman, and sadomasochism (Brownell, Hayes, and Barlow, 1977). The authors describe the latter problem as follows:

> During intercourse with his wife, he had tied her to the bed, handcuffed her, and had her wear an animal leash with a collar. He had also tied himself with ropes, chains, handcuffs, and wires while he was cross-dressed, and he was concerned that he would injure himself seriously. (p.1146)

---

[3]The significance of this form of learning has not been lost on Madison Avenue advertising experts. Think of the sexist, but successful, pairing of products for men—for example, razors, shaving cream, alcohol, cigarettes, and others—with beautiful, receptive women on television.

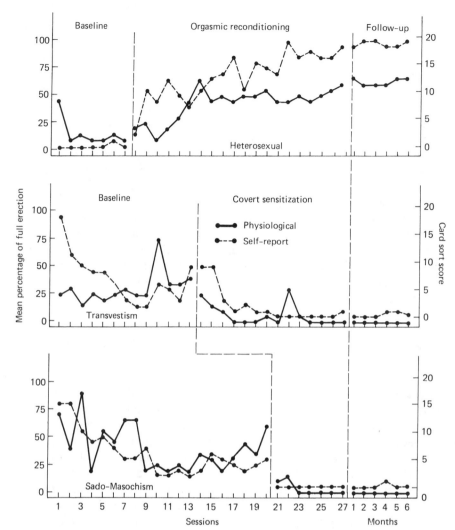

FIGURE 6.5
Mean penile circumference changes and card sort ratings of sexual
arousal in response to deviant and heterosexual stimuli for Subject 5.
(Brownell, K. D., Hayes, S. C., and Barlow, D. H. Patterns of appropriate
and deviant sexual arousal: The behavioral treatment of multiple sexual
deviations. Reprinted with permission from *Journal of Consulting and
Clinical Psychology*, 1977, 45:1144–1155. Copyright 1977 by the
American Psychological Association.)

The client was instructed to continue to masturbate to his deviant fantasies of cross-dressing and sadomasochism in his usual fashion. However, just
prior to the point of ejaculatory inevitability, that is, that point at which the
male ejaculates involuntarily, he was instructed to switch to an erotic fantasy
of more conventional heterosexual behavior. This switch was then gradually
made earlier in the sequence until the client could initiate masturbation and
reach orgasm exclusively using heterosexual fantasies. The client was given

pictures from magazines of nude women to facilitate the switch to heterosexual fantasies.

The results of this treatment are shown in the top third of Fig. 6–5. This single-case experimental design using a multiple baseline demonstrates that measures of sexual arousal to conventional heterosexual stimuli were increased significantly as a result of treatment and maintained at a six-month follow-up. Penile erection was measured by means of the penile plethysmograph. The card sort measure consisted of the client's subjective ratings of the degree of sexual arousal he experienced when instructed to imagine scenes involving appropriate and deviant sexual behavior.

Although several other clinical reports are consistent with this success of orgasmic reconditioning in increasing heterosexual arousal, Conrad and Wincze (1976) obtained negative results with four homosexuals. This technique has been used mainly with men, although Wilson (1973) and Zeiss, Zeiss, and Rosen (1977) have reported its successful application to facilitating orgasmic responsiveness in women.

Aversion Therapy

Aversion therapy based on classical conditioning principles was a significant part of behavior therapy in its early years. It was applied to problems such as addictive behaviors (for example, alcoholism and cigarette smoking) and sexual deviance (for example, transvestism and exhibitionism). The goal of classical aversion conditioning is to eliminate or decrease an undesirable response (for example, excessive alcoholic drinking) by repeatedly pairing it with an aversive event (for example, physical discomfort produced by electric shock or nausea). Several different forms of aversion conditioning using electrical, chemical, and imaginal aversive stimuli have been applied to a variety of problems (see Hallam and Rachman, 1976).

ELECTRICAL AVERSION CONDITIONING

Electric shock as an aversive stimulus has been widely employed in the treatment of different forms of sexual deviance. An example of this method of treatment is provided by Marks and Gelder (1967). Five transvestites and fetishists were administered electric shocks, which were just above the pain threshold, on a variable-ratio schedule in which one-quarter of all trials were shock-free. In the initial stages of treatment the shock was paired with the client imagining himself performing the deviant activities, while in the second stage, clients were shocked for performing these behaviors in reality.[4] Commendably, multiple measures of outcome, including penile erection, attitudinal, and subjective ratings, were made throughout the two-week treatment period. The use of a multiple baseline design showed that the aversion conditioning procedure was responsible for eliminating arousal to deviant stimuli without interfering with the clients' responses to conventional heterosexual stimuli. Following treatment, clients either had difficulty or were unable to obtain clear images of the formerly arousing deviant sexual stimuli. However, contrary to what might be expected from straightforward classical conditioning theory, no conditioned anxiety responses to the deviant stimuli were established. Clients simply reported neutral attitudes towards these stimuli after therapy. Deviant behavior in which all but one patient had engaged for at least twenty years was completely eliminated at the end of treatment, although two patients showed a reversal to some of their former patterns of behavior within a year after therapy.

In a two-year follow-up of twenty-four clients treated in the manner described above, Marks, Gelder, and Bancroft (1970) reported that transvestites, fetishists, and sadomasochists were all either "improved" (that is, deviant behavior infrequent and significantly less than before therapy), or "greatly improved" (deviant behavior rare or absent). They also maintained their changed attitudes towards deviant stimuli. Although most patients occasionally experienced deviant thoughts, these were usually transient and accompanied by little sexual arousal. Seven transsexuals, however, all failed to show lasting improvement as a result of therapy and returned to their previous modes of behavior within two or three months following treatment. The differential response to treatment of transvestites and transsexuals can probably be ascribed to the fact that the former present a fairly circumscribed set of behaviors which can be modified without necessarily involving or affecting other aspects of the individual's behavioral repertoire. In the latter, however, sexual desire is secondary to the overall gender-role reversal that requires a multifaceted treatment program aimed at changing social and sexual behaviors (see Barlow and others, 1973). Electrical aversion conditioning has also shown some clinical success in the treatment of exhibitionists (Rooth and Marks, 1974).

Electrical aversion conditioning was also once used to modify homosexual behavior. The results of several studies are equivocal, with interpretation hampered by the lack of adequate experimental controls and poor outcome measures. Although there are data that suggest that aversion therapy may be superior to placebo treatment, the clinical value of aversion conditioning cannot be said to have been satisfactorily established (see Bancroft, 1974). Aside

---

[4]The alert reader will have noticed that this treatment method involved both classical and instrumental conditioning components. Pairing shock with images of deviant stimuli is a classical conditioning procedure. Presenting shock contingent on the performance of a specific deviant response is an example of a punishment procedure (instrumental conditioning).

from this lack of empirical support, other reasons exist for what essentially has been the discontinuance of electrical aversion conditioning treatment with homosexuals.

Homosexuality was once widely regarded as a form of psychopathology that needed to be cured. However, social attitudes toward homosexuality have changed, and behavior therapists have been in the forefront of professional opposition to the sickness, illness, or disease concept of homosexuality. It is the client who is primarily responsible for setting the goals of treatment. In behavior therapy, the homosexual has the choice to remain exclusively homosexually oriented or to attempt to develop heterosexual interests. A survey of the attitudes of members of behavior therapy organizations in the United States and Great Britain indicated that the majority would, and in fact do, attempt to promote improved homosexual functioning, where appropriate, and reject treating homosexuals against their wishes (Davison and Wilson, 1973). In the event that the homosexual client wishes to broaden his or her sexual interests, aversion therapy is not used. Instead, positive procedures are employed in which the focus is on reducing anxiety about interacting with members of the opposite sex—through methods like desensitization, increasing social and sexual skills via modeling and information, or enhancing heterosexual arousal with orgasmic reconditioning. This flexibility of behavioral methods which is more consistent with personal freedom of expression is illustrated in a daring case study of a homosexual pedophile by Kohlenberg (1974). Initial treatment of this client, who had been arrested for sexually molesting young male children, involved aversion therapy. After this treatment failed to decrease the client's attraction to young male children, the therapist reassessed the case and decided to help the client develop an alternative pattern of sexual expression with consenting adult partners. Accordingly, a modified version of the Masters and Johnson (1970) program was used (see Box 6–1) in which the client brought an adult male friend to therapy sessions to act as a surrogate partner. As a result of this treatment, the client became sexually aroused to men of his own age and, at a six-month follow-up, reported no desire to sexually approach children.

Electrical aversion conditioning has been extensively used in the treatment of alcoholics and to a much lesser degree in the treatment of drug addicts. Well-controlled experimental investigations have shown that this form of aversion therapy is no more effective with alcoholics than a placebo treatment (see Wilson, 1978a). There is little reason to believe that it is any more effective with drug addicts (O'Leary and Wilson, 1975).

CHEMICAL AVERSION CONDITIONING

The use of nausea-inducing drugs as an aversive stimulus has been confined primarily to the treatment of alcoholics. The typical procedure is one in which the client is first given Emetine, a drug that reliably induces strong feelings of nausea. As the nausea reaction builds up, the client is instructed to concentrate on the sight, smell, and thought of alcohol. (S)he then tastes and swallows the alcohol with the result that vomiting occurs, and the alcohol is regurgitated. Approximately five such conditioning trials are conducted on alternate days with a range of different alcoholic beverages used as the conditioned stimulus in order to enhance generalization of the conditioned aversion reaction.

Lemere and Voegtlin (1950) reported the results of 4096 alcoholics whom they treated with this aversion conditioning method. Total abstinence from alcohol was achieved by 51 percent of all clients over a one- to ten-year follow-up. More specifically, 60 percent remained abstinent for one to two years 51 percent, for two to five years; and 38 percent, for five to 10 years. Participation by the clients in booster aversion conditioning sessions during the year immediately following treatment (when most reversions to drinking occurred) significantly facilitated the maintenance of long-term sobriety. Specific steps were taken to ensure the accuracy of these outcome findings, and they probably represent a conservative estimate of treatment success (see O'Leary and Wilson, 1975). More recent data on essentially the same treatment approach indicate comparable success rates (Wiens and others, 1976). These are extremely impressive clinical findings since alcoholism is a difficult problem to treat and is associated with a notoriously high relapse rate, after initial treatment success. However, several reservations must be had in interpreting the results. First, the lack of any control group makes it impossible to attribute success to the specific treatment method employed. Second, clients received other forms of treatment, aside from aversion conditioning. Thus it is unclear whether aversion conditioning was the effective agent of behavior change.

Theoretical Considerations. There are theoretical reasons to support the apparent superiority of chemical aversion, as opposed to electrical aversion, conditioning with alcoholics. Wilson and Davison (1969) have pointed out that electric shock may not be the best means of conditioning an aversion to the taste and smell of food or liquids. Evidence from animal conditioning studies suggests that successful aversion conditioning to taste and smell cues is facilitated by the use of "biologically appropriate" or "prepared" aversive stimuli such as nausea or sickness. Of course, this is exactly what the use of nausea-inducing drugs provides. However, it is not necessary to attribute the apparent superiority of nausea as an aversive stimulus to selective biological preparedness. In terms of Bandura's (1977b) social learning theory, an optimal aversive stimulus is one that can be easily recalled in imagery and cognitively rehearsed, as we explain in the following section. Nausea or sickness is a natural feeling that everyone has experienced at one time or another. It is often all too easy to remember what feeling nauseated is like! Electric shock on the other hand, is an artificial stimulus that most people rarely, if ever, experience. It is more difficult to recreate symbolically what the sensations of shock are like.

As we have discussed earlier in this chapter, classical conditioning does not result in S–R bonds that are automatically elicited. The film "A Clockwork Orange" misleadingly depicted an aversion conditioning "treatment" in which a strong aversive reaction was automatically conditioned in a young man against his will. Science fiction like this might entertain, but it needlessly arouses public apprehension and misrepresents psychological knowledge. All the evidence shows that conditioned aversive reactions are not developed that easily (Evans, 1976). Chemical aversion using Emetine is one of the most powerful forms of conditioning based on repeated pairings of alcohol with an intensely aversive physical reaction (nausea, hot flushes, sweating, and vomiting). Yet even with this intensely aversive procedure, not all clients develop conditioned aversions to alcohol. Conditioned responses are most likely to be created with the client's deliberate, conscious cooperation. Even if alcoholics do develop an initial conditioned aversion to alcohol as a result of aversion therapy, they are able to extinguish such a response whenever they wish either by "desensitizing" themselves to alcohol, by taking gradually increasing quantities, or by "flooding," that is, rapidly consuming large quantities until the nausea disappears.

SYMBOLICALLY GENERATED AVERSIVE CONDITIONING

Since conditioned aversive reactions are not automatically established by simply pairing two external stimuli together and since the client's self-directed involvement in the learning process is probably crucial, symbolically generated aversive reactions are the preferred form of treatment. In this procedure the client is asked to imagine the aversive consequence. An alcoholic might be asked to imagine experiencing nausea at the thought of a drink. As illustrated in the case of Mr. B in Chap. 1, an exhibitionist might be asked to imagine being apprehended by the police. This method is often referred to as covert sensitization. Several advantages recommend such a method: it is more practical and can be implemented by the client in any setting without cumbersome apparatus; it focuses directly on the self-activation of a reaction that social learning theory regards as a crucial process in conditioning; and it is more humane since it spares both the client and the therapist the unpleasant experience of electric shock or drug-induced nausea.

Efficacy of Imaginal Aversion Conditioning. Covert sensitization has been most effective in the treatment of forms of sexual deviance. Its use is illustrated by Brownell and others' (1977) treatment of five clients with multiple sexual deviations. One of these clients was the transvestite/sadomasochistic policeman discussed earlier (see Fig. 6–5). As can be seen from the multiple baseline design in Fig. 6–5, orgasmic reconditioning increased heterosexual arousal but had little effect on the two patterns of deviant sexual arousal. Covert sensitization was then applied to the transvestite arousal pattern. After this response was effectively decreased, aversive imagery was paired with the sadomasochistic arousal pattern. Each imagery scene was presented for three minutes. Stable reductions in deviant arousal was obtained in all five clients. No incidents of deviant behavior were reported, and all clients experienced satisfactory heterosexual interactions following treatment. The use of the multiple baseline design shows that these behavioral changes were attributable to the specific aversive imagery procedure and not to placebo influences or spontaneous improvement over time.

Whereas covert sensitization has been shown to be effective in the treatment of specific forms of sexual deviance, it has proved to be no more effective than placebo factors in the treatment of obesity (Foreyt and Hagen, 1973). Aversive imagery has also been applied to the treatment of other addictive behaviors, including alcoholism, drug abuse, and cigarette smoking. Its usefulness with these disorders remains to be demonstrated (O'Leary and Wilson, 1975). The efficacy of aversive imagery with sexual deviance, but not with an addictive disorder like obesity, is a function of the nature of the disorder being treated. First, deviant sexual behavior is usually elicited by a relatively narrow range of specific stimuli which can be reliably paired with aversive imagery. However, a problem like overeating frequently involves too diverse a set of antecedant stimuli to be treated in this manner. Second, sexual behavior, especially in males, is powerfully influenced by symbolic processes (Wilson, 1978c). Although cognitive mediating factors are important in other addictive disorders, their influence may not always be as powerful and as direct, as they are in many forms of sexual responses. The fact that a particular technique is effective with some well-defined problems, but not with others, highlights the need for specificity in evaluating therapy outcome. The important outcome question is not whether one global approach (behavior therapy) is better than another ill-defined approach (psychotherapy), but how effective is a specific technique applied to a particular problem and at what cost.

Theoretical Considerations. The efficacy of client-controlled aversive imagery in changing patterns of sexual responsiveness emphasizes the significant role cognitive mediating factors play in aversion therapy. Instead of being viewed as a form of automatic conditioning, aversion therapy is more accurately seen as providing the client with a means of self-control. This distinction is not only of theoretical importance but also has major consequences for the clinical practice of aversion therapy (see Bandura, 1969). If aversion therapy is regarded as a form of conditioning that automatically stamps in S–R bonds, the emphasis in therapy will be on ensuring that the crucial parameters of classical conditioning are not violated, for example, optimal inter-stimulus intervals between the conditioned and unconditioned stimuli and precision in specifying the intensity and duration of all stimuli. The reason why electrical aversion conditioning was once defended as the optimal method of aversion therapy (for example, Eysenck and Beech, 1971) was that it allowed precise control over these parameters. Such precision is not possible with chemical or symbolic aversion.

These parameters of classical conditioning, however, were all derived from experimental work on animals and are of questionable relevance to humans. As we noted in our critical analysis of classical conditioning theory, symbolic processes in humans are of major importance. Instead of precise timing of stimulus events, it may be far more important whether treatment procedures are readily recalled and can be rehearsed cognitively. Attempts to increase resistance to extinction through the use of unpredictable or intermittent pairings of the conditioned stimulus with the unconditional stimulus is rendered largely irrelevant by the human capacity to make complex discriminations. In terms of social learning theory, maintenance of treatment-produced behavior change will depend more on what the client does *between* and *after* therapy sessions than on the precise temporal parameters between conditioned and unconditioned stimuli *during* therapy sessions. Specifically, maintenance will be heavily influenced by the degree to which the client acquires and utilizes cognitive self-control strategies that persist long after the conditioning procedure is ended. When aversion therapy is viewed as a method of training self-control, a major task of therapy is to arrange conditions and incentives that ensure that the client implements potentially effective methods of self-control. For example, as the case of Mr. B in Chap. 1 indicated, the therapists deliberately took steps to make it likely that the client continued practicing aversive imagery procedures well after treatment was over. Viewed within this context, aversion therapy would best be used as one component of a multifaceted treatment program, designed to provide the client with alternative reinforcers and coping skills, and consisting of other self-control methods and specific maintenance strategies, designed to ensure long-term success. Aversion therapy alone will have only temporary effects on behavior.

Summary

Classical conditioning principles played an important role in the early formulations of behavior therapy, serving as a model of the development of phobias and influencing the introduction of innovative treatment methods. Subsequently, however, the classical conditioning model has been shown to be inadequate in accounting for the development of phobias. There is no evidence that lasting fears can be reliably conditioned, conditioned fears are easily extinguished in contrast to phobic reactions, and many clinical cases show no sign of any traumatic experience that could have produced conditioned fear.

Two-factor theory involves two assumptions: (a) anxiety is an acquired drive that is created by a classical conditioning process in which a neutral stimulus is paired with an unconditioned stimulus; and (b) this anxiety motivates overt avoidance behavior that is in turn reinforced by the reduction of the anxiety drive. However, two-factor theory still cannot account for the unusual resistance to extinction, shown by phobias. Even though the avoidance response removes the person from the anxiety-eliciting stimuli, some nonreinforced exposure to the anxiety stimuli does occur, and extinction should ensue. Another problem is that conditioned fear (autonomic arousal) does not mediate avoidance behavior. Rather, both autonomic arousal and avoidance behavior are correlated coeffects of a central mediating state. Attempts to salvage conditioning theory through the postulation of the incubation and preparedness hypotheses are speculative and lack sufficient empirical support.

In terms of a social learning analysis, pairing two stimuli together in the classical conditioning procedure results in learned expectations instead of S–R bonds. This learning is cognitively mediated and does not occur automatically as a result of temporal contiguity. Simple exposure to the fear-provoking stimuli does not necessarily result in extinction. Extinction occurs only if the information derived from this exposure leads the person to believe that (s)he can cope successfully with the situation. Aside from direct experience with fear-producing stimuli, fear reactions are acquired through modeling effects and through instruction and information about frightening events.

Regardless of the validity of the classical conditioning explanation of the development of phobias, it had an important influence on the introduction of novel treatment methods. Systematic desensitization is a widely used fear-reduction technique that was originally derived from classical conditioning principles. Clients are first trained to relax and then are asked to imagine progressively fearful scenes. If any scene elicits anxiety, it is repeated until the client can imagine it without experiencing undue anxiety. Systematic desensitization has been shown to be effective in the treatment of a wide range of problems involving anxiety as a central feature. It can be used in a group context and in self-administered desensitization, clients treat themselves. Contrary to Wolpe's reciprocal inhibition hypothesis, neither relaxation training nor the hierarchy of anxiety-eliciting stimuli are necessary for successful treatment. The crucial element is exposure, either in imagination or real life, to the anxiety-eliciting stimuli. The relaxation training and the hierarchy facilitate this exposure in cases of severe anxiety.

Flooding is a fear-reduction technique that involves exposure to high intensity anxiety-eliciting stimuli without the use of a hierarchy or relaxation training. Flooding is based on the principle of extinction that states that a conditioned response will be extinguished by repeated exposures to the fearful situation or object. This method has been demonstrated to be even more effective than systematic desensitization, particularly with obsessive-compulsive disorders. Factors that maximize the efficacy of flooding include *in vivo*, rather than imaginal exposure; lengthy rather than brief exposure to the fear-producing stimuli; and the administration of the technique by a live therapist, rather than by a tape recording.

Classical conditioning procedures have been used to increase sexual responsiveness to appropriate stimuli. This learning by association is thought to play a major role in the development of conventional and unconventional sexual behavior in males and females. In orgasmic reconditioning, fantasies of the desired sexual behavior are systematically paired with the powerful biological reinforcer of orgasm produced by masturbation.

Aversion therapy based on classical conditioning principles has been applied to problems such as addictive behavior and sexual deviance. The goal of classical aversive conditioning is to eliminate or decrease an undesirable or unwanted response by associating it with an aversive event. In electrical aversion conditioning, this aversive event is a painful, but harmless, electric shock. Despite some success in some cases of sexual deviance, such as transvestism and fetishism, electrical aversion conditioning has been shown to be largely ineffective and is rarely used nowadays. Chemical aversion conditioning attempts to associate drug-induced nausea with the undesirable response. Despite positive clinical evidence from the treatment of alcoholism, there is little scientific support for this method. Symbolically generated aversion pairs the undesirable response with an imaginal aversive event, such as nausea or being apprehended by the police, in the case of an exhibitionist. The evidence indicates that this is a useful technique in treating sexual deviance but not with addictive behavior.

Suggested Readings

Theoretical issues in the development, maintenance, and modification of neurotic disorders:

BANDURA, A. *Social learning theory*. Englewood Cliffs, NJ: Prentice-Hall 1977.

RACHMAN, S. (Ed.). Perceived self-efficacy: Analysis of Bandura's theory of behavioral change. *Advances in Behaviour Research and Therapy*, 1978, 1, 139–269.

The behavioral treatment of phobic disorders:

MARKS, I. Behavioral psychotherapy of adult neurosis. In S.L. Garfield and A.E. Bergin (Eds.), *Handbook of psychotherapy and behavior change*. New York: Wiley, 1978.

The behavioral treatment of obsessive-compulsive neuroses:

RACHMAN, S., and HODGSON, R. *Obsessions and compulsions*. Englewood Cliffs, NJ: Prentice-Hall, 1980.

Aversion therapy for alcoholism and sexual deviance:

HALLAM, R., and RACHMAN, S. Current status of aversion therapy. In M. Hersen, R.M. Eisler, and P.M. Miller (Eds.), *Progress in behavior modification,* Vol.2. New York: Academic Press, 1975.

WILSON, G.T. Aversion therapy for alcoholism: Issues, ethics, and evidence. In G.A. Marlatt and P.E. Nathan (Eds.), *Behavioral assessment and treatment of alcoholism.* New Brunswick, NJ: Center for Alcohol Studies, 1978.

7

Modeling

Introduction

Chris Evert, Frank Sinatra, Elvis Presley, and Barbra Streisand are individuals in the sports and entertainment fields whose behavior is imitated by thousands. Teenagers imitate such stars unabashedly, but adults also often mimic the vocal styles of singers and the actions of athletes. Young children regularly imitate other youngsters they observe on TV. Sons and daughters may copy the behaviors of their parents with such exactness that it is often difficult to distinguish the senior family member from the junior member when either is heard on the phone or seen from a distance.

While it is apparent that people important to us serve as models, it is also possible for cartoon figures and written or oral descriptions of individual behavior to provide us with information that guides our behavior. For example, children readily imitate the behavior of cartoon figures they observe on TV. Individuals hear or read about major crimes, such as skyjacking, and in turn engage in such behavior. *Modeling* thus refers to the learning process in which an individual changes as a function of observing, hearing, or reading about the behavior of another individual or humanlike figure.

A more expansive conceptualization of the modeling process is provided by Rosenthal and Bandura (1978), who defined a model as follows:

> A model is any stimulus array so organized that an observer can extract and act upon the main information conveyed by environmental events without needing to first perform overtly. (p. 3)

This definition of a model very strongly emphasizes the cognitive activities of the observer and includes any stimulus array (for example, a product such as a flower display, a well-decorated room, a road map, an instruction, or a self-help manual). It goes beyond the earlier emphasis on observing behavior of others (for example, Liebert, 1972) and may serve the heuristic function of prompting research on modeling through diverse nonsocial means (for example, how an individual can watch the demonstration of a physical principle, such as the angle of reflection of a ball from a cue stick, and in turn improve his or her pool game). This broader definition is important because it is offered by Bandura, whose conceptualizations and research regarding modeling have been very influential in psychology. However, in behavioral treatment, modeling has been almost exclusively effected through social means, that is, observation of others, and in this chapter the emphasis will be on modeling as a social learning process.

Models are especially important because they provide us with information so that we can acquire behaviors rapidly, without having to perform them and without having to have our behavior shaped in a trial and error fashion. The modeling effect is determined both by characteristics of the model and by cognitive activities of the observer. As we will detail later, the impact of models is influenced by such model characteristics as status and similarity to the observer and by the observer's ability to attend to, extract, and remember what he or she sees.

Because noted learning theorists stated that stable learning required overt performance, the role of modeling in psychological interventions based on learning theory was not considered to be especially important until the past decade. Bandura and Walters' book *Social Learning and Personality* published in 1963 was a seminal influence on psychologists in that it graphically described the extent to which social learning resulted from the observation of models. In particular, Bandura and Walters showed that children were influenced by viewing films in which either human or cartoon figures displayed aggressive behavior. Their book spurred a host of investigations into the role of modeling in the learning of aggressive behavior, and those investigations prompted a social action movement of consumers and researchers whose goal is to decrease the amount of aggression on prime time TV. However, before elaborating on the social impact of modeling research, let us first examine the basic effects of modeling in terms of how it can be used both to increase and to decrease the frequency of certain behaviors.

Increases in Behavior by Modeling

Increases in behavior through modeling can be considered under three different rubrics: (1) acquisition effects, (2) disinhibitory effects, and (3) facilitation effects. These modeling influences will now be explored.

ACQUISITION EFFECTS

The *acquisition effect* refers to the learning of a novel sequence of behavior as a result of observing a model. Of course, the observer would have to know how to perform the simple behaviors in this sequence, but the unique combinations of these behaviors which follow the observation of models demonstrate the influence of modeling. An experiment by Kaye (1971) clearly illustrated the acquisition of a novel behavior sequence by infants. When six-month-old children were presented with a toy that was obstructed by a transparent screen, they reached for the toy but were frustrated in their attempts to obtain it. Initially, none of the children reached around the screen to get the toy. However, when an experimenter modeled the behavior of reaching around the screen, within a few trials the infants imitated the behavior, and all obtained the toy without difficulty.

The learning of speech by a mute child represents the acquisition of a

novel sequence of behavior as a result of observing a model and being reinforced for imitation. Lovaas and his colleagues (see Lovaas and Newsom,
1976) developed a therapeutic program for autistic children, who are characterized by lack of speech, impairment in the comprehension of sounds, and
limited emotional attachment. The therapeutic program relies heavily on modeling and imitation in the development of speech. The verbal imitation training
consists of four steps:

1. The therapist first uses food to reinforce any vocalization.
2. Vocalizations are reinforced only if they occur within five seconds of the
   therapist's vocalizations.
3. The child has to make closer approximations to the therapist's speech sound;
   that is, when the therapist says, "a," the child has to make a sound which
   resembles "a."
4. The child has to make sounds and later words which very closely resemble
   those of the therapist. As can be seen in the figure, the autistic child learned
   the first sounds and words slowly, but later his imitative skills progressed very
   rapidly (See Fig. 7–1/redrawn from Lovaas, 1973).

Bandura, Ross, and Ross (1963) demonstrated the acquisition effect in
a study of the modeling of aggression. When preschool children observed a
model behaving aggressively toward a life-size plastic doll (Bobo doll), the
children imitated the identical aggressive behaviors displayed by the model.
The modeled behaviors included sitting on the doll, punching the doll repeatedly, kicking the doll around the room, and using the accompanying aggressive
verbal behavior (for example, "Sock him in the nose."). Both males and
females served as aggressive models. One part of the Bandura and others study
involved comparing the behavior of children who saw aggressive models with
the behavior of control children who were not exposed to the aggressive models
but were simply given the same objects with which to play (a table, chair,
tinker toy set, mallet, and the five-foot Bobo doll). The rates of aggressive
behavior similar to that performed by the models are depicted in Table 7–1
for boys and girls in the control and modeling conditions:

TABLE 7-1
Frequency of Imitative Aggression

	Children Who Observed Aggressive Models	Control Children
Girls	14.2	1.8
Boys	28.4	3.9

The aggressive model clearly influenced the children's behavior dramatically, and boys were more strongly affected than were girls. While it is possible
that the children in the modeling condition had previously displayed aggres-

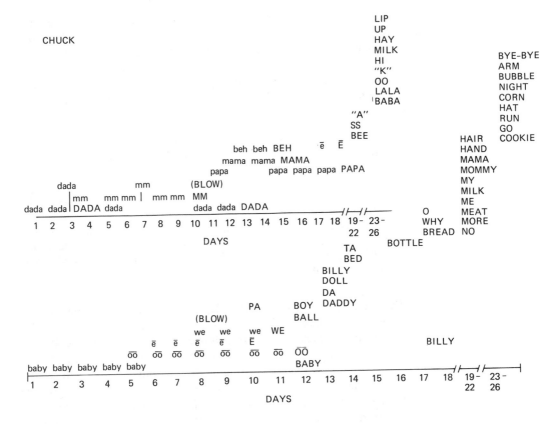

FIGURE 7.1
The first 26 days of verbal imitation training for Billy and Chuck, psychotic boys who were mute before training. The sounds and words are printed in lower case letters on the days they were introduced and in capitals on the days they were mastered (Lovaas, O. I., *Behavioral treatment of autistic children,* published by General Learning Press. © 1973 General Learning Corporation. Reprinted by permission of Silver Burdett Company.)

sive behavior at home that was similar to the aggression against the Bobo doll, the behaviors displayed after watching the model were novel combinations of aggressive behavior toward an inanimate object. Furthermore, Hicks (1965; 1968) found that children displayed the novel aggressive behaviors that they observed on film even when the assessment of the observational effect occurred six or eight months after the film was viewed.

Finally, let us consider a novel therapeutic use of filmed models in the treatment of women unable to achieve orgasm through intercourse or masturbation. McMullen and Rosen in press assigned sixty inorgasmic women to one of three conditions ($N = 20$ per group):

190

(a) Videotape sequences of a woman learning to stimulate herself to orgasm. During a six-week treatment, an actress portrayed an individual who initially had some difficulty with masturbation but who later was easily able to reach orgasm. The coping modeling sequence followed a masturbation program described by Heiman, LoPiccolo, and LoPiccolo (1976). First, the actress portrayed how she became comfortable and relaxed while touching her genitals; then she learned to self-stimulate to orgasm; and finally, she learned to achieve orgasm with her partner.

(b) Written instructions excerpted from the videotapes regarding self-stimulation.

(c) A wait-list control group (that is, a group who waited six weeks before being assigned to treatment).

(d) There was no direct contact with the experimenter following the pretreatment assessment so that all treatment was self-administered. Sixty percent of the women in the treatment groups became orgasmic by the end of the six-week period, and the percentage increased at the one-year follow-up. None of the women in the wait-list control group became orgasmic during the six-week period. The videotape modeling and written instructions treatments did not differ in their effectiveness. Thus, both the modeling treatment and specific written instructions offer viable self-administered treatments for inorgasmic women.

DISINHIBITORY EFFECTS

A *disinhibitory effect* occurs when the observer's inhibited behavior becomes more frequent after viewing a model perform the behavior in question without suffering any adverse consequences. A common example of the disinhibition effect is seen at parties when people begin to tell sexual jokes after listening to one individual tell such a joke. The rate of traffic signal violations is influenced by models who jaywalk. Awareness that many well-known politicians accept bribes and report only part of their incomes without any negative consequences undoubtedly encourages others to engage in similar illegal behavior. The disinhibitory role of modeling in behavior therapy has been extensively documented. Approach to feared objects, social interactions in children, and assertive behavior in adults can be increased through the use of modeling.

Bandura and his associates have shown that many children and adults with snake phobias can learn to approach and hold a snake in their laps after viewing a model gradually approach a snake (Ritter, 1968; Bandura, Blanchard, and Ritter, 1969). However, as will be discussed later, if a snake phobic

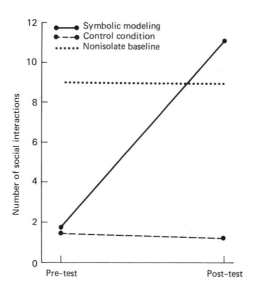

FIGURE 7.2
Mean number of social interactions displayed by subjects in the modeling and control conditions, before and after the experimental sessions. The dotted line represents the level of interactions manifested by 26 non-isolate children who were observed at the pretest phase of the study. (O'Connor, R. D., Modification of social withdrawal through symbolic modeling. *Journal of Applied Behavior Analysis,* 1969, 2, 19. Copyright 1969 by the Society for the Experimental Analysis of Behavior, Inc.)

can observe a live model who aids the subject in handling the snake and who gives the subject information about the snake, the subject is able to approach the snake much more easily than if he or she simply views a filmed model gradually approach the snake.

O'Connor (1969) selected extremely withdrawn preschool children whose behavioral deficits presumably were caused, in part, by fear of social interactions. Half of the children were assigned to view a film in which an initially fearful child interacted more and more frequently with peers. In the film the child first observed others interact; then he joined in certain sedentary activities, such as sharing a book; and finally, he joined many other children having fun in active endeavors. The other half of the children observed a control film depicting a dolphin performance. Following the film viewing, the children's social interactions were observed in their classrooms. As can be seen in Fig. 7–2, the children who observed the film of the model who learned to interact with others markedly increased their classroom social interactions. In contrast, the children who viewed the control film did not change their social behavior. This study, with variations, has been replicated (Evers and Schwarz,

1973; Keller and Carlson, 1974), and it has been found that improvements in interaction rates were maintained at a four-week follow-up (Evers and Schwarz, 1973).

Assertive behavior has been increased through treatment programs in which modeling has often played a central role. Hersen, Eisler, and Miller (1974) assigned psychiatric patients matched for age, sex, and assertiveness to one of five conditions: (1) Modeling and instructions to imitate the model; (2) Modeling, instructions and generalized instructions (to apply what you have learned in new situations and stand up for your rights); (3) Practice control, that is, role-playing assertive behavior, without receiving feedback; (4) Practice control with generalized instructions; and (5) No-treatment control. The patients' behavior was assessed in interpersonal situations that would typically prompt assertion. Patients who viewed the model with either instructions or generalized instructions showed the greatest increases in assertiveness.

Goldsmith and McFall (1975) evaluated the effects of an interpersonal skill-training program to teach assertiveness to psychiatric inpatients. The program involved modeling, behavior rehearsal, coaching, recorded response playback, and corrective feedback. The investigators compared the effects of this interpersonal skill training program with a pseudotherapy control in which subjects discussed their feelings about the same audiotaped interpersonal problem situations that the skill-training group used to practice assertiveness. A third group of subjects, the no-treatment control, was simply assessed twice. The subjects who received the interpersonal skill training evidenced greater increases in assertiveness than either of the two control groups. Of special importance was the finding that the subjects displayed assertiveness both in situations similar to those in which they had been trained and in situations for which no training was given (See Box 7–1 on *Assertion Training*).

FACILITATION EFFECTS

A *facilitation effect* refers to the observation of another which results in an increase in a socially acceptable behavior. In contrast to the acquisition and disinhibitory effects, the facilitation effect does not involve the learning of a novel sequence of behavior or the increase in behaviors that are unencumbered by restraints or are socially unacceptable. Common examples of the facilitation effect are an individual's volunteering of services or monetary contributions, recounting past experiences, and laughing, after observing another individual display any of these behaviors.

Children's cooperative behavior is influenced by observing film sequences in which taking turns is exemplified. A short film sequence developed for public television depicts a boy and girl initially fighting over a swing. Later, one child suggests that they take turns and that the other go first. Children

Box 7–1 *Assertion Training*

Books on assertion training have grown so rapidly in popularity that Landau (1976) provided a consumer guide for the potential purchaser of nine such books. *Looking Out for Number One* by Ringer (1977) was on the *New York Times Book Review* Best Seller list (*N.Y. Times* 1978), and of the books on that particular list, it had been there longest. Much of the assertion material in the popular literature is purportedly based on behavior therapy research. In fact, modeling has been a very important ingredient in many assertion studies by behavior therapists (for example, Field and Test, 1975; Goldsmith and McFall, 1975; Hersen, Eisler, and Miller, 1974; Longin and Rooney, 1975; Thorpe, 1975; Twentyman and McFall, 1975). More specifically, modeling played a central role in the assertion training programs of Hersen, Eisler, and Miller (1974) and Goldsmith and McFall (1975). Unfortunately, assertion training has become faddish, and its proponents often have blithely advocated its use under the behavior therapy aegis. As Franks and Wilson (1976) noted, "Unfortunately, the procedures touted in some of these books are *not* behavior therapy; assertion training per se is *not* the 'key' to blissful content; and it is certainly *not* new" (p. 148). Consider the following quotation from Newcomb's *How to Be a Man; A Book for Boys* written in 1847:

> If you find any difficulty in uttering (No), . . . go by yourself, and practice saying no, no, NO! till you can articulate clearly, distinctly, and without hesitation; and have it always ready on your tongue's end, to utter with emphasis to every boy or girl, man or woman, or evil spirit that presumes to propose to do you anything that is wrong. Only be careful to say it respectfully and courteously, with the usual *prefixes* and *suffixes,* which properly belong to the persons to whom you are speaking. (p. 211)

While caution should be used in the development and promulgation of assertion training programs, systematic research on assertion training is definitely needed. While many shy, withdrawn individuals apparently can profit markedly from assertion training programs, the evidence suggests that the effects of such training often does not generalize to nontrained areas. Further clinical experience leads us to suggest that whenever there are serious interpersonal problems between individuals, increases in assertive behavior should occur within an integrated therapy program in which the ethical and social consequences of increased assertion would be examined. Many marriages have been inadvertently ruined by one partner's poorly executed increases in assertive behavior!

who viewed this film sequence cooperated more in a game than children who saw a children's commercial (Liebert and Poulos, 1975).

There are numerous examples of the practical use of response facilitation. Coatroom attendants place dollar bills and large coins in their tip trays in the hope of evoking large tips from their clients. Television producers use canned laughter to facilitate laughter from home viewers. People are often paid to show their approval of concert performances or plays enthusiastically to encourage similar behavior in the rest of the audience.

Facilitation of helping in a naturalistic setting via modeling was documented by Bryan and Test (1967) in a study, "Lady in Distress: A Flat Tire Study." An adult female stood next to a car with a flat tire and an inflated tire leaning against the car. During the experimental period, about a quarter of a mile away, a model (a male) was helping a young woman change a flat tire. In the control period, at approximately the same time of day, the helping model was absent. The study took place in a residential area of a large city, and the presence of the helping model increased the number of individuals who stopped to help the woman in distress.

Decreases in Behavior by Modeling

Decreases in behavior through modeling can be considered under two rubrics: (1) inhibitory effects, and (2) incompatible behavior effects. In the first, a subject may observe a model being punished for a behavior and then will tend to engage in the modeled behavior less frequently. For example, the inhibitory effect is used by the government and various health agencies to decrease behaviors like smoking cigarettes through films showing the negative consequences of habitual smoking. An inhibitory effect may also result from observing a model engage in behavior without being reinforced for that behavior (for example, a child's use of an incorrect problem-solving strategy decreases as he or she watches a peer unsuccessfully use the same strategy), or from observing a model engage in a behavior at a low rate (for example, a heavy smoker may smoke less when observing his or her host smoking infrequently). The second modeling effect here considered, the incompatible behavior effect, results from the modeling of behavior incompatible with the target or problem behavior (a fearful subject observes a model cope with fear). This observation of the coping model tends to decrease the subject's fear of the situation.

INHIBITORY EFFECT

A "Juvenile Awareness" program for teenagers with minor legal infractions, which has been conceived and run by criminals with life sentences, utilizes the potential impact of the inhibitory effects of certain types of modeling. The "lifers" meet the fourteen- to sixteen-year-old youths in the prison for an hour and a half and describe in explicit detail the horrors of the prison. They depict their humiliation, their misery, and the terror of their existence. After the lecture by the lifers, a prison employee escorts the teenagers through the worst areas of the prison—especially "the hole," or solitary confinement cells. Initial reports by parents, teenagers, and prison officials, as well as recent police records, document the success of the program (Sheppard, 1977).

Another intriguing illustration of the use of models was provided by Garlington and Dericco (1977). Interview data from several sources strongly suggest that the drinking patterns of peers are one of the most important determinants of alcohol consumption in young people. Thus, these investigators experimentally evaluated the effects of a model's rate of drinking on three college students who volunteered to participate in a study on normal drinking habits. The study took place in a simulated tavern setting and involved the three college student volunteers and three "confederates" who were students paid to interact with the three subjects and to serve as possible models. The confederates were instructed not to discuss drinking during any of the sessions, but in other ways, the social interactions between confederates and subjects were presumably fairly typical of tavern interactions. The confederates were initially told to match the subjects' rate of beer consumption over a period of five days and then to decrease their own rate by one third. The subjects' drinking rate was markedly influenced by the models, as exemplified in Fig. 7–3. As noted in the figure, the confederate matched the subject's rate in the initial and second baseline phases, and the lowered drinking rate of the confederate in the second condition (slow rate) was associated with a reduction in the subject's drinking, although the effect was not clear until the last four sessions.

One could infer from this and a related study by Caudill and Marlatt (1975) that college students' drinking in taverns and housing units can be increased or decreased through modeling. As a host or hostess, one also sets an example and probably influences the type and amount of drinking of one's guests. Before one could predict whether modeling alone would influence a subject's drinking rate, the sex and prestige of the model, the number of models, and the normal drinking rate of the subject probably would have to be known. Presumably, however, models who drink slowly can influence their friends and relatives simply by the example being set.

MODELING OF INCOMPATIBLE BEHAVIOR

A wide variety of clients' fears have been reduced by having models display behaviors that are incompatible with the fearful behavior of the clients. One of the best designed therapeutic experiments regarding children's fears was

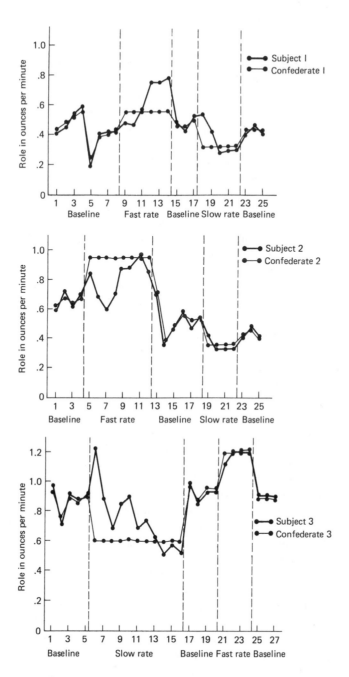

FIGURE 7.3
Drinking rate of subjects and confederates for all baseline and experimental conditions. (Garlington, W. K., Dericco, D. A., The effect of modeling on drinking rate. *Journal of Applied Behavior Analysis,* 1977, 10, 210. Copyright 1977 by the Society for the Experimental Analysis of Behavior, Inc.)

that of Melamed and Siegel (1975) who prepared the film "Ethan Has An Operation" which depicted the experiences of a seven-year-old boy undergoing a hernia operation. The child, Ethan, described his own feelings, the fears that he experienced at each stage, and his resolution of them. The observer viewed Ethan progress through the admission process, ward orientation, examinations by the surgeon and anesthesiologist, return to the recovery room, reunion with his parents, and hospital discharge.

Upon hospital admission, thirty children about to undergo surgery for hernias, tonsillectomies, or urinary problems were shown either the film about Ethan or a control film about a boy's trip in the country. In addition, all children received preoperative preparation. This preparation included demonstrations and explanations of the surgery and recovery process by a social worker, and a visit from the surgeon who again explained the surgery to the child and his or her parents.

Melamed and Siegel (1975) collected children's self-reports of anxiety; staff observations of the children's anxiety; and a physiological measure of anxiety, the Palmar Sweat Index, a measure of the sweat gland activity of the hand and of transitory physiological arousal. All three measures of anxiety showed greater reduction of anxiety both at preoperative (night before operation) and postoperative (three to four week examination post surgery) assessments for the experimental group (See Figs. 7–4 and 7–5).

In related studies, Melamed and her associates have shown that children's fear of dentists and anxiety about dental treatment can be significantly reduced. They used videotaped demonstrations of young children who successfully coped with their anxieties while undergoing dental restorative procedures (Melamed, Weinstein, and others, 1975; Melamed, Hawes, and others, 1975). Vernon illustrated the efficacy of having children observe film models who receive general anesthesia or injections. He showed that children's levels of pain and/or upset were reduced by viewing the modeling films (Vernon, 1973; 1974; Vernon and Bailey, 1974). Briefly, modeling is an efficient and effective way to reduce children's fears of medical and dental personnel and practices. In fact, given the repeated demonstrations of effectiveness of the modeling films and the ease with which such brief films could be shown in a small cassette audiovisual display unit in any office, such films should be used routinely in medical and dental practice.

Modeling of incompatible behavior has also been used successfully in reducing women's debilitating sexual anxiety. For example, Wincze and Caird (1976) and Nemetz, Craig, and Reith (1978) had women relax and then view thirty to forty-five videotaped vignettes in which couples engage in graduated sequences of heterosexual behavior. The women were given systematic desensitization training in the Wincze and Caird study and simply were told to relax between vignettes in the Nemetz and others study. Women in the Nemetz and others study were also instructed to complete

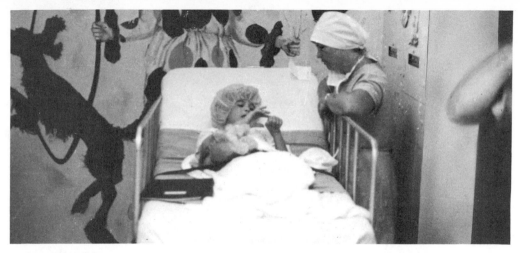

Child being informed about operation.

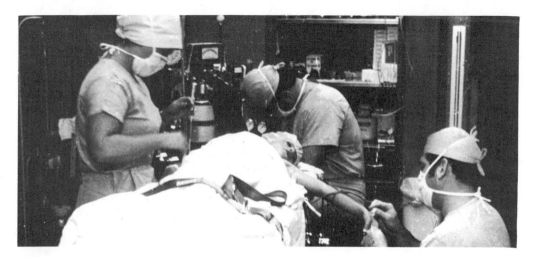

Child in operating room.

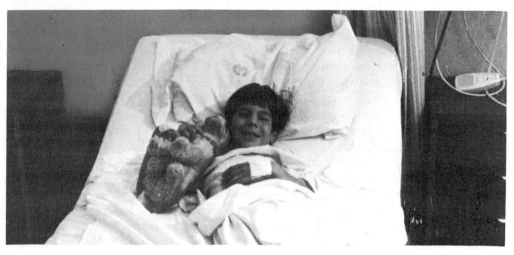

Child following operation.
(*From* "Ethan Has An Operation," Melamed and Siegel, 1975.)

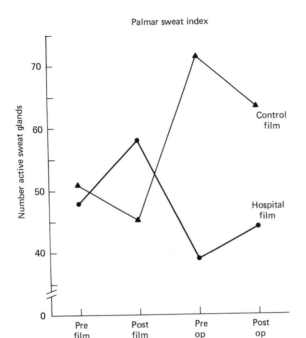

Palmar sweat index

FIGURE 7.4
Number of active sweat glands for the experimental and control groups across the four measurement periods. (Melamed, B. G., Siegel, L. J., Reduction of anxiety in children facing hospitalization and surgery by use of filmed modeling. *Journal of Consulting and Clinical Psychology*, 1975, 43, 516. Copyright 1975 by the American Psychological Association. Reprinted by permission.)

tasks at home with their partners similar to those depicted on the videotapes. In both studies, there were significant decreases in heterosexual anxiety, and Nemetz and others found that such decreases in anxiety maintained at a one-year follow-up.

In summary, there are two ways in which the frequency of certain behavior is decreased through modeling—inhibition and modeling of incompatible behavior. The three aforementioned categories of modeling effects that result in increases in behavior are the observational learning effect, disinhibition, and facilitation. Depending upon the target behaviors assessed, it may be possible to categorize certain studies in more than one of these subsections. For example, in the O'Connor (1969) study of socially isolated children described in the section on disinhibition, the children may have increased their social interactions because their fears were reduced by viewing the coping model (that is, modeling of incompatible behavior). However, we have placed the O'Connor study in the disinhibition section because he measured an *increase* in interactional behavior; we do not know for certain that the children experienced a fear reduction. Had there been a measure documenting fear reduc-

200

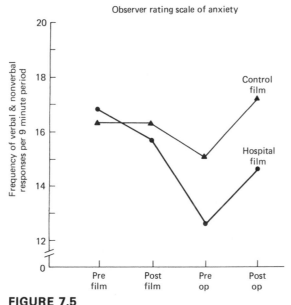

Observer rating scale of anxiety

FIGURE 7.5
Frequency of observer-rated verbal and nonverbal anxiety responses
for the experimental and control groups across the four measurement
periods. (Melamed, B. G., Siegel, L. J., Reduction of anxiety in children
facing hospitalization and surgery by use of filmed modeling. *Journal
of Consulting and Clinical Psychology,* 1975, 43, 518. Copyright
1975 by the American Psychological Association. Reprinted by permission.)

tion, the study could then have been classified as an example of how models
can be used both to increase and decrease behavior.

Covert Modeling

As you can readily imagine, a therapist cannot easily arrange a variety of
models for clients. While modeling films or videotapes about frequent clinical
problems can be made available through commercial firms, a therapist will
often encounter clients who have problems unlike those for which films have
been prepared. Because of this problem, Cautela (1971) suggested that clients
imagine models engaging in the behaviors the clients wish to develop. If one
conceptualizes modeling as the transmission of information, then it would be
possible to have a client imagine a sequence of events and thus use *covert
modeling.* Of course, the ability of a client to imagine, the plausability of the
rationale for covert modeling, and the vividness and clarity of the information
in the imagined sequences will all have an influence on the effectiveness of the
procedure. However, it is theoretically possible that covert modeling could be

201

clinically useful, and it might have an effect similar to that of live models.

With college students who have good imagining skills, covert modeling has proven effective in reducing fears (Kazdin, 1974a,b). In a clinical setting, submissive clients who were asked to imagine a model similar in age and sex to themselves making assertive responses showed improvement both on self-report and on behavioral tests of assertiveness (Kazdin, 1976a). Although there are few direct comparisons between overt and covert modeling, under some conditions live and covert modeling yield generally equivalent results with adults (Cautela, Flannery, and Hanley, 1974). On the other hand, with very young children and retardates whose attention span is short and whose symbolic imagery is presumably poor, covert modeling would probably be ineffective or inferior to overt modeling (Rosenthal and Bandura, 1978).

Controlled research involving evaluation of parameters that influence covert modeling is sparse, but the available evidence provided almost solely by Kazdin suggests that parameters that affect live modeling also affect covert modeling in similar ways. First, a coping covert model is more effective than a mastery covert model (the coping model initially shows fear and apprehension, whereas the mastery model boldly approaches a feared object). Second, the greater the perceived similarity between the client and the covert model, the greater the fear reduction. Third, when clients are asked to imagine reinforcing consequences to the model for assertiveness, they show more improvement than clients who simply are asked to imagine assertive models. Fourth, multiple covert models are more effective than single covert models (Kazdin, 1976a).

While there is considerable evidence that covert modeling procedures can lead to reduction of fears of snakes and increases in assertion in college students, it is still not clear what covert modeling is effective with clinical populations. With such populations, research comparing covert modeling with wait-list controls or other therapeutic procedures is meager; it is not seen as a very important procedure to be taught in a graduate clinical training program (Pomeranz, 1975); and procedures which rely on actual, rather than imagined, events are almost always superior.

Participant Modeling

Participant modeling treatment involves both the active shaping and guiding of a client as well as direct modeling of the critical behaviors. Bandura (1977a) reported that this treatment is more effective than having a client simply observe the model perform the critical behaviors. More specifically, a participant modeling program involving displays of the behavior by a model, performance by the client, and corrective feedback to the client is more effective than modeling alone, symbolic desensitization, and covert modeling. As importantly, clients who are not helped by treatments using imaginal exposure to feared stimuli are readily aided by participant modeling. Let us consider a classic study which illustrates the comparative treatment advantages of participant modeling.

Bandura, Blanchard, and Ritter (1969) treated adolescents and adults who had snake phobias that generally restricted them in significant activities, such as gardening, hiking, and camping. In a comprehensive evaluation of behavioral change, Bandura and others (1969) assigned the clients to one of four treatments:

1. **Self-administered Symbolic Modeling.** In this modeling intervention, the subjects viewed a film of children, adolescents, and adults engaging in progressively more threatening interactions with a large snake. To maximize the effectiveness of the film, subjects were asked to remain relaxed during the viewing. Whenever they felt anxious, they were to stop the film, relax, and go to the beginning of the scene which made them anxious.

2. **Modeling with Guided Participation.** In this intervention, a live model initially demonstrated the desired behavior while the subject watched from a "safe" location. Later, the subject was asked to join the model and was helped by the model to touch the snake's body, first wearing a glove and then with a bare hand. If a subject felt unable to touch the snake, he or she was asked to place a hand on the model's hand while the model's hand gradually approached the snake's body. Later, the subject and model touched the snake's head and tail, and as the subject felt less anxious, the snake was allowed to move freely in the room. Progress through the graded approach tasks was always determined by the subject's anxiety.

3. **Desensitization.** Subjects in this group received the standard deep muscle relaxation and imaginal pairing of images of snakes in progressively more threatening situations (Wolpe, 1958).

4. **Control Condition.** Subjects in this group served as a control for possible changes resulting from repeated measurements of approach toward the snake. These subjects' fears were simply assessed on two occasions.

As shown in Fig. 7–6, the Modeling with Guided Participation group showed the greatest improvement in approach behaviors toward the snake. In fact, 92 percent of the subjects in this condition were able to perform the behavior they originally rated as most threatening. In contrast, only 33 percent of the subjects in the Symbolic Modeling condition, 25 percent in the Desensitization condition, and none in the control condition were able to perform the most threatening behavior at the post test.

In participant modeling treatment, the presence of a therapist while a client is overcoming a fear can be especially comforting. A sensitive therapist can help the client judge the comparative utility of progressing with very minor steps or facing larger, more demanding, challenges rather early in the program. Response induction aids, such as modeling threatening activities in easily mastered steps, joint approaches toward the feared object, using protective clothing, and controlling of the feared object, can be readily used by a therapist in participant modeling treatments (Bandura, Jeffery, and Wright, 1974). As with all external prompting devices, however, the performance aids have to be gradually removed to assure maximal client performance under natural condi-

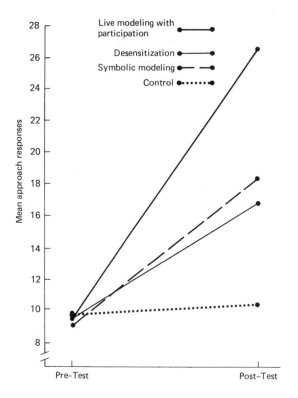

FIGURE 7.6
Mean number of snake-approach responses performed by subjects before and after receiving different treatments (Bandura, Blanchard, Ritter, The relative efficacy of desensitization and modeling approaches for inducing behavioral, affective, and attitudinal changes. *Journal of Personality and Social Psychology,* 1969, 13, 173–199. Copyright 1969 by the American Psychological Association. Reprinted by permission.)

tions. To facilitate performance of fearful clients after treatment involving induction aids, Bandura, Jeffery, and Gajdos (1975) had clients engage in self-directed practice. Such independent practice facilitated specific and generalized fear reduction and feelings of self-competency.

Cognitive Explanation of Modeling Effects

As evidenced in the Bandura and others (1969) study, the greater the emphasis on actual performance of desired behaviors in modeling treatments, the more likely the improvement. In fact, as we shall see in Chap. 9, Bandura (1977a) has emphasized that regardless of the treatment method involved, comparative studies attest to the superiority of performance-based treatments. Bandura's theoretical rationale for improvement in therapy is that successful psychological treatment enables individuals to strengthen their expectations of personal effectiveness, and changes in such expectations occur most readily through performance-based treatments. Bandura stated that our expectations of efficacy influence how we will strive and how long we will persist at tasks, despite frustrations and adverse feedback.

In fact, after generally successful treatment but before a posttest evaluation, when fearful adults were asked whether they considered themselves capable of performing various fear-arousing tasks, Bandura and his associates (Bandura and Adams, 1977; Bandura, Adams, and Beyer, 1977) found that clients' judgments of self-efficacy were accurate predictors of posttest performance in almost 90 percent of the tasks whether in participant modeling, modeling alone, or desensitization treatment. Bandura argued that regardless of the type of treatment, the feeling of self-efficacy was a critical mediator of therapeutic improvement. However, it is important to note that the treatment emphasis of the therapist should be on encouraging the client to perform critical target behaviors (that is, overt behavior) even though the cognitive construct of self-efficacy may account for changes in anxiety treatment programs. As Bandura (1977a) stated, "The apparent divergence of theory and practice can be reconciled by postulating that cognitive processes mediate change but that cognitive events are induced and altered most readily by experience of mastery arising from effective performance" (p. 191). In brief, the reciprocal interaction between feelings of self-efficacy and behavior change during the treatment process is here emphasized. Because of this complex interaction, it is difficult to analyze the function of perceived self-efficacy. The construct of self-efficacy is new in the behavioral literature, and it is not clear whether it will retain its predictive power with children or with adult clinical problems, other than anxiety. However, Bandura's data on self-efficacy will undoubtedly prompt many behavior therapists to address cognitive explanations for therapeutic change in modeling, as well as in other treatments.

Factors Influencing Modeling

Determinants of the effectiveness of modeling can be subsumed under three headings: (1) model characteristics, (2) observer characteristics, and (3) procedural characteristics.

MODEL CHARACTERISTICS

Let us now briefly consider factors about the model(s) which influence the modeling process. Models identical in age, sex, and ethnicity to the subject are more likely to be imitated than models dissimilar to the subject with regard to these characteristics. A model who is a celebrity or who has purported expertise or social status is also likely to bring about greater modeling effects than is a model of lower status. However, as Zimmerman (1977) has aptly noted, one should not conclude from the research on model characteristics that models must have these qualities to be effective. He reports that the differences in imitation attributable to model characteristics have been small and often inconsistent. Fortunately, as long as there is some similarity in age, and the observer and model are the same sex, modeling is a robust phenomenon which is relatively immune to certain factors, such as ethnicity. That is, a model will generally be imitated even if the observer is somewhat different in age, ethnicity, or social status from the model.

A characteristic of the model which has been influential in a number of studies is the coping versus mastery distinction. A coping model is one who verbalizes some apprehension while learning to approach the feared object, whereas as mastery model is a model who boldly approaches the feared object (see Meichenbaum, 1977a). However, evidence regarding the relative merits of coping models and mastery models is equivocal (Kornhaber and Schroeder 1975; Bruch, 1975; Meichenbaum, 1971). Despite the lack of clear support for the superior effectiveness of coping models, modeling programs of demonstrated clinical utility have employed coping models—especially in the modeling of incompatible behavior (for example, Melamed and Siegel, 1975). There are several possible explanations for the continued use of coping models by clinicians and researchers:

1. The use of coping models is compatible with the gradual shaping of behavior emphasized by many psychologists.
2. The coping model procedure often includes the demonstration of self-control and coping techniques.
3. Children often will not look at displays of bold approach behavior, whereas they will attend to a model who initially shows fear but later overcomes it (Bandura, Grusec, and Menlove, 1967).

OBSERVER CHARACTERISTICS

Bandura (1976) outlined four determinants of the effectiveness of modeling which are summarized below. Knowledge about these factors is especially important in devising treatment programs. Let us consider the four determinants:

1. **Attention Processes.** Exposure to a model does not guarantee that an observer will be influenced by the model; the observer must attend to and comprehend the information provided by the model. Lighting contrasts, sound changes, repetition of crucial elements, and explanatory summaries will enhance the likelihood that one will attend to the most relevant information conveyed by the model (Bandura, 1977b).

2. **Retention Processes.** Once an observer attends to relevant model information and can comprehend the relevant cues, the observer must then be able to remember that material. It is clear that active processing of information by coding, classifying, attaching pictorial (iconic) images to verbal material, and using mnemonic devices and capsule summaries can enhance one's memory of material. Further, individuals who first use coding and then acronyms to help them retain information about modeled sequences retain much more information than people who use either coding or acronyms alone (Bandura, Jeffery, and Bachicha, 1974). As Rosenthal and Bandura (1978) noted, "Higher order symbols, like other mediators, depend upon organizing frameworks," and knowledge of the effects of such organizing skills on retention should be used to build effective modeling treatments. Through the use of instructions and modeling, subjects can be taught to code, classify, and order information that will facilitate their retention.

3. **Motoric Reproduction.** With certain complex motoric behavior like riding a bicycle, it is clear that unless an individual has the requisite skills, such as balancing and the ability to steer and stop the bicycle, he or she will not learn how to ride a bicycle from observing others. Similarly, performance of other motor behaviors demands motoric skill that requires overt practice and proprioceptive feedback for proficiency. However, performance of complex motor behaviors can be facilitated by modeling and symbolic rehearsal of the motor activity.

4. **Motivation Processes.** Even when an observer attends to a model, comprehends the information conveyed by the model, retains such information, and has the motoric skill to execute the modeled activity, the observer may not perform the modeled behavior because he or she

expects aversive consequences to follow the behavior. On the other hand, when individuals expect positive consequences for engaging in modeled behavior, they are likely to perform the behavior in question.

PROCEDURAL CHARACTERISTICS

Certain procedures related to the circumstances in which modeling occurs can influence the modeling effect. Consequences to the model have been repeatedly shown to influence a model's effectiveness. More specifically, a model who is rewarded for his or her action is more likely to be imitated than a model who is punished. Finally, having models display the behaviors to be modeled in a variety of settings will enhance modeling effects, as will the inclusion of multiple models, rather than a single model.

Individuals abstract rules for guiding their own behavior from observing models, and these rules function to influence the observer's behavior in very predictable ways. In brief, when an observer can deduce a rule or discover a general plan of action from the model's behavior, the model's actions are very effective in influencing the observer; there is rapid acquisition and excellent transfer and retention of the information conveyed by the modeling sequence. Alternatively stated, the functional value of the model's actions is very great when the observer can extract information or rules from the model. Noting critical features of the model's behavior, giving parsimonious rules that best describe the model's actions, and providing reasons for engaging in certain behaviors greatly facilitate the observer's learning.

Social Impact of Modeling Research

TV AGGRESSION

The role of aggression and violence on television has been a hotly contested subject for almost a decade. Many studies have documented the presence of aggressive models on TV. In 1972, Gerbner reported that there were eight acts of violence per hour on prime time television dramas and thirty violent acts per hour on children's Saturday morning cartoons. In 1976, Slaby, Quaforth, and McConnachie reported a remarkably similar rate of violent acts per hour on children's Saturday morning cartoons; namely, 21.5 violent acts per hour. Domineik (1973) found that 60 percent of prime time drama and comedy shows portrayed at least one crime. In brief, both children and adults are exposed to large amounts of violence and/or criminal activity. Furthermore, there is evidence from many sources that exposure to aggression directly from television does lead to increases in aggressiveness in the viewers (Liebert and Poulos, 1975). One classic study by Lefkowitz, Eron, Walder, and Huesmann (1972) well exemplifies the impact of exposure to televised violence. Lefkowitz and his associates collected a wide variety of data from 400 nine-year-olds including peer ratings, television viewing habits, and parental disciplinary practices. Ten years later they collected similar data on the same individuals, then nineteen years old. For boys, exposure to televised violence at nine years of age was significantly related to aggressive behavior at age nineteen. Sophisticated statistical analyses of these data by independent investigators led to the conclusion that exposure to televised violence was causally related to aggression, not merely a factor associated with aggression (Neale, 1972).

Although the TV industry has been slow to reduce or regulate aggression, in 1975 the National Association of Broadcasters created "Family Viewing" during prime time or early evening broadcasting. Violence was reduced during Family Viewing Time, and the public has reacted very positively to the Family Viewing Concept (Wiley, 1977). However, in 1977 the U.S. District Court in Los Angeles ruled the family viewing hour unconstitutional, but the decision has been appealed.

WOMEN'S ROLES

Sternglanz and Serbin (1974) analyzed popular children's television shows and found that the female characters were punished for high levels of activity and were portrayed as less effective and more deferent than males. Women were victimized more than men, and single women were most likely to be victims. In an examination of children's readers and prize-winning books, males predominated in central roles (Liebert and Schwartzberg, 1977). Such findings have prompted women's organizations to urge television producers and publishing firms to show female characters functioning effectively in important roles.

In terms of occupational roles, TV males are generally employed and have highly prestigious jobs, such as physicians, attorneys, and law enforcement officers. In contrast, only one third of TV females are clearly employed, and when they are, they seldom hold prestigious jobs (Rubenstein and Sprafkin, 1978). With regard to marriage, the power of male TV models who are married is less than that of unmarried male models. On the other hand, married women are portrayed as more powerful than single women (Gerbner, 1972).

In brief, books and TV have portrayed models who are restricted in their occupation, roles, and emotional behavior. These media should use their great potential to provide us with both male and female models who portray the widest range of behaviors.

THE UNHEALTHY PERSUADER

Choate (1974) estimated that a child observes over 5000 commercials a year, and cereals, candy, other foods, and toys each make up the subject matter of about 20 percent of such commercials (Barcus, 1971). An outstanding example of the impact of these TV commercials was provided by Galst and White (1976), who analyzed the effects of modeling on purchase-influence attempts at the supermarket by children. They found that children who watched large amounts of television and who liked to view commercials made greater attempts to influence the purchases of their mothers. Cereals and candy were the most heavily requested items, and 48 percent of the children's attempts to get their mothers to purchase a requested cereal were successful. As Galst and White noted, since most of the advertisements are for sweetened foods, and it is known that consumption of these foods contributes to dental caries, diabetes, and heart disease, television is presently "a vehicle for unhealthy persuasion." Such research has spurred two nonprofit groups, Center for Science in the Public Interest and Action for Children's Television, to urge public hearings by the Federal Trade Commission (FTC) regarding curtailment of television advertisements aimed at children. Interestingly, the banning of all advertisements directed at very young children is supported by the FTC Chairman (*Newsday,* March 1, 1978).

PROSOCIAL ACTION

While the majority of investigations of the effects of television initially focused on the negative effects, the television medium is also an excellent source for teaching prosocial skills. Stein and Friedrich (1972) exposed approximately one hundred preschool children to one of three programs for twelve consecutive viewings: (1) Aggressive *(Batman* and *Superman),* (2) Prosocial *(Mister Rogers Neighborhood),* (3) Neutral (activities such as children working on a farm). They observed all children in the nursery school before and after the television program sequences, and they showed that children became less compliant and less tolerant of frustration after viewing the aggressive cartoons. In contrast, exposure to the prosocial programs resulted in higher levels of task persistence than did exposure to the neutral programs. Another example of the potential prosocial effect of TV was provided by an evaluation of a *Lassie* program. First- and second-grade children exposed to a *Lassie* program containing a dramatic helping scene were more helpful in a test situation than were children exposed to scenes without helpful models (Sprafkin, Liebert, and Poulos, 1975).

210

Summary

Modeling is a phenomenon which was considered relatively unimportant until the past decade because many influential psychologists felt that stable learning required overt performance. However, in the early 1960s, it was repeatedly demonstrated that social learning resulted from simply observing models. Increases in behavior were considered under three rubrics: (1) acquisition effects, (2) disinhibitory effects, and (3) facilitation effects. The acquisition of novel behavior was exemplified by the development of speech in autistic children; disinhibitory effects were shown in programs to teach assertion and to encourage approach behavior of phobic clients; facilitation effects were illustrated by practical examples of tipping in restaurants and laughter in TV audiences. Decreases in behavior through modeling were considered under two rubrics: (1) inhibitory effects and (2) incompatible behavior effects. The inhibitory effect was illustrated by a program for teenage offenders in which prisoners depicted their life of misery and terror. The effects of modeling of incompatible behaviors have been demonstrated by the reduction of a wide variety of fears.

Covert modeling has been shown to be effective under certain conditions, but its efficacy with clinical populations has not been documented. Participant modeling in which a therapist models, guides, and shapes a client's behavior is a multifaceted treatment procedure which has proven more successful than modeling alone. Model, observer, and procedural factors were seen to influence modeling. Finally, the social impact of modeling research on TV programming and policy regarding aggression and women's roles, the influence of TV advertisements on children's behavior, and the prosocial effects of TV were considered.

Suggested Readings

Basic Principles:

ROSENTHAL, T. L., and BANDURA, A. 1978. Psychological modeling: Theory and practice. In *Handbook of psychotherapy and behavior change*, eds. S.L. Garfield and A. E. Bergin, rev. ed. New York: Wiley.

Clinical Applications:

KIRKLAND, K. D., and THELEN, M. H. 1977. Uses of modeling in child treatment. *Advances in clinical child psychology*, eds. B. B. Lahey and A. E. Kazdin, chap. 8. *Advances in clinical child psychology*, New York: Plenum.

Television Modeling:

LIEBERT, R. M., and POULOS, R. W. 1975. Television and personality development: The socializing effects of an entertainment medium. In *Child personality and psychopathology: Current topics,* ed. A. Davids. vol. 2. chap. 2. New York: Wiley.

8

Self-Control, Biofeedback, and Relaxation

Self-Control

The term *self-control* generally connotes self-restraint. When asked to describe individuals who exercise self-control, we often think of people who deny immediate gratification for the purpose of achieving a long-term goal. Individuals who study while others are having a party or while others are asleep appear to demonstrate self-control. When an aggressive child is very angry at another child but does not hit him or her, we say the child has exercised restraint or self-control. When we know that someone loves a particular dessert but refuses it in order to lose weight, we say the person is displaying self-control. The examples cited are consistent with dictionary definitions of self-control, which are "restraint exercised over oneself" and/or "restraint and coordination of one's acts and impulses." The more a person struggles in exercising restraint, the more likely we are to say he or she is exhibiting self-control. Let us consider some examples of self-controlling behaviors or strategies varying in difficulty that you might use to lose weight:

1. You buy dietetic ice cream at the grocery store.
2. You don't eat ice cream while preparing dinner.
3. You wait fifteen minutes after dinner to have your dessert (the ice cream).
4. You give yourself one scoop of ice cream instead of two scoops.

This hierarchy of self-controlling behaviors is arranged according to presumably increasing degrees of "struggle" that an individual would experience in controlling eating ice cream. The latter behaviors in this hierarchy may involve considerable struggle, but behavior therapists often see the "easy" behaviors as being more effective in controlling eating. Behaviors that occur early in a chain of behavior (not purchasing *any* ice cream or purchasing dietic ice cream) and that involve minimal struggle may be most effective in controlling our behavior, because we can perform them more reliably than we do ones involving great struggle.

While struggle may often be thought of as important in self-control, self-control does not necessarily involve a struggle. For example, a person who refrains from eating before going out for a gourmet dinner may exercise self-control without necessarily struggling. An author may set aside a particular time and place to write several pages of a novel, and such self-control may not involve any struggle. In brief, self-control may be exercised by some with ease and can be a pleasant and productive process. In fact, the most effective and relatively painless self-control may result from critical self-controlling action taken by individuals, long before they are placed in frustrating or tempting situations (for example, not taking money to the race track, not buying high calorie food, not drinking at all to preclude stripping or streaking at parties, refusing to even get involved minimally with a sexually appealing person when such a relationship might lead to intercourse and disaster!)

In addition to the issue of "struggle," psychologists have an ongoing debate regarding how important the "self" is in self-control. For example, Thoresen and Mahoney (1974) stated, "Self-control refers to changes in overt or covert behavior that are relatively independent of external forces." On the other hand, Skinner (1971) argued that most self-controlling behaviors can be linked directly to external influences rendering the "self" superfluous. Suppose that John Jones refuses a delicious dessert that he usually loves and states, "I can't eat this dessert because I want to lose a pound this week." Is John exhibiting self-control, or is he responding primarily to his wife's statement that he doesn't look as good as he did when she married him?

As we have seen repeatedly throughout this book, behavior is clearly influenced by the environment. However, we often arrange our own environment, and we respond to selected factors in our environment after evaluating the consequences our actions will have. The reciprocal influence process (Bandura, 1978) is depicted below with John Jones' behavior serving to illustrate the interdependencies of the roles of behavior, cognition, and the external environment. (See Fig. 8–1 below.)

Figure 8–1

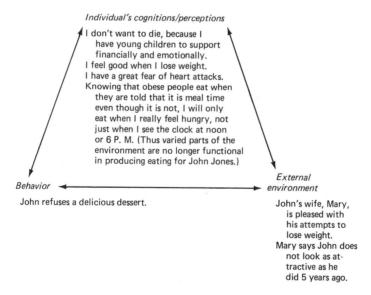

In the above framework, behavioral, cognitive, *and* environmental factors are interlocking determinants of one another. Thus, searches for either cognitive or environmental factors that are seen as sole determinants of an individual's behavior are here judged to be generally futile. In this interactional process, complex triadic influences are always operative in which events can be viewed as causes or effects depending upon where in the chain of events the analysis is begun.

Realizing that the analysis of behavior is an arbitrary one which can be initiated at different points, we have adopted the following definition of self-control: Self-control is a behavior change procedure that is initiated primarily by the individual for the purpose of influencing his or her own behavior. Conceptualizing any behavior as influenced by some admixture of internal and external variables can result in viewing behavior as ranging from being almost totally externally controlled (for example, blinking when a bright light is flashed in one's eyes) to being largely internally controlled (for example, self-instructions and meditation used to achieve relaxation). To study self-control in a meaningful sense, investigators have evaluated behavior change procedures that can be taught to an individual but which require the individual to initiate those procedures largely in the absence of external prompts and reinforcers. In line with the above conceptualizations, the fewer and less frequent the external prompts and reinforcers, the more we are apt to label the procedure a self-control technique.

RESEARCH AND CLINICAL TRENDS IN SELF-CONTROL

Much of the initial research in behavior therapy focused on methods of changing a client's environment in order to foster desired behavior. This focus led to behavior changes of clinical significance in children and adults who spent much of their time with key change agents (for example, ward attendants, teachers) who had control over reinforcers. Further, this emphasis on changing an individual's environment led to changes in behaviors of ecological import (for example, gas, electrical, and highway utilization). However, behavior therapy researchers now have an avowed concern with means of teaching self-control. Of course, good practitioners have long concerned themselves with a client's ability to manage his or her own behavior, and case studies and theoretical accounts of self-control or self-management have appeared sporadically in the behavior therapy literature since the early 1960s (for example, Cautela, 1967; Ferster, Nurnberger, and Levitt, 1962; Goldiamond, 1965; Homme, 1965). However, research on self-control has only recently begun to assume a central role in the behavior therapy literature.

Much of the best early research on self-control was designed to address questions about how one acquired self-control and to assess background factors that contributed to self-control (for example, type of parental discipline, adoption of interval standards, and modeling of self-reinforcement). That is, self-controlling behaviors were studied as dependent measures and the determinants of the self-controlling behaviors were examined (O'Leary and Dubey, 1979). More recently, clinical and educational researchers have studied what clients may do to influence their own behavior in a significant way. Thus, the behaviors individuals engage in for the purpose of influencing themselves are now studied as independent variables. Before we discuss how self-control procedures can be used in this latter sense, let us examine some of the reasons for the growing emphasis on self-control.

First, for a number of client problems, programs which rely solely on changes in external factors, such as reinforcement from others, do not result in maintenance of behavior changes when the programs are no longer in effect. For example, it is probable that token reinforcement programs for children in home and classroom settings will not be effective after the token reinforcement program is withdrawn unless there has been some emphasis on the development of self-control while the token program is in existence. Second, with outpatient adults, it is usually impossible to change external factors in their environment, such as their rewards (for example, paychecks and supervisory praise) and their punishments (loss of a sale, a transfer, or a demotion). Consequently, it is the therapist's role to teach clients how to alter their behavior and emotional reactions to certain events in the absence of systematic changes in the environment. Third, there is a very high value on self-control, as evidenced by the admiration we give to individuals who through their own apparent perseverance overcame great odds (for example, Abraham Lincoln and Helen Keller), and by the daily admiration we show to children, friends, colleagues, and relatives who complete tasks or meet challenges largely on their own. Among the numerous reasons why self-control is admired in others is the need to have people obey norms. If there were no self-control, the incidence of crime would be much higher. Furthermore, working for long-term goals is valued by society, as this is viewed as more productive than a hedonistic life style based on immediate gratification.

In behavioral treatment programs, both child and adult clients are taught that they must play an active part in determining their treatment goals and in implementing the treatment program. As noted in the case of Mr. B, the exhibitionist, in Chap. 1, clients must be involved in the treatment program, and they must be convinced that they have the potential to be an agent of change, not just the object or product of others' actions. Most importantly, in order to be able to obtain goals that we desire, we have to regulate our behavior in a fashion that is instrumental in achieving that result. Since we preside over our own activities, we are in an excellent position to influence our behavior through self-regulatory procedures.

The procedures that behavior therapists have generally included under self-control or self-management are stimulus control, self-selection of standards, self-instruction, self-recording, self-evaluation, and self-production of consequences. These procedures will be discussed in detail in this chapter. Cognitive restructuring procedures to be discussed in Chap. 9 are also methods of self-regulation, but they differ from the aforementioned procedures in that restructuring emphasizes the discovery and changing of illogical thinking and self-defeating verbalizations.

STIMULUS CONTROL

Stimulus control in a self-control paradigm refers to the rearrangement of environmental cues by an individual in order to prompt or reduce certain of his or her own behaviors. Stimulus control procedures have been used widely in programs that aid clients in reducing eating or smoking. As most individuals know, smoking may be prompted by seeing an ashtray or sitting in a chair that has been associated with smoking. Similarly, purchasing certain foods and eating can be influenced by environmental events such as attractive food displays.

In a classic study, Stuart (1967) designed a weight reduction program emphasizing—*among other tactics*—rearrangement of stimuli. A brief summary of some of his stimulus control procedures follows:

1. Remove food from all places in the house except the kitchen.
2. Try to keep foods which require some preparation.
3. Make eating a "pure experience," that is, not associated with other activities, such as reading, listening to the radio, or talking on the phone.

Stuart's weight control program was completed by eight obese women who lost an average of 38 pounds over 12 months of treatment. The *least* successful woman lost 26 pounds; the most successful lost 47 pounds (See Fig. 8–2 from Stuart). These weight losses were clearly dramatic, and this program served as the impetus both for studies on stimulus control factors associated with eating and for scores of treatment programs. Most subsequent behavioral treatment programs have not been as successful as Stuart's was. However, they have been consistently associated with significant, albeit modest, weight losses (that is, 11–12 lbs), that can be maintained over a one-year period (Jefferey, Wing, and Stunkard, 1978).

Similar stimulus control procedures have been used in programs to overcome insomnia. A brief summary of rules for establishing good sleep habits via stimulus control procedures follows (Coates and Thoresen, 1977). The rules involve many self-control factors, but a goal of the program is to establish the bed as a clear stimulus for sleep (of course, we realize that the bed often is a stimulus for more arousing and exciting physical endeavors than sleep).

SELF-SELECTION OF STANDARDS

Often when we decide to do certain tasks, such as jogging or studying, we set a goal or standard for ourselves, for example, I will run 1.5 miles; I will run 1 mile in 12 minutes; I will read twenty pages; I will write three paragraphs. There have been several studies regarding the effects of goal or standard setting, and it appears that goal setting per se is relatively ineffective or produces a transitory effect (Bandura and Perloff, 1967; Sagotsky, Patterson, and Lepper, 1978).

Using a somewhat different paradigm involving both goal setting and reinforcement, many studies have been conducted to compare the effects of self-determined and externally determined standards for reinforcement. The basic research design involves one individual or group of individuals who select their own standards for reinforcement, and another individual or group of individuals who have standards of reinforcement determined by the experimenter. An individual in the self-selection group decides how hard he or she wishes to work (for example, how many problems he or she wishes to complete) before receiving a reinforcer. A second individual is later given the same

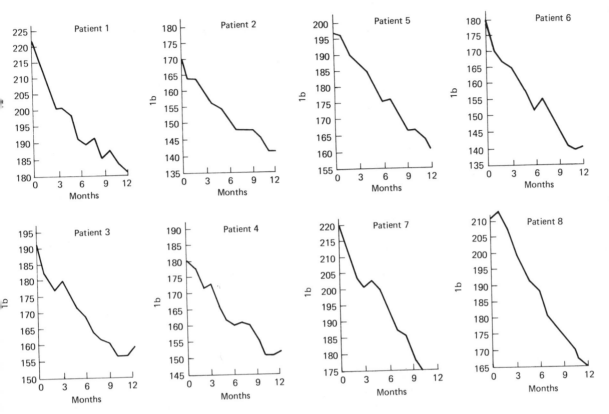

FIGURE 8.2
Weight profile of eight women undergoing behavior therapy for overeating. (Reprinted with permission from *Behaviour Research and Therapy*, 5, 357–364, Stuart, Richard B., Behavioral control of overeating. Copyright 1967, Pergamon Press, Ltd.)

standard for reinforcement as was chosen by the first. The standards that are externally imposed are yoked or matched to the self-selected standards to assure comparability. Studies in applied settings indicate that both self- and externally imposed standards of reinforcement increase selected performance, but the two methods do not differ from each other (Bandura and Perloff, 1967; Farnum, Brigham, and Johnson, 1977; Felixbrod and O'Leary, 1973; Frederiksen and Frederickson, 1975). However, on *some* laboratory tasks, self-determined reinforcement contingencies have been shown to produce greater resistance to extinction than externally determined contingencies (see Review by Rosenbaum and Drabman, 1978). Of special interest is the finding that children exposed to both self- and externally imposed reinforcement contingencies prefer self-determined contingencies (Felixbrod and O'Leary, 1974). However, if children are given the freedom to choose and repeatedly change their standards of reinforcement, they will generally select progressively more lenient standards (Felixbrod and O'Leary, 1973).

Bandura and Simon (1977) conducted a study to evaluate the effects of goal setting and simple monitoring of eating. They found that obese subjects who simply monitored food intake did not lose weight over a one-month period. In contrast, subjects who monitored food intake and, in addition, set weekly and/or daily goals did lose weight. It is important to note that when subjects who had lost weight in the goal-setting conditions failed to set goals even when continuing to record their food intake, they overate and failed to lose weight. Further, subjects who focused on long-range rather than immediate goals rarely lost weight.

The above finding is consistent with the use of immediate goal setting in many self-help programs. This strategy is probably best known through the program of Alcoholics Anonymous which emphasizes that the member should "take each day at a time." Goals, such as, "I will not drink for a year," are discouraged. Similar goal setting is used in the programs of Overeaters Anonymous and Weight Watchers.

SELF-INSTRUCTIONS

We all talk to ourselves. This talking takes many forms, but *self-instruction* refers to the self-talk which takes the form of prompts, guides, or demands (for example, I will not steal; I have to hold the bat more firmly; I have to make a line straight down and then put a line across the top [a youngster talking to himself while making a "T."]). Self-instructional training has been used to alter impulsive styles of aggressive and hyperactive children, cognitive functioning of schizophrenics, writing deficiencies of young children, and anger in adults (Meichenbaum, 1977).

Self-instructional training is well exemplified by Meichenbaum and Goodman's (1971) program for teaching impulsive children to modify their nonverbal behavior. The program included: (1) an adult modeling a task while talking to himself out loud; (2) the child performing the task under direction of the model (guidance from adult); and (3) the child performing the task while instructing himself aloud, and finally covertly. In a task which required copying lined patterns, the adult performed the task while modeling self-instructions as follows:

> Okay, what is it I have to do? You want me to copy the picture with the different lines. I have to go slowly and carefully. Okay, draw the line down, down, good; then to the right, that's it; now down some more and to the left. Good, I'm doing fine so far. Remember, go slowly. Now back up again. No, I was supposed to go down. That's okay. Just erase the line carefully. . . . Good. Even if I make an error I can go on slowly and carefully. I have to go down now. Finished. I did it! (Meichenbaum 1977, p. 32).

This training procedure, which emphasized self-instruction, resulted in significant improvement on tasks requiring fine motor coordination and reflective problem-solving skills. Further, in a second study Meichenbaum and Goodman (1971) found that simply modeling the self-instructions was not as effective as combining modeling and actual practice in implementing the self-instructions.

Many of the self-instructional training programs are multifaceted treatment programs in which self-instruction apparently plays a key role. The functional role of self-instructions per se, however, has rarely been documented in applied studies. In laboratory studies, however, self-instruction has been clearly linked to changes in moral behavior (O'Leary, 1968), increased tolerance of the dark (Kanfer, Karoly, and Newman, 1975), impulsivity (Bender, 1976), and resistance to temptation (Hartig and Kanfer, 1973). Self-instructions do not have much impact in other instances, such as on complex cognitive tasks like arithmetic and reading (Friedling and O'Leary, 1979). New Year's resolutions provide an example of self-instructions that are often ineffective. These instructions (for example, I will study more) may not change our behavior because we are not sufficiently committed to following them, because they are too general, and because they cover a very large time period that is too far in the future. Further, resolutions usually concern complex behaviors, and the component sets of skills, such as reading for main ideas, setting aside particular times and places for studying, and learning requisite background material, may not be established. Given the apparent variability in the effects of self-instructional training, it is important to specify both the advantages and limitations of the procedure. At present, we can state that self-instructions which guide or prompt behavior may be ineffective if the set of motor skills to be executed is very poorly established (for example, hitting a tennis ball). Additionally, self-instructions are likely to be ineffective if the motivation to perform the motoric behavior is minimal. However, self-instructions can serve an effective guidance or directive function when an individual is executing either simple motor tasks or more complex tasks for which the component skills are well established. They can also be used to help an individual remember how he or she is to proceed when a difficult set of instructions from someone else is to be followed (for example, a depressed person or an individual with a short attention span can repeat to himself or herself the instructions given by another person). In this case self-instructions are especially advantageous because they can be used by an individual at any time he or she so desires.

SELF-RECORDING AND SELF-EVALUATION

Self-recording refers to the monitoring of behavior that requires relatively simple judgments (for example, pages read, miles jogged, cigarettes smoked).

In contrast, *self-evaluation* refers to a procedure requiring an individual to make judgments about his or her behavior on a subjective basis (for example, evaluate your behavior on a 1–10 scale, evaluate your essay in terms of its creativity and organization). As Bandura and Simon (1977) noted, self-recording or self-evaluation alone is unlikely to have any appreciable impact on behavior unless internal positive or aversive contingencies become engaged in the activity. It is presumed that the consequence component of the activity induces the behavior change. For example, Ewart (1978) gave subjects positive, negative, and neutral evaluations of time awareness, defined as the frequency with which a person checks time. Time checking is easily self-observed, and it was found to be perceived as relatively neutral behavior before any experimenter evaluations were given. (Interestingly, undergraduate college students check the time of day approximately thirty-five times per day.) Following the request by the experimenter to self-record time checking and the introduction of positive, negative, and neutral evaluations, the subjects changed their time-checking behavior in accord with the evaluations of that behavior given by the experimenter.

An illustration of the effects of self-recording was provided by Romanczyk, Tracey, Wilson, and Thorpe (1973) and Romanczyk (1974), who found that when obese subjects simply recorded caloric intake and set proximal goals, they lost significant amounts of weight. In contrast, Mahoney, Moura, and Wade (1973) found no therapeutic value in simply self-recording or self-monitoring of caloric intake. Briefly, setting proximal goals appeared to be the critical facilitative difference in the two studies.

As noted earlier in this book (Chap. 2), self-recording is a procedure that has been used by famous novelists, such as Irving Wallace, author of *The Prize,* to prompt and reinforce their behavior. Of special interest is Wallace's comment that he never told anybody about his self-recording and daily charts of writing productivity because he "feared that their existence would be considered eccentric or unliterary." He stated:

> Once, long ago, deceived by the instructors, professors, by an old romantic tradition, I had believed that a writer writes only when he feels like it, only when he is touched by mystic inspiration. But then, after studying the work habits of novelists in the past, I realized that most successful writers invest their work with professionalism. . . . In short, no matter how they effected their routines, the vast majority of published authors have kept, and do keep, some semblance of regular daily hours. . . . Occasionally the hourkeepers were inspired when they went to their desks, but if they were not, they simply wrote as well as they could, as craftsmen, and hoped for the best. (Wallace 1977, pp. 518–19)

In sum, Wallace's comments highlight the use of self-recording by many creative writers to help them plan their writing and to facilitate productivity.

Self-evaluation refers to judgments of one's behavior on a subjective basis. As just discussed, self-evaluative behaviors may be influential in altering diverse behaviors because the evaluation serves to prompt other self-controlling behaviors, for example, positive self-statements. However, several studies have shown that when children are asked to evaluate their own behavior, the evaluations do not necessarily result in any behavior change—even though the evaluations are accurate (for example, Santogrossi and others, 1973). It may be the case that self-evaluation is effective only when the use of self-evaluative strategies is self-motivated, rather than when externally introduced. Alternatively, it may be that self-evaluation procedures, whether prompted by others or by oneself, are effective only when the individual engaging in the self-evaluative behavior desires to change the behavior which is the target of the self-evaluation. Clearly, self-evaluative control was critical in producing many revisions of this book, and our goal was to repeatedly improve our writing. In contrast, when children with severe behavior problems are asked to utter self-evaluative statements about their academic progress, if they don't care about improving such academic or social behavior, the self-evaluative comments may prove useless in altering their behavior.

Self-evaluation when combined with rewards for academic and social behavior has proven quite effective (Bolstad and Johnson, 1972; Drabman, Spitalnik, and O'Leary, 1973). For example, when children with severe emotional problems are taught to evaluate their classroom behavior on a 1–10 rating scale and are given feedback and rewards for appropriate evaluations and behavior, they can maintain the behavioral change that was effected through a token reinforcement program. Further, it appears that once accurate self-evaluation skills have been taught, changes in academic and social behavior may be maintained even after a token program is removed (Turkewitz, O'Leary, and Ironsmith, 1975; Wood and Flynn, 1978). Presumably, the children adopt some of the values that are being taught in the self-evaluation program.

SELF-ADMINISTERED CONSEQUENCES

Just as others react in ways which influence us, we also can provide ourselves with consequences which can change our own behavior. Such self-administered consequences may be overt or covert, as exemplified by the purchase or denial of an item or by a statement to oneself. These consequences generally occur in conjunction with goal setting and self-evaluation, although there are occasions when we can consequate our behavior even though we did not set particular goals, for example, when we accidentally make an error and then engage in self-punitive statements. Interestingly, some entertainers (for example, Sammy Davis, Jr.) or baseball players (for example, Lyman Bostock of the California Angels) have refunded money to night club patrons or have given their salary for a specific period to charity when they evaluated their own behavior as inferior (Nack, 1978).

Mahoney, Moura, and Wade (1973) studied the effects of self-reward, self-punishment, and self-monitoring on weight loss. Self-reward or self-punishment consisted of having subjects financially reward or fine themselves for progress or lack thereof at weekly weight checks (progress was defined as weight loss and adaptive behavior, such as "thin thoughts and restraint"). The money was initially obtained from the subjects who placed a deposit with the experimenter. If progress were made, subjects in the self-reward group asked to have money placed in an account for themselves, whereas self-punishment subjects fined themselves for lack of improvement, or weight gain, and the money was placed in a common subject pool. After four weeks of the intervention, the self-reward subjects lost more weight than did subjects in the self-monitoring group but not more than did the self-punishment subjects. However, at a four-month follow-up, the self-reward subjects had lost more weight than the self-punishment group. In a subsequent study, Mahoney (1974) compared the effects of (1) self-reward for weight loss, (2) self-reward for habit improvement, and (3) self-monitoring of weight loss and eating habits with a wait-list control group. All treatment groups received information about stimulus control techniques for weight loss, and they self-monitored their weight and eating habits. In addition, self-reward subjects awarded themselves portions of their own deposit for either weight loss (Group 1) or habit improvement (Group 2). Subjects who self-rewarded for habit improvement lost more weight and showed greater maintenance of weight loss than did subjects who rewarded weight loss or who simply self-monitored.

With regard to the two aforementioned studies, one may reasonably ask whether the obese subjects were free to reward themselves without external constraint or monitoring. In the Mahoney study, after the weigh-in, the subjects in the self-reward conditions

> had the opportunity to privately reinforce themselves by taking a special envelope from behind a large metal partition. Five envelopes containing cash and gift certificates from local stores were present. Although the experimenter could not monitor subjects' self-rewarding responses, an inventory of remaining envelopes after each subject's departure served as an objective index of this operation. (pp. 50–51)

While it was possible for the subjects to freely reward or fine themselves, they could have guessed that their self-rewarding behavior was being monitored—as in fact it was. Under the conditions described, transgressions defined as unmerited self-reward or self-denial were quite few and were most often self-denial transgressions. As mentioned in the introduction to this chapter, self-control refers to behavior that is *relatively* independent of external factors. In this sense, there is a continuum of control in which individuals and the environment always exert some influence on behavior, and it becomes important to assess when the individual is largely the influential factor in bringing about behavioral change. In the aforementioned study by Mahoney, the obese subjects had the opportunity to obtain rewards as they saw fit, but they were constrained by the amounts of money in the envelopes and their perception of being monitored. When children have the opportunity to maximize "rewards," and they perceive that there will be no aversive consequence for "free loading," or inappropriately awarding themselves points, they often do so (Santogrossi and others, 1973). When children and adolescents are taught self-evaluative and self-reinforcement skills *and* are intermittently checked for performing such skills accurately, the subjects show important changes in academic and social behavior (Santogrossi and O'Leary, 1978).

In summary, self-rewarding, like other self-controlling behaviors, is a function of a complex of behavioral, cognitive, and external factors. The less an individual's behavior results from external factors, the more likely we are to label the behavior self-control. In any self-reward study, individuals may perceive that their self-rewarding behavior is being monitored, so the interaction between external and internal factors is always present. Given this interaction, it would be useful for researchers who wish to argue that behavior changes were due to self-control to obtain subjects' perceptions of the extent to which they felt they were free to behave without external constraint in self-reinforcement studies.

SUMMARY: SELF-CONTROL

Research on self-control has developed at a very rapid pace in the past decade. This trend is in large part due to the frequent difficulty in obtaining maintenance of behavior following programs emphasizing external rewards. Self-control is best viewed as a behavior change procedure initiated primarily by the individual for the purpose of influencing his or her own behavior. While self-control has generally been divided into stimulus control, self-selection of standards, self-instruction, self-monitoring, self-evaluation, and self-reinforcement, it should be emphasized that these processes are often interactive. That is, when individuals monitor their own behavior, they usually engage in self-evaluative and self-reinforcing behaviors as well. Nonetheless, studies have been conducted in which the above types of self-control are isolated enough to make general conclusions about the relative efficacy of the various types of self-control. Self-selection of standards and self-instructions per se have been relatively ineffective in altering complex clinical problems over extended periods. On the other hand, impulsive cognitive styles and motoric tasks repeatedly have been influenced by self-instructions, and self-instructions should probably be used as adjunctive procedures in many treatment programs. Stimulus control has been used extensively in multifaceted treatment programs, and it is presumably an effective component of such programs. Self-recording has been effective in altering certain problems. probably because self-monitoring prompts self-evaluative and self-reinforcing contingencies. Self-administration of consequences generally occurs in combination with goal setting, and self-reinforcement, when combined with intermittent checking by others, has proven to be a useful treatment procedure.

Biofeedback

As mentioned in Chap. 4 on operant conditioning, classic experiments by Neal Miller and his colleagues in the 1960s indicated that visceral responses of animals, such as heart rate, blood pressure, and salivation, could be altered by making rewards and punishments contingent upon changes in these visceral responses. This research was especially important, and it generated excitement both in scientific and lay circles because it suggested that people could control a number of physiological responses formerly thought to be involuntary. In 1971, Benson, Shapiro, Tursky, and Schwartz reported that hypertensive patients had dramatically lower blood pressure after several weeks of training in which they received money as a reward for lowering blood pressure in the laboratory. To aid the patients in learning to lower their blood pressure, moment to moment feedback regarding their blood pressure level was provided which they termed *biofeedback*.

Since the early 1970s, rewards, punishments, and knowledge of physiological change have been called biofeedback, but more specifically, biofeedback refers to immediate feedback about a biological function provided by a device (Miller, 1978). Generally, this feedback is in the forms of lights, tones, and graphic displays of response patterns. Biofeedback has been used to help people correctly perceive both their visceral responses (for example, blood pressure, heart rate, and salivation) and skeletal musculature responses. Biofeedback is included in a chapter on self-control because it is a set of procedures used to enable individuals to control their own physiological responses.

Biofeedback has been heralded by some as a potential means of obtaining clinically significant changes in many disorders such as hypertension, migraine headaches, and hyperactivity, and biofeedback consulting firms and clinics have appeared in almost all major metropolitan areas of the United States. Further, biofeedback workshops are very popular among postgraduates in psychology and psychiatry. At this point, according to Miller, one of the foremost authorities in the world on biofeedback, although most clinical research on biofeedback has included controlled comparisons between biofeedback and other treatment procedures, the number of patients and the range of therapists employed in most studies are too small to enable practitioners to adopt treatment procedures without certain skepticism because of ambiguity regarding biofeedback's clinical efficacy (Miller, 1978; Blanchard and Young, 1974). The use of biofeedback will be illustrated in the treatment of three problems: hypertension, migraine headaches, and tension headaches.

HYPERTENSION

Hypertension, or high blood pressure, has been referred to as "the quiet killer" (*Time,* 1975), because most people with hypertension are unaware that they have it. However, it is estimated that 23 million Americans suffer from this condition which usually does not have obvious physical or psychological symptoms until clear damage occurs (for example, heart attack or stroke).

Research assistant, Martin Kluger, monitoring and adjusting biofeedback equipment.

There are two measurements of the force of blood against the walls of the arteries. The first pressure recorded is the pressure during the heart's contraction and is called the *systolic pressure;* the second pressure recorded is the pressure between heart beats when the heart is relaxed and is called the *diastolic pressure.* Normal blood pressure increases slightly with age but is about 120/80 for a person thirty-five years of age. Diastolic blood pressure is clinically significant since it is the most important predictor of heart attacks and strokes. When the blood pressure is greater than 140/90 at any age, a physician should be consulted (Byassee, 1977).

When high blood pressure is treated via biofeedback, information regarding blood pressure on each heart beat is given to patients by a special programmed apparatus (Shapiro and Surwit, 1976). The initial studies on biofeedback used normal subjects. Several different physiological responses were measured simultaneously, and the subjects' task was to make feedback in the forms of lights and tones occur as frequently as possible. Sometimes this feedback was given when their blood pressure was higher than their median; and sometimes, when it was lower, although the subjects were not told that feedback was being given to aid in decreasing or increasing blood pressure.

Using this method, subjects increased their diastolic blood pressure by 25 percent and reduced it by 15 percent (Shapiro, Schwartz, and Tursky, 1972). These data prompted clinical case study trials with hypertensive patients. For example, after seven weeks of daily recordings of blood pressure, Kristt and Engel (1975) trained four patients in a laboratory to voluntarily increase *and* decrease blood pressure for three weeks. All four patients were receiving antihypertensive medication. During twelve weeks of follow-up, patients took their blood pressure at home and were told to practice lowering it on a daily basis. The average decreases in systolic and diastolic pressure were 18.8 mm and 7.5 mm, respectively. At a three-month follow-up, three of the four patients had continually maintained their decreases in blood pressure. While medication was still necessary for these patients, the reductions in blood pressure were clearly significant.

Blanchard and Miller (1977) summarized the results of fourteen studies on the effects of biofeedback for hypertension. With one exception, all studies showed statistically significant *and* clinically significant decreases in blood pressure through the use of biofeedback. Both systolic and diastolic blood pressure changes occurred. Some of the patients were receiving antihypertensive medication, while others were not. With the exception of two studies, no adequate follow-up data were obtained. However, in informal follow-up evaluations of two studies, treatment gains had been lost at six-month follow-up. In brief, biofeedback can induce changes in blood pressure, but special programs must be followed to enable patients to maintain such gains.

Despite the clear successes obtained with biofeedback in lowering blood pressure (Tarler-Benlolo, 1978), there also have been failures in treating hyper-

Subject in biofeedback laboratory at State University of New York at Stony Brook. Finger pulse volume (blood flow) and finger temperature were recorded from index fingers. EMG was recorded from fontalis muscle.

tensives with biofeedback (Blanchard, 1979; Surwit, Shapiro, and Good, 1978). It may be that some of the failures are a function of the type of instrumentation used to provide patients with feedback. Alternatively, differences in patient populations, length of subject adaptation to having blood pressure measured, and therapists' belief in the efficacy of biofeedback may account for some of the treatment failures. Whatever the reasons for the failures, biofeedback must be viewed with considerable caution as a singular treatment for patients with severe hypertension (Birbaumer, 1977; Blanchard, 1979; Miller, 1978). It is often recommended, however, as an adjunctive treatment with medication.

MIGRAINE HEADACHES

A *migraine* is a pulsating, severe, sometimes excruciating, headache which is often accompanied by visual distortion, vomiting, and motor imbalance. Migraine headaches occur most frequently in women and are often associated with stress and menstrual period onset. It is generally felt that the discomfort is caused by dilation of arteries, thus increasing blood flow to the brain— particularly dilation of extracranial arteries of the temporal area.

Biofeedback treatment of migraine headaches has been designed to teach patients to warm their hands through temperature feedback. It is theorized that the hand warming is associated with increased blood flow to the hands which in turn leads to a lessening of arterial pressure in the brain.

Treatment of migraine is well illustrated in a study by Blanchard, Theobald, Williamson, Silver, and Brown (1978) who compared the effects of biofeedback, relaxation training, and a wait-list control group. Thirty patients with frequent migraine headaches were assigned to one of the three aforementioned conditions. The essence of the biofeedback treatment involved hand warming by temperature biofeedback and practice of this exercise at home for six weeks. Relaxation followed the standard Jacobsen relaxation procedure described in Chap. 6. Patients were asked to practice the relaxation exercises daily for six weeks. The wait-list control group simply recorded their headaches for six weeks, after which they began treatment in either biofeedback or relaxation. At the end of treatment, on measures of headache duration and intensity, both treated groups improved, while the wait-list control group did not. All three groups showed a significant reduction in headache frequency. The relaxation subjects initially improved more than the biofeedback subjects, but three months after treatment, there was no difference in the relaxation and biofeedback groups. This lack of a difference led the authors to conclude that the common ingredient of the two treatments is to teach the patients to relax and to assume a calm relaxed attitude.

TENSION HEADACHES

According to survey results reported by Kashiwagi, McClure, and Wetzel (1972), 50 to 70 percent of adults experience headaches, 40 percent of which are tension headaches. "Tension headache is typically characterized by persistent sensations of bandlike pain or tightness located bilaterally in the occipital

---

Box 8–2   *The Emerging Field of Behavioral*
Medicine

The recent renewal of interest in the impact of psychological and social factors on physical diseases has been fostered in part by advances in biofeedback. This interest is illustrated by the formation of new journals (for example, *Journal of Behavioral Medicine,* 1978) and the establishment of the Academy of Behavioral Medicine Scientists in 1978. In a recent editorial by Schwartz and Weiss (1977) in *Psychosomatic Medicine,* they noted that behavioral medicine has been stimulated by input from behavioral sciences, especially learning, biofeedback methodology, basic research on psychophysiology, and social and clinical psychology. Behavioral medicine is concerned directly with treatment and, importantly, with prevention of physical disease. Further, Schwartz and Weiss (1977) contended that the emergence of behavioral medicine will prompt a greater degree of cooperation and collaboration between behavioral and biomedical sciences than did psychosomatic medicine which was developed primarily from the psychoanalytic theories of Freud.

---

and/or forehead regions. It is gradual in onset and may last for hours, weeks, or even months" (Holroyd, Andrasik, and Westbook 1977, p. 121). Tension headaches are less severe than migraine headaches and usually they are not accompanied by visual distortion, nausea, and motor imbalance. The exact etiology of tension headaches is not clear,[1] but in the past there has seemed to be general agreement that it might result from sustained contraction of skeletal muscles of the face, scalp, neck, and shoulders (Bakal, 1975; Martin, 1972) in response to psychological distress (Ad Hoc Committee on the Classification of Headache, 1962; Wolff, 1963).

Biofeedback treatment of tension headaches has generally been seen as one of the most successful applications of biofeedback (Birbaumer, 1977). This treatment involves auditory or visual feedback regarding muscle tension called electromyographic feedback (EMG feedback; Budzynski and Stoyva, 1969). An important early study illustrating the clinical value of biofeedback was conducted by Budzynski, Stoyva, and Adler (1970), who used EMG feedback from the frontalis muscle area (forehead) with five patients. A shaping procedure was used in which a continuous tone informed them of reductions in muscle tension, and as progress occurred, the feedback was faded. Thirty-minute training sessions were conducted from one to two months, and patients were told to practice relaxation at home once a day. All five patients had significant reductions both in frontalis EMG levels and head-

---

[1]Empirical differentiation of migraine and tension headaches is very meager, and classic assumptions about such headaches were questioned by Philips (1978).

232

aches, and the results were maintained at a three-month follow-up.

In order to isolate critical ingredients of biofeedback treatments, like those just mentioned, Cox, Freundlich and Meyer (1975) compared the effects of EMG feedback and relaxation, progressive relaxation alone, and a placebo (glucose capsule) treatment with three groups of patients. On the basis of frontalis EMG recordings, headache frequency and duration, and amount of medication needed, the biofeedback and relaxation groups were superior to the placebo groups, although they were not different from one another.

Holroyd, Andrasik, and Westbrook (1977) compared the efficacy of frontalis EMG biofeedback training with "Stress Coping Training" for tension headaches. Stress Coping Training emphasized that tension headaches result from stress and that stress responses are determined by cognitions about an event. Unreasonable expectations (for example, I should be perfect and liked by everyone) were discussed and viewed as stress-producing. Clients were encouraged to view their headaches as being due to "cognitive aberrations," rather than due to external factors or an inner disposition to become stressed. They were also taught to employ self-statements designed to minimize stress (for example, calm down; concentrate on the present; there is no point in catastrophizing). The biofeedback and Stress Coping Training groups were compared with a wait-list control group; only the Stress Coping group showed a significant decrease in headache frequency as compared to the wait-list group.

Although there are certain methodological problems with the Holroyd study, such as having the senior therapists conduct the stress training and having laboratory assistants conduct the biofeedback training, the value of cognitively oriented treatments for tension headaches is apparent. In addition, the findings that only the biofeedback group showed significant reductions in frontalis EMG activity and that reduction in frontalis tension was not associated with headache improvement for either treatment group raise serious questions about the particular type of biofeedback training for tension headache sufferers. This concern was echoed by Philips (1977) who questioned the role of muscular contraction as the major cause of most tension headaches, because she also found low correlations between level of muscle tension and headaches. As she noted, "Tension headaches are heterogeneous in respect to the implicated muscle and in the way in which the muscular abnormality is manifested (at rest, in reaction, or both)" (p. 119). While biofeedback procedures have proven effective with certain individuals suffering from tension headaches, the causes of tension headaches are not clear. Many individuals appear to suffer from a combination of tension *and* migraine headaches which may require different treatments than tension headaches alone. Further, cognitive factors may play a much more important role than previously assumed.

The need for differential treatment of tension and migraine headaches that occur in the same individuals is well illustrated by Sturgis, Tollison,

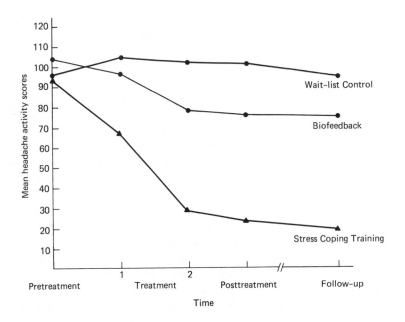

FIGURE 8.3
Mean weekly headache activity scores in 2-week blocks. (*From* Holroyd, K., Andrasik, F., Westbrook, T. Cognitive control of tension headaches, in *Cognitive Therapy and Research,* 1, 121–133. New York: Plenum, 1977.)

and Adams (1978). With two subjects, they showed how migraine headaches decreased with reductions of blood volume pressure in the temporal artery, and muscle contraction headaches decreased with decrements in frontalis muscle activity. Both subjects learned to control blood volume pulse (BVP) during BVP feedback and frontalis muscle action potention (EMG) during EMG feedback, but their tension or migraine headaches decreased only when they received biofeedback training relevant to the presumed etiological cause of the headache, namely, muscle contraction or blood volume pressure.

Relaxation

The rapidly growing interest in methods of relaxing and meditating has popularized Zen, yoga, Transcendental Meditation, and progressive relaxation. Behavior therapists have relied heavily on the use of progressive relaxation, which Wolpe adapted from Jacobson (1938), for treating anxiety, tension, insomnia, fears, and tics. The reasons for its use by behavior therapists are clear: it is generally effective; it is easy to teach; and clients usually find it enjoyable and helpful.

Progressive relaxation consists of teaching an individual to alternately tense and relax different muscle groups of the body in a systematic fashion. By engaging in this tensing-relaxing procedure, the person learns to become especially attentive to feelings of tension and to substitute feelings of relaxation for the tense state. The four major muscle groups that an individual learns to relax are: (a) hands and arms; (b) head, face, and throat; (c) shoulders, chest, and stomach; and (d) legs and feet. The following excerpt from the instructions for progressive relaxation training adapted from Arnold Lazarus (1971) illustrates learning to relax the hands:

> Now, settle back as comfortably as you can, close your eyes, and listen to what I'm going to be telling you. I'm going to make you aware of certain sensations in your body and then show you how you can reduce these sensations. First direct your attention to your left arm, your left hand in particular. Clench your left fist. Clench it tightly and study the tension in the hand and in the forearm. Study those sensations of tension. And now let go. Relax the left hand and let it rest on the arm of the chair. And note the difference between the tension and the relaxation. (10-second pause) Once again now, clench your left hand into a fist, tightly, noticing the tensions in the hand and in the forearm. Study those tensions, and now let go. Let your fingers spread out, relaxed, and note the difference once again between muscular tension and muscular relaxation. (Goldfried and Davison, 1976, p. 88)

Learning to regulate one's breathing is an important element in progressive relaxation. This technique is illustrated in the following excerpt from progressive relaxation training for the chest and stomach muscles:

> And now, take a deep breath, filling your lungs, and hold it. Hold it and study the tension all through your chest and down into your stomach area. Study that tension, and now relax, let go. Exhale and continue breathing as you were. Note once again the difference between the tension and the relaxation. (Goldfried and Davison, 1976, p. 91)

Once the person has learned to relax in this manner, the next stage involves relaxing without first tensing the muscles; in this stage relaxation is achieved by simply "letting go" and relaxing the muscles directly. The person is encouraged to associate a word, such as "calm" or "relax," with the experience of complete relaxation. In particular, this word is paired with controlled breathing, that is, with exhaling after a deep breath. Relaxation can also be facilitated by having the person imagine a pleasant, calming scene. Finally, the person is taught to extend relaxation skills gradually into everyday activities. The ultimate goal is for the person to use these newly acquired relaxation skills to remain relatively calm in the face of anxiety-evoking situations. Relaxation has been used to alter many clinical problems, but its use with hypertension and insomnia will be discussed here.

HYPERTENSION

Jacob, Kraemer, and Agras (1977) reviewed the effects of relaxation and relaxationlike procedures (for example, meditation) in the treatment of hypertension. They found that relaxation procedures resulted in significantly greater reductions in blood pressure than placebo or other control procedures. Further, they found that the magnitude of reductions in blood pressure were clinically significant, and the reductions compared favorably with reductions found with antihypertensive medication. Relaxation led to clinically significant reductions in both systolic and diastolic blood pressure of patients on hypertensive medication. Such reductions persisted six months following treatment (-18 mm systolic, -10 mm diastolic; Brauer and others, in press). At present, relaxation therapy has not been evaluated well enough to know whether it can replace pharmacological therapy, for, like biofeedback, it is not known whether relaxation therapy leads to reductions in blood pressure in situations other than those where the blood pressure measurements are taken. As Jacob and others (1977) noted, 24-hour measurements of blood pressure are needed to clearly assess the magnitude and generalizability of effects of relaxation therapy. At a minimum, however, relaxation is a very useful adjunct to medication in the treatment of hypertension in patients whose blood pressure remains high despite medication.

    Little research has been conducted regarding the critical components of relaxation therapy for hypertensive patients, but muscular relaxation, mental focusing, and task awareness appear to be the most important ingredients. In the laboratory, task awareness in the form of expectation of success and knowledge of the goal of treatment appear to be especially important. Redmond, Gaylor, and McDonald (1974) simply instructed hypertensive patients to raise and lower their blood pressure without being in a state of deep muscular relaxation. The patients could alter their own systolic and diastolic blood pressures as a result of instructions alone. Interestingly, patients reported that they used mental imagery to aid them in changing their blood pressure. For example, they visualized themselves in stimulating situations to help them increase blood pressure and in relaxing situations, such as, lying on the beach, to help them decrease their blood pressure. This finding highlights the use of cognitive mediational activities to change behavior. However, given the superiority of relaxation therapy when compared with control procedures, such as instructions to self-induce blood pressure changes in whatever way possible, Jacob and others (1977) concluded that task awareness of the purpose of the study and self-induced attempts to use imagery to lower

Box 8–3 *The Relaxation Response*

Relaxation became well known to many with the publication of the book *The Relaxation Response* by Herbert Benson in 1975. Benson was one of the first investigators to utilize biofeedback with hypertension (Benson and others, 1971). In numerous experiments on biofeedback with hypertensives, Benson and his collaborators found that subjects said they lowered their blood pressure by simply relaxing. Given the reports of these subjects, the high cost of biofeedback equipment, and the fact that only one physiological response can be efficiently monitored at a time, relaxation alone was evaluated for its clinical efficacy. Of course, relaxation is not a discovery of this century. Zen, yoga, and Transcendental Meditation have long been known for their relaxation effects. However, it was not until the past decade that systematic physiological and psychological data have been gathered with subjects using varied methods of obtaining a relaxed state.

Devotees of Transcendental Meditation approached Benson to be studied in his laboratory. He found that with a relatively simple meditation procedure in which a secret word, or *mantra,* is repeated over and over again while sitting in a comfortable position, subjects showed decreases in oxygen consumption, respiratory rate, heart rate, and blood pressure (in patients with initially high blood pressure). Consequently, the commonalities in various cultural ways of achieving tranquillity were studied, and the following four elements were found to be crucial in obtaining what Benson called

The Relaxation Response:

1. A quiet environment.
2. Something to dwell on (for example, directing one's attention to a sound, a feeling, or an object).
3. A passive attitude (while thoughts and feelings may drift into awareness, they should not become the focus of concentration but be allowed to pass on).
4. A comfortable position.

There is little controlled research comparing the progressive relaxation procedures described by Jacobson (1938) and the relaxation method outlined by Benson which does not include tensing and relaxing of various muscle groups. However, initial research provides suggestive evidence for the efficacy of relaxation without muscle tensing for decreasing smoking, drinking, and hypertension (Benson, 1975; Surwit, Shapiro, and Good, 1978), and the practice of meditation and relaxation is viewed quite positively by subjects (Marlatt and Marques, 1977).

blood pressure cannot account for the entire relaxation therapy effect.

The role of therapist factors in relaxation for hypertensives was illustrated by Brauer and others (in press). They compared the effects of therapist-conducted relaxation, identical relaxation procedures implemented in the home by use of audio cassettes, and nonspecific individual psychotherapy which largely involved talking about stress. The therapist-conducted relaxation group showed the greatest reductions in blood pressure. Further, patients of experienced therapists showed greater reductions in blood pressure than patients of an inexperienced therapist.

INSOMNIA

Millions of dollars are spent on sedatives, tranquilizers, and nonprescription sleeping pills to enable people to cope with *insomnia,* or the inability to sleep. Nonetheless, the nonprescription nostrums are generally short-lived, and some of the prescription sleeping aids have clearly addictive characteristics. Furthermore, many individuals experience an *increase* in insomnia when sleeping medication is withdrawn; and concern that this may happen serves to increase psychological stress while the individual is taking medication. Another effect of sleeping medication is a suppression of the relative amount of Rapid Eye Movement sleep (REM). REM sleep is sometimes called paradoxical sleep (Jouvet, 1967) because the large muscles are deeply relaxed while electroencephalographic (EEG) activity closely resembles waking patterns. When subjects are awakened during periods of REM sleep, they report to be dreaming more often than when awakened during other stages of sleep (Dement and Kleitman, 1957). When medication is withdrawn, the percentage of REM sleep increases sharply, and some clinicians have reported this "rebound" effect to be associated with an increase in dreams and nightmares (Coates and Thoresen, 1977). In short, sedatives and tranquilizers have serious side effects and are viewed by many physicians and psychologists as the most overprescribed drugs (Walen, Hauserman, and Lavin, 1977). Sleeping medication is best used as a means of enabling an individual to cope with stress over a short period, rather than as a means of enabling people to cope with chronic insomnia.

In a review of the sleep literature, Bootzin and Nicassio (1978) concluded that relaxation has clearly been demonstrated to result in improvement among mild to severe cases of insomnia. Unfortunately, the majority of studies have used only self-report measures of sleep onset and latency. Borkovec, Grayson, O'Brien, and Weerts (1979) stated that reliance on such measures may have been a serious methodological error, since Dement (1972) found that approximately 50 percent of his self-described insomniacs showed few sleep deficits when measured by EEG criteria. That is, while all his subjects reported requiring a long time to fall asleep and sleeping very little throughout the night, 50 percent of the subjects' EEGs revealed sleep onset and activity close to normal limits. These individuals were thus called "pseudoinsomniacs."

In order to assess differential treatment effects on objectively and subjectively defined sleep deficits, Borkovec and others (1979) classified subjects as pseudoinsomniacs and idiopathic insomniacs (cases in which EEG measurements are in accord with subjective complaints). Subjects were assigned to one of the following conditions: progressive relaxation training, no-tension-release relaxation training (a procedure identical to progressive relaxation but omitting muscle tension-release), and no treatment. As predicted, relaxation without muscle tensing influenced self-reports of sleep latency and onset in both pseudoinsomniacs and idiopathic insomniacs. However, only relaxation training with muscle tensing improved objective measures of sleep in the idiopathic insomniacs. Thus, future research should utilize both objective and subjective measures of sleep disturbances.

DIVERSE CLINICAL APPLICATIONS OF BIOFEEDBACK AND/OR RELAXATION

Relaxation and biofeedback have been used to aid individuals with a host of problems too long to be reviewed here. Instead, the diversity of applications briefly noted below illustrates typical problems being treated.

Myopia. Biofeedback and instructions to relax the muscle around the eyes both appear to be procedures which enable near-sighted individuals (myopes) to increase their visual acuity from 15 to 50 percent. At certain times, some subjects have even demonstrated changes in acuity as much as 100 percent (see Lanyon and Giddings, 1974, for review).

General tension and anxiety. Progressive relaxation has been used effectively in the treatment of pervasive, yet mild, cases of tension (Borkovec, Grayson, and Cooper, 1978). With only four sessions of training, subjects reported significant reductions in tension which were maintained at seven-month follow-up. Similarly, subjects showed significant reductions in anxiety after four sessions of progressive relaxation training (Lehrer, 1978). Relaxation can be used as a general means of coping with stress, and when combined with an analysis of one's self-management and beliefs and standards, it can be a very useful procedure for individuals who simply feel stressed by their normal routines (Woolfolk and Richardson, 1978). More specifically, tension can often be reduced by a lowering of one's expectations about what should be done each day and an increased belief in the value of recreation and relaxation.

Bruxism. The nonfunctional gnashing and grinding of teeth, sometimes occurring during sleep, is called *bruxism.* Such grinding often results in abnormal wear on the teeth and damage to the structures surrounding the teeth. Biofeedback regarding the musculature surrounding the mastication area combined with relaxation has been used successfully in one study using self-reporting of grinding (see Glaros and Rao, 1977, for review of bruxism). While promising, these results need to be replicated with objective measures.

Snoring. The intensity of snoring has been reduced by immediate feedback in the form of a loud noise. Of course, the noise initially disrupts one's sleep (as well as others' if in the same room), but the individual can learn to snore less intensely in as few as fourteen biofeedback sessions (Josephson and Rosen, 1978).

Neuromuscular disorders. Some individuals with abnormal muscle activity in the form of spasms and tremors have been aided by biofeedback. While the evidence is still suggestive of the clinical efficacy of biofeedback with muscular problems, experts agree that it has clear and perhaps unique value with this problem (Birbaumer, 1977; Miller, 1978).

Aggression. Relaxation can be used as a means of helping an individual stop a reaction to frustration, such as hitting or name-calling, after which social problem solving can be used to help choose appropriate responses to the situation (Robin, Schneider, and Dolnick, 1976).

SUMMARY: BIOFEEDBACK AND RELAXATION

Biofeedback has been an especially important development, because its use with humans clearly illustrates the viability of teaching individuals to control physiological responses formerly thought to be involuntary. Biofeedback has proven useful for patients with hypertension, migraines, and tension headaches, but because of the patients' reports that relaxation was important in their improvement, relaxation in many forms has become a critical research and clinical focus. Relaxation has proven clinically effective in the treatment of a host of problems including hypertension and insomnia, and relaxation will probably be used much more frequently than biofeedback in the future for many clinical problems, because it can be used more readily than biofeedback which involves very costly equipment. Instead of being seen as an all-purpose treatment procedure, biofeedback is now beginning to be viewed as a scientific methodology for investigating the relationships between physiology and behavior under tightly controlled laboratory circumstances (Lang, 1976). In both relaxation and biofeedback procedures, cognitive mechanisms, such as self-suggestion and expectation, have yet to be systematically evaluated. Since it has been known for years that individuals can significantly alter the skin temperature of their limbs (the procedure used to treat migraine) under suggestion to do so (Barber, 1976), clients' cognitive activities (for example, thinking my hand is under a heat lamp or in a bucket of cold water) will probably become a more frequent focus of biofeedback and relaxation research.

Suggested Readings

Self-control:

STUART, R. B. 1977. *Behavioral self-management: Strategies, techniques, and outcomes.* New York: Brunner/Mazel.

MAHONEY, M. J., and THORESEN, C. E. 1974. *Self-control: Power to the person.* Monterey, California: Brooks-Cole.

Biofeedback:

STOYVA, J., ed. 1978. *Biofeedback and self-control.* Chicago, Illinois: Aldine.

MILLER, N. E. 1978. Biofeedback and visceral learning. *Annual Review of Psychology* 29:373–404.

Relaxation:

BENSON, H. 1975. *The relaxation response.* New York: Avon.

GOLDFRIED, M. R., and DAVISON, G. C. 1976. *Clinical behavior therapy.* New York: Holt, Rinehart, and Winston.

9

Cognitive Learning Therapies

Psychology, it has been recently said, has "gone cognitive" (Dember, 1974). Judging from the theoretical and clinical literature, much of behavior therapy seems to have followed suit. The term "cognitive" refers to private or internal processes such as imagery, symbolic representation of external events, and verbal coding of experience. The emphasis on these cognitive factors in behavior therapy has been the most distinctive feature of behavior therapy in the 1970s. The terms "cognitive behavior therapy" and "cognitive behavior modification" are frequently used to describe this recent development. A new journal devoted exclusively to this approach has been founded,[1] and several books on the subject are still hot off the press.

In fact, the major shift in behavior therapy from an S–R psychology dominated by animal conditioning models to a more cognitive framework was formally ushered in by Bandura's (1969) influential book. During the late 1960s several developments had emphasized the limitations of a strict conditioning approach and resulted in increased interest in cognitive mechanisms (for example, Davison, 1969; Lang, 1969; Lazarus, 1968; Mischel, 1968; Peterson, 1968).

In this chapter we shall examine the role of cognitive factors in behavior therapy, describe the most important methods of "cognitive behavior therapy," and evaluate its theoretical claims and empirical foundations. Not all of behavior therapy has embraced this cognitive connection, and radical behavioristic objections to this development are reviewed. Finally, the question is raised whether emphasis on cognitive factors provides a bridge or merger between behavior therapy and traditional psychotherapy.

Cognitive Processes and Behavioral
Treatment Procedures

In earlier chapters we have indicated that recent analyses of many behavior therapy procedures have increasingly emphasized the role of cognitive mediating processes as explanatory mechanisms (Bandura, 1977b; Brewer, 1974; Bower, 1978). This emphasis on cognitive factors has been especially marked in the self-control techniques (for example, Mahoney and Arnkoff, 1978) and those methods based on vicarious learning (for example, Rosenthal and Zimmerman, 1978). However, in terms of social learning theory, cognitive processes are seen to play an important part even in behavior therapy techniques that are based on classical and operant conditioning procedures.

In Chap. 4, it was pointed out that reinforcement does not involve an

---

[1]This new journal is entitled *Cognitive Therapy and Research* (Mahoney, 1977) and may be contrasted with the title of the first behavioral journal, *Behaviour Research and Therapy* (Eysenck and Rachman, 1963).

automatic strengthening of behavior and that learning from response consequences is attributable to the informative and incentive functions of rewards.
By observing the consequences of behavior, the person learns what action is
appropriate in what situation. By symbolic representation of anticipated future
outcomes of behavior, the person helps to generate the motivation to initiate
and sustain current actions. In Chap. 6, it was pointed out that classical
conditioning in people usually requires that the person realize that the two
stimuli are correlated. Simple contiguity between two stimuli is not enough.
Thus a conditioned stimulus does not automatically control the response;
rather, it enables the person to predict the occurrence of the correlated event.
In this cognitive formulation the influence of the conditioned stimulus cannot
be understood without taking account of the person's active appraisal of the
nature of that stimulus.

Behavior change that takes place as a result of the association of two
stimuli (classical conditioning) or the link between a response and its environmental consequences (operant conditioning) often appears to be dependent
upon the cognitive representation of the contingencies. An example of the
overriding importance of the cognitive representation of a contingency is
described in Box 9–1. This study by Moore, Mischel, and Zeiss (1976) shows
that the manner in which children cognitively represent rewards is a significantly more potent determinant of self-control behavior than is the actual
reward stimulus to which the child is physically exposed. It is not the objective
reality of *what* the child sees but *how* the child perceives the reward that
governs behavior. The findings of this study illustrate a fundamental principle
of human learning: that we tend to react, not to the *actual* environment, but
to the environment as we *perceive* it. It follows from this principle that by
altering the way in which the environment is perceived, behavior can be
changed. Remember the use of the method of symbolic stimulus transformation in the case of Mr. B, the exhibitionist (Chap. 1). Since Mr. B could expose
himself early if the woman was unknown to him, the therapist taught him to
imagine that she was talking to him and telling him about herself. Clearly not
all problem behaviors can be overcome by simple cognitive transformation of
powerful environmental stimuli, such as alcohol-related situations in the case
of the alcoholic or food for an obese person. Nonetheless, it must be remembered that it is not always necessary to alter the environment in order to modify
behavior. The importance of this principle in therapeutic intervention is documented throughout this chapter.

This recent emphasis on cognitive factors in behavior therapy has been
criticized by some behaviorists as a step in the wrong direction (for example,
Catania, 1975; Ledwidge, 1978; Wolpe, 1976). According to this view, the use
of cognitive concepts is at best, irrelevant to the development of a true science
of human behavior; at worst, an emphasis on unobservable cognitive processes
is regarded as a potential hindrance to the development of effective forms of
treatment. Clearly, the inclusion of unobservable cognitive processes in an
applied science, such as behavior therapy, must be approached with all due

In a study of self-control processes, specifically the ability to delay gratification, Moore, Mischel, and Zeiss (1976) allowed children (mean age four years, eight months) to choose between two rewards. In order to obtain the preferred reward, a subject had to wait alone until the experimenter, who had left the room, returned. However, the child could obtain the less preferred reward at any time by ringing a bell that would immediately recall the experimenter. In other words, the children were faced with a common choice: a less attractive but *immediate* reward or a more attractive but *delayed* reward. (For the overweight person, this translates into a piece of appetizing pie now or weight loss later; for the cigarette smoker, it is the immediate satisfaction of a cancer-causing cigarette or the benefit of sensible health care by refusing to smoke; and for the overburdened college student, it is the dilemma of goofing off tonight and not studying for a psychology exam or staying home, studying, and obtaining a good grade.)

There were four major experimental conditions during the experimenter's absence: in two conditions, the children were instructed to see what was placed in front of them—either the *actual* rewards or a *picture* of the two rewards. In the other two conditions, children were instructed to transform the reward stimuli in front of them, cognitively representing the actual rewards as pictures, the pictures as actual rewards. The main measure in this study was the time elapsed from the moment the experimenter left the room to the point where each subject rang the bell (or waited for a maximum of 20 minutes).

Previous research had clearly established that allowing children to see the actual rewards during the delay period (that is, when they were trying to make a choice) greatly decreased the amount of time children would wait. Yet this same research, for reasons that are not relevant to this discussion, showed that presenting children with a picture of the rewards during the delay period produced a sizeable increase in the length of time they would wait.

The results of this study showed that *what* was in front of the children —either the actual rewards or a picture of the rewards—had little effect on their behavior. The important finding was that *how* the children cognitively construed the rewards had a significant effect on their behavior. Children who were instructed to imagine that they were seeing a picture of the rewards waited much longer than children instructed to imagine that they were seeing the actual rewards, irrespective of what was in front of them. Simply asking these young children to transform an actual reward stimulus into a picture of that stimulus in their mind significantly changed their delay of gratification. These results provide strong support for the powerful role of cognitive representational processes in self-regulation.

caution. However, provided that terms are well-defined, all treatment procedures are carefully specified and replicable, and therapeutic claims are subjected to rigorous experimental evaluation, there would seem to be no problem in including cognitive processes in behavior therapy. Indeed, investigating psychological phenomena along scientific lines like this is in the best tradition of *methodological* behaviorism. In the long run, the test of whether it is useful to emphasize cognitive factors in the explanation and application of behavior therapy techniques will be whether they generate innovative and effective treatment strategies and expand our capability to treat a broader range of clinical problems than would otherwise be the case. In the remainder of this chapter, we describe the current "cognitive connection" in behavior therapy and evaluate the success of the treatment methods it has generated. It will be suggested that the emphasis on cognitive factors has given rise to important experimental research and innovative clinical strategies. These cognitive learning strategies have already proved to be useful and show promise of still further theoretical and therapeutic advances.

Covert[2] Conditioning Methods

In previous chapters a number of behavior change techniques have been described that are usually referred to as *covert conditioning methods.* The distinguishing feature of these techniques is that either the antecedent stimuli, the target responses, or the reinforcing consequences exist only in symbolic form. In systematic desensitization, for instance, clients are instructed to imagine the phobic stimulus and treatment proceeds according to their self-report of the fear that is elicited by this imagery. Imaginal representation of the stimulus object or event is frequently used in aversive counterconditioning, while in covert sensitization, the stimulus (for example, a bottle of alcohol), the response (for example, consuming the alcohol), and the aversive consequences (for example, nausea) are all symbolic events that are conjured up by the client in the form of imagery. Similarly, covert modeling entails the client's imagining a model performing a specific target behavior followed by reinforcing consequences. Several other methods that are included in this category of covert conditioning methods include *covert reinforcement* (positive and negative), *covert extinction, covert response cost,* and *coverant* (=covert operant) *control* (Cautela, 1973; Homme, 1965, Mahoney, 1974). The tendency of some behavior therapists to take traditional conditioning principles and convert them into "covert" methods prompted the suggestion that we develop a proce-

---

[2]The term *covert* is an unfortunate one. Strictly speaking, the word means something that is "veiled, not open, or explicit." In fact these methods are very explicit. *Symbolic* or *cognitive* are more accurate, descriptive terms. (Lazarus, 1979)

dure called "covert therapy" in which the client imagines receiving successful therapy without ever undergoing actual treatment. However, one therapist was quick to point out that a problem with this was that the payment for therapy might also be "covert!"

Although a symbolic process like imagery is a fundamental part of these techniques, their originators like Wolpe and Cautela conceptualized them within a conditioning framework. This emphasis on conditioning, as opposed to cognitions, as the conceptual basis of these behavioral methods is not surprising in view of the early reliance on principles and procedures from the animal conditioning laboratory. More recently, the conditioning interpretation of these methods has been challenged, and alternative cognitive explanations put forward. The respective advantages and disadvantages of the conditioning interpretation of these methods that rely on the client's imaginal representation of events are discussed next.

An obvious advantage of the conditioning model is that a great deal is known about laboratory conditioning methods. Variables and parameters that have been shown to affect the modification of observable behavior may be applied to symbolic events with similar outcomes. An excellent example of this *heuristic function* of the conditioning model is seen in Kazdin's (1974a and b) studies on covert modeling (see Chap. 7). This program of research indicates that the *number* of covert models, the *type* of model, and the *nature of the consequences* following the modeled behavior all significantly influence the efficacy of covert modeling. Multiple models of the coping type who are reinforced for their behavior constitute the most powerful covert modeling procedure, as is the case with live modeling.

Systematic desensitization provides another instance of the heuristic value of the conditioning model. Some critics have argued that the operations of desensitization are so far removed from the animal laboratory that the terms stimulus and response are only metaphorical and do not retain their original, highly specific meaning, in the laboratory. It is true that sounding a buzzer as a conditioned fear stimulus for one of Wolpe's (1958) cats is a topographically different event from instructing a client with a fear of flying to imagine roaring down the runway in a Boeing 747. However, similar *functional relationships* between antecedent and consequent events have been shown to exist. For example, repeated presentations of either "stimulus" without any adverse consequence will result in the reduction of fear, that is, extinction. The important issue is whether or not we can specify the lawful effects of these variables on measurable behavior. As described in Chap 6, subjects instructed to imagine an aversive stimulus show a fear response pattern almost indistinguishable from that produced by the application of a physical aversive stimulus. Moreover, Lang, Melamed, and Hart (1970) showed that subjects' autonomic responses to imaginal fear stimuli bear a close resemblance to the parameters of classical conditioning. These data do *not* prove that the conditioning model is the best way of viewing symbolic events. However, they indicate that condi-

tioning formulations have been fruitful in translating complex symbolic processes into practical behavior change techniques.

The covert conditioning model is based on a major assumption about
psychological functioning, namely, the *homogeneity assumption*. According to
this assumtion, symbolic activities obey the same psychological laws as do
observable behaviors; they can be modified in the same manner by the same
procedures as overt behavior. Actually, there is no logical necessity for this
assumption. Even if conditioning principles did provide an adequate explanation of overt behavior, it would not follow logically that internal processes
operate along the same lines. Empirically, there appears to be some evidence
suggesting at least a rough correspondence between these principles and those
of overt behavior and internal processes. For example, there are Kazdin's
(1974 a and b) findings with covert modeling and Lang and others (1970)
desensitization data. In research discussed later in this chapter, Meichenbaum
(1977) successfully modified clients' private speech using modeling and reinforcement procedures.

Despite the heuristic value of the homogeneity assumption in behavior
therapy, there is good reason to doubt that the complexity of internal symbolic
processes could ever be adequately accounted by the relatively simple conditioning model. Some of the more obvious problems with the covert conditioning model can be mentioned.

In some imagery-based techniques it is difficult to know what are stimuli
and what are responses. In orgasmic reconditioning, for example, is the target
erotic fantasy a stimulus that is being paired with an unconditioned response
(orgasm) or is it a response that is being shaped up by contingent positive
reinforcement (orgasm)? In covert reinforcement the client is instructed to
imagine the target behavior and then imagine a pleasant scene as a reinforcing
consequence. Yet the evidence shows that behavior change occurs irrespective
of whether the client imagines the supposedly reinforcing scene before or after
the target response (Mahoney 1974). This violates the basic concept of a
reinforcement contingency in which reinforcement is delivered *only after* the
desired response. Another conceptual problem involves the definition of a
reinforcing stimulus. In operant conditioning a reinforcer is defined by its
effects on behavior. As Kazdin (1977a) points out, in covert conditioning
methods, the "reinforcement" is based on the client's self-report of what (s)he
finds rewarding or pleasant. There is no necessary relationship between the
client's subjective evaluation of an event and its functional relation to behavior.
Because of this and its emphasis on unobservable events, the covert conditioning model is rejected by radical behaviorists.

Another major problem with the covert conditioning interpretation is
that the model from which it derives has been increasingly criticized. As noted
in the beginning of this chapter, conditioning principles do not appear to
provide an adequate explanation of overt behavior, let alone complex symbolic
processes. In particular, it has been pointed out that neither classical condi-

tioning nor positive reinforcement automatically alter behavior. Rather, it appears that the person has to make some connection between two correlated events. Yet a major assumption underlying the covert conditioning methods is that imaginal events are automatically changed by simple association with some other imaginal or external event.

The evidence for the efficacy of methods like systematic desensitization, orgasmic reconditioning, covert sensitization, and covert modeling has been evaluated in previous chapters. The data on other covert conditioning techniques, such as covert reinforcement and coverant control, fail to document their efficacy. Experimental studies in these areas are relatively sparse and poorly controlled. As a result positive findings can plausibly be explained by placebo factors or inadequate assessment of outcome.

Regardless of the conceptual difficulties associated with the covert conditioning model, it has been heuristic in generating numerous treatment methods. Historically, it has also been useful in providing a link between a strict behaviorist approach that concentrated on overt behavior and the more recent social learning approach that has included an emphasis on cognitive mediating processes. But is the covert conditioning perspective still a useful one, or has it run its course? If it is no longer useful in generating novel procedures, then rigid adherence to its principles will be unnecessarily restrictive. The cognitive concepts that are discussed in the remainder of this chapter are alternatives to the covert conditioning perspective.

Cognitive Restructuring

The procedures that have received most attention in the recent development of cognitive behavior therapy and that are most important are those referred to as *cognitive restructuring*. The therapies in this category are all based on the assumption that emotional disorders are the result of maladaptive thought patterns. This assumption can be traced back to the philosopher Epictetus (A.D. 60) who declared that "Men are disturbed not by things, but by the views they take of them." The task of therapy is to restructure these maladaptive cognitions.

ELLIS' RATIONAL-EMOTIVE THERAPY

The oldest and most prominent of the cognitive restructuring therapies is Ellis' (1970) rational-emotive therapy (RET) that until the 1970s existed outside the mainstream of behavior therapy. According to Ellis, the road to Hell is paved, not with good intentions, but with irrational assumptions. These assumptions or self-statements are said to be irrational because they are distortions of objective reality. Ellis (1970) lists twelve irrational core assumptions that are said to be at the root of most emotional disturbance. These dirty dozen are summarized in Box 9–2.

Box 9–2   *Irrational Ideas That Cause and Maintain Emotional Disturbance According to Ellis' Rational-Emotive Therapy*

1. It is a dire necessity for an adult to be loved by everyone for everything he does.
2. Certain acts are awful or wicked, and people who perform such acts should be severely punished.
3. It is horrible when things are not the way one would like them to be.
4. Human misery is externally caused and is forced on one by outside people and events.
5. If something is or may be dangerous or fearsome, one should be terribly upset about it.
6. It is easier to avoid than to face life difficulties and self-responsibilities.
7. One needs something other or stronger or greater than oneself on which to rely.
8. One should be thoroughly competent, intelligent, and achieving in all possible respects.
9. Because something once strongly affected one's life, it should indefinitely affect it.
10. One must have certain and perfect control over things.
11. Human happiness can be achieved by inertia and inaction.
12. One has virtually no control over one's emotions, and one cannot help feeling certain things.

In terms of this approach it is not experience but the client's perception of that experience that causes neurotic disorders. This process is illustrated by Ellis' A-B-C analysis of depression. "A" refers to a real-life event (for example, a broken love affair). "B" symbolizes the irrational interpretation of that event (for example, the belief that nothing has meaning any more; that there will never be anybody else like him or her again). The person *catastrophizes,* that is, greatly exaggerates the negative meaning of the event. "C" is the upset and depression that is caused by the extremely negative perception of the broken love affair, not the actual break-up itself. Clients do not always consciously or deliberately tell themselves these irrational assumptions in everyday situations. These internal self-statements or beliefs appear to be automatic and pervasive in their influence because they have been repeated so often that they assume the status of an overlearned response.

Treatment consists of assisting the client to identify these irrational ideas and to replace them with more constructive, rational thoughts. The therapy consists of the following procedural steps:

a. verbal persuasion aimed at convincing the client of the philosophical tenets of RET;

b. identification of irrational thoughts through client self-monitoring and the therapist's feedback;

c. direct challenges to the client's irrational ideas and models and rational reinterpretations of disturbing events;

d. repeated cognitive rehearsal aimed at substituting rational self-statements for previously irrational interpretation;

e. behavioral tasks designed to develop rational reactions to replace formerly irrational, distress-producing assumptions.[3]

Systematic rational restructuring, a procedure developed by Goldfried (1977), is a variation of RET. The technique of systematic rational restructuring is more clearly specified and structured than is Ellis' method. In a manner similar to the procedure in systematic desensitization, the client is asked to imagine a hierarchy of anxiety-eliciting situations. At each step the client is instructed to identify irrational thoughts associated with the specific situation, to dispute them, and to reevaluate the situation more rationally. In addition, clients are instructed to practice rational restructuring in specific *in vivo* situations that elicit anxiety. Although procedurally different, systematic rational restructuring shares the same rationale as RET, and the two methods are not distinguished in the following evaluation.

RET: A Critical Evaluation

Theoretical Limitations. The theoretical framework for RET is not well-developed. In short, RET boils down to the conclusion that thoughts influence behavior. Ellis' theory does not at present provide a formal theoretical model for guiding innovative empirical research. There appears to be little doubt that faulty or maladaptive thoughts contribute to emotional disorders. However, current research does not provide strong support for the loose theoretical assumptions on which RET rests. For example, there is no convincing evidence

[3]RET is usually viewed as a therapeutic approach that rests primarily on the use of verbal persuasion, logical analysis, and rational restructuring of faulty thought patterns. Recently, Ellis (1977) has argued that this is too narrow a view of RET and that behavioral homework assignments have always been part of RET. In his most recent formulation of RET, Ellis asserts that RET includes the use of all behavior therapy techniques, Gestalt therapy methods, encounter group exercises, unconditional acceptance of the client (a method that derives from Carl Rogers' client-centered therapy), and others! If RET is this all-inclusive, it would be impossible to evaluate. For present purposes we concentrate on the specific assumptions about faulty thought patterns that are the basis of RET and the explicitly cognitive techniques that Ellis has repeatedly emphasized as the major methods of therapeutic change (for example, Ellis, 1962, 1970). It is this insistence on the primary role of cognitive processes in clinical disorders and their treatment that distinguishes RET from alternative treatment approaches.

that Ellis' list of irrational assumptions cause neurotic conflicts. Goldfried and Sobocinski (1975) found that the tendency to hold irrational beliefs of this nature was correlated with different forms of anxiety, but this was only a correlation. One cannot argue from correlation to cause. Rogers and Craighead (1977) showed that negative self-statements increased physiological arousal, but their findings suggest that this relationship might be more complex than is noted in RET. Nor is there any evidence that most neurotics even share the irrational assumptions described by Ellis. These are Ellis' ideas about what is troubling the client. Many of them may be irrelevant to a particular client's problems. Many clients protest that they do not hold such beliefs. Goldfried and Davison (1976) report that two of Ellis' notions are especially characteristic of neurotic clients—that "everybody must love me" and "I must be perfect in everything I do." Yet these beliefs are still too global and imprecise. For example, few clients really believe that "everybody must love me." Rather, this translates to the individual client wishing that a few highly significant people love him or her. Similarly, the desire to be perfect in everything usually means that the client has unduly high and strict standards of self-reinforcement with respect to specific areas of functioning.

Empirical Status. Ellis (1977) has recently concluded that the research evidence that supports his system of therapy is "immense—indeed, almost awesome." However, a more dispassionate analysis of the evidence that supports RET shows that it is difficult to assess the efficacy of RET because the appropriate outcome studies have been sparse, often lacking in the necessary controls, and frequently based on nonbehavioral measures of treatment efficacy. The following are some examples of the better controlled outcome studies on RET.

DiLoreto (1971) performed a frequently cited outcome study on the treatment of interpersonal anxiety in college students. The different treatment groups in this study were as follows: (a) RET; (b) systematic desensitization; (c) client-centered therapy; (d) attention-placebo; and (e) no treatment. Each treatment was conducted in a group setting with therapy lasting for nine weeks. DiLoreto also investigated the interaction between specific treatments and the personality type of the subjects by assigning an equal number of introverted and extroverted subjects to each treatment group. The assessment of whether a subject was introverted or extroverted was made on the basis of a questionnaire measure of this personality dimension. The outcome measures consisted of subjects' self-reports of anxiety, a behavioral checklist of interpersonal anxiety, and several questionnaire measures of general anxiety.

The results indicated that all three treatment groups (RET, systematic desensitization, and client-centered therapy) differed significantly from the control groups on all outcome measures with the exception that the client-centered group was not superior on the self-report scale of anxiety. Overall, however, systematic desensitization was significantly more effective in reduc-

Specific thought patterns directly influence physiological activity and our experience of emotion. Schwartz, Fair, Salt, Mandel, and Klerman (1976) measured subtle changes in facial muscle activity ("covert facial expression") in normal and depressed subjects while they generated different thought patterns. Muscle tension was monitored using electrodes that were attached to four sites on the face: the forehead (F), the eyebrows (E), the jaw (J), and the chin (C). When instructed to think happy thoughts, the normal subjects showed a pattern of muscle tension that was quite different from the pattern generated when they were asked to think sad and angry thoughts. Asked to think about a typical day, the normals made a "happy face."

The results were different in the depressed subjects. Almost identical to normals when instructed to think sad and angry thoughts, the depressed subjects showed a markedly attenuated muscle pattern when asked to think happy thoughts. Moreover, the sadness pattern was associated with thoughts about a typical day (see Fig. 9–1).

This study demonstrates that specific cognitive processes are associated with discrete patterns of physiological activity. It follows that modifying these thought patterns may reduce maladaptive muscular tension and also autonomic arousal. As Schwartz and others comment, "If as a result of consciously regulating specific thoughts and emotions, the brain generates specific motor and visceral output devices, we have the psychobiological foundation for teaching a person to regulate his health" (p. 299). This suggests how cognitive restructuring methods and cognitive relaxation procedures, like meditation, may be helpful in the treatment of psychosomatic disorders (see Chap. 8).

ing anxiety than either RET or client-centered therapy. For example, systematic desensitization was equally effective with introverted and extroverted subjects. RET, however, proved to be effective only with the introverted subjects. The results of a similar study of the treatment of interpersonal anxiety, by Kanter and Goldfried (1979), proved to be more favorable to a variation of RET, namely rational restructuring. Compared to a desentization treatment and a waiting list control condition, rational restructuring was more consistently effective across a broad range of behavioral and subjective measures of anxiety in interpersonal interactions at posttreatment and at a two-month follow-up.

The efficacy of systematic rational restructuring in treating unassertive women was evaluated in a well-controlled study by Linehan, Goldfried, and Goldfried (1979). Women who were unassertive and who experienced emotional discomfort in social interactions requiring assertive behavior received one of five forms of treatment: (a) rational restructuring; (b) behavior rehearsal, the focus of which was to equip subjects with the necessary behavioral skills that being assertive requires; (c) a combination of rational restructuring and behavior rehearsal; (d) a modified client-centered treatment condition that provided a supportive therapeutic relationship; and (e) a waiting-list control condition. The overall pattern of results showed that the combined rational restructuring and behavior rehearsal treatment produced the greatest increase in assertive behavior and a corresponding decrease in emotional discomfort. Rational restructuring alone was as effective as behavior rehearsal, and both were superior to the control conditions on most outcome measures. Improvement was maintained at a two-month follow-up.

The vast majority of outcome studies on RET has focused on the treat-

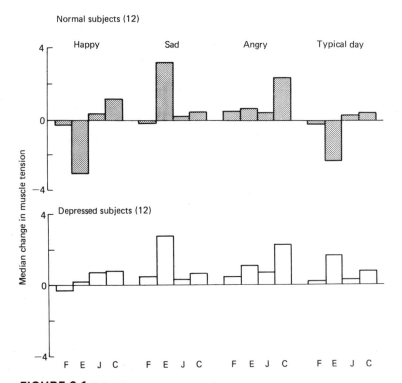

FIGURE 9.1
Changes in pattern of facial muscle tension in normal and depressed subjects instructed to generate imagery for happiness, sadness, anger, and a typical day. (*Adapted from* Schwartz, Fair, Salt, Mandel and Klerman, 1976. Facial muscle patterning to affective imagery in depressed and nondepressed subjects. *Science* 192: 489–491. Copyright 1976 by the American Association for the Advancement of Science.)

ment of mild-to-moderate anxiety problems, often among college students, as illustrated by the DiLoreto (1971) study. In marked contrast, Brandsma, Maultsby, and Welsh (1978) commendably completed a comparative outcome study of RET with so-called "revolving door" alcoholics; namely, clients who recurrently enter and then drop out of treatment. In this study, subjects were described as confirmed alcoholics of "lower middle class . . . of low normal intelligence . . . having legal troubles (e.g. arrested for drunkeness) but fairly socially and psychologically adept." There is wide consensus among professionals that this sort of alcoholic client is unusually difficult to treat successfully—hence the phenomenon of the "revolving door" alcoholic. Subjects (262 were accepted into treatment) were randomly assigned to one of five different treatment conditions: (a) RET conducted by professional therapists who were skilled in the practice of RET; (b) Insight therapy given by experienced professional therapists of diverse backgrounds but who were instructed to adopt a psychodynamic approach; (c) RET led by a lay therapist who, as an ex-drug abuser, had been successfully treated by RET himself; (d) Alcoholics Anonymous (AA) started by two volunteers from a local AA group; and (e) a Control group whose members received no specific treatment and were provided with a list of different community agencies that offered services to alcoholics. The maximum duration of therapy was 30 hours, consisting, by and large, of weekly sessions on an individual basis. (The AA treatment condition, of course, was carried out in a group context.) Multiple measures of outcome were obtained, including numerous objective and subjective indices of improvement.

The results? Of the 262 subjects who were initially accepted for treatment, 104 completed ten or more therapy sessions. There were significantly more drop-outs in the AA condition than in the other treatments. At the end of treatment, measures of drinking behavior consistently showed that all four treatment groups drank significantly less than the control group. The two treatments conducted by professional therapists (RET and Insight) produced the greatest number of *dry days,* namely those days on which subjects consumed no alcohol at all. All four treatment groups showed significant improvement compared to the control group in terms of arrests for drunkeness. Of these four treatment groups, the Insight group showed the greatest reduction in legal problems, such as being picked up by the police, being jailed, or making court appearances related to drinking. As an indicator of economic improvement, the professionally administered RET and Insight treatments were superior to the other groups with respect to owning a car.

Of the 104 subjects who completed ten or more sessions of therapy, 81 (77.9 percent) participated in follow-up sessions at three, six, nine, and twelve months after the end of therapy. The same pattern of results observed at posttreatment was apparent, with the four treatment groups proving superior to the control group and with the professionally administered RET and Insight groups having the edge in efficacy.

In another investigation using a clinical population, Emmelkamp et al. (1978) treated 24 agoraphobics with both cognitive restructuring and prolonged exposure *in vivo* using a cross-over design. Patients received five group sessions of each treatment, evaluations of outcome being made after each treatment and at a one-month follow-up. Outcome was assessed in terms of multiple measures of *in vivo* behavioral performance, independent ratings of phobic anxiety and avoidance in different situations, and a variety of patient self-rating scales. Twenty patients completed the full treatment program.

Prolonged *in vivo* exposure, irrespective of whether it was the first or second treatment, produced significant improvement on the majority of outcome measures, including the behavioral measure of how long patients would persist in a planned walk away from the hospital, where the treatment was conducted, towards town. Cognitive restructuring did not result in significant improvement on the behavioral measure and produced relatively few significant changes on ratings of phobic anxiety or avoidance. These improvements were obtained mainly when cognitive restructuring was the first treatment to be administered. When cognitive restructuring followed prolonged exposure *in vivo* in the cross-over design, hardly any incremental change was noted. Comparatively, prolonged exposure *in vivo* was significantly more effective than cognitive restructuring on a variety of objective and subjective measures at posttreatment and follow-up.

The efficacy of the *in vivo* exposure therapy is consistent with previous findings (see Chap. 6). Several factors may explain the less than favorable showing by cognitive restructuring. Emmelkamp et al. (1978) suggest that this cognitive method might be less appropriate for a disorder such as agoraphobia than for the less severe, social or evaluative anxiety problems that have been successfully treated by Goldfried (1977) and others. The reason, Emmelkamp et al. suggest, is that the degree of physiological arousal might be greater among agoraphobics and that this physiological arousal is less amenable to cognitive methods of modification. This issue of matching treatment techniques to particular types of problems is addressed later in this chapter.

Another reason for the relative ineffectiveness of cognitive restructuring in this study, as Ellis (1979) has pointed out, may have been the absence of specific behavioral homework assignments. The importance of such a behavioral component is underscored by Emmelkamp et al.'s observation that although the patients were able to think rationally while imagining phobic situations, they found it far more difficult to use rational self-statements in real life situations (e.g., on the way home from the hospital). Whether a combined cognitive-behavioral treatment would result in greater efficacy remains to be determined.

In reviewing the evidence, Rachman and Wilson (in press) concluded that the available studies "do not provide adequate information on which to reach firm conclusions about the efficacy of RET as a treatment method. Evidence on the long-term efficacy of RET is especially lacking. Encouragingly the evidence suggests that RET is more effective than no treatment or a placebo effect on key measures in most studies. However, it is impossible to conclude at this point that RET is superior to alternative treatment methods such as desensitization, prolonged exposure, or behaviour rehearsal."

Nonetheless, RET is currently riding the crest of a wave of popularity among practicing clinical psychologists (Garfield and Kurtz, 1976). It is sobering to reflect upon the fact that there is no greater empirical justification for the present enthusiastic reception accorded RET than there was for its almost complete neglect by practitioners over a decade ago. The history of clinical psychology and psychiatry has been marked by the recurrent rise and decline of one fad after another. It is precisely to avoid faddish or uncritical acceptance or rejection of treatment methods that the rigorous experimental evaluation of the theories and methods of behavior change is so important.

MEICHENBAUM'S SELF-INSTRUCTIONAL TRAINING

A second form of cognitive restructuring is self-instructional training, a method developed by Meichenbaum (1977). The rationale for this approach derives from two main sources: (1) Ellis' (1970) RET and its emphasis on irrational self-talk as the cause of emotional disturbance; and (2) the developmental sequence according to which children develop internal speech and verbal-symbolic control over their behavior (Luria, 1961). In terms of this latter analysis, children's behavior is first regulated by the instructions of other people; subsequently they acquire control over their own behavior through the use of overt self-instructions which they ultimately internalize as covert self-instructions.

Self-instructional training involves the following steps:

a. training the client to identify and become aware of maladaptive thoughts (self-statements);

b. the therapist models appropriate behavior while verbalizing effective action strategies; these verbalizations include an appraisal of task requirements, self-instructions that guide graded performance, self-statements that stress personal adequacy and counteract worry over failure, and covert self-reinforcement for successful performance;

c. the client then performs the target behavior first while verbalizing aloud the appropriate self-instructions and then by covertly rehearsing them. Therapist feedback during this phase assists in ensuring that constructive problem-solving self-talk replaces previously anxiety-inducing cognitions associated with that behavior.

A large number of studies exist indicating that self-instructional training can significantly modify a wide range of different behaviors in both children and adults. It has been used successfully to reduce diverse anxiety-related problems, such as test anxiety (for example, Holroyd, 1976), interpersonal anxiety (for example, Thorpe, 1975), and speech anxiety (for example, Meichenbaum, Gilmore and Fedoravicius, 1971). To take an example of the research in this area, Meichenbaum and others (1971) compared self-instructional training to imaginal systematic desensitization, an attention-placebo, and a waiting-list control condition in the treatment of speech anxiety in undergraduate students. The results are shown in Fig. 9–2. Both self-instructional training and systematic desensitization were significantly more effective than the control conditions in producing greater reductions in speech anxiety, as assessed by behavioral and self-report measures at the end of treatment and at three-months follow-up. Self-instructional training did not differ from systematic desensitization in efficacy.

Research on the cognitive functioning of schizophrenics provides another demonstration of the positive effects of self-instructional training (Meichenbaum and Cameron, 1973). Hospitalized schizophrenics were assigned either to the self-instructional training condition or a control group in which subjects merely practiced without instruction. The self-instructional training consisted of teaching subjects to emit task-relevant verbalizations during the course of the structured interview, for example, "pay attention, repeat instructions, disregard distraction." Subjects were initially trained to say these self-instructions aloud and then covertly, or "privately," to themselves as they learned to deal with increasingly more demanding performance tasks. These tasks range from a simple sensorimotor task to more complex cognitive activities, such as interpreting proverbs and responding to the experimenter. The purpose of this training was to aid the schizophrenics in learning to monitor and evaluate their own behavior so that they could screen out inferior and irrelevant cognitions and become more efficient problem-solvers.

The control group subjects were given the same amount of practice on the different performance tasks as the experimental group and received comparable social reinforcement for correct responses, but they were not exposed to explicit modeling and rehearsal of self-statements aimed at reducing disorganized thinking and facilitating problem-solving ability. Both treatment conditions were carried out over eight 45-minute sessions during a three-week period. The dependent measures of performance were readministered immediately posttreatment and again after a three-week interval.

The results at both posttreatment and follow-up showed that the self-instructional training produced significantly greater improvement on measures of attention, thought, and language. In addition, changes on specific target

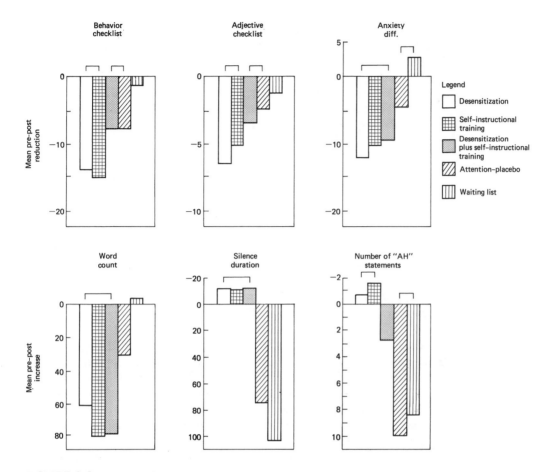

FIGURE 9.2
Mean reduction and increase in manifestations of anxiety from pre-treatment to posttreatment on test speech measures (groups not connected by solid line are significantly different at .05 level). (Meichenbaum, D., Gilmore, J., and Fedoravicius, A. Group insight vs. group desensitization in treating speech anxiety. Reprinted with permission from *Journal of Consulting and Clinical Psychology*, 1971, 36: 410–421. Copyright 1971 by the American Psychological Association.)

behaviors generalized to similar nontreated behaviors. These findings not only show the efficacy of self-instructional training but also indicate that it may.be applicable to severely disturbed individuals.

In other studies, self-instructional training has been used successfully to enhance creativity, develop methods for coping with stress and pain, and increase self-control in impulsive children (Meichenbaum, 1977). A variant of self-instructional training, stress innoculation, is described in Box 9–4.

259

Reviewing the outcome evidence on self-instructional training, Rachman and Wilson (in press) noted that over 50 percent of the available studies consisted of laboratory investigations of problems of test, public-speaking, interpersonal anxiety, and fear of snakes or animals. And, as in the case of RET, the relative absence of long-term follow-ups limits the clinical significance of these studies. It is clear that future studies of more severe problems across different client populations with longer follow-up evaluations are needed. Nonetheless, Rachman and Wilson were able to conclude that

> . . . the overall pattern of results is encouraging. Self-instructional was compared with various control conditions and alternative forms of treatment including systematic desensitization, behavior rehearsal, EMG biofeedback, and operant conditioning procedures. The findings suggest that self-instructional training was consistently superior to control conditions and equalled or out-performed comparison treatments.

COGNITIVE RESTRUCTURING AND GENERALIZATION OF TREATMENT EFFECTS

Do cognitive methods such as RET and self-instructional training produce greater generalization of treatment effects than direct behavioral techniques? It has been suggested that the alteration of cognitive mediating processes will result in change that is less stimulus-bound than that produced by behavioral techniques that modify actions directly. It is therefore of theoretical and practical importance to find out whether cognitive methods produce significant generalization effects.

Some studies of self-instructional training, including the Meichenbaum and Cameron (1973) study described above, have demonstrated generalization of treatment effects. However, as Rachman and Wilson (in press) have pointed out, most of the evidence does not show significant generalization effects. Nor can it be said that either RET or self-instructional training is superior to behavioral techniques in producing generalization of treatment effects. For example, studies with impulsive or learning disabled children have generally failed to show much generalization across responses or settings, e.g., from improvement on a specific laboratory task to actual performance in the classroom (e.g., Friedling and O'Leary, 1979). In the Linehan et al. (1979) study described above, behavior rehearsal appeared to facilitate more generalization of increased assertive skills than rational restructuring.

What this means is that generalization of treatment effects cannot be taken for granted in using cognitive treatment methods. As in the case of behavioral techniques, specific steps must be taken to facilitate better generalization and maintenance of treatment effects (Meichenbaum and Asarnow, 1979).

Box 9–4 *Stress Inoculation Training: Coping*
with Anger

Stress inoculation training is a cognitive-behavioral treatment method for enhancing the client's coping skills in response to stressful events. The procedure involves exposing the client to regulated "doses" of stress that test, but do not overwhelm, their capacity to cope effectively. The procedure is illustrated in Novaco's (1977) successful treatment of severe anger disorders.

The treatment involves three basic phases: cognitive preparation, skill acquisition, and application practice.

COGNITIVE PREPARATION

This phase includes several steps: (a) explaining the nature and purpose of the treatment to the client; (b) identifying the persons and situations that arouse anger. (The client keeps a daily diary in which all anger-related events are recorded—another instance of self-monitoring); (c) discriminating justified from less justified anger; (d) recognizing the early signs of anger.

SKILL ACQUISITION

The Cognitive Level. Clients are taught to view provocative situations from different perspectives. Self-instructional training is used to develop coping self-statements at each stage of the provocation sequence: (a) preparing for provocation—for example, "I can work out a plan to handle this. Easy does it;" (b) impact and confrontation—for example, "As long as I keep my cool, *I'm* in control of the situation;" (c) coping with arousal—for example, "My anger is a signal of what I need to do. Time for problem solving;" (d) conflict unresolved—for example, "Forget about the irritation. Thinking about it only makes you upset;" and (e) conflict resolved—for example, "I handled that one pretty well. That's doing a good job."

The Emotional Level. Clients are taught to use progressive relaxation training (see Chap. 8) as a response that is incompatible with anger.

The Behavioral Level. Clients are taught to identify the onset of anger, to express it in a nonhostile manner. This prevents the build-up of excessive anger that results in an aggressive overreaction. Assertion training is the means of accomplishing this goal. Frequently clients do not know of any other way to deal with difficult interpersonal situations other than by using anger to control the interaction. Just as assertion training provides the submissive, unassertive person an alternative mode of self-expression and communication, so does it equip the aggressive client with alternative, more constructive social skills. This behavioral training also emphasizes a task-oriented set that facilitates problem-solving actions. Sticking to the issues and not taking provocation too personally is the key to retaining one's composure.

APPLICATION PRACTICE

This is carried out by means of imaginal and role-playing inductions of anger. A hierarchy of anger situations that the client is likely to encounter in real life is first constructed. Then the various coping skills that have been learned are practiced in behavior rehearsal sessions with the therapist. As in systematic desensitization, practice begins with situations that arouse the least anger and gradually progress to the most anger-arousing situations.

EXPERIMENTAL EVALUATION

Novaco (1976) has shown that this treatment method is significantly more effective in reducing excessive anger reactions than an attention-placebo control group. The combined cognitive-behavioral procedure appears to be more effective than either the cognitive or the relaxation training components alone.

BECK'S COGNITIVE THERAPY

A third approach to cognitive restructuring is Beck's (1976) "cognitive therapy." Beck (1963) developed this cognitive approach independently of Ellis' RET. Despite the name, the approach is behaviorally based in large part. As in RET and self-instructional training, the ultimate goal of cognitive therapy is the development of rational, adaptive thought patterns. Cognitive therapy progresses through the following phases:

    a. clients become aware of their thoughts;
    b. they learn to identify inaccurate or distorted thoughts;
    c. these inaccurate thoughts are replaced by accurate, more objective cognitions;
    d. therapist feedback and reinforcement is a necessary part of this process.

The specific procedures used to accomplish these therapeutic objectives are both behavioral and cognitive in nature. The former include the prescription of an explicit activity schedule, graded tasks aimed at providing mastery and

262

success experiences, and various homework assignments. The latter include several techniques of which "distancing" and "decentering" are examples.

Distancing is the ability to view one's thoughts more objectively, to draw a distinction between "I believe" (an opinion that is open to disconfirmation) and "I know" (an "irrefutable" fact). Teaching clients to separate themselves from vicariously experiencing the adversities of others is known as *decentering*. For example, an agoraphobic woman hearing that a friend of her neighbour's died of a heart attack becomes anxious that the same thing will happen to her or her family.

Beck developed this approach in the course of his treatment of depression, one of the most common yet least understood and most difficult to treat of all psychological disorders. Finding that negative conceptions of the self, the external world, and the future were defining features of depressive reactions, Beck devised a method for modifying these cognitions directly.

Empirical Support. Rush, Beck, Kovacs, and Hollon (1977) compared this form of cognitive restructuring to pharmacotherapy in the treatment of depression. On average, the clients had been continually or intermittently depressed for about nine years, and 75 percent reported suicidal ideas. The majority had had previous psychotherapy without success, and 22 percent had been hospitalized on account of their depression. Treatment for both groups averaged eleven weeks.

Depression was substantially reduced by both treatments; however, cognitive therapy produced significantly greater improvement on self-ratings and clinical ratings of depression. Seventy-nine percent of the clients in the cognitive therapy condition underwent marked improvement or complete remission, as compared to 23 percent of the clients in the pharmacotherapy condition. These treatment differences were maintained at three- and six-month follow-ups. Aside from being more effective, cognitive therapy was associated with a significantly lower drop-out rate over the course of the study. This is an important finding since there is good evidence that clients who drop out of treatment are almost inevitably treatment failures. If statistical analysis of outcome results is based only on those clients who complete treatment, a biased picture may emerge. In this study by Rush and others (1977), cognitive therapy was superior to pharmacotherapy irrespective of whether the dropouts were included in the analysis—an impressive finding.[4]

Two other features of this study should be noted. The first point is that

[4]Consistent with these results, McLean and Hakstian (1979) found that a multifaceted therapy program, consisting of both behavioral and cognitive components, was more effective than drug (amitriptyline) therapy and short-term psychotherapy in the treatment of clinically depressed clients. Moreover, the combined cognitive-behavioral treatment resulted in significantly fewer dropouts from therapy. These data indicate that a cognitive-behavioral treatment is effective with depressed clients. There are different types of depression, and it is clear that drugs are the preferred treatment in some types (e.g., manic depression).

pharmacotherapy provided a powerful treatment method against which to compare cognitive therapy. Tricyclic antidepressant drugs (for example, Imipramine) have been shown to be more effective than are other treatments, including traditional psychotherapy, and are widely viewed as the recommended therapy for depression. Moreover, the results obtained with pharmacotherapy in this study were comparable to previous findings with antidepressant drugs. As a consequence, we may tentatively infer that it was the superiority of the cognitive therapy rather than the inadequacy of the drug treatment that accounted for the difference in treatment outcome. The second point is that cognitive therapy was administered by eighteen different therapists. The majority of these therapists were committed to the psychodynamic approach, had no expertise in cognitive behavior therapy, and participated in the study as part of their psychiatric training. This tends to rule out an explanation of treatment differences in terms of some therapist factor, as opposed to the cognitive restructuring method. In terms of a cost-effectiveness analysis, it shows that with brief training, inexperienced therapists or psychodynamic therapists lacking training in behavior therapy can use cognitive restructuring effectively.

Beck's cognitive restructuring method has also been compared to a behavioral approach for the treatment of depression that emphasized social skills and reinforcement (Shaw, 1977). The social skills and/or reinforcement group was based on Lewinsohn's (1974) behavioral analysis of depression. According to that view, the lack of social skills that would allow the person to obtain social reinforcement is said to be an important antecedent of depression. Losses of a deeply personal nature (for example, a death, divorce, broken love affair, or a lost job) are assumed to represent a major reduction in social reinforcement. Those individuals who react to these losses with depression are those who are unable to secure alternative sources of reinforcement. Obtaining social reinforcement depends on one's social skills. For the person who does not have these skills, a decrease in social reinforcement represents a disproportionately severe loss, and depression might be the consequence. The specific treatment techniques used included directed activity schedules and behavior rehearsal techniques designed to teach better communication and social reinforcement skills. An attention-placebo and a no-treatment control group completed the experimental design. The attention-placebo condition consisted of a nondirective group discussion of the subjects' feelings about their depression and why they were depressed. Subjects were college students (ages eighteen to twenty-six years), a much younger population than Rush and others (1977). All treatments involved 16 hours of therapy over a four-week period.

The results showed that the cognitive restructuring group produced significantly greater decreases in depression than either the social skills and/or reinforcement or attention-placebo groups, as measured by self-ratings and clinical ratings. There was no difference between the social skills and/or reinforcement and attention-placebo groups. The degree of improvement was similar to that obtained by Rush and others (1977). A one-month follow-up indicated that the cognitive group was still superior to the social skills and/or reinforcement group although the difference was not statistically significant. These findings provide further support for Beck's cognitive therapy, but they must be interpreted with caution. First, one month is too short a follow-up period. The fact that the cognitive method was no longer significantly more effective than the social skills and/or reinforcement procedure at this point raises questions about its long-term superiority. Secondly, the investigator was the single therapist for all treatment groups, and it is difficult to discount inadvertent bias of the therapist-investigator as an influence on the outcome of therapy.

In a similar comparative outcome study, Taylor and Marshall (1977) compared four treatment conditions: (a) a cognitive method, based on Beck's approach; (b) a social skills and/or reinforcement method, based on Lewinsohn's approach; (c) a combined cognitive-behavioral group; and (d) a no-treatment control group. Subjects were undergraduate or graduate students who were less depressed than subjects in either the Rush and others (1977) or Shaw (1977) studies. Results showed that the combined group was the most effective. However, the lack of any follow-up measures and the fact that a single therapist conducted all treatment groups renders those results tentative.

A COMPARISON OF THE COGNITIVE RESTRUCTURING METHODS OF ELLIS, MEICHENBAUM, AND BECK

The similarity among these three approaches is that they all share a common goal, the therapeutic modification of maladaptive thought patterns. However, there are some important differences among these cognitive restructuring methods.

Procedural Differences. (a) The primary strategy in RET has typically consisted of a verbal attack on the client's irrational thinking. The therapist actively disputes irrational assumptions and attempts to cajole the client into thinking more logically. In contrast, both Meichenbaum and Beck place greater emphasis on using behavioral methods such as modeling, behavior rehearsal, and graded task assignments in teaching the client more constructive cognitive and behavioral skills. (b) Unlike Ellis' style of direct confrontation, Beck adopts a Socratic approach in which therapy is structured so that clients discover for themselves the inaccuracies and distortions in their thinking. In this latter approach, the client is helped to identify and alter automatic thoughts through a more gentle and strategic progression of therapeutic interventions. That this may be a more desirable strategy is indicated by the findings from social psychology that a person who perceives that (s)he is being coerced into changing his or her beliefs may actively resist the influence attempt. This phenomenon is known as *reactance* (Brehm, 1966). In systematic rational restructuring Goldfried (1977), like Beck (1976), uses a less challenging, more Socratic approach to prompt clients to reevaluate their perceptions of problem situations. This difference, combined with the greater structure and specification of treatment procedures in systematic rational restructuring, makes it the preferred method to Ellis' practice of RET.

Conceptual Differences. The goal of RET is a total change in the client's philosophical outlook. The prescribed philosophy is one of logic and rationality, which are equated with adaptiveness. Consider, for example, the treatment of a client complaining about his sexual impotence. According to Ellis (1977), treatment would include the use of the Masters and Johnson-type techniques described in Box 6–1. In addition, however, RET would involve changing the client's whole outlook on sex. To quote Ellis directly:

> I would also try to show this sexually malfunctioning male that even if he never became fully potent, that would be very inconvenient but not "awful" or "horrible"; that he could fully accept himself no matter what his sex partners or anyone else thought of him; and that there is no reason why he must or has to succeed sexually—or, for that matter, should succeed in any other goal that he wishes or prefers to succeed at. In . . . RET, therefore, I would try to help him change his fundamental disturbance-creating philosophies, about sex or any other aspect of his life, and try to show him how to deal fairly comfortably, unneurotically, and nonself-downingly with any present or future difficulty that might arise. (p. 74)

Neither Meichenbaum nor Beck emphasize such a radical philosophical shift. Self-instructional training is geared towards modifying specific verbal responses and teaching specific cognitive skills. There is little concern about whether the client's thoughts are logical or not. In the example of the impotent client, the thrust of therapy would not be to persuade the client to accept that impotence is not "awful." Rather, self-instructional training would be directed at reducing specific self-statements which were causing anxiety that interfered with the natural sexual response of erection. Similarly, Beck's treatment is focused more specifically on particular maladaptive thoughts, rather than a broad change in philosophy. He notes that "if a patient's incorrect assumptions or personal mythology are not related to his difficulties, it is not necessary to change them. The therapist's mandate does not require that he educate his patient to be a Renaissance man" (p. 247). The success that has been obtained with RET does not appear to result from the "thorough-going philosophic reorientation of a person's outlook on life" that Ellis strives to achieve. Where they occur, changes are relatively limited and specific and are the probable consequence of the behavioral tasks clients are instructed to perform.

Cognitive Restructuring and Social Learning Theory

The cognitive restructuring methods are the essence of what has been called *cognitive behavior therapy* or *cognitive behavior modification*. These developments are best viewed as extensions and clinically relevant applications of the social learning conceptualization of behavior therapy (Bandura, 1969; O'Leary and Wilson, 1975). Viewing the cognitive therapies within the social learning framework has important consequences. The conceptual models of behavior therapy in the 1970s can each be said to place primary emphasis on one dimension of psychological functioning to the relative neglect of the others. Thus applied behavior analysis concentrates on overt behavior; Wolpe's counterconditioning approach emphasizes autonomic or emotional habits; and the cognitive therapists, of course, focus on the causal role of maladaptive thought patterns. A major advantages of social learning theory is that it integrates these three regulatory systems of antecedent, consequent, and mediational influence in a comprehensive yet testable framework.

BEHAVIORAL PROCEDURES VERSUS COGNITIVE PROCESSES

A basic assumption of the social learning approach is that while cognitive mechanisms are postulated to explain the development and maintenance of abnormal behavior, the most powerful methods of behavior change are those that rely upon direct behavioral intervention. In other words, an important distinction must be drawn between treatment *procedure* and theoretical *process.*

Behaviorally based treatment methods appear to be more effective than procedures that involve verbal, imaginal, or vicarious operations. A clear example of this superiority of direct behavioral methods is that of participant modeling. As discussed in Chap. 7, participant modeling is more effective in reducing phobic behavior than either symbolic modeling or imaginal systematic desensitization (Bandura, Blanchard, and Ritter, 1969). Similarly, participant modeling has been demonstrated to have greater efficacy than covert modeling in the reduction of phobic behavior (Thase and Moss, 1976), and Rachman and Hodgson (1980) have shown the superiority of performance-based treatment over imaginal and vicarious methods in the modification of obsessive-compulsive disorders. Other studies have shown the superiority of performance-based treatment over imaginal desensitization (for example, Crowe and others, 1972) and imaginal flooding (for example, Emmelkamp and Wessels, 1975; Marshall and others 1977; Stern and Marks, 1973). Finally,

Kockott, Dittmar, and Nusselt (1975), Mathews, Bancroft, Whitehead, Hackmann, Julier, Bancroft, Gath, and Shaw (1976), and Marks (1978) reported that sexual dysfunction was most effectively treated by a Masters and Johnson-type program that relied on directed practice *in vivo,* as opposed to imaginal, systematic desensitization.

INTERDEPENDENCE AMONG COGNITIVE, BEHAVIORAL, AND ENVIRONMENTAL REGULATORY INFLUENCES

Behavior is a function of interdependent influence processes, and most actions are a product of joint regulatory factors. Thus cognitions do not operate independently. In a complete analysis of the cognitive control of behavior, mediating processes must be tied to observable action. Furthermore, the determinants of these cognitive mediating processes must be spelled out. Unless this reciprocal determinism between cognitive and environmental factors is explicitly built into treatment programs, the client will usually be left buried in introspective analyses of his or her thought patterns without engaging in the necessary corrective behaviors.

Consider, for example, a client's belief or anticipation about a behavioral event, how it affects that event, and how that behavioral consequence in turn influences that belief. Clinicians are familiar with the client who is deeply suspicious and distrustful about becoming involved in an intimate relationship with a woman. Typically, he has been previously hurt when the woman with whom he was emotionally involved broke off the relationship for someone else. As a consequence of the sense of personal rejection he experienced, he has become defensive and resentful towards women, since he anticipates another rejection based on past experience. The result of this anticipation is that he behaves in such a way as to turn off women and to elicit unfriendly reactions from them. His behavior confirms his original belief, and so he continues to act suspiciously, without showing any trust or openness in interpersonal relationships. This makes it even more certain that women will reject him. He is locked into a vicious cycle that ends up with his seeking therapy for his inability to get close to people and enjoy an emotionally satisfying relationship.

The important point here is that the client's belief, or anticipation about being rejected, creates the social environment that now maintains his behavior. This behavioral sequence, in which anticipation creates reality in a self-confirming manner, is more commonly summarized as a self-fulfilling prophecy. An experimental demonstration of the complex interaction between cognition and behavior is described in Box 9–5. Treatment of this client would require that he learn to identify the interactional sequence, realize how his own actions contribute to the maintenance of his problem, stop blaming women for his woes, and learn to alter his actions. The most effective way of accomplishing these objectives is to teach the client *directly* how to *behave* differently towards women, thereby eliciting reciprocal positive responses. The manner in which this sort of corrective feedback from behavioral performance changes defensive behavior is illustrated in Bandura's (1977a) theory of self-efficacy and behavior change. This theory is discussed next.

SELF-EFFICACY: AN INTEGRATED THEORY OF BEHAVIORAL CHANGE

As noted in Chap. 7 on modeling, Bandura (1977a) proposes that behavioral treatment methods such as desensitization, flooding, and modeling are effective because they increase the client's expectations of *personal efficacy*. Efficacy expectations reflect the subjective estimate that one has the ability to cope successfully with a threatening situation. They are differentiated from *outcome expectations* which are defined as the client's belief that a particular behavior will result in a certain outcome. The difference between efficacy and outcome expectations is shown in Fig. 9–3.

In this social learning analysis, efficacy expectations play a major part in the initiation, generalization, and maintenance of coping behavior. Take the phobic client, for example, who avoids a particular situation in which (s)he believes that (s)he cannot cope effectively, that is (s)he becomes anxious and loses control. To the extent that therapy strengthens or restores efficacy expectations, the client will cease avoiding and will confront the previously feared situation. Expectations of self-efficacy also generalize to other situations and help explain the process of generalized behavior change.

Traditionally, generalized behavior change has been explained on the basis of the learning principles of S–R generalization (see Chap. 4). These well-known principles were derived from animal conditioning research in the laboratory and have been developed into a technology for generalization in applied behavior analysis (Stokes and Baer, 1977). However, it has always been difficult to account adequately for the generalization of behavior change in one specific situation to radically different situations, solely on the basis of S–R

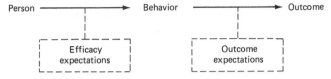

FIGURE 9.3
Diagrammatic representation of the difference between efficacy expectations and outcome expectations. (Bandura, A., 1977a. Self-efficacy: Toward a unifying theory of behavioral change. *Psychological Review,* 84: 191–215. Copyright 1977 by the American Psychological Association. Reprinted by permission.)

Box 9–5 *Cognition and Behavior: When Belief
Creates Reality*

As human beings we constantly search for the causes of our own and
others' behavior; we actively draw inferences about people and events; and
we act upon these inferences. The process whereby we draw inferences and
derive impressions about other people has been extensively studied by social
psychologists. But what of the *consequences* of this cognitive process of
impression formation? Is it possible that individuals who hold certain beliefs
behave in such a fashion as to elicit responses from other people that then
confirm the original beliefs? To answer this question, Snyder, Tanke, and
Berscheid (1977) performed the following experiment.

Numerous studies have shown that a widely held belief or social
stereotype in our culture involves physical attractiveness. Both men and
women believe that physically attractive people (men and women) possess
more socially desirable personality traits and lead better, more interesting
lives than people who are less physically attractive. Physically attractive
young adults are more popular and are more eagerly sought after for dates.
In testing the validity and consequences of this belief, Snyder and others
(1977) arranged for male-female pairs of college students to participate in
what they believed was a study on acquaintance processes in social relationships.

Specifically, the two students engaged in a telephone conversation
with the goal of getting to know each other. Unbeknownst to the women,
the men were led to believe that they were talking with either a physically
attractive or a physically unattractive woman. This was accomplished by
showing the two groups fake photographs of either attractive or unattractive coeds as rated by independent observers. All conversations were tape-
recorded and later analyzed by naive judges who were unaware of the
experimental conditions and the purpose of the research.

After seeing photographs of their partners, but prior to the conversation, the men who anticipated talking to a physically attractive partner
expected to find her sociable and humorous; the men who anticipated
talking to physically unattractive partners expected to find them unsociable,
serious, and socially inept. In other words, the men showed evidence of the
social stereotype about physical attractiveness.

The important finding is that analyses of the tape-recordings showed
that the women who were perceived (unknown to them) to be physically
attractive were rated as more friendly, likeable, and sociable than the
women who were perceived as physically unattractive. "What had initially
been reality in the minds of the men had now become reality in the behavior
of the women with whom they had interacted—a behavioral reality discern-
ible even by naive judges who had access *only* to tape-recordings of just the

woman's contributions to the conversations." To assess *how* the men's beliefs came to influence their partners' behavior, the ratings of the conversations were evaluated. The results showed that the men who believed that their partner was physically attractive were rated as more sociable, interesting, sexually permissive, and humorous than were their counterparts who believed that their partners were physically unattractive. In other words, belief leads to action that elicits behavior from other people that confirms the initial belief.

Despite overwhelming evidence that argues against the reality of personality traits (that is, consistencies in behavior across different situations (Mischel, 1968), people continue to view the actions of others in terms of global traits. The findings of this study indicate that people might impose a consistency upon others in their interpersonal interactions. It is possible that our cognitive stereotypes of others cause them to behave in "trait-like" ways that are consistent with our impressions.

generalization. For example, Bandura, Jeffery, and Gajdos (1975) showed that after snake phobic subjects had been successfully treated using participant modeling, they coped more effectively with fears of other animals, as well as their social anxieties. This is an example of *mediated generalization*. Bandura (1977a) suggests that the mediating process in this type of generalization is an increase in self-efficacy. As one of the subjects in the Bandura and others (1975) said, "The biggest benefit to me of the successfulness of the treatment was the feeling that if I could lick snakes, I could lick anything. It gave me the confidence to tackle, also successfully, some personal stuff (p. 150)."

Another important prediction from this theory is that the strength of efficacy expectations will help determine how long clients will engage in active coping behavior in the face of obstacles and adverse psychological experiences. As such, this prediction bears importantly on the maintenance of treatment-produced improvement. Unless treatment creates strong expectations of efficacy, coping behaviors may be easily extinguished following the termination of therapy. The phenomenon of relapse is a problem for all methods of psychological treatment, including behavior therapy. Self-efficacy theory is a means of conceptualizing the relapse process and suggests procedures for facilitating the long-term maintenance of behavior change (Wilson, 1979).

Efficacy expectations are based on four major sources of information: behavioral performance, vicarious experience, physiological arousal, and verbal persuasion. Fig. 9–4 shows the hypothesized mode of operation on efficacy expectations of behavior therapy techniques for fear reduction.

In an experimental test of self-efficacy theory, snake phobic subjects received treatments designed to create differential levels of efficacy expectations and relate them to behavioral change (Bandura, Adams, and Beyer, 1977). The three treatment methods were participant modeling, symbolic

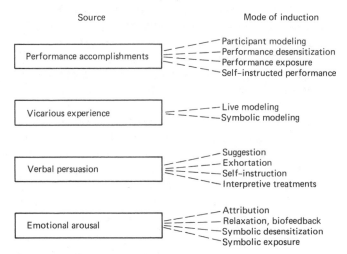

Efficacy Expectations

Source   Mode of induction

Performance accomplishments
— Participant modeling
— Performance desensitization
— Performance exposure
— Self-instructed performance

Vicarious experience
— Live modeling
— Symbolic modeling

Verbal persuasion
— Suggestion
— Exhortation
— Self-instruction
— Interpretive treatments

Emotional arousal
— Attribution
— Relaxation, biofeedback
— Symbolic desensitization
— Symbolic exposure

FIGURE 9.4

Major sources of efficacy information and the principal sources through which different modes of treatment operate. (Bandura, A. Self-efficacy: Toward a unifying theory of behavioral change. Reprinted by permission form *Psychological Review,* 1977, 84: 191–215. Copyright 1977 by the American Psychological Association.)

modeling, and a no-treatment control group. Predictably, participant modeling produced significantly stronger efficacy expectations of coping successfully with the phobic object and more generalized behavioral changes than did symbolic modeling. The latter resulted in greater expectations of personal efficacy and behavioral change than the control condition. As shown in Fig. 9–5, the degree of treatment-produced change in efficacy expectations was closely related to a reduction in phobic behavior. The greater the increase in self-efficacy, the greater the reduction in phobic behavior. Consistent with the theory, a detailed analysis shows that increases in efficacy expectations were predictive of behavioral change, irrespective of whether they were created by participant or symbolic modeling.

SELF-EFFICACY THEORY VERSUS TWO-FACTOR CONDITIONING THEORY

In a treatment study designed to compare these two alternative theories, Bandura and Adams (1977) treated snake phobic subjects with systematic desensitization until they completed the stimulus hierarchy; that is, they

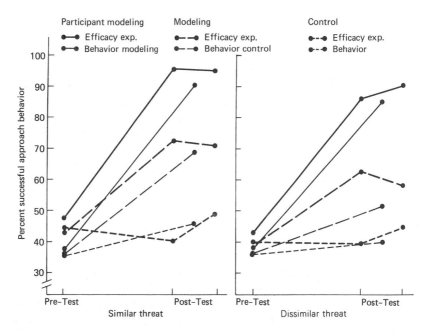

FIGURE 9.5
Level of efficacy expectations and approach behavior displayed by subjects toward threats after receiving vicarious or enactive treatments, or no treatment. (Bandura, A., Adams, N. E., and Beyer, J. 1977. Cognitive processes mediating behavioral change. *Journal of Personality and Social Psychology,* 35: 125–239. Copyright 1977 by the American Psychological Association. Reprinted by permission.)

showed no anxiety to imaginal representation of the most aversive scenes. In addition to measures of behavioral avoidance, subjects' self-efficacy expectations were assessed before treatment, after treatment but prior to the posttest, and following the posttest. Although all subjects had been equally desensitized, the reductions in avoidance behavior that they showed were typically variable. Subjects' self-efficacy expectations, however, were accurate predictors of subsequent performance on 89 percent of the behavioral tasks. These results support the cognitive theory that treatment-induced reduction of physiological arousal changes phobic behavior by increasing efficacy expectations, rather than by extinguishing a conditioned autonomic drive as postulated by the reciprocal inhibition or two-factor theory of avoidance learning (see Chap. 6). These findings need to be replicated in other settings with other problems. However, they suggest that self-efficacy theory may provide a more powerful explanation of the often variable effects of behavioral treatment methods than does existing conditioning theory.

SELIGMAN'S THEORY OF LEARNED HELPLESSNESS

Another major theory of behavioral and emotional disorders that is based on the cognitive construct of *expectations* is Seligman's (1975) notion of learned helplessness. According to this theory, a person who is subjected to uncontrollable aversive consequences learns that his or her responses are futile and comes to expect that future responding will be similarly futile. This expectation, or learned helplessness, can result in severe emotional and motivational effects, including stress, adverse physiological consequences, and extreme passivity or the failure to initiate coping responses even when behavioral consequences are controllable.

Seligman's theory can be represented in the following diagram:

I	II	III
Information about the response-outcome contingency, that is, they are independent.	Cognitive representation of the contingency (the person's expectation).	Behavior, for example, depression, passivity, anxiety, and other adverse effects.

The first component (I) is a property of the external environment. Objectively, a person's response has no effect on the consequences (s)he experiences. The second component (II) represents the way in which the person perceives or appraises the objective information (I). This is a cognitive process. In terms of Seligman's theory, it is the causal condition for the adverse emotional and motivational effects seen in component III. Why, it should be asked, need we infer this cognitive process at II instead of simply relating observable events at I to observable events at III? The latter would be the radical behaviorist view. The reason for inferring a causal cognitive process at II is that the evidence clearly shows that simple exposure to information about an uncontrollable contingency at I is insufficient for producing learned helplessness. A person can be exposed to such a contingency yet not develop learned helplessness. Conversely, a person can develop helplessness without being exposed to the objective contingency. (S)he need only *believe* that responding will not affect outcome in order to develop helplessness (Seligman, 1975). This is another example of the fact that it is our perception of the external world rather than actual reality that determines our actions (see Box 9–1). Clinical problems often arise when a significant discrepancy between a person's perceptions of events and objective reality develops. Seligman and others have proposed that this is what happens in some forms of depression. In this formulation the depressive is someone who has come to believe that trying to cope with the problems (s)he encounters is useless. (S)he has learned that responding and reinforcement are independent. It follows that the main goal of therapy is for the client to regain the belief that (s)he can control events that are important to her. The recommended treatment is precisely that used by Beck and his associates: directive therapy aimed at prompting the client to initiate behavior that results in a success experience and which serves to dispel negative attitudes.

In terms of self-efficacy theory, learned helplessness consists of faulty response-outcome expectations. It seems important to expand upon this analysis and to distinguish between efficacy and outcome expectations. The significance of such a distinction is emphasized by Bandura (1977a):

> People can give up trying because they lack a sense of efficacy in achieving the required behavior, or they may be assured of their capabilities but give up trying because they expect their behavior to have no effect on an unresponsive environment or to be consistently punished. These two separable expectancy sources of futility have quite different antecedents and remedial implications. To alter efficacy-based futility requires development of competencies and expectations of personal effectiveness. By contrast, to change outcome-based futility necessitates changes in prevailing environmental contingencies that restore the instrumental value of the competencies that people already possess. (p. 204)

Cognitive Learning Therapies and Behaviorism

The conceptual models discussed in this chapter all depart fundamentally from a radical behavioristic framework. Every treatment method in cognitive behavior therapy makes the assumption that cognitions have a causal influence on behavior. This position is explicitly rejected by radical behaviorists.

Consider self-efficacy theory. According to a behavioristic analysis, the verbal expression of self-efficacy may be reliably related to subsequent avoidance behavior, but it cannot be a cause (controlling variable) of that avoidance behavior. Both the verbal statement *and* the avoidance behavior are said to be a function of some other environmental variable. For every generalization in which a cognition is related to behavior, it is assumed that there must exist a corresponding behavior-environment generalization. In this way, cognitive variables can be overlooked without missing any lawful psychological relationships (Lacey and Rachlin, 1978). However, the challenge to this position from the social learning analysis of self-efficacy is that the initial findings suggest that a cognitive variable (self-efficacy) may be superior to a simple behavior-environment generalization in predicting and controlling phobic behavior.

The basic premise of the cognitive restructuring methods is that people react not to the *actual* but to the *perceived* environment. These perceptions may be inaccurate or irrational, in which case emotional distress may be elicited. The behaviorist dispenses with cognitive variables, such as perceptions, in favor of the person's *past history of environmental interaction.* Take, for example, the client who is phobic about flying. This client typically becomes highly anxious when he hears a sudden noise as the plane leaves the ground on take off—actually the perfectly normal retracting of the plane's landing-gear. A cognitive behavior therapist might attribute this anxiety reaction to the client's inaccurate perception that something is wrong with the plane. The radical behaviorist would suggest that the client is reacting, not only to the present environment (the sudden noise), but also to stories he has heard in the past about engines falling off and planes crashing. Rachlin (1977) summarizes this view by stating that "Inferences about past experiences may be as speculative about present cognitions, but at least they are potentially observable and suggest methods of observation and modification short of brain surgery (p. 374)."

Three important points must be noted in this connection. The first is that this dependence on a person's past history of reinforcement is inconsistent with the clinical practice of behavior therapy, a cardinal principle of which is the emphasis on the variables that are *currently* maintaining the client's problems. The focus on the here and now is a distinguishing characteristic of behavior therapy, as the descriptions of treatment strategies and assessment procedures in Chaps. 1 and 2 make clear. The second point is that radical behavioristic explanation, as Rachlin (1977) makes clear, necessarily involves an inference. Radical behaviorism is not free from inferential reasoning, as is commonly supposed. The question is not whether inferences will be made in trying to account for human behavior, but what sort of inference is the most useful. This is an empirical question that will be decided ultimately by appropriate research, rather than by theoretical arguments. The third point is that the radical behaviorist is betting that inferences that do not involve cognitive variables will lead to more effective treatment methods than those that do. There are good grounds for challenging this latter position.

When all is said and done about cognitions as opposed to conditioning, it is the criterion of *utility* and *heuristic value* that provides the acid test of the relative merits of competing theoretical approaches in contemporary behavior therapy. Noncognitive conditioning approaches have been extremely successful in generating a wealth of experimental-clinical research and in developing innovative and effective treatment methods. Yet there is reason to believe that the heuristic value of these conditioning approaches is now less than it once was. Fresh conceptual frameworks are needed to continue and extend the impetus towards a more effective form of psychological treatment that conditioning theory began. Cognitive concepts are featured prominently in this process.

Some examples can be briefly mentioned. The demonstrably successful use of vicarious observation methods, including covert, symbolic, and live modeling were derived, not from operant conditioning or applied behavior analysis, but from social learning theory with its emphasis on cognitive mediating processes (Rosenthal and Zimmerman, 1978). Therapeutic techniques that rely upon visual imagery and cognitive transformations of external events are explained away by applied behavior analysts as instances of the instructional control of behavior.[5] But it was a commitment to a mediational model of behavior that initially resulted in the development of these methods; and it is a cognitive-mediational model that continues to suggest innovative treatment strategies like those of Beck's and Meichenbaum's. It can be argued that cognitive restructuring methods, like that of Beck's, are reducible to conventional behavioral procedures. Yet Beck derived his method from a cognitive theory of human behavior. Moreover, both clinical and experimental evidence indicate that this method may be superior to conventional behavioral procedures that have remained conceptually narrow and therapeutically limited. The fact that these methods can be accommodated within the post hoc parsimony of a noncognitive, conditioning framework is less important than the failure of the latter approach to generate such techniques (Wilson, 1979).

Cognitive Learning Therapies: An Evaluation

In the evaluation of treatment outcome there is little to be gained by comparing arbitrarily defined categories of "cognitive" versus "behavioral" techniques. For example, Ledwidge (1978) compared what he calls "cognitive behavior modification" (a major part of which is cognitive restructuring) with "behavior therapy" and concluded that the former is a "step in the wrong direction." The many difficulties with Ledwidge's analysis are discussed more fully by Rachman and Wilson (in press). Illustrating these difficulties is Ledwidge's attempt to distinguish between "behavior therapy" and "cognitive behavior modification" by the focus of intervention. Thus he defines behavior therapy as the treatment of maladaptive behavior

[5]It is true, of course, that we cannot observe or change images or thoughts directly. What happens is that we observe a client's reactions to specific instructions to image a scene or rethink an assumption. Radical behaviorists argue that we need only pay attention to these instructions in explaining the determinants of behavior without inferring cognitive mediation processes. However, this position can be criticized in the same way as the concept of a past history of reinforcement was faulted as a means of explaining a person's current perceptions. Bandura (1978) has noted that "Instructions are merely sources of information that become influences through cognitive processing rather than by reflexive adoption" (p. 351). Consistent with this view, there is abundant evidence showing that people do not react mechanically to instructions but often improvise on the information they contain in unusual and unpredictable ways. People play an active role in interpreting and responding to instructions. The fact that this activity is based on previous learning (reinforcement history) does not permit the scientist or the clinician to overlook the overriding importance of an individual's current perception of instructions or any other external influence.

itself rather than some activity assumed to mediate the behavioral problem. Cognitive behavior modification is described as treatment aimed at altering thought patterns that mediate behavior. The difficulty with this distinction is that many of the methods Ledwidge defines as behavior therapy are explicitly based on a mediational model of human behavior! Systematic desensitization is a case in point. Aside from the obvious fact that this procedure includes cognitive elements such as asking the client to imagine anxiety eliciting situations, in Wolpe's original formulation the purpose of the technique was to extinguish the anxiety that was assumed to mediate overt phobic behavior. This is an example of two-factor theory that we have discussed above and which is clearly a mediational theory. Another technique that Ledwidge classifies as "behavior therapy" and not "cognitive" is modeling. However, the cognitive nature and origin of modeling are well-established (Rosenthal and Zimmerman, 1978).

Another difficulty that a simplistic categorization of diverse therapeutic techniques encounters is that most treatment methods are multifaceted, consisting of behavioral, affective, and cognitive components. As such they defy compartmentalization into simple categories. Beck's (1976) cognitive therapy is a case in point. Despite the name, it is a deliberate amalgam of explicit behavioral methods (e.g., graded *in vivo* behavioral assignments) and cognitive restructuring strategies (e.g., decentering and distancing). Then there is the previously emphasized point that behavioral *procedures* might be effective because they produce changes in cognitive *processes* that govern behavior. For instance, in discussing the results of their study comparing prolonged *in vivo* exposure with a cognitive restructuring treatment, Emmelkamp et al. (1978) point out that "Giving a form of treatment a name is not the same as elucidating the therapeutic process involved. Whether the treatment 'cognitive restructuring' does actually produce a modification of cognitive processes is a debatable point. On the other hand, the effects of prolonged exposure *in vivo* could at least partly be explained in terms of cognitive restructuring. During treatment with prolonged exposure *in vivo* clients notice, for example, that their anxiety diminishes after a time and that the events which they fear, such as fainting or having a heart attack, do not take place. This may lead them to transform their unproductive self-statements into more productive ones: 'There you are, nothing will go wrong with me'. A number of clients reported spontaneously that their 'thoughts' had undergone a much greater change during prolonged exposure *in vivo* than during cognitive restructuring. It is possible that a more effective cognitive modification takes place through prolonged exposure *in vivo* than through a procedure which is focused directly on such a change" (p. 40).

As a result of the problems involved in identifying the critical processes that are responsible for successful treatment procedures, a more useful approach to evaluation would entail a detailed analysis of methods in which the contribution of specific treatment components is assessed.

When this is done, behaviorally based methods are usually found to be more effective than those that rely upon imagery or verbal operations. However, the efficacy of any technique will partly depend on the particular problem to which it is applied. For example, there is convincing evidence that cognitive restructuring methods are especially effective with the treatment of test anxiety. The reason appears to be that test anxiety is more a function of deficits in attentional processes than anxiety produced by autonomic arousal (Holroyd and others, 1978). On the other hand, with a disorder like agoraphobia, which does involve high levels of autonomic arousal and motivational problems, cognitive restructuring seems to be less effective than the preferred treatment method of *in vivo* exposure.

In conclusion, it is premature to announce that an emphasis on cognitive learning therapies is a mistake. We have indicated a number of reasons why such an emphasis makes sense at this time. As Rachman and Wilson (in press) observe, not the least of these reasons "is a welcome willingness on the part of many proponents of cognitive methods to engage in the necessary research and to conduct rigorous evaluations of their procedures. In view of the fact that clinical psychiatry and psychology have often been retarded by the reliance upon personal preference, unscientific practices and an inexcusable neglect of appropriate evaluation, this commitment and receptivity to research represents a development of potentially far-reaching significance."

A Cautionary Note

This chapter has shown that there are compelling theoretical and practical reasons for behavior therapists to pay attention to cognitive factors. By rejecting the role of cognitive processes, strict behavioristic approaches needlessly delimit the scope and efficacy of their treatment methods. However, some cognitive therapists have overreacted to this behavioral bias. By failing to emphasize the greater efficacy of behavioral *procedures* in helping clients change, these cognitive therapists run the risk of overlooking the most effective treatment methods yet developed. If unchecked, this tendency threatens to return therapy to the verbal, interview-based model of treatment in opposition to which behavior therapy was originally developed. This is especially evident in Ellis' RET, in which abnormal behavior is viewed as nothing but a problem of irrational cognitions and where the treatment methods emphasized most heavily are cognitive in nature—verbal persuasion, rational argument, and logical reasoning.

Enthusiasm for the cognitive connection in behavior therapy has also given rise to renewed suggestions about a merger between behavior therapy and traditional psychodynamic treatment approaches. Thus attention has been drawn to the cognitive nature of much of psychodynamic theory and therapy, particularly that of the ego-analysts (see Wachtel, 1977). However, we have to be careful that this appeal to eclecticism does not obscure the very real differences between psychodynamic and behavior therapy. Among the differences are the following:

a) cognitive methods in behavior therapy are concerned primarily with conscious thought processes, rather than unconscious, symbolic meanings;

b) cognitive methods in behavior therapy emphasize the regulatory influence of current cognitions. It is unnecessary to determine the unconscious roots of inaccurate or irrational interpretations of reality. It is a general characteristic of behavior therapy that the therapist focuses on how the client distorts cognitively and what to do about it, rather than on why the distortion occurs;

c) cognitive methods in behavior therapy are explicitly formulated and testable in contrast to the looser, more vaguely formulated concepts in psychodynamic approaches;

d) initial studies show that some cognitive methods in behavior therapy are significantly more effective than previous traditional procedures;

e) cognitive methods in behavior therapy are more efficient than psychodynamic approaches, both in terms of the duration of therapy and the time required to train therapists in their use (Beck, 1976).

In conclusion, the social learning conceptualization of behavior therapy is broader than the strict behavioristic view without repeating the conceptual errors of past psychodynamic therapies. The image of human functioning that emerges from this social learning view of behavior therapy is neatly described by Mischel (1977):

> This image is one of the human being as an active, aware problem-solver, capable of profiting from an enormous range of experiences and cognitive capacities, possessing great potential for good or ill, actively constructing his or her psychological world, and influencing the environment but also being influenced by it in lawful ways—even if the laws are difficult to discover and hard to generalize. It views the person as so complex and multifaceted as to defy easy classifications and comparisons on any single or simple common dimension, as multiply influenced by a host of interacting determinants, as uniquely organized on the basis of prior experiences and future expectations, and yet as rule-guided in systematic, potentially comprehensible ways that are open to study by the methods of science. It is an image that has moved a long way from the instinctual drive-reduction models, the static global traits, and the automatic stimulus-response bonds of traditional personality theories. (p. 253)

Summary

A recent emphasis on cognitive processes and procedures has resulted in the emergence of what is called *cognitive behavior therapy*. In fact, cognitive factors have been a central part of the social learning framework of behavior therapy since Bandura's (1969) landmark text. In terms of this framework, classical and operant conditioning, self-control methods, and modeling techniques all involve cognitive mediating processes.

From the start behavior therapy techniques such as systematic desensitization have relied upon symbolic processes such as visual imagery. However, these symbolic processes were conceptualized in terms of conditioning principles—the covert conditioning model. This model is based on the homogeneity assumption: that cognitive processes obey the same psychological laws as overt behavior. Although this covert conditioning model has been extremely useful in generating innovative treatment techniques, recent findings make it increasingly unlikely that it provides an accurate analysis of symbolic functioning.

Cognitive restructuring treatment techniques have been the vanguard of the cognitive behavior therapy development. All these methods are based upon the assumption that emotional disorders are the result of distorted or maladaptive thought patterns. Despite procedural differences, all are directed towards modifying or restructuring these faulty cognitions. In Ellis' RET, therapy is an attempt to change clients' philosophic outlook such that they think rationally rather than irrationally. Rationality is said to be incompatible with neurotic disturbances, and treatment consists primarily of verbal persuasion and logical argument aimed at altering clients' self-statements or beliefs. Well-controlled outcome studies on RET are sparse, and convincing supportive evidence is lacking. Yet this form of therapy appears to be highly regarded by practitioners at present.

Meichenbaum's self-instructional training consists of the modification of specific speech and thought patterns using behavioral methods, like modeling and social reinforcement. The literature attests to the efficacy of this approach in successfully changing a variety of clinical problems including anxiety, anger, pain, impulsivity in children, and attentional disorders in schizophrenic patients. In Beck's cognitive therapy, both behavioral and cognitive procedures are used to correct faulty thought processes and develop alternative coping skills. Initial outcome studies indicate that this approach is effective in the treatment of depression, a disorder marked by negative and self-defeating attitudes and hitherto resistant to psychological treatment methods.

Cognitive restructuring methods are viewed as extensions of the social learning approach. This approach integrates different treatment methods that are almost exclusively based on overt behavior (for example, operant conditioning), autonomic conditioning (for example, counterconditioning), and cognitive processes (for example, cognitive restructuring). A distinction is drawn between behavioral treatment *procedures* and cognitive *theoretical* mechanisms. Behaviorally based treatment methods are more effective than those based on verbal, imaginal or vicarious operations. There appears to be little difference between methods using visual imagery (for example, systematic desensitization) and those involving verbal processes (for example, self-instructional training).

Cognitions do not function independently. Behavior is a product of interdependent influence processes. Beliefs often shape external reality in a self-confirming manner.

Self-efficacy is an integrative theory of behavior change that suggests that different behavior therapy techniques are effective because they increase expectations of personal efficacy; namely the belief that one can cope successfully with a threatening situation. Efficacy expectations are differentiated from outcome expectations which are defined as one's belief that a particular action will result in a certain outcome. Efficacy expectations are based upon four sources of information: behavioral accomplishments, vicarious experience, physiological arousal, and verbal persuasion. Behavioral performance has been shown to influence efficacy expectations most powerfully. Reductions in phobic behavior are closely related to changes in self-efficacy. Initial research findings indicate that self-efficacy theory may provide a better explanation of the effects of fear reduction methods like participant modeling and systematic desensitization than does conditioning theory.

Seligman's theory of learned helplessness is also based on the cognitive construct of expectations. An organism exposed to uncontrollable aversive consequences learns that all attempts to cope are futile, "gives up," and shows adverse emotional effects. This helplessness persists even when the situation changes to one in which coping responses would be effective. In terms of self-efficacy theory, learned helplessness is a matter of faulty response-outcome expectations.

Strict behavioristic approaches deny that cognitions can have causal influence on behavior change. Cognitive variables, such as perceptions and expectations, are explained away in terms of the person's past history of environmental interaction. However, this analysis is as inferential as social learning theory. Moreover, it can be argued that a strict behavioristic, or operant conditioning, approach is not as heuristic as social learning theory. It can explain findings on a post hoc basis but is less successful in generating novel treatment techniques.

It is important that in the current enthusiasm for cognitive variables, the greater efficacy of behavioral *procedures* is ignored. There is a tendency in some cognitive methods to return therapy to an interview-based, verbal method, in opposition to which behavior therapy was started. Suggestions that the recent emphasis on cognitive factors might usher in a merger between behavior therapy and psychodynamic therapy are premature. Specific differences between these alternative orientations are outlined.

Suggested Readings

Cognitive processes in classical and operant conditioning, modeling, and self-control:

BANDURA, A. 1977. *Social learning theory.* Englewood Cliffs: Prentice-Hall.

Cognitive restructuring techniques:

BECK, A. T. 1976. *Cognitive therapy.* New York: International Universities Press.

ELLIS, A., and HARPER, R. A. 1975. *A new guide to rational living.* Englewood Cliffs: Prentice-Hall.

MEICHENBAUM, D. H. 1977. *Cognitive behavior modification.* New York: Plenum Press.

Critical evaluations of cognitive behavior therapy:

MAHONEY, M. J., and ARNKOFF, D. 1978. Cognitive and self-control therapies. In *Handbook of psychotherapy and behavior change,* eds. S. L. Garfield and A. E. Bergin, 2nd ed. New York: Wiley.

RACHMAN, S., and WILSON, G.T. *The effects of psychotherapy.* London: Pergamon Press, in press.

10

Ethical Issues in the Practice of Behavior Therapy

The preceding chapters have been devoted to describing the principles of behavior therapy, illustrating treatment procedures, and analyzing research strategies designed to evaluate the effectiveness of behavioral methods. The focus has been on showing how the findings and methods of experimental psychology can be applied to a wide range of clinical and educational problems in creative and successful ways. In short, we have attempted to describe and explain the nature of behavior therapy as an applied science. But what about the ethical and humanistic considerations that govern the use of all therapies, including behavior therapy? Scientific principles of behavior change cannot be evaluated without regard for the social context. Behavioral scientists have to take responsibility for considering *how* behavior change methods are applied, with *whom,* under *what* circumstances, and for *which* purposes.

In this chapter we discuss some fundamental requirements for the humane and ethical practice of behavior therapy. The important concerns include the following: (a) definition of the problem and selection of the goals of treatment; (b) informed consent and the protection of the client's human rights; (c) accountability and quality control of treatment services; and (d) factors affecting the choice of different therapeutic strategies.

Who Defines the Problems and Sets the Goals of Treatment?

As an applied science, behavior therapy is simply a collection of principles and techniques about how to change behavior; it says nothing about who should modify what behavior, why, or when. It is the client, and not the therapist, who ultimately should decide the goal of therapy. Selecting effective techniques with which to change behavior is an empirical question in which the therapist is presumably an expert; choosing therapeutic objectives is a matter of value judgement and ought to be determined primarily by the client.

While ideally the client has priority over the therapist in identifying the problem and selecting the goal of treatment, it would be naive to imagine that the therapist plays no part in influencing this process. The manner in which this occurs is one of the ways in which the therapist influences the client. The major contribution of the therapist is in helping clients to develop appropriate problem-solving strategies for establishing realistic and personally satisfying life goals for themselves. This is accomplished by assisting clients to generate several alternative courses of action and in attempting to analyze and predict the consequences to the client of pursuing different objectives. The therapist is called on to perform this function particularly with those clients who enter therapy not knowing what they really want and who hope to have the therapist make a decision for them. In cases such as these, the therapist's own values and personal experiences will almost certainly be reflected in the alternatives that are explored and how their different consequences may be evaluated.

It is incumbent on the behavior therapist to declare what his or her own values are and to state how his or her opinions might be influencing the analysis of the selection of appropriate goals. The behavior therapist might decide against furthering goals which are at odds with his or her code of ethics and refuse to work with the client or refer the client elsewhere. This openness on the part of the therapist allows the client a degree of choice in finding a suitable therapist. Performing this delicate task obviously demands self-knowledge and self-understanding on the part of the behavior therapist.

This commitment to the client's choice of goals directly contradicts the criticism that behavior therapy is a coercive form of treatment in which arbitrary treatment goals are imposed on passive, uninvolved clients. Consider the case of homosexuality, the continuing source of professional disagreement and political and social controversy. Traditional psychodynamic approaches, for example, have assumed that homosexuality represents a pathological, or "abnormal" deviation from the "normal" heterosexual psychosexual developmental process (for example, Bieber, 1962). In terms of the social learning approach, "normal" and "abnormal" are viewed as labels which reflect society's prevailing value judgments; they tell us more about the labeler's behavior and the value system it reflects than about the person being labeled. There is no evidence to contradict the assumption that homosexual responsiveness is socially acquired in the same manner as is heterosexuality. Accordingly, behavior therapists appear open to helping homosexuals adjust more satisfactorily to a permanent homosexual identity (Davison and Wilson, 1973; Russell and Winkler, 1977). The willingness to accept the client's goal, albeit unconventional, is illustrated in the case of Chuck (see Box 10–1). In this instance the therapist accepted the client's personal goal of a homosexual life, despite the fact that Chuck's parents defined this as maladaptive behavior in need of therapy. What if Chuck or any other homosexual had expressed a desire to become a heterosexual? If the therapist were satisfied that this were a mature decision arrived at after careful consideration, (s)he would try to help the client reorient to heterosexuality. This feature of behavior therapy distinguishes it not only from traditional therapeutic thinking in which homosexuality is considered prima facie evidence of psychopathology which needs to be "cured," but also from the opposition of certain extremist members of gay liberation groups who deny the right of the individual homosexual to seek treatment aimed at heterosexual reorientation (Wilson and Davison, 1974). Thus an emphasis is placed on the client's *choice.*

INFORMED CONSENT: THE ETHICAL IMPERATIVE

Before implementing any program of behavior change, it is imperative to obtain the client's freely given *informed consent,* a legal term that refers to the

Box 10–1 *Gay Rights—The Case of Chuck*

Chuck was a nineteen-year-old junior at a prominent east coast university. Returning home during the summer, Chuck disclosed to his parents that he was a homosexual. Not atypically, the parents were shocked and dismayed. The father, a successful medical internist, tried to persuade Chuck to see a therapist, but he refused, asserting that he was content with his homosexuality and that he did not want some "shrink" messing around with his head. Chuck attempted to get his parents to accept his homosexuality, but his father remained unconvinced, and his mother alternated between outbursts of anger and expressions of self-guilt. At this point, after fairly extensive reading on the subject, the father consulted one of the authors.

In brief, the parents described the full sequence of events to the therapist and appealed to him to see their son in therapy. Chuck's father, a rational man, stated that he was not asking the therapist to force or induce his son to change sexual orientation, even though this is what he really hoped would happen. Rather, he claimed that he doubted whether Chuck knew what he wanted. He felt Chuck was confused about his sexual identity. Both parents had numerous questions. They wanted to know, for example, how someone becomes homosexual instead of heterosexual? Can people change sexual preferences? In particular, the father wanted more information about the use of aversion conditioning therapy about which he had read. The therapist answered these questions as best he could, given the available scientific literature. He also made clear to the parents what his personal views on homosexuality were; that he regarded it as an alternative life style that a client is free to choose, rather than a sickness that needed to be "cured." The therapist agreed to meet with Chuck if he voluntarily sought an appointment. However, he explained to the parents that he would give Chuck the same information that he had given them concerning homosexuality; namely, that it was up to Chuck to decide what he wanted.

Two weeks later Chuck contacted the therapist for an appointment. He acknowledged that he had been reluctant to see any therapist but had changed his mind after speaking to his father, who had given him a very accurate description of what the therapist had told him and his wife. The therapist reviewed his position on the issues and answered questions Chuck had. Chuck explained that he had known that he was homosexual from the time he was thirteen years old. He had never been attracted to girls, only to other boys. He had dated in high school but only because he was supposed to. Interestingly, Chuck was very popular among the girls since he was tall, good-looking, and active in sports. During a summer vacation in Europe as a college student, Chuck had attempted to have sexual intercourse with several women, including prostitutes. He experienced no sexual arousal and was usually unable to obtain an adequate erection. Upon returning home he began to associate with a gay organization at his university and soon developed a sexually satisfying relationship with another man to whom he was attracted. It was at this point that he decided to share his feelings with his parents, with whom he had always enjoyed an open and harmonious relationship.

Chuck impressed the therapist as a bright and articulate young man. It was clear that he had given the subject of his homosexuality careful thought, that he had explored heterosexual alternatives without success, and that he was fully aware of the consequences involved in coming out of the closet in today's society. He was genuinely concerned about his parents feelings and asked the therapist if there was anything to be done to help them accept his decision. The therapist expressed his opinion that Chuck appeared to have considered the various alternatives open to him in a responsible and intelligent fashion and that he would communicate this to Chuck's parents. With Chuck's agreement he also suggested to the parents that they consult a therapist to explore ways of better accepting Chuck's homosexuality, especially since his mother experienced periods of depression.

clients' right to decide whether they want to participate in a proposed program, after they have been told what is going to be involved. More specifically, informed consent is considered to have three components: knowledge, voluntariness, and competency (Friedman, 1975). *Knowledge* refers to the information describing the program and its goals. The client must realize that (s)he is at liberty to decline or withdraw from treatment at any point. Alternative treatments should be discussed and the relative merits of each fairly evaluated. For example, a therapist who proposes to treat a hyperactive child along behavioral lines should alert the parents to the benefits and risks of pharmacological treatment of hyperactivity, a widely used alternative with some empirical support. *Voluntariness* refers to the absence of coercion, or duress, when the decision to consent is made. *Competency* reflects an assessment that the clients can understand the information that has been given to them and are in a position to make a responsible judgment about it.

Selecting therapeutic goals is considerably more difficult in the case of institutionalized individuals (for example, prisoners and mental hospital inmates) and with clients who are too young or too disturbed (for example, many psychotics) to participate meaningfully in determining behavioral objectives. In many of these instances it might be necessary to waive the requirement of obtaining the client's freely given, informed consent. In such cases behavioral procedures and goals might be approved by a guardian or an independent review committee, fairly representing all parties responsible for and concerned with the client's treatment. Review panels of this nature would be specifically created to safeguard the individual's civil rights and general well-being.

Behavior modification is oriented toward changing behavior in the natural environment. It actively attempts to use those social influence processes in the client's community which affect behavior, which in turn will influence community members. Behavior and environment interact in a reciprocal fashion. Therefore, it is important to involve relevant community groups in the planning and execution of behavior modification programs. A revealing example of how this joint decision-making procedure operates is provided by Achievement Place in Kansas, which is a community-based, family-style behavior modification center for predelinquent children (see Box 5-2, Chap. 5). Relevant community interest groups cooperated with the professional behavior modifiers who were directing the project, and the delinquent boys themselves participated in establishing goals which were mutually acceptable to all parties concerned, yet beneficial in modifying their behavior.

The emphasis here on the interests of the individual client, on informed consent, and the right to withdraw from treatment are the defining characteristics of therapy. As such, therapy is to be distinguished from social regulation in which it is the social group's, rather than the individual's, interests that are recognized and in which coercive procedures may play a prominent role.

Selection of Intervention Methods

Once the problem is defined and the goals of treatment set, the appropriate therapeutic techniques have to be selected by the therapist. The efficacy and efficiency of a treatment method are the most important factors that need to be taken into account in making this selection. Another consideration that is relevant to the choice of therapeutic techniques is the relative intrusiveness of alternative methods. *Intrusiveness* refers to methods that involve a high degree of obvious external control, especially those based on aversive control. Self-administered relaxation therapy, for example, would be an instance of a benign, minimally intrusive technique whereas the therapist-administered use of a punishment procedure using aversive electric shock would qualify as highly intrusive and restrictive. Similarly, praise or social reinforcement is less intrusive than is a token economy program based on tangible rewards. Recent legal rulings have emphasized the importance of using the least intrusive of available treatment methods (Wexler, 1973).

This principle of the "least intrusive alternative treatment" dictates that more intrusive methods be applied only after less intrusive methods have been shown to be ineffective. There are occasions, however, when more intrusive, or even aversive, procedures are appropriate. For example, in the case of Mr. B, the exhibitionist, (Chap. 1), the use of aversive behavior rehearsal, an extremely intrusive technique, was justified by the urgency of the situation and the seriousness of the consequences if he were to expose himself again. Even here, however, the client was requested to give his informed consent to this specific procedure. He was deliberately reminded that he could refuse to participate in that particular therapeutic technique without sacrificing his opportunity to be treated with other less intrusive behavioral methods. This procedure provides a necessary safeguard against the unchecked use of arbitrary or coercive methods.

An example of the use of an aversive method after a more benign approach had proved ineffective is provided by the case study of Peter, a self-injurious six-year-old boy. In this case the more benign procedure, differential positive reinforcement, proved ineffective. In the absence of alternative methods and given the life-threatening nature of the problem, a more restrictive and aversive technique was adopted. Note that in making this decision, the therapist obtained informed consent from the parents, had tried an alternative method first, and was able to document the fact that previous experimental and clinical research showed that response-contingent electric shock was an effective form of treatment (Bachman, 1972). Although a treatment might be effective in changing a target behavior, it is important to assess whether any adverse side-effects are associated with its use. In other words, the likely benefits must be weighed against possible risks. This risk-benefit analysis will vary according to the nature of the target behavior, the particular treatment technique, and the therapeutic setting. In the case of Peter, the research literature indicated that negative side-effects of the punishment procedure were unlikely (Risley, 1968). In view of the severity of the problem, the lack of an alternative, and the availability of an effective method with little probability of any negative side-effects, the use of the momentarily painful punishment procedure was professionally responsible and humane (see Friedman, 1975).

The principle of the least treatment method available has broad applicability in behavior therapy. In general, methods directed towards developing positive, alternative behaviors are favored over aversive techniques aimed at reducing or suppressing some unwanted or undesirable behavior. In turn, there is a hierarchy of priorities within each of these general categories of treatment procedures. Consider, for example, the use of reinforcement programs in the classroom as an illustration of positive methods for increasing appropriate behavior. The sequencing of intervention strategies from the least to the more restrictive requires that a token reinforcement program using tangible rewards be instituted only if systematic attempts to praise good behavior and ignore bad behavior have failed. This advice is given because token reinforcement programs require considerable teacher effort and the fading of external rewards. Moreover, on occasion, the use of external rewards may reduce the likelihood that behavioral improvements will generalize to other situations where there are no token reinforcement programs (O'Leary, Poulous, and Devine, 1972).

This principle of sequencing of interventions is best viewed as a general guide for treatment, as opposed to an iron-clad rule. The possibility exists that

Box 10–2 *The Case of Peter the Self-Injurious*
Six-Year-Old

Six and a half years old, Peter was referred to the Psychological Clinic at Rutgers University because of his self-injurious behavior. Peter's language was nonfunctional; he had no self-help skills and had to be force-fed since he would spit out all food that he was offered. More disturbing, however, was the fact that he would hit and scratch himself unless physically restrained. He hit his head so hard with his hand or knee, or against any solid object, that it posed a threat to his life. His condition had been diagnosed by a previous treatment agency as "infantile autism with functional retardation."

Initial treatment focused upon counseling the parents and attempting to reinforce behavior incompatible with hitting and scratching, using food as a reward (differential reinforcement of other behavior). At the end of one treatment session while Peter was in the care of both his mother and the therapist, he hit his head with sufficient force to require immediate hospitalization. Since even constant adult supervision could not ensure Peter's safety, it was decided that differential reinforcement was an inappropriate method. Elimination or suppression of life-threatening, self-injurious behavior was urgently required. After consultation with Peter's parents and with their fully informed consent, following the advice of other professional behavior therapists, and with the knowledge of the child's pediatrician, the therapist decided to use response-contingent electric shock as a treatment method. Experimental evidence showed that this was an effective means of reducing severe self-injurious behavior.

The details of this complex and time-consuming treatment program are beyond the scope of this book. To summarize, shock electrodes were strapped to the hand that Peter usually used to hit himself. Each self-injurious response was punished by a brief, nonharmful shock. As the self-injurious behavior decreased, Peter's mother was taught how to administer the treatment so that she could implement it at home. Both parents observed all details of the treatment procedure. Following approximately three months of this treatment, Peter had improved enough to be admitted to the Child Behavior Research and Learning Center at Rutgers University, a special school for severely disturbed children. Two months later, Peter almost completely ceased self-injurious behavior, scratching, spitting, screaming, and throwing things. He was eating solid foods and had made considerable progress in speech, self-help, and simple academic and social skills. Detailed records were kept of Peter's behavior during all treatment phases, both at home and in the clinic, in order to evaluate the effects of treatment.

For reasons that remain unclear, Peter's behavior began to deteriorate at this point. The reintroduction of electric shock helped somewhat but failed to suppress self-injurious behavior as effectively as before. Because of the constant supervision that was now involved and the limited effectiveness of the punishment procedure, Peter's parents had him admitted to an institution, on the advice of the therapist. With partial restraint, Peter was able to attend the school at the institution and engage in simple tasks. A careful follow-up revealed that during home visits, the intensity and frequency of Peter's self-injurious behavior remained considerably improved, compared to pretreatment level. Details of the treatment and results of this case are described by Romanczyk and Goren (1975).

this sequencing strategy may, under some circumstances, undermine the efficacy of a program. For example, O'Leary, Becker, Evans, and Saudargas (1969) introduced rules, structure, and a combination of praising and ignoring as treatment components prior to instituting a token economy. Disruptive behavior was reduced only during the token economy. The question is whether an earlier introduction of the token program might not have produced more efficient and effective behavior change than a sequence of less powerful procedures did. Although controlled comparisons were not made, there was the impression that the token economy eventually introduced in the O'Leary and others (1969) study resulted in less behavior change than had occurred in previous studies with similar populations in which token programs were introduced earlier in the treatment. Thus, inflexibly sequencing intervention strategies from the least to the most intrusive might well have adverse effects, in the sense that a program so sequenced might be less effective than one that began with a stronger intervention. In the ultimate analysis, the choice of treatment methods must be based upon the therapist's professional appraisal of the specific circumstances surrounding each situation.

A final word on intrusiveness is in order. We have defined intrusiveness in terms of obvious external control, especially involving the use of aversive methods. Simply because a technique is a direct method or behavior change does not necessarily make it very intrusive. For example, orgasmic reconditioning, in particular, and behavioral sex therapy, in general, have been criticized as highly intrusive, compared to psychotherapy which is assumed to be far less intrusive (Bailey, 1978). However, the issue is more complex than this simplistic dichotomy implies (Wilson, 1978d).

Orgasmic reconditioning is a well-specified technique that is *self-administered* by two informed sexual partners. It has a limited goal (orgasm); its effects on sexual behavior are reasonably predictable and clearly observable to the client. Compare these procedural criteria with traditional psychotherapy. The success of psychodynamic therapy is predicated upon the development of a workable transference relationship. During the course of this intense emotional relationship, unconscious thoughts, forbidden impulses, hidden fantasies, and a wealth of deeply intimate material is probed. Therapy has the

292

relatively vague goal of insight without specific operational referents that are immediately observable to the client (see Bandura, 1969). Is this not intrusive? Might this not have a broader effect on the client's values and beliefs than the limited attempt to enhance orgasm during specific sexual interactions?

The treatment of Peter raises an important point that is often overlooked in discussions of ethics in behavior therapy: What are the consequences of *not* using a particular technique for a given problem just because it appears to be intrusive or involves an aversive stimulus. Many therapists arbitrarily reject direct, intrusive methods because they are not to their personal liking. We would argue that it is *un*professional and *un*ethical not to use an effective technique where one exists. To draw an analogy from medicine, surgery may be painful and dangerous, but it is often necessary to save lives or restore vital bodily functioning. To refuse to operate on a seriously ill patient where that operation might save a life, just because the physician concerned has a subjective distaste for surgery, would be rightly rejected as ridiculous. Psychological therapy is not as advanced as medical treatment, but numerous behavioral techniques that have been demonstrated to be effective now exist (see Kazdin and Wilson, 1978; Leitenberg, 1976b).

Note that in this analysis of the ethical factors governing the selection of treatment techniques, decisions about treatment depend mainly on what the research literature shows. Answers to questions like "How effective is this method?" and "Are any side-effects associated with its use?" are vital to an informed decision about what methods to employ. This point should serve to emphasize the clinical and practical importance of the scientific research discussed in the preceding chapters of this book.

Accountability and Quality Control in Treatment

There are two important issues here: (1) Appropriate assessment of the effects of treatment intervention; and (2) Implementation of treatment methods by competent and qualified therapists or other behavior change agents. In order to resolve these issues and ensure quality control, it is necessary to collect *data* on the effects of treatment on both the target behavior and other behaviors that may be affected by changes in the target behavior.

ASSESSMENT OF TREATMENT EFFECTS

One of the defining characteristics of behavior therapy is a commitment to the continual measurement and evaluation of the specific effects of treatment. This concern with assessment is illustrated in the treatment of Peter, the self-injurious little boy (see Box 10–2). Detailed records were kept showing the frequencies of operationally defined self-injurious behavior and the number of punishments administered in both the home and the clinic setting. These data showed that compared to Peter's behavior prior to treatment (baseline), the introduction of the punishment procedure greatly reduced self-injurious behavior. It was on the basis of these detailed behavioral observations that changes were made in the treatment program; these observations also provided an early warning of Peter's deterioration following his earlier progress. Similarly, in the case of Mr. B (see Chap. 1), the measurement of penile erection to specific sexual stimuli during the course of therapy provided an objective index of whether the treatment was having the desired effects.

Side-Effects. Side-effects, or changes in behaviors that are not directly targeted for change, are possible in all forms of treatment, including behavior therapy. Accordingly, relevant related behaviors should be assessed in addition to the specifically treated behavior. In behavior therapy, these side-effects, or concomitant changes in behavior, have almost always been reported to be positive. In the treatment of obesity, for example, traditional therapists have warned that clients who lose weight may become depressed. However, careful monitoring of the emotional patterns of clients in weight reduction programs has indicated positive emotional consequences of weight loss (Stunkard and Mahoney, 1976). It has been alleged that one of the side-effects of the behavioral treatment of sexual dysfunction is that it undermines the traditional institutions of marriage, family, and religious values. Yet behavioral sex therapy has been shown to enhance marital satisfaction and often prevent divorce and family disruption (Masters and Johnson, 1970).

In rare instances, maladaptive behavior has been reported to occur following behavior therapy. For example Brady (1971) observed that some husbands became impotent after their wives' sexual responsiveness was increased. This phenomenon exemplifies the fact that psychological functioning represents a continuous reciprocal interaction between people's behavior and its controlling environmental consequences, and reinforces Masters and Johnson's (1970) insistence that "there is no such thing as an uninvolved partner in any marriage in which there is some form of sexual inadequacy." Behavior change does not occur in a vacuum but within the context of an ongoing network of complicated social relationships. More often than not, the development of behavioral competence engenders positive, reinforcing social feedback; it may also, however, draw attention to behavioral deficits in a marital partner for whom the original problem was of functional value, and who will often require treatment in his own right. This requires careful assessment of the effects of therapy on both the client's functioning and his or her spouse's behavior.

Information on the direct and indirect effects of treatment makes the therapist or treatment agency accountable to the consumer. This consumer may be the person receiving treatment, or parents, or representatives of institutions who are employing the therapist to change someone else's behavior. Another advantage of collecting data on treatment effects is that it may allow the therapist to make more informed decisions about treatment. Data provide feedback about client progress and can be used to indicate whether therapy should be continued, intensified, or completely altered. In most traditional approaches, which are less empirically oriented, a switch in therapeutic tactics, if this occurs at all, is usually made according to more arbitrary and subjective criteria.

Of course, clinical practitioners are not always able to collect objective data on a continuous basis, as they were in the case of Mr. B or little Peter, both of whom were treated in university facilities where the therapists had the necessary time and back-up resources, that is, a psychophysiological laboratory and trained behavioral observers. However, asking the client to keep daily records of problem behaviors (self-monitoring) or obtaining reports from a spouse or family member of the client (with the client's permission) are acceptable alternatives that yield valuable information.

WHO IS QUALIFIED TO USE BEHAVIORAL METHODS?

Scientific research establishes which treatment procedures are effective and which are not. However, in order to evaluate the quality of a behavioral treatment program one also has to assess the competence of the therapist who implements the behavioral techniques. Effective therapy usually depends on the skill of the therapist in conducting a complete behavioral assessment, selecting the appropriate treatment techniques, and implementing these methods at the right time in the right way for each individual client. Behavior therapy sometimes appears to be deceptively simple to do. In fact, its effective use is usually a complex and challenging task that requires as much ingenuity and skill as any other form of therapy. A discussion of these factors is beyond the scope of this book. (For a more detailed analysis of the therapist's contributions to effective behavior therapy see Goldfried and Davison [1976] and Wilson and Evans [1976].) Suffice it to state here that specifying the personal and professional qualifications that comprise a competent behavior therapist is not an easy task. Agras (1973) has commented that a well-qualified behavior therapist

> . . . must have knowledge of the principles underlying behavior modification, experience in the application of such knowledge to human behavior problems, and experience in the experimental analysis of deviant human behavior, both for research purposes and as an approach to the on-going evaluation of clinical care.

(S)he must also, however, demonstrate certain less well-defined characteristics, usually referred to as general clinical skills. (p. 169)

These "clinical skills" are usually acquired in formal graduate training programs in clinical and school psychology, in psychiatric residency training, or in graduate programs in social work. Although they do not guarantee competence, other practical pointers to finding a competent therapist include certification or licensing by a state boards and membership in professional organizations.

As we have described in Chap. 1, a characteristic feature of behavior therapy is the widespread use of nonprofessional psychological assistants as mediators of behavior change programs. They include parents, teachers, nurses, psychiatric aides, and even members of children's peer groups. The training and competence of these assistants requires systematic attention. Behavior therapists in charge of an intervention program must ensure the adequacy of training of their staff and continued supervision of on-going programs. To collect the data that are necessary for assessing treatment effects, to supervise and to monitor the quality of a behavioral program that is implemented by nonprofessional assistants requires considerable time and effort. If the behavior therapist is unable to invest the necessary time and effort, (s)he is best advised not to initiate the treatment program at all.

The sense of the discussion thus far is summarized in Box 10–3. This inset lists a number of basic questions that are addressed to the critical ethical issues inherent in *any* treatment approach. These questions should be borne in mind in the practice of all forms of psychological treatment.

Therapist Influence on the Client: To Be or Not to Be?

Unlike the case of Shakespeare's *Hamlet,* this is *not* the question when it comes to psychological therapies. It is now widely accepted that all forms of therapy involve direct social influence of the client by the therapist. This is true even for Rogerian, or "client-centered," therapy in which the therapist may unwittingly reinforce particular sorts of verbalizations that are believed to be therapeutic (Truax, 1966). The question is thus not whether clients' behavior should or should not be influenced, it unquestionably is. The important question then becomes whether the therapist is aware of this influence and the behaviors it is used to develop. The influence process should be explicitly recognized, and emphasis placed on specific, client-defined objectives. The inadvertent influence of the therapist's own value system will be greater when treatment goals are not specified in clear behavioral terms. A particular problem with this form of influence in vaguely formulated and unstructured thera-

Box 10–3 *Ethical Issues for Human Services*

A. Have the goals of treatment been adequately considered?

   1. To insure that the goals are explicit, are they written?
   2. Has the client's understanding of the goals been assured by having the client restate them orally or in writing?
   3. Have the therapist and client agreed on the goals of therapy?
   4. Will serving the client's interests be contrary to the interests of other persons?
   5. Will serving the client's immediate interests be contrary to the client's long-term interest?

B. Has the choice of treatment methods been adequately considered?

   1. Does the published literature show the procedure to be the best one available for that problem?
   2. If no literature exists regarding the treatment method, is the method consistent with generally accepted practice?
   3. Has the client been told of alternative procedures that might be preferred by the client on the basis of significant differences in discomfort, treatment time, cost, or degree of demonstrated effectiveness?
   4. If a treatment procedure is publicly, legally, or professionally controversial, has formal professional consultation been obtained, has the reaction of the affected segment of the public been adequately considered, and have the alternative treatment methods been more closely reexamined and reconsidered?

C. Is the client's participation voluntary?

   1. Have possible sources of coercion on the client's participation been considered?
   2. If treatment is legally mandated, has the available range of treatments and therapists been offered?
   3. Can the client withdraw from treatment without a penalty or financial loss that exceeds actual clinical costs?

D. When another person or an agency is empowered to arrange for therapy, have the interests of the subordinated client been sufficiently considered?

   1. Has the subordinated client been informed of the treatment objectives and participated in the choice of treatment procedures?
   2. Where the subordinated client's competence to decide is limited, have the client as well as the guardian participated in the treatment discussions to the extent that the client's abilities permit?

3. If the interests of the subordinated person and the superordinate persons or agency conflict, have attempts been made to reduce the conflict by dealing with both interests?

E. Has the adequacy of treatment been evaluated?

1. Have quantitative measures of the problem and its progress been obtained?
2. Have the measures of the problem and its progress been made available to the client during treatment?

F. Has the confidentiality of the treatment relationship been protected?

1. Has the client been told who has access to the records?
2. Are records available only to authorized persons?

G. Does the therapist refer the clients to other therapists when necessary?

1. If treatment is unsuccessful, is the client referred to other therapists?
2. Has the client been told that if dissatisfied with the treatment, referral will be made?

H. Is the therapist qualified to provide treatment?

1. Has the therapist had training or experience in treating problems like those of the client?
2. If deficits exist in the therapist's qualifications, has the client been informed?
3. If the therapist is not adequately qualified, is the client referred to other therapists, or has supervision by a qualified therapist been provided? Is the client informed of the supervisory relation?
4. If the treatment is administered by mediators, have the mediators been adequately supervised by a qualified therapist?

Reprinted from *Behavior Therapy*, 1977, 8, V–VI.

pies is that it involves a subtle and often insidious manipulation of the client's beliefs.

Causal Models of Human Behavior

In part, the birth of behavior therapy was a reaction against the psychoanalytic model of human behavior. According to this causal model, behavior is determined by largely autonomous and unconscious intrapsychic forces; and, logically, therapy focuses on these internal processes to the relative neglect of environmental factors. In rejecting this model, many behavior therapists sought refuge in the causal model of radical behaviorism. However, like the psychoanalytic model, radical behaviorism, or the strict operant conditioning approach, is *unidirectional* causal model of human behavior. Whereas the psychoanalytic view emphasizes internal, psychic determinants of behavior, the behavioristic approach holds that the environment is the ultimate determinant of behavior. As Skinner (1971) bluntly put it, "A person does not act upon the world, the world acts upon him" (p. 211). Not surprisingly, often exaggerated descriptions of this model evoked unflattering images of people as passive automatons, responding reflexively to external influences beyond their control. Such a position seems to deny our everyday experience that we at least partly determine our own actions.

As discussed in Chap. 1, the social learning approach to behavior therapy is based on the model of *reciprocal determinism.* According to this model, psychological functioning involves a continuous reciprocal interaction among behavioral, cognitive, and environmental influences. Self-efficacy theory, which was discussed in Chap. 9, provides an excellent example of this *interdependence* among causal influences. Behavior is partly a function of the environment, but it is also true that the environment is partly created by our behavior. Thus behavior helps determine the environment which then influences behavior in a continuous reciprocal interaction process. Box 9-3 provides an example of reciprocal determinism. In that example, the males' beliefs influenced their behavior which changed the behavior of their female partners. The change in the males' social environment, in turn, influenced their own beliefs and behavior.

There is not an inevitable prime determinant of behavior although the relative influence of cognitive, behavioral, and environmental factors will vary across individuals, activities, and situations. The importance of this social learning model of human behavior is that people are viewed as having the capability of self-direction—of being able to shape their own destinies by affecting the external environment. Chapter 7 describes the nature of behavioral self-control strategies and the evidence of their effectiveness. The newcomer to behavior therapy might be surprised to learn of this emphasis on self-regulation of behavior and to discover that one of the most prominent areas of research on behavioral principles is devoted to the exploration and development of self-regulatory skills for more personally satisfying emotional and behavioral adjustment—or what Mahoney and Thoresen (1974) have aptly called "power to the person."

The reciprocal determinism model of causal processes in human behavior must be borne in mind in evaluating ethical issues in behavior therapy. One of the major objections critics had of behavior therapy was that a scientific technology of behavior modification would give treatment agencies unilateral power to change the behavior of clients. Typical of this response is the fear expressed by the psychoanalyst Wheelis (1973) who charged that behavior therapy is "a coercive treatment in which the therapist acts as agent for society, and the goal is adjustment." If this were the case, there would certainly be cause for concern. Happily, however, these fears are greatly exaggerated and based upon grossly distorted interpretations of the field. The fundamental flaw in charges of this nature is that they assume a unidirectional causal model of behavior and exaggerate the reality of automatic conditioning processes. The automatic nature of both classical and operant conditioning has been shown to be largely false (see Chaps. 4 and 6). The alleged power of behavior modification methods to control human behavior has been exaggerated by both extreme proponents as well as the opponents of behavior therapy.

Even an extreme behaviorist such as Skinner (1971) has acknowledged what he calls the capacity for countercontrol. To *countercontrol* means to react against the influence of environmental influence. However, this concept does not go far enough in accommodating the well-documented ability of people to resist unwanted external control over their lives (Bandura, 1977b). In therapy, for example, it is vital that the behavior therapist have the cooperation and active participation of the client. This is one of the reasons the therapist-client relationship is important in behavior therapy (Wilson and Evans, 1976). A hallmark of behavior therapy is that the client is asked to *do* something, such as imagine aversive scenes in desensitization, refuse to accede to an unreasonable request in assertion training, self-monitor caloric intake in self-control programs for the treatment of obesity, and so on. If clients do not follow these specific treatment suggestions, little if any change can be expected. This is especially true with adult outpatients. Whenever possible, the behavior therapist is also well-advised to seek out the active cooperation of children and even institutionalized clients whose own behavior is to be altered, despite the fact that someone else (parents or institutional authorities) has initiated the therapy (Stolz and others, 1977). To summarize this section, it is clear that for behavior therapy to be successful, the client's freely given, informed consent and continued cooperation with a therapist who is trusted is a minimal necessity.

In an attempt to emphasize the links between laboratory research and applied behavior analysis, some behavior modifiers have described the behavior therapist as a "social reinforcement machine," a "behavioral engineer," or a behavioral "programmer." The use of this operant jargon has been doubly unfortunate. First, these figurative terms are misleading since they emphasize unilateral control of the therapist over a relatively passive and powerless client. As we have indicated, this model of human behavior is one-sided; it does not reflect the interdependence among behavior, cognitive processes, and the environment. Secondly, this language of "control" helps perpetuate an unfavorable (and inaccurate) image of behavior therapy. People are so put off that they might reject behavioral methods that can contribute significantly to a happier and more rewarding life. The unfortunate effects of the impersonal and mechanistic language of radical behaviorism are illustrated in the study by Woolfolk, Woolfolk, and Wilson (1977). (See Box 10–4).

Box 10-4 *A Rose by Any Other Name*

Mention the term *behavior modification,* and many people become uncomfortable, with thoughts of the sort of "mind control" shown in the film *A Clockwork Orange.* But what if the name were changed? Would people still have negative reactions to the methods of behavior therapy?

In a study by Woolfolk, Woolfolk, and Wilson (1977), college students in a teacher-education program were asked to evaluate a videotape illustrating a teaching approach used in an elementary school special education class. The tape included three 10-minute segments showing the teacher working with emotionally disturbed second graders who left their own class to join her program one to three hours a day. Two descriptions of the videotape were prepared, one identifying the teaching strategy as an example of "behavior modification" and the other labeling it "humanistic and affective education." Approximately half the subjects received the behavior modification description when they viewed the videotape, while the rest were given the humanistic education account.

The description of behavior modification emphasized the work of B.F. Skinner as indicated by the following excerpt:

> Success in controlling the behavior of laboratory animals has led Skinner and other psychologists to the conclusion that, in order to be maximally effective, the teacher should function in the classroom in much the same way as the experimental psychologist functions in the laboratory. That is, the teacher should determine the final behaviors that she desires from her students and then systematically shape their behavior by presenting the appropriate stimuli and reinforcing student responses that lead to the specified outcomes."

The description of humanistic education focused on the importance of feelings and contained phrases such as self-awareness, growth, and successes and accomplishments.

The subjects' responses to questionnaires indicated that they liked both the teacher and the technique better if the videotape was presented as an illustration of humanistic education. The teacher was perceived as more competent, more personally attractive, and more flexible; the intervention method was viewed as more effective. These results suggest that the terms used to describe behavior therapy techniques might have more negative connotations for many people than do the actual methods. Few people might object to the system of rewards and punishments that teachers have used for centuries. But people do react negatively to descriptions of behavior change processes that sound like human engineering, that emphasize control by others, and that are devoid of any concern about a client's or a student's feelings.

There is no need to resort to mechanistic metaphors and technocratic jargon in order to describe behavior in precise and accurate terms. In contemporary behavior therapy, with its explicit recognition of cognitive mediation and its emphasis on self-control processes, therapists are no longer seen as simple "shapers" of attitudes and behavior, although their influence on the client may be profound. Instead, the therapist is seen as a consultant, not as a controller.

Behavior Therapy as a Humanistic Science

Bandura (1969) has pointed out that far from being inconsistent with a humanistic philosophy, behavior therapy is a very effective means of promoting personal freedom and emotional growth because of its efficacy in enhancing freedom of choice. Consider, for example, the agoraphobic client who is at the mercy of her unpredictable terrors and confined to her home or the unassertive person who cannot express his genuine feelings and is often treated like a doormat. Removing the agoraphobic's crippling fears or teaching the dependent person to be appropriately assertive and hence savor the satisfaction of experiencing a sense of human dignity, rather than personal humiliation, is to increase dramatically the range of activities in which those individuals can engage. They can now choose to stay at home or travel; they can now elect to refuse an unreasonable request or freely express their genuine feelings of approval or disapproval, joy or sorrow, without experiencing guilt or embarrassment.

Or, think of the psychotic or retarded child, who, as a result of not knowing basic self-care skills, having learning deficiencies, and being unable to talk or communicate properly, is inexorably destined to a life of squalid emptiness in some understaffed, impersonal state institution. A behavior therapy program which can successfully teach self-care, social skills, and communicative competencies can give that child a chance of avoiding institutionalization and of finding a rewarding role for himself in society (Lovaas, Koegel, Simmons, and Long, 1973). In other words, behavior therapy, when successfully applied, does not oppressively mold clients according to some rigid, impersonal formula. Rather, it seeks to free clients from the restrictions placed upon them by their problems by helping them to overcome obstacles to self-fulfillment.

As with any body of knowledge, the principles and procedures of behavior therapy can be abused. Specific instances of the unethical and illegal use of behavior modification methods have been reported in institutional settings. In response to these abuses, behavior therapists have been active in attempts to formulate procedures that guarantee the human rights and personal dignity of all clients, especially those of the retarded and mental hospital populations that are often subjected to relative neglect (for example, Azrin, Stolz, and Stuart, 1977; Davison and Stuart, 1975; May and others, 1975; Stolz and others, 1977). Finally, it must be remembered that these ethical imperatives of informed consent, accountability, and quality control of treatment should be common to *all* forms of psychological and psychiatric treatment. There is little that is unique about behavior therapy when it comes to concern about these matters.

Summary

There is more to the practice of clinical behavior therapy than the simple application of the principles and procedures of experimentally based psychology. Ethical and legal considerations require that the therapist be concerned about how these procedures are applied, toward what ends, and for which purposes. Four areas in particular demand attention. These involve the question of who determines the goals of treatment; informed consent; the selection of specific therapeutic techniques; and accountability and quality control of treatment.

In behavior therapy the *goal of treatment is determined primarily by the client.* The role of the therapist is in helping the client to generate alternative courses of action and to attempt to analyze their probable consequences. In other words, the therapist assists the client to develop general strategies of how you go about setting goals and does not choose goals for the client. Inevitably, the therapist does influence the client in the process of setting the goals of therapy. However, the therapist attempts to indicate what his or her personal biases and values are and how they might be influencing the analysis of the selection of goals.

Informed consent is defined legally as consent given by a competent and knowledgeable person on a strictly voluntary basis. Informed consent requires that the client be made aware of the availability of alternative forms of treatment and of his or her right to decline or withdraw from treatment at any point. With young children or individuals who are too disturbed (for example, some psychotics) or too retarded to participate meaningfully in the selection of treatment goals, the right to informed consent has to be waived. In the case of young children, the parents must give their informed consent for treatment. With institutionalized clients, a review committee representing those people responsible for and concerned about the client's treatment should ideally approve treatment goals and procedures.

The guiding ethical and legal principle in the selection of treatment methods is that the *least intrusive method(s)* should be used to accomplish therapeutic objectives. In practice this means that procedures involving the development of positive behavioral alternatives are preferred to aversive techniques aimed at the reduction or elimination of unwanted or undesirable behavior. In those instances in which more restrictive or intrusive procedures are warranted (for example, punishment procedures with a self-injurious child), the anticipated benefits must be weighed carefully against potential risks or adverse side-effects. However, the failure to employ an effective aversive (intrusive) technique when more benign methods have proved unsuccessful is unprofessional and unethical.

Accountability requires that the effects of treatment on the target behavior and other related activities be systematically monitored and assessed. This information is vital in deciding whether to continue, modify, or intensify therapy. It also provides the client with specific information on his or her progress. *Quality control* necessitates that the therapist be competent and well-trained in scientific psychology and general clinical skills. In behavioral programs in which the procedures are implemented by psychological assistants (for example, parents and teachers), the behavior therapist is responsible for ensuring that the assistants are well-trained and closely supervised throughout the course of the treatment program.

Behavior therapists often arouse concern because they avowedly change behavior. However, *all* forms of psychological treatment involve therapist influence on the client. In explicitly acknowledging this influence process and in emphasizing specific, client-defined goals, behavior therapy is an open and "up-front" approach in which the client is an active and cooperative participant. This specificity and openness in behavior therapy can be contrasted with the more subtle, but none the less very real, influence process in alternative forms of treatment in which it is assumed that the therapist, and not the client, is the best judge of what is good adjustment or "mental health."

Behavior therapy is a humanistic form of treatment that promotes personal growth and fulfillment by enhancing freedom of choice. Rather than imposing arbitrary therapeutic goals or molding clients according to some impersonal formula, behavior therapy expands clients' life choices by reducing debilitating inhibitions and fears and broadening behavioral repertoires.

Suggested Readings

Behavior therapy and legal regulation:

FRIEDMAN, P.R. 1975. Legal regulation of applied behavior analysis in mental institutions and prisons. *Arizona Law Review* 17:39–104.

MARTIN, R. 1974. *Behavior modification: Human rights and legal responsibilities.* Champaign, Ill: Research Press.

WEXLER, D. 1974. Token and taboo: Behavior modification, token economies, and the law. In *Annual review of behavior therapy: Theory and practice, Vol. II.* eds. C. M. Franks & G. T. Wilson. New York: Brunner/Mazel.

Dealing with ethical issues in the practice of behavior therapy:

BANDURA, A. 1969. *Principles of behavior modification.* chap. 2. New York: Holt, Rinehart and Winston.

STOLZ, B., and others. 1977. Report of the American Psychological Association Commission on Behavior Modification.

The therapist's contribution to effective behavior therapy:

WILSON, G.T., and EVANS, I.M. The therapist-client relationship in adult behavior therapy. *Annual review of behavior therapy: Theory and Practice, Vol. IV.* eds. C.M. Franks & G.T. Wilson. New York: Brunner/Mazel.

BIBLIOGRAPHY

AD HOC COMMITTEE ON CLASSIFICATION OF HEADACHE. 1962. *Journal of the American Medical Association* 179:717–718.

AGRAS, W.S. 1973. Toward the certification of behavior therapists? *Journal of Applied Behavior Analysis* 6:167–173.

ANESKO, K., and O'LEARY, S.G. 1978. *Assessment of homework problems and evaluation of a remedial training manual for parents.* Unpublished manuscript, State University of New York at Stony Brook, Stony Brook, N.Y.

ATTHOWE, J.M., JR., and KRASNER, L. 1968. Preliminary report on the application of contingent reinforcement procedures (token economy) on a "chronic" psychiatric ward. *Journal of Abnormal Psychology* 73:37–43.

AYLLON, T., and AZRIN, N.H. 1969. The measurement and reinforcement of behavior of psychotics. *Journal of the Experimental Analysis of Behavior* 8:357–383.

AYLLON, T., and AZRIN, N.H. 1968. *The token economy: A motivational system for therapy and rehabilitation.* New York: Appleton-Century-Crofts.

AYLLON, T. and AZRIN, N.H. 1965. The measurement and reinforcement of behavior of psychotics. *Journal of the Experimental Analysis of Behavior,* 8:357–383.

AZRIN, N.H. 1976. Improvements in the community-reinforcement approach to alcoholism. *Behaviour Research and Therapy* 14:339–348.

AZRIN, N.H. 1977. A strategy for applied research: Learning based but outcome oriented. *American Psychologist* 32:140–149.

AZRIN, N.H., HOLZ, W., ULRICH, R., and GOLDIAMOND, I. 1961. The control of the content of conversation through reinforcement. *Journal of the Experimental Analysis of Behavior* 4:25–30.

AZRIN, N.H., and POWELL, J. 1968. Behavioral engineering: The reduction of smoking behavior by a conditioning apparatus and procedure. *Journal of Applied Behavior Analysis* 1:193–200.

AZRIN, N.H., and POWELL, J. 1969. Behavioral engineering: The use of response priming to improve prescribed self-medication. *Journal of Applied Behavior Analysis* 2:39–42.

AZRIN, N.H., STUART, R. B., RISLEY, T., and STOLZ, S. 1977. Ethical issues for human services. *Behavior Therapy* 8:v–vi.

AZRIN, N.H., and WESOLOWSKI, M.D. 1974. Theft reversal: An overcorrection procedure for eliminating stealing by retarded persons. *Journal of Applied Behavior Analysis* 4:577–581.

BACHMAN, J.A. 1972. Self-injurious behavior: A behavioral analysis. *Journal of Abnormal Psychology* 80:211–224.

BAER, D.M. 1962. Laboratory control of thumb sucking with withdrawal and representation of reinforcement. *Journal of the Experimental Analysis of Behavior* 5:525–528.

BAER, D.M., PETERSON, R.R., and SHERMAN, J.A. 1967. The development of imitation by reinforcing behavioral similarity to a model. *Journal of Experimental Analysis of Behavior* 10:405–416.

BAILEY, K.G. 1978. Psychotherapy or massage parlor technology: Comments on the Zeiss, Rosen, and Zeiss treatment procedure. *Journal of Consulting and Clinical Psychology,* 46:1502–1506.

BAK, R.C., and STEWART, W.A. 1974. Fetishism, transvestism and voyeurism: A psychoanalytic approach. In *American Handbook of Psychology*, ed. S. Arieti, Vol. 3. New York: Basic Books.

BAKAL, D. 1975. Headache: A biopsychological perspective. *Psychological Bulletin*, 82:369–382.

BANCROFT, J.H. 1974. *Deviant sexual behaviour*. Oxford: Oxford University Press.

BANDURA, A. 1971. Psychotherapy based on modeling principles. In *Handbook of psychotherapy and behavior change*, eds. A.E. Bergin and S.L.Garfield. New York: Wiley.

BANDURA, A. 1972. Modeling theory: Some traditions, trends, and disputes. In *Recent trends in social learning theory*, ed. R.D. Parke. New York: Academic Press.

BANDURA, A. 1976. Effecting change through participant modeling. In *Counseling methods*, eds. J.D. Krumboltz and C.E. Thoresen. New York: Holt, Rinehart and Winston.

BANDURA, A. 1977a. Self-efficacy: Toward a unifying theory of behavioral change. *Psychological Review*. 84:191–215(a).

BANDURA, A. 1977b. *Social learning theory*. Englewood Cliffs: Prentice-Hall.

BANDURA, A. 1978a. Reflections on self-efficacy. *Advances in Behaviour Research and Therapy* 1:237–269.

BANDURA, A. 1978b. The self system in reciprocal determinism. *American Psychologist* 33:344–358.

BANDURA, A., and Adams, N.E. 1977. Analysis of self-efficacy theory of behavioral change. *Cognitive Therapy and Research*, 1:287–310.

BANDURA, A., ADAMS, N.E., and BEYER, J. 1977. Cognitive processes mediating behavioral change. *Journal of Personality and Social Psychology* 35:125–139.

BANDURA, A., BLANCHARD, E.B., and RITTER, B. 1969. The relative efficacy of desensitization and modeling approaches for inducing behavioral, affective, and cognitive changes. *Journal of Personality and Social Psychology* 13:173–199.

BANDURA, A., GRUSEC, J.E., and MENLOVE, F.L. 1967. Vicarious extinction of avoidance behavior. *Journal of Personality and Social Psychology* 5:16–23.

BANDURA, A., JEFFERY, R.W., and BACHICHA, D.L. 1974. Analysis of memory codes and cumulative rehearsal in observational learning. *Journal of Research in Personality* 7:295–305.

BANDURA, A., JEFFERY, R.W., and GAJDOS, E. 1975. Generalizing change through participant modeling with self-directed mastery. *Behaviour Research and Therapy* 13:141–152.

BANDURA, A., JEFFERY, R.W., and WRIGHT, C.L. 1974. Efficacy of participant modeling as a function of response induction aids. *Journal of Abnormal Psychology* 83:56–64.

BANDURA, A., and PERLOFF, B. 1967. Relative efficacy of self-monitored and externally imposed reinforcement systems. *Journal of Personality and Social Psychology* 7:111–116.

BANDURA, A., ROSS, D., and ROSS, S.A. 1963. Imitation of film-mediated aggressive models. *Journal of Abnormal and Social Psychology* 66:3–11.

BANDURA, A., and SIMON, K.M. 1977. The role of proximal intentions in self-regulation of refractory behavior. *Cognitive Therapy and Research* 1:177–193.

BANDURA, A., and WALTERS, R.H. 1963. *Social learning and personality development*. New York: Holt, Rinehart and Winston.

BARBER, T.X. 1975/1976. Responding to "hypnotic" suggestions: An introspective report. In *Biofeedback & self-control,* eds. T.X. Barber, L.V. Dicara, J. Kamiya, N.E. Miller, D. Shapiro, and J. Stoyve. Chicago: Aldine, 1976.

BARCUS, F.E. 1971. *Saturday Children's Television.* Newtonville, Mass.: Action for Children's Television.

BARLOW, D.H., REYNOLDS, E.J., and AGRAS, W.S. 1973. Gender identity change in a transsexual. *Archives of General Psychiatry* 28:569–576.

BARLOW, D.H. 1977. Behavioral assessment in clinical settings: Developing issues. In *Behavioral assessment: New directions in clinical psychology,* eds. J.D. Cone and R.P. Hawkins. New York: Brunner/Mazel.

BARTON, E.S., GUESS, D., GARCIA, E., and BAER, D.M. 1970. Improvement of retardates' mealtime behaviors by time-out procedures using multiple baseline techniques. *Journal of Applied Behavior Analysis* 3:77–84.

BAUM, W.M. 1973. The correlation-based law of effect. *Journal of the Experimental Analysis of Behavior* 20:137–153.

BECK, A.T. 1963. Thinking and depression: 1. Idiosyncratic content and cognitive distortions. *Archives of General Psychiatry* 9:324–333.

BECK, A.T. 1976. *Cognitive therapy and the emotional disorders.* New York: International Universities Press.

BENDER, N. 1976. Self-verbalization versus tutor verbalization in modifying impulsivity. *Journal of Educational Psychology* 68:347–354.

BENSON, H. 1975. *The relaxation response.* New York: Avon.

BENSON, H., SHAPIRO, D., TURSKY, B., SCHWARTZ, G.E. 1971. Decreased systolic blood pressure through operant conditioning techniques in patients with essential hypertension. *Science* 173:740–742.

BERNSTEIN, D.A. and PAUL, G.L. 1971. Some comments on therapy analogue research with small animal "phobias." *Journal of Behavior Therapy and Experimental Psychiatry* 2:225–237.

BERNSTEIN, L. BERNSTEIN, R.S., and DANA, R.H. 1974. *Interviewing: A guide for health professionals* (2nd ed.). New York: Appleton-Century-Crofts.

BIEBER, I., DAIN, H.J., DINCE, P.R., DRELLICH, M.G., GRAND, H.G., GUPDLACH, R.H., KREMER, M.W., RIFKIN, A.H., WILBUR, C.B., and BIEBER, T.B. 1962. *Homosexuality: A psychoanalytic study.* New York: Basic Books.

BIJOU, S.W. 1965. Experimental studies of child behavior, normal and deviant. In *Research in behavior modification,* eds. L. Krasner and L.P. Ullmann. New York: Holt, Rinehart and Winston.

BIRBAUMER, N. 1977. Biofeedback training: A critical review of its clinical application and some possible future directions. *European Journal of Behavioural Analysis and Modification* 4:235–251.

BIRNBRAUER, J.S., WOLF, M.M., KIDDER, J.D., and TAGUE, C.E. 1965. Classroom behavior of retarded pupils with token reinforcement. *Journal of Experimental Child Psychology* 2:219–235.

BLACK, A.H. 1971. Autonomic aversive conditioning in infrahuman subjects. In *Aversive conditioning and learning,* ed. F.R. Brush. New York: Academic Press.

BLANCHARD, E.B., and MILLER, S.T. 1977. Psychological treatment of cardiovascular disease. *Archives of General Psychiatry* 34:1402–1413.

BLANCHARD, E.B., MILLER, S.T., ABEL, G.G., HAYNES, M.R., and WICKER, R. 1979. Evaluation of biofeedback in the treatment of borderline essential hypertension. *Journal of Applied Behavior Analysis,* 12:99–109.

BLANCHARD, E.B., and YOUNG, L.D. 1974. Clinical applications of biofeedback training. *Archives of General Psychiatry* 30:573–589.

BLANCHARD, E.B., THEOBOLD, D.E., WILLIAMSON, D.A., SILVER, B.V., and BROWN, D.A. 1978. Temperature biofeedback in the treatment of migraine headaches. *Archives of General Psychiatry* 35:581–588.

BOERSMA, K., DENHEDGST, S., DEKKER, J., and EMMELKAP, P.M.G. 1976. Exposure and response prevention in the natural environment: a comparison with obsessive-compulsive patients. *Behaviour Research and Therapy* 14:19–24.

BOLSTAD, O.D., and JOHNSON, S.M. 1972. Self-regulation in the modification of disruptive classroom behavior. *Journal of Applied Behavior Analysis* 5:443–454.

BOOTZIN, R.R., and NICASSIO, P.M. 1978. Behavioral treatments for insomnia. In *Progress in behavior modification,* eds. M. Hersen, R. Eisler, and P. Miller. New York: Academic Press, Vol. 6.

BOREN, J.J., and COLMAN, A.D. 1970. Some experiments on reinforcement principles with a psychiatric ward for delinquent soldiers. *Journal of Applied Behavior Analysis* 3:29–37.

BORKOVEC, T.D., GRAYSON, J.B., and COOPER, K.M. 1978. Treatment of general tension: Subjective and physiological effects of progressive relaxation. *Journal of Consulting and Clinical Psychology* 46:518–528.

BORKOVEC, T.D., GRAYSON, J.B., O'BRIEN, G.T., and WEERTS, T.C. 1979. Treatment of pseudoinsomnia and idiopathic insomnia via progressive relaxation with and without muscle tension-release: An electroencephalographic evaluation. *Journal of Applied Behavior Analysis,* 12:37–54.

BORKOVEC, T.D., and O'BRIEN, G.T. 1977. Relation of autonomic perception and its manipulation to the maintenance and reduction of fear. *Journal of Abnormal Psychology* 86:163–171.

BORNSTEIN, P.H., and QUEVILLON, R.P. 1976. The effects of a self-instructional package on overactive preschool boys. *Journal of Applied Behavior Analysis* 9:179–188.

BOWER, G.H. 1978. Contacts of cognitive psychology with social learning theory. *Cognitive Therapy and Research* 2:123–146.

BRADY, J.P. Brevital-aided systematic desensitization. In *Advances in behavior therapy,* eds. R.D. Rubin, H. Fensterheim, A.A. Lazarus, and C.M. Franks. New York: Academic Press.

BRANDSMA, J.M., MAULTSBY, M.C. and WELSH, R. 1978. *Self-help techniques in the treatment of alcoholism.* Unpublished manuscript, University of Kentucky: Lexington.

BRAUER, A.P., HORLICK, L.F., NELSON, E., FARQUHAR, J.W., and AGRAS, W.S. Relaxation therapy for essential hypertension: A Veterans Administration Outpatient study. *Journal of Behavioral Medicine,* in press.

BREHM, J.W. 1966. *A theory of psychological reactance.* New York: Academic Press.

BREWER, W.F. 1974. There is no convincing evidence for operant or classical conditioning in adult humans. *Cognition and the symbolic processes,* eds. W.B. Weimer and D.S. Palermo. Hillsdale. NJ: Lawrence Erlbaum Associates.

BRIGHAM, T., and CATANIA, C., eds. 1979. *Handbook of applied behavior research: Social and instructional processes.* New York: Irvington Press/Halstead Press.

BROWNELL, K.D., HAYES, S.C., and BARLOW, D.H. 1977. Patterns of appropriate and deviant sexual arousal: The behavioral treatment of multiple sexual deviations. *Journal of Consulting and Clinical Psychology* 45:1144–1155.

BRUCH, M. 1975. Influence of model characteristics on psychiatric inpatients' interview anxiety. *Journal of Abnormal Psychology* 84:290–294.

BRYAN, J.H., and TEST, M.A. 1967. Models and helping: Naturalistic studies in aiding behavior. *Journal of Personality and Social Psychology* 6:400–407.

BUDZYNSKI, T.H., and STOYVA, J.M. 1969. An instrument for producing deep relaxation by means of analog information feedback. *Journal of Applied Behavior Analysis,* 2:231–237.

BUDZYNSKI, T.H., STOYVA, J., and ADLER, C. 1970. Feedback-induced muscle relaxation: Application to tension headache. *Journal of Behavior Therapy and Experimental Psychiatry* 1:203–211.

BURCHARD, J.D. 1967. Systematic socialization: A programmed environment for the habilitation of antisocial retardates. *Psychological Record* 17:461–476.

BYASSEE, J.E. 1977. Essential hypertension. In *Behavioral approaches to medical treatment,* eds. R.B. Williams, Jr. and W.D. Gentry.Cambridge, Mass.: Ballinger Publishing Co.

CAMERON, N. 1963. *Personality development and psychopathology.* Boston: Houghton Mifflin Company.

CAMPBELL, D.T., and STANLEY, J.C. 1963. Experimental and quasi-experimental designs for research and teaching. In *Handbook of research on teaching,* ed. N.L. Gage. Chicago: Rand McNally.

CATANIA, A.C. 1975. The myth of self-reinforcement. *Behaviorism* 3:192–199.

CAUDILL, B.D., and MARLATT, G.A. 1975. Modeling influences in social drinking: An experimental analogue. *Journal of Consulting and Clinical Psychology* 43:405–415.

CAUTELA, J. 1973. Covert processes and behavior modification. *Journal of Nervous and Mental Disease* 157:27–36.

CAUTELA, J.R. 1967. Covert sensitization. *Psychological Reports* 20:459–468.

CAUTELA, J.R. 1971. *Covert modeling.* Paper presented to the Association for the Advancement of Behavior Therapy, Washington, D.C.

CAUTELA, J.R., FLANNERY, R.B., and HANLEY, S. 1974. Covert modeling: An experimental test. *Behavior Therapy* 5:494–502.

CHEYNE, J.A., and WALTERS, R.H. 1970. Punishment and prohibition: Some origins of self-control. In *New Directions in Psychology 4.* New York: Holt, Rinehart and Winston.

CHOATE, R.B. Refrigerator roulette: The sugar-coated children's hour. *Nation,* January 31, 1974, 146–148.

CIMINERO, A.R., CALHOUN, K.S., and ADAMS, H.E., eds. 1977. *Handbook of behavioral assessment.* New York: Wiley.

CIMINERO, A.R., NELSON, R.O., and LIPINSKI, D.P. 1977. Self-monitoring procedures. In *Handbook of behavioral assessment,* eds. A.R. Ciminero, K.S. Calhoun, and H.E. Adams. New York: Wiley.

CLARKE, R.N., BURGESS, R.L., and HENDEE, J.C. 1972. An experimental analysis of antilitter procedures. *Journal of Applied Behavior Analysis* 5:1–7.

COATES, T.J., and THORESEN, C.E. 1977. *How to sleep better.* Englewood Cliffs: Prentice-Hall.

COHEN, H.L., and FILIPCZAK, J. 1971. *A new learning environment.* San Francisco: Jossey Bass.

CONE, J.D., and HAWKINS, R.P., eds. 1977. *Behavioral assessment.* New York: Brunner/Mazel.

CONNERS, C.K. 1969. A teacher rating scale for use in drug studies with children. *American Journal of Psychiatry* 6:884–888.

CONNERS, C.K., and GOYETTE, C. 1977. Food dye challenge in hyperkinesis. *NCDEU Intercom* 7:18–19. U.S. Department of Health, Education, and Welfare, ADAMHA, Rockville, MD.

CONRAD, S.R., and WINCZE, J.P. 1976. Orgasmic reconditioning: A controlled study of its effects upon the sexual arousal and behavior of adult male homosexuals. *Behavior Therapy* 7:155–166.

CORTES, J.B., and GATTI, F.M. 1972. *Delinquency and crime: A biosocial approach.* New York: Seminar Press.

COX, D.J., FREUNDLICH, A., and MEYER, R.G. 1975. Differential effectiveness of electromyograph feedback, verbal relaxation instructions, and medication placebo with tension headaches. *Journal of Consulting and Clinical Psychology* 43:892–898.

CRONBACH, L.J. 1970. *Essentials of psychological testing.* 3rd ed. New York: Harper and Row.

CROWE, M.J., MARKS, I.M., AGRAS, W.S., and LEITENBERG, H. 1972. Time-limited desensitization, implosion and shaping for phobic patients: A crossover study. *Behaviour Research and Therapy* 10:319–328.

DAVIDSON, R.S. 1972 *Aversive modification of alcoholic behavior: Punishment of an alcohol-reinforced operant.* Unpublished manuscript, U.S. Veterans Administration Hospital, Miami, Florida.

DAVISON, G.C. 1968. Systematic desensitization as a counterconditioning process. *Journal of Abnormal Psychology* 73:91–99.

DAVISON, G.C. 1969. Behavior modification techniques in institutional settings. *Behavior therapy: Appraisal and status,* ed. C.M. Franks. New York: McGraw-Hill.

DAVISON, G.C. 1973. Counter control in behavior modification. In *Behavior change: Methodology, concepts and practice,* eds. L.A. Hamerlynck, L.C. Handy, and E.J. Mash. Champaign, Ill.: Research Press.

DAVISON, G.C., and NEALE, J.M. 1974 *Abnormal psychology: An experimental clinical approach.* New York: Wiley.

DAVISON, G.C., and STUART, R.B. 1975. Behavior therapy and civil liberties. *American Psychologist* 30:755–763.

DAVISON, G.C., and WILSON, G.T. 1973. Attitudes of behavior therapists towards homosexuality. *Behavior Therapy* 4:686–696 (a).

DAVISON, G.C., and WILSON, G.T. 1973. Processes of fear reduction in systematic desensitization: Cognitive and social reinforcement factors in humans. *Behavior Therapy* 4:1–21(b).

DAVISON, G.C., and WILSON, G.T. 1974. Goals and strategies in behavioral treatment of homosexual pedophilia: Comments on a case study. *Journal of Abnormal Psychology* 83:196–198.

DEMBER, W.N. 1974. Motivation and the cognitive revolution. *American Psychologist* 29:161–168.

DEMENT, W.C. 1972. *Some must watch, while some must sleep.* Stanford: Stanford Alumni Association.

DEMENT, W., and KLEITMAN, N. 1957. Cyclic variations in EEG during sleep and their relation to eye movements, body motility, and dreaming. *Electroencephalography and Clinical Neurophysiology* 9:673–690.

DENNEY, D.R. Self-control approaches to the treatment of test anxiety. In *Test anxiety: Theory, research and applications,* ed. I.G. Sarason. Hillsdale, NJ: Lawrence Erlbaum Associates, in press.

DeSILVA, P., RACHMAN, S., and SELIGMAN, M.E.P. 1977. Prepared phobias and obsessions: Therapeutic outcome. *Behaviour Research and Therapy* 15:65–77.

DEUR, J.L., and PARKE, R.D. 1970. The effects of inconsistent punishment on aggression in children. *Developmental Psychology* 2:403–411.

DiLORETO, A. 1971. *Comparative psychotherapy.* New York: Aldine-Atherton.

DOLLARD, J., and MILLER, N.E. 1950. *Personality and psychotherapy.* New York: McGraw-Hill.

DOMINEIK, J.R. 1973. Crime and law enforcement on prime-time television. *Public Opinion Quarterly* 37:241–250.

DRABMAN, R.S., and SPITALNIK, R. 1973. Social isolation as a punishment procedure: A controlled study. *Journal of Experimental Child Psychology* 16:236–249.

DRABMAN, R.S., SPITALNIK, R., and O'LEARY, K.D. 1973. Teaching self-control to disruptive children. 1973. *Journal of Abnormal Psychology* 82:10–16.

DUBEY, D.R., KENT, R.D., O'LEARY, S.G., BRODERICK, J., and O'LEARY, K.D. 1977. Reactions of children to classroom observers: A series of controlled investigations. *Behavior Therapy* 8:887–897.

DULANY, D.E. 1968. Awareness, rules, and propositional control: A confrontation with S-R behavior theory. In *Verbal behavior and general behavior theory,* eds. T.R. Dixon and D.L. Horton, pp. 340–387. Englewood Cliffs: Prentice-Hall.

DULANY, D.E. 1974. On the support of cognitive theory in opposition to behavior theory: A methodological problem. In *Cognition and the symbolic process,* eds. W.B. Weimar and D.S. Palermo, pp. 43–56. Hillsdale, NJ.: Lawrence Erlbaum Associates.

EGAN, G. 1975. *The skilled helper.* Monterey, CA: Brooks/Cole Publishing Co.

ELLIOT, R., and VASTA, R. 1970. The modeling of sharing: Effects associated with vicarious reinforcement, symbolization, age, and generalization. *Journal of Experimental Child Psychology* 10:8–15.

ELLIS, A. 1962. *Reason and emotion in psychotherapy.* New York: Lyle Stuart.

ELLIS, A. 1970. *The essence of rational psychotherapy: A comprehensive approach to treatment.* New York: Institute for Rational Living.

ELLIS, A. 1977. Rational-emotive therapy: Research data that support the clinical and personality hypothesis of RET and other modes of cognitive behavior therapy. *The Counseling Psychologist* 7:2–42.

ELLIS, A. 1979. A note on the treatment of agoraphobics with cognitive modification versus prolonged exposure in vivo. *Behaviour Research and Therapy* 17: 162–163.

EMMELKAMP, P.M.G., and KRAANEN, J. 1977. Therapist-controlled exposure *in vivo* versus self-controlled exposure *in vivo:* a comparison with obsessive-compulsive patients. *Behaviour Research and Therapy* 15:491–495.

EMMELKAMP, P.M.G., KUIPERS, A.C.M., and EGGERAAT, J.B. 1978 Cognitive modification versus prolonged exposure *in vivo:* A comparison with agoraphobics as subjects. *Behaviour Research and Therapy* 16:33–42.

EMMELKAMP, P.M.G., and WESSELS, H. 1975. Flooding in imagination vs. flooding *in vivo:* A comparison with agoraphobics. *Behaviour Research and Therapy* 13:7–15.

EVANS, I.M. 1976. Classical conditioning. In *The theoretical and experimental bases of behavior therapy,* eds. M.P. Feldman and A. Broadhurst. New York: Wiley.

EVERS, W.L., and SCHWARZ, J.C. 1973. Modifying social withdrawal in preschoolers: The effects of filmed modeling and teacher praise. *Journal of Abnormal Child Psychology* 1:248–256.

EWART, C. 1978. Self-observation in natural environments: Reactive effects of behavior desirability and goal setting. *Cognitive Therapy and Research* 2:39–56.

EYSENCK, H.J. 1952. The effects of psychotherapy: An evaluation. *Journal of Consulting Psychology* 16:319–324.

EYSENCK, H.J. 1959. Learning theory and behaviour therapy. *British Journal of Mental Science* 105:61–75.

EYSENCK, H.J. 1960. *Behaviour therapy and the neuroses.* Oxford: Pergamon Press.

EYSENCK, H.J. 1964. *Experiments in behaviour therapy.* Oxford: Pergamon Press.

EYSENCK, H.J. 1976. The learning theory model of neurosis—a new approach. *Behaviour Research and Therapy* 14:251–268.

EYSENCK, H.J., and BEECH, H.R. 1971. Counter conditioning and related methods. In *Handbook of psychotherapy and behavior change,* eds. A.E. Bergin and S.L. Garfield. New York: Wiley.

EYSENCK, H.J., and EYSENCK, S.B.G. 1976. *Psychoticism as a dimension of personality.* London: Hodder and Stoughton.

EYSENCK, H.J., and RACHMAN, S. 1965. *The causes and cures of neurosis.* London: Routledge and Kegan Paul.

FAIRWEATHER, G.W., SANDERS, D.H., MAYNARD, H., and CRESSLER, D.L. 1969. *Community life for the mentally ill: An alternative to institutional care.* Chicago: Aldine.

Family Health/Today's Health Magazine. Health Matters: Deactivating the overactive child. July 1977, pp. 56–58.

FARNUM, M., BRIGHAM, T.A., and JOHNSON, G. 1977. *A comparison of the effects of teacher determined and student determined contingencies on arithmetic performance.* Unpublished manuscript, Washington State University. Pullman, Washington.

FEINGOLD, B. 1975. *Why your child is hyperactive.* New York: Random House.

FELIXBROD, J.J., and O'LEARY, K.D. 1973. Effects of reinforcement on children's academic behavior as a function of self-determined and externally imposed systems. *Journal of Applied Behavior Analysis* 6:241–250.

FELIXBROD, J.J., and O'LEARY, K.D. 1974. Self-determination of academic standards by children: Toward freedom from external control. *Journal of Educational Psychology* 66:845–850.

FERSTER, C.B., NURNBERGER, J.I., and LEVITT, E.B. 1962. The control of eating. *Journal of Mathetics* 1:87–109.

FERSTER, C.B., and SKINNER, B.F. 1957. *Schedules of reinforcement.* New York: Appleton-Century-Crofts.

FICHTER, M.M., WALLACE, C.J., LIBERMAN, R.P., and DAVIS, J.R. 1976. Improving social interaction in a chronic psychotic using discriminated avoidance ("nagging"): Experimental analysis and generalization. *Journal of Applied Behavior Analysis* 9:377–386.

FIELD, G.D., and TEST, M.A. 1975. Group assertive training for severely disturbed patients. *Journal of Behavior Therapy and Experimental Psychiatry* 6:129–134.

FOREYT, J.P., and HAGEN, R.L. 1973. Covert sensitization: Conditioning and suggestion? *Journal of Abnormal Psychology* 82:17–23.

FOXX, R.M., and AZRIN, N.H. 1972. Restitution: A method of eliminating aggressive-disruptive behaivor in retarded and brain-damaged patients. *Behaviour Research & Therapy* 10:15–27.

FOXX, R.M., and JONES, J.R. 1978. A remediation program for increasing the spelling achievement of elementary and junior high school students. *Behavior Modification* 2:211–230.

FRANKS, C.M., and WILSON, G.T. 1973. *Annual review of behavior therapy: Theory and practice,* vol. I. New York: Brunner/Mazel.

FRANKS, C.M., and WILSON, G.T. 1974. *Annual review of behavior therapy: Theory and practice,* vol. II. New York: Brunner/Mazel.

FRANKS, C.M., and WILSON, G.T. 1975. *Annual review of behavior therapy: Theory and practice,* vol. III. New York: Brunner/Mazel.

FRANKS, C.M., and WILSON, G.T. 1976. *Annual review of behavior therapy: Theory and practice,* vol. IV. New York: Brunner/Mazel.

FRANKS, C.M., and WILSON, G.T. 1977. *Annual review of behavior therapy: Theory and practice,* vol. V. New York: Brunner/Mazel.

FRANKS, C.M., and WILSON, G.T. 1978. *Annual review of behavior therapy: Theory and practice,* vol. VI, New York: Brunner/Mazel.

FREDERIKSEN, L.W., and FREDERIKSEN, C.B. 1975. Teacher-determined and self-determined token reinforcement in a special education classroom. *Behavior Therapy* 6:310–314.

FREEDMAN, B.J. 1974. *An analysis of social-behavioral skill deficits in delinquent and non-delinquent adolescent boys.* Unpublished doctoral dissertation, University of Wisconsin, Madison.

FREEMAN, W., and MEYER, R.G. 1975. A behavioral alteration of sexual preferences in the human male. *Behavior Therapy,* 6:202–212.

FRIEDLING, C., and O'LEARY, S.G. 1979. Effects of self-instructional training on second and third grade hyperactive children: A failure to replicate. *Journal of Applied Behavior Analysis,* 12:211–219.

FRIEDMAN, P.R. 1975. Legal regulation of applied behavior analysis. *Arizona Law Review* 17:39–104.

GALST, J.P., and WHITE, M.A. 1976. The unhealthy persuader: The reinforcing value of television and children's purchase-influencing attempts at the supermarket. *Child Development,* 47:1089–1096.

GARFIELD, S.L., and KURTZ, R. 1976. Clinical psychologists in the 1970s. *American Psychologist* 31:1–9.

GARLINGTON, W.K., and DERICCO, D.A. 1977. The effect of modelling on drinking rate. *Journal of Applied Behavior Analysis* 10:207–211.

GEER, J.H. 1965. The development of a scale to measure fear. *Behaviour Research and Therapy* 3:45–53.

GEER, J.H. 1977. Sexual functioning: Some data and speculations on psychophysiological assessment. In *Behavioral assessment: New directions in clinical psychology,* eds. J.D. Cone and R.P. Hawkins. New York: Brunner/Mazel.

GEER, J.H., MOROKOFF, D., and GREENWOOD, P. 1974. Sexual arousal in women. The development of a measurement device for vaginal blood-volume. *Archives of Sexual Behavior* 3:559–564.

GELDER, M.G., BANCROFT, J.H.J., GATH, D., JOHNSTON, D.W., MATHEWS, A.M., and SHAW, P.M. 1973. Specific and non-specific factors in behaviour therapy. *British Journal of Psychiatry* 123:445–462.

GELFAND, D.M., and HARTMANN, D.B. 1975. *Child behavior analysis and therapy.* Elmsford, New York: Pergamon.

GERBNER, G. 1972 Violence in television drama: Trends and symbolic functions. In *Television and social behavior,* eds. G.A. Comstock and E.A. Rubinstein, *vol. 1:Media content and control.* Washington, D.C.: GPO.

GLAROS, A.G., and RAO, S.M. 1977. Bruxism: A critical review. *Psychological Bulletin* 84:767–781.

GLAVIN, J.P., and MOYER, L.S. 1975. Facilitating extinction of infant crying by changing reinforcement schedules. *Journal of Behavior Therapy and Experimental Psychiatry* 6:357–358.

GOLDFRIED, M.R. 1971. Systematic desensitization as training in self-control. *Journal of Consulting and Clinical Psychology* 37:228–234.

GOLDFRIED, M.R. 1977. The use of relaxation and cognitive relabeling as coping skills. In *Behavioral self management,* ed. R.B. Stuart. New York: Brunner/Mazel.

GOLDFRIED, M.R., and DAVISON, G.C. 1976. *Clinical behavior therapy.* New York: Holt, Rinehart and Winston.

GOLDFRIED, M.R., and LINEHAN, M.M. 1977. Basic issues in behavioral assessment. In *Handbook of behavioral assessment,* eds. A.R. Ciminero, K.S. Calhoun, and H.E. Adams. New York: Wiley-Interscience.

GOLDFRIED, M.R., and SOBOCINSKI, D. 1975. Effect of irrational beliefs on emotional arousal. *Journal of Consulting and Clinical Psychology* 43:504–510.

GOLDIAMOND, I. 1965. Self-control procedures in personal behavior problems. *Psychological Reports* 17:851–868.

GOLDSMITH, J.B., and McFALL, R.M. 1975. Development and evaluation of an interpersonal skill-training program for psychiatric inpatients. *Journal of Abnormal Psychology* 84:51–58.

GOTTMAN, J.M. 1973. N-of-one and N-of-two research in psychology. *Psychological Bulletin,* 80:93–105.

GREENBERG, D.S. 1977. The rush to cure cancer. *Newsday,* Nov. 11, p. 63.

GREENE, B.F., CLARK, H.B., and RISLEY, T.R. 1977. *Shopping with children: Advice for parents.* San Rafael, CA: Academic Therapy Publications.

GREENE, L. 1978. Temporal and stimulus factors in self-monitoring of obese persons. *Behavior Therapy* 9:328–341.

GREY, S., SARTORY, G., and RACHMAN S. 1979. Synchronous and desynchronous changes during fear reduction. *Behaviour Research and Therapy,* 17:137–148.

GURMAN, A.S., KNUDSON, R.M., and KNISKERN, D.P. 1978. Behavioral marriage therapy, IV. Take two aspirin and call us in the morning. *Family Process,* 17:165–180.

HACKMAN, J.R., and SUTTLE, J.L. 1977. *Improving life at work: Behavioral science approaches to organizational change.* Santa Monica, CA: Goodyear.

HAGEN, R.L., CRAIGHEAD, W.E., and PAUL, G.L. 1975. Staff reactivity to evaluative behavioral observations. *Behavior Therapy* 6:201–205.

HALLAM, R.S. 1978. Agoraphobia: A critical review of the concept. *British Journal of Psychiatry,* 133:314–319.

HALLAM, R. and RACHMAN, S. 1976. Current status of aversion therapy. In *Progress in behavior modification,* eds. M. Hersen, R.M. Eisler, and P.M. Miller, vol. 2. New York: Academic Press.

HAND, I., LAMONTAGNE, Y., and MARKS, I.M. 1974. Group exposure (flooding) *in vivo* for agoraphobics. *British Journal of Psychiatry* 124:588–602.

HARRIS, S.L., and ROMANCZYK, R.G. 1976. Treating self-injurious behavior of a retarded boy by overcorrection. *Behavior Therapy* 7:235–239.

HARTIG, M., and KANFER, F.H. 1973. The role of verbal self-instructions in children's resistance to temptation. *Journal of Personality and Social Psychology* 25:259–267.

HAYES, S.C., and CONE, J.D. 1977. Reducing residential electrical energy use: Payments, information, and feedback. *Journal of Applied Behavior Analysis* 10:425–435.

HECKEL, R.V., WIGGINS, S.L., and SALZBERG, H.C. 1972. Conditioning against silences in group therapy. *Journal of Clinical Psychology* 18:216–217.

HEIMAN, J., LoPICCOLO, L., and LoPICCOLO, J. 1976. *On becoming orgasmic: A program of sexual growth for women.* Englewood Cliffs: Prentice-Hall.

HELLER, K., and MONOHAN, J. 1977. *Psychology and community change.* Homewood, Illinois: Dorsey.

HERJANIC, B., HERJANIC, M., BROWN, F., and WHEATT, T. 1975. Are children reliable reporters? *Journal of Abnormal Child Psychology* 3:41–48.

HERRNSTEIN, R.J. 1969. Method and theory in the study of avoidance. *Psychological Review* 76:46–69.

HERSEN, M., and BARLOW, D.H. 1976. *Single case experimental designs: Strategies for studying behavior change.* New York: Pergamon Press.

HERSEN, M., EISLER, R.M., and MILLER, P.M. 1974. An experimental analysis of generalization in assertive training. *Behaviour Research and Therapy* 12:295–310.

HICKS, D. 1965. Imitation and retention of film-mediated and aggressive peer and adult models. *Journal of Personality and Social Psychology* 2:97–100.

HICKS, D. 1968. Short and long-term retention of affectively varied modeled behavior. *Psychonomic Science* 11:369–370.

HODGSON, R., RACHMAN, S., and MARKS, I. 1972. The treatment of chronic obsessive-compulsive neurosis: Follow-up and further findings. *Behaviour Research and Therapy* 10:181–189.

HOFFMAN, M.L. 1960. Power assertion by the parent and its impact on the child. *Child Development* 31:129–143.

HOGAN, R., DESOTO, C.B., and SOLANTO, C. 1977. Traits, tests, and personality research. *American Psychologist* 32:255–264.

HOLAHAN, C.J. 1976. Environmental effects on outdoor social behavior in a low income urban neighborhood: A naturalistic investigation. *Journal of Applied Social Psychology* 6:48–63.

HOLROYD, K.A. 1976. Cognition and desensitization in the group treatment of test anxiety. *Journal of Consulting and Clinical Psychology* 44:991–1001.

HOLROYD, K.A., ANDRASIK, F., and WESTBROOK T. 1977. Cognitive control of tension headache. *Cognitive Therapy and Research* 1:121–133.

HOLROYD, K.A., WESTBROOK, T., WOLF, M., and BADHOM, E. 1978. Performance, cognition, and physiological responding in test anxiety. *Journal of Abnormal Psychology* 87:442–451.

HOMME, L.E. 1965. Perspectives in psychology: XXIV. Control of coverants, the operants of the mind. *Psychological Record* 15:501–511.

HONIG, W.K., and STADDON, F.E.R., eds. 1977. *Handbook of operant behavior.* Englewood Cliffs: Prentice-Hall.

HUGDAHL, K. 1978. Electrodermal conditioning to potentially phobic stimuli: Effects of instructed extinction. *Behaviour Research and Therapy,* 16:315–321.

HULL, C. 1943. *Principles of behavior.* New York: Appleton-Century-Crofts.

HUMPHREYS, L.G. 1939. Acquisition and extinction of verbal expectations in a situation analogous to conditioning. *Journal of Experimental Psychology* 25:294–301.

HUNT, J. McV. 1961. *Intelligence and experience.* New York: Ronald Press.

HYGGE, S., and OHMAN, A. 1978. Modeling processes in the acquisition of fears: Vicarious electrodermal conditioning to fear-relevant stimuli. *Journal of Personality and Social Psychology,* 36:271–279.

IWATA, B.A., and BAILEY, J.S. 1974. Reward versus cost token systems: An analysis of the effects on students and teacher. *Journal of Applied Behavior Analysis* 7:567–576.

JACOB, R., KRAEMER, H., and AGRAS, W.S. 1977. Relaxation therapy in the treatment of hypertension. *Archives of General Psychiatry* 34:1417–1427.

JACOB, R.G., O'LEARY, K.D., and ROSENBLAD, C. 1978. Formal and informal classroom settings: Effects on hyperactivity. *Journal of Abnormal Child Psychology* 6:47–59.

JACOBSON, E. 1938. *Progressive relaxation.* Chicago: University of Chicago Press.

JEFFERY, R.W., WING, R.R., and STUNKARD, A.J. 1978. Behavioral treatment of obesity: The state of the art 1976. *Behavior Therapy* 9:189–199.

JONES, F.H., and MILLER, W.H. 1974. The effective use of negative attention for reducing group disruption in special elementary school classrooms. *The Psychological Record* 24:435–448.

JONES, M.C. 1924. The elimination of children's fears. *Journal of Experimental Psychology* 1:383–390.

JOSEPHSON, S.C., and ROSEN, R.C. 1978. The experimental modification of sonorous breathing. Paper presented at American Association for the Advancement of Behavior Therapy, Chicago, Illinois, December, 1978.

JOUVET, M. 1967. Mechanisms of the states of sleep: A neuropharmacological approach. *Research Publications of the Association for Research in Nervous and Mental Disease* 45:86–126.

KANFER, F., KAROLY, P., and NEWMAN, A. 1975. Reduction of children's fear of the dark by competence related and situational threat related verbal cues. *Journal of Consulting and Clinical Psychology* 43:251–258.

KANTER, N.J., and GOLDFRIED, M.R. 1979. Relative effectiveness of rational restructuring and self-control desensitization for the reduction of interpersonal anxiety. *Behavior Therapy* 10:472–490.

KASHIWAGI, T., MCCLURE, J.N., and WETZEL, R.D. 1972. Headache and psychiatric disorders. *Diseases of the Nervous System* 33:659–663.

KAUFMAN, K.F., and O'LEARY, K.D. 1972. Reward, cost, and self-evaluation procedures for disruptive adolescents in a psychiatric hospital school. *Journal of Applied Behavior Analysis* 5:293–309.

KAYE, K. 1971. *Learning by imitation in infants and young children.* Paper presented at the meeting of the Society for Research in Child Development, Minneapolis, April, 1971.

KAZDIN, A.E. 1974a. Covert modeling, model similarity, and reduction of avoidance behavior. *Behavior Therapy* 5:325–340.

KAZDIN, A.E. 1974b. Effects of covert modeling and modeling reinforcement on assertive behavior. *Journal of Abnormal Psychology* 83:240–252.

KAZDIN, A.E. 1976a. Effects of covert modeling, multiple models, and model reinforcement on assertive behavior. *Behavior Therapy* 7:211–222.

KAZDIN, A.E. 1976b. Statistical analyses for single-case experimental designs. In *Single-case experimental designs: Strategies for studying behavior change,* eds. M. Hersen and D.H. Barlow. New York: Pergamon Press.

KAZDIN, A.E. 1977a. Research issues in covert conditioning. *Cognitive Therapy and Research,* 1:45–58.

KAZDIN, A.E. 1977b. *The token economy.* New York: Plenum Press.

KAZDIN, A.E., and WILCOXON, L.A. 1976. Systematic desensitization and nonspecific treatment effects: A methodological evaluation. *Psychological Bulletin* 83:729–758.

KAZDIN, A.E., and WILSON, G.T. 1978. *Evaluation of behavior therapy: Issues, evidence, and research strategies.* Cambridge, Mass.: Ballinger.

KELLER, M.F., and CARLSON, P.M. 1974. The use of symbolic modeling to promote social skills in preschool children with low levels of social responsiveness. *Child Development* 45:912–919.

KENT, R.N., and FOSTER, S. 1977. Direct observational procedures: Methodological issues in naturalistic settings. *Handbook of behavioral assessment,* eds. A.R. Ciminero, K.S. Calhoun, and H.E. Adams. New York: Wiley.

KENT, R.N., and O'LEARY, K.D. 1976. A controlled evaluation of behavior modification with conduct problem children. *Journal of Consulting and Clinical Psychology* 44:586–596.

KINGSLEY, R.G., and WILSON, G.T. 1977. Behavior therapy for obesity: A comparative investigation of long-term efficacy. *Journal of Consulting and Clinical Psychology* 45:288–298.

KINSEY, A.C., POMEROY, W.B., MARTIN, C.E., and GEBHARD, P.H. 1953. *Sexual behavior in the human female.* Philadelphia: Saunders.

KIRKLAND, K.D., and THELAN, M.H. 1977. Uses of modeling in child treatment. In *Advances in clinical child psychology,* eds. B.B. Lahey and A.E. Kazdin. New York: Plenum.

KLOTZ, J., and SHANTZ, D.W. 1973. Cooperative behavior of emotionally disturbed boys as a function of contingent application of social approval. *Journal of Behavior Therapy and Experimental Psychiatry* 4:33–37.

KOCKOTT, G., DITTMAR, F., and NUSSELT, L. 1975. Systematic desensitization of erectile impotence: A controlled study. *Archives of Sexual Behavior* 4:493–500.

KOHLENBERG, R.J. 1974. Treatment of a homosexual pedophiliac rising *in vivo* desensitization: A case study. *Journal of Abnormal Psychology,* 83:192–195.

KORCHIN, S.J. 1976. *Modern clinical psychology.* New York: Basic Books.

KORNHABER, R., and SCHROEDER, H. 1975. Importance of model similarity on extinction of avoidance behavior in children. *Journal of Consulting and Clinical Psychology* 43:601–607.

KRAGER, J.M., SAFER, D., and EARHARDT, J. 1979. Medication used to treat hyperactive children: Follow-up survey results. Paper presented at School Health Association Annual Meeting, Detroit, Spring, 1979.

KRANTZ, P.J., and RISLEY, T.R. 1977. Behavioral ecology in the classroom. In *Classroom Management: The successful use of behavior modification,* eds. K.D. O'Leary and S.G. O'Leary. Elmsford, New York: Pergamon.

KRASNER, L. 1971. Behavior therapy. In *Annual Review of Psychology,* eds. P.H. Mussen and M.R. Rosenzweig, pp. 453–532 Palo Alto, CA: Annual Reviews 483–532.

KRISTT, D.A., and ENGEL, B.T. 1975. Learned control of blood pressure in patients with high blood pressure. *Circulation* 51:370–378.

KUHN, T.S. 1962. *The structure of scientific revolutions.* Chicago: University of Chicago Press.

LACEY, H.M., and RACHLIN, H. 1978. Behavior, cognition, and theories of choice. *Behaviorism,* 6:177–202.

LANDAU, P. 1976. A guide for the assertive book buyer. *Human Behavior.* May 1976, 67–71.

LANG, P.E. 1969. The mechanics of desensitization and the laboratory study of fear. In *Behavior therapy: Appraisal and status,* ed. C.M. Franks. New York: McGraw-Hill.

LANG, P.J. 1976. Biofeedback and testing of experimental hypotheses. *European Journal of Behavioural Analysis and Modification* 4:252–254.

LANG, P.J. 1977. Physiological measurement of anxiety and fear. In *Behavioral Assessment,* eds. J.P. Cone and R.P. Hawkins. New York: Brunner/Mazel.

LANG, P.J., MELAMED, B.G., and HART, J. 1970. A psychophysiological analysis of fear modification using an automated desensitization procedure. *Journal of Abnormal Psychology* 76:220–234.

LANYON, R.I., and GIDDINGS, J.W. 1974. Psychological approaches to myopia: A review. *American Journal of Optometry and Physiological Optics* 51:271–281.

LAZARUS, A.A. 1961. Group therapy of phobic disorders by systematic desensitization. *Journal of Abnormal and Social Psychology* 63:504–510.

LAZARUS, A.A. 1968. Scientism and psychotherapy. *Psychological Reports* 22:1015–1016.

LAZARUS, A.A. 1971. *Behavior therapy and beyond.* New York: McGraw-Hill.

LAZARUS, A.A. 1976. *Multimodal behavior therapy.* New York: Springer.

LAZARUS, A.A. Personal communication.

LAZARUS, A.A., and DAVISON, G.C. 1971. Clinical innovation in research and practice. *Handbook of psychotherapy and behavior change.* eds. A.A Bergin and S.L. Garfield. New York: Wiley.

LEDWIDGE, B. 1978. Cognitive behavior modification: A step in the wrong direction? *Psychological Bulletin* 85:353–375.

LEFKOWITZ, M.M., ERON, L.D., WALDER, L.O., and HUESMAN, L.R. 1972. Television violence and child aggression: A follow-up study. In *Television and social behavior, Vol. 3:Television and adolescent aggressiveness.* eds. G.A. Comstock and E.A. Rubinstein. Washington, D.C.: GPO.

LEFKOWITZ, M.M., WALDER, L.O., and ERON, L.D. 1963. Punishment, identification, and aggression. *Merrill-Palmer Quarterly* 9:159–174.

LEHRER, P.M. 1978. Psychophysiological effects of progressive relaxation in anxiety neurotic patients and of progressive relaxation and alpha feedback in nonpatients. *Journal of Consulting and Clinical Psychology* 46:389–404.

LEITENBERG, H. 1976a. Behavioral approaches to treatment of neuroses. In *Handbook of behavior modification and behavior therapy,* ed. H. Leitenberg. Englewood Cliffs: Prentice-Hall.

LEITENBERG, H. 1976b. *Handbook of behavior modification and behavior therapy.* Englewood Cliffs: Prentice-Hall.

LEITENBERG, H., AGRAS, S., BUTZ, R., and WINCZ, J. 1971. Relationship between heart rate and behavioral change during the treatment of phobias. *Journal of Abnormal Psychology* 78:59–68.

LEMERE, F., and VOEGTLIN, W.L. 1950. An evaluation of the aversion treatment of alcoholism. *Quarterly Journal of Studies on Alcohol* 11:199–204.

LEVINE, F.M., and FASNACHT, G. 1974. Token rewards may lead to token learning. *American Psychologist* 29:816–820.

LEVIS, D.J., and HARE, N. 1977. A review of the theoretical rationale and empirical support for the extinction approach of implosive (flooding) therapy. In *Progress in behavior modification,* eds. M. Hersen, R.M. Eisler, and P.M. Miller, vol. IV. New York: Academic Press.

LEVITSKY, A., and PERLS, F.S. 1970. The rules and games of Gestalt therapy. In *Gestalt therapy now,* eds. J. Fagan and I.L. Sheperd. Palo Alto, CA: Science and Behavior Books.

LEWINSOHN, P.M. 1974. A behavioral approach to depression. In *The psychology of depression: Contemporary theory and research.* eds. R.J. Friedman and M.M. Katz. New York: Wiley.

LICHTENSTEIN, F.E. 1950. Studies of anxiety: I. The production of feeding inhibition in dogs. *Journal of Comparative and Physiological Psychology* 43:16–29.

LIEBERT, R.M. 1972. Television and social learning: Some relationships between viewing violence and behaving aggressively. In *Television and social behavior. Vol. II: Television and social learning,* eds. J.P. Murray, E.A. Rubinstein, and G.A. Comstock. Washington D.C.: U.S. Government Printing Office.

LIEBERT, R.M., and POULOS, R.W. 1975. Television and personality development: The socializing effects of an entertainment medium. In *Child personality and psychopathology: Current topics. Vol. 2,* ed. A. Davids. New York: Wiley.

LIEBERT, R.M., and SCHWARTZBERG, N.S. 1977. Effects of mass media. *Annual Review of Psychology* 28:141–173.

LINEHAN, M.M., GOLDFRIED, M.R., and GOLDFRIED, A.P. 1979 Assertion therapy: Skill training or cognitive restructuring? *Behavior Therapy,* 10: 372–388.

LIPINSKI, D., and NELSON, R. 1974. The reactivity and unreliability of self-recording. *Journal of Consulting and Clinical Psychology* 42:110–123.

LOBITZ, G.K., and JOHNSON, S.M. 1975. Normal versus deviant children: a multimethod comparison. *Journal of Abnormal Child Psychology* 3(4):353–373.

LONGIN, H.E., and ROONEY, W.M. 1975. Teaching denial assertion to chronic hospitalized patients. *Journal of Behavior Therapy and Experimental Psychiatry* 6: 219–222.

LOVAAS, O.I., KOEGEL, R., SIMMONS, J.Q., and LONG, J.S. 1973. Some generalization and follow-up measures on autistic children in behavior therapy. *Journal of Applied Behavior Analysis* 6:131–166.

LOVAAS, O.I., and NEWSOM, C.D. 1976. Behavior modification with psychotic children. In *Handbook of behavior modification and behavior therapy,* ed. H. Leitenberg. Englewood Cliffs: Prentice-Hall.

LURIA, A. 1961. *The role of speech in the regulation of normal and abnormal behavior.* New York: Liverright.

MACDONALD, M. 1978. Measuring assertion; A model and method. *Behavior Therapy,* 9:889–899.

MACPHERSON, E.M., CANDEE, B.L., and HOLMAN, R.J. 1974. A comparison of three methods of eliminating disruptive lunchroom behavior. *Journal of Applied Behavior Analysis* 1:287–297.

MADSEN, C.H., BECKER, W.C., THOMAS, D.R., KOSER, L., and PLAGER, E. 1968. An analysis of the reinforcing function of "sit down" commands. In *Readings in educational psychology,* ed. R.K. Parker. Boston: Allyn and Bacon.

MADSEN, C.H., MADSEN, C.K., SAUDARGAS, R.A., HAMMOND, W.R., and EDGAR, D.E. 1970. *Classroom RAID (Rules, Approval, Ignore, Disapproval): A cooperative approach for professionals and volunteers.* Journal of School Psychology, 8(3): 180.

MAHONEY, M.J. 1974. *Cognition and behavior modification.* Cambridge, Mass: Ballinger.

MAHONEY, M.J. 1974. Self-reward and self-monitoring techniques for weight control *Behavior Therapy* 5:48–57.

MAHONEY, M.J. 1977. *Cognitive and non-cognitive views in behavior modification.* Paper presented at the Annual Meeting of the American Psychological Association, San Francisco, 1977.

MAHONEY, M.J., and ARNKOFF, D. 1978. Cognitive and self-control therapies. In *Handbook of psychotherapy and behavior change,* eds. S.L. Garfield and A.E. Bergin, 2nd ed. New York: Wiley.

MAHONEY, M.J., KAZDIN A.E., and LESSWING, N.J. 1974. Behavior modification: Delusion or deliverance? In *Annual review of behavior therapy: Theory and practice,* vol. 2, eds. C.M. Franks and G.T. Wilson, pp. 11–40. New York: Brunner/Mazel.

MAHONEY, M.J., MOURA, N.G., and WADE, T.C. 1973. Relative efficiency of self reward, self punishment, and self monitoring techniques for weight loss. *Journal of Consulting and Clinical Psychology* 40:404–407.

MAHONEY, M.J., and THORESEN, C.E. 1974. *Self-control: Power to the person.* Monterey, CA: Brooks/Cole.

MARKMAN, H. 1977 *A behavioral exchange model applied to the longitudinal study of couples planning to marry.* Unpublished doctoral dissertation, University of Indiana, Bloomington, Indiana.

MARKS, I.M. 1969. *Fears and phobias.* New York: Academic Press.

MARKS, I.M. 1976. Management of sexual disorders. In *Handbook of behavior modification and behavior therapy,* ed. H. Leitenberg. Englewood Cliffs: Prentice-Hall.

MARKS, I. 1978. Behavioral psychotherapy of adult neurosis. In *Handbook of psychotherapy and behavior change,* eds. S.L. Garfield and A.E. Bergin, 2nd ed. New York: Wiley.

MARKS, I., and GELDER, M. 1967. Transvestism and fetishism: clinical and psychological changes during faradic aversion. *British Journal of Psychiatry* 113:711–739.

MARKS, I., GELDER, M.G., and BANCROFT, J. 1970. Sexual deviants two years after electrical aversion. *British Journal of Psychiatry* 117:73–85.

MARKS, I.M., HALLAM, R.S., CONNOLLY, J., and PHILPOTT, R. 1977. *Nursing in behavioural therapy.* London: The Royal College of Nursing of the United Kingdom.

MARKS, I., HODGSON, R., and RACHMAN, S. 1975. Treatment of chronic obsessive-compulsive neurosis by *in vivo* exposure. *British Journal of Psychiatry* 127: 349–364.

MARLATT, G.A., and MARQUES, J.K. 1977. Meditation, self-control, and alcohol use. In *Behavioral self-management: Strategies, techniques and outcome,* ed. R.B. Stuart. New York: Brunner/Mazel.

MARSHALL, W.L., GAUTHIER, J., CHRISTIE, M.M., CURRIE, D.W., and GORDON, P. 1977. Flooding therapy: effectiveness, stimulus characteristics, and the value of brief *in vivo* exposure. *Behaviour Research and Therapy* 15:79–87.

MARTIN, M.J. 1972. Muscle contractions headache. *Psychosomatics* 13:16–19.

MASSERMAN, J.H. 1943. *Behavior and neurosis.* Chicago: University of Chicago Press.

MASTERS, W., and JOHNSON, V. 1970. *Human sexual inadequacy.* Boston: Little Brown.

MATHEWS, A. 1978. Fear-reduction research and clinical phobias. *Psychological Bulletin,* 85:390–404.

MATHEWS, A.M., BANCROFT, J., WHITEHEAD, A., HACKMANN, A., JULIER, D., BANCROFT, J., GATH, D., and SHAW, P. 1976. The behavioural treatment of sexual inadequacy: a comparative study. *Behaviour Research and Therapy* 14:-427–436.

MAURER, A. 1974. Corporal punishment. *American Psychologist* 29:614–626.

MAY, J.G., RISLEY, T.R., TWARDOSZ, S., FRIEDMAN, P., BIJOU, S.W. and WEXLER,

D. 1975. Guidelines for the use of behavioral procedures in state programs for retarded persons. *M.R. Research,* vol. 1.

MCCALDEN, M., and DAVIS, C. 1972. *Report on priority lane experiment on the San Francisco-Oakland Bay Bridge.* California: Department of Public Works.

MCCORD, W., MCCORD, J., and ZOLA, I.K. 1959. *Origins of crime: A new evaluation of the Cambridge-Somerville Youth Study.* New York: Columbia University Press.

MCCULLOUGH, W. 1975. *Penal law of the state of New York.* Flushing, New York: Looseleaf Law Publications, Inc.

MCCUTCHEON, B., and ADAMS, H. 1975. The physiological basis of implosive therapy. *Behaviour Research and Therapy,* 13:93–100.

MCFALL, R.M. 1970. Effects of self-monitoring on normal smoking behavior. *Journal of Consulting and Clinical Psychology* 35:135–142.

MCFALL, R.M., and LILLESAND, D.B. 1971. Behavior rehearsal with modeling and coaching in assertive training. *Journal of Abnormal Psychology* 77:313–323.

MCGUIRE, R., CARLISLE, J.M., and YOUNG, B.G. 1965. Sexual deviation as conditioned behavior: A hypothesis. *Behaviour Research and Therapy* 2: 185–190.

MCLAUGHLIN, F.T., and MALABY, J. 1972. Reducing and measuring inappropriate verbalizations in a token classroom. *Journal of Applied Behavior Analysis,* 5: 329–333.

MCLEAN, P.D., and HAKSTIAN, A.R. 1979. Clinical depression: Comparative efficacy of outpatient treatments. Unpublished manuscript, University of British Columbia, Vancouver, Canada.

MCMULLEN, S., and ROSEN, R. Self-administered masturbation training in the treatment of primary orgasmic dysfunction. *Journal of Consulting and Clinical Psychology,* in press.

MCSWEENEY, A.J. 1978. Effects of response cost on the behavior of a million persons: Charging for directory assistance in Cincinnati. *Journal of Applied Behavior Analysis* 11:47–52.

MEICHENBAUM, D. 1971. Examination of model characteristics in reducing avoidance behavior. *Journal of Personality and Social Psychology* 17:298–307.

MEICHENBAUM, D. 1977a. *Cognitive-behavior modification.* New York: Plenum Press.

MEICHENBAUM, D., and ASARNOW, J. 1979. Cognitive-behavior modification and metacognitive development: Implications for the classroom. In P.C. Kendall and S.D. Hollon (Eds.), *Cognitive-behavioral interventions: Theory, research and procedures.* New York: Academic Press.

MEICHENBAUM, D., and CAMERON, R. 1973. Training schizophrenics to talk to themselves: A means of developing attentional controls. *Behavior Therapy,* 4:515–534.

MEICHENBAUM, D., GILMORE, J., and FEDORAVICIUS, A. 1971. Group insight vs. group desensitization in treating speech anxiety. *Journal of Consulting and Clinical Psychology* 36:410–421.

MEICHENBAUM, D.H., and GOODMAN, J. 1971. Training impulsive children to talk to themselves: A means of developing self-control. *Journal of Abnormal Psychology* 77:115–126.

MELAMED, B.G., HAWES, R.R., HEIBY, E., and GLICK, J. 1975. Use of filmed modeling to reduce uncooperative behavior of children during dental treatment. *Journal of Dental Research* 54:797–801.

MELAMED, B.G., and SIEGEL, L.J. 1975. Reduction of anxiety in children facing hospitalization and surgery by use of filmed modeling. *Journal of Consulting and Clinical Psychology* 43:511–521.

MELAMED, B.G., WEINSTEIN, D., HAWES, R.R., and KATIN-BORLAND, M. 1975. Reduction of fear-related dental management problems with use of filmed modeling. *Journal of the American Dental Association* 90:822–826.

MERCATORIS, M., and CRAIGHEAD, W.E. 1974. The effects of nonparticipant observation on teacher and pupil classroom behavior. *Journal of Educational Psychology* 66:512–519.

MILLER, L.K. 1975. *Principles of everyday behavior analysis.* Belmont, California: Wadsworth.

MILLER, N.E. 1948. Studies of fear as an acquirable drive: I. Fear as motivation and fear reduction as reinforcement in the learning of new responses. *Journal of Experimental Psychology* 38:89–101.

MILLER, N.E. 1969. Learning of visceral and glandular responses. *Science* 163:434–445.

MILLER, N.E. 1978. Biofeedback and visceral learning. *Annual Review of Psychology* 29:373–404.

MILLS, H.L., AGRAS, W.S., BARLOW, D.H., and MILLS, J.R. 1973. Compulsive rituals treated by response prevention. *Archives of General Psychiatry,* 28:524–529.

MISCHEL, W. 1968. *Personality and assessment.* New York: Wiley.

MISCHEL, W. 1977. On the future of personality measurement. *American Psychologist* 32:246–254.

MISCHEL, W., and BENTLER, P. 1960. The ability of persons to predict their own behavior. Unpublished manuscript. Stanford University, Stanford, CA.

MISCHEL, W., EBBESEN, E.B., and ZEISS, A. 1972. Comparative effects of the reward stimulus and its cognitive presentation in voluntary delay. *Journal of Personality and Social Psychology* 21:204–218.

MOORE, B., MISCHEL, W., and ZEISS, A. 1976. Comparative effects of the reward stimulus and its cognitive representation in voluntary delay. *Journal of Personality and Social Psychology* 34:419–424.

MORENO, J.L. 1946. *Psychodrama.* Beacon, N.Y. Beacon House.

MOWRER, O.H. 1939. A stimulus-response analysis of anxiety and its role as a reinforcing agent. *Psychological Review* 46:553–565.

MOWRER, O.H. 1946. On the dual nature of learning—a reinterpretation of "conditioning" and "problem solving." *Harvard Educational Review* 17:102–148.

MUNJACK, D., CRISTOL, A., GOLDSTEIN, A., PHILLIPS, D., GOLDBERG, A., WHIPPLE, K., STAPLES, F., and KANNO, P. 1976. Behavioural treatment of orgasmic dysfunction: A controlled study. *British Journal of Psychiatry* 129:497–502.

MURRAY, E.J. 1956. A content-analysis method for studying psychotherapy. *Psychological Monographs* 70 Whole No. 420.

MURRAY, R.G., and HOBBS, S.A. 1977. The use of a self-imposed time-out procedure in the modification of excessive alcohol consumption. *Behavior Therapy and Experimental Psychiatry* 8:377–380.

NACK, B. 1978. Now, Bostock can laugh at April. *Newsday,* June 17, p. 23.

NATHAN, P.E., & HARRIS, S.L. 1975. *Psychopathology and society.* New York: McGraw-Hill.

NBC News, January 17, 1977.

NEALE, J.M. 1972. Comment on "Television violence and child aggression: A follow-up." In *Television and social behavior, vol. 3:Television and adolescent aggressiveness,* eds. G.A. Comstock and E.A. Rubinstein. Washington, D.C.: U.S. Government Printing Office.

NELSON, R.O., KAPUST, J.A., and DORSEY, B.L. 1978. Minimal reactivity of overt classroom observations on student and teacher behaviors. *Behavior Therapy,* 9:695–702.

NEMETZ, G.H., CRAIG, K.D., and REITH, G. 1978. Treatment of female sexual dysfunction through symbolic modeling. *Journal of Consulting and Clinical Psychology* 46:62–73.

NEWCOMB, H. 1847. *How to be a man: A book for boys.* Boston: Gould, Kendall and Lincoln.

Newsday. FTC plans hearings on child TV ads. March 1, 1978, p. 7.

New York Times. Book Review List, Feb. 19, 1978, p. 40.

NIETZEL, M.T., WINETT, R.A., MACDONALD, M.L., and DAVIDSON, W.S. 1977. *Behavioral approaches to community psychology.* New York: Pergamon Press.

NOVACO, R.W. 1976. Treatment of chronic anger through cognitive and relaxation controls. *Journal of Consulting and Clinical Psychology* 44:681.

NOVACO, R.W. 1977. Stress inoculation: A cognitive therapy for anger and its application in a case of depression. *Journal of Consulting and Clinical Psychology* 45:600–608.

O'CONNOR, R.D. 1969. Modification of social withdrawal through symbolic modeling. *Journal of Applied Behavior Analysis* 2:15–22.

O'LEARY, K.D. 1968. The effects of self-instruction on immoral behavior. *Journal of Experimental Child Psychology* 6:297–301.

O'LEARY, K.D. 1978. Token reinforcement programs in the classroom. In *Handbook of applied behavior analysis: Social and instructional processes,* eds. A.C. Catania and T.A. Brigham, pp. 179–207. New York: Irvington Publishers.

O'LEARY, K.D., and BECKER, W.C. 1967. Behavior modification of an adjustment class. A token reinforcement program. *Exceptional Children* 9:637–642.

O'LEARY, K.D., BECKER, W.C, EVANS, M.B., and SAUDARGAS, R.A. re1969. A token reinforcement program in a public school: Replication and systematic analysis. *Journal of Applied Behavior Analysis* 2:3–13.

O'LEARY, K.D., and BORKOVEC, T.C. 1978 Conceptual, methodological, and ethical problems of placebo groups in psychotherapy research. *American Psychologist,* 33:821–830.

O'LEARY, K.D., and DRABMAN, R. 1971. Token reinforcement programs in the classroom: A review. *Psychological Bulletin* 75:379–398.

O'LEARY, K.D., and JOHNSON, S.B. 1979. Psychological assessment. In *Psychopathological disorders of children,* 2nd Ed., eds. H.C. Quay and J.S. Werry. New York: Wiley.

O'LEARY, K.D., KAUFMAN, K.F., KASS, R.E., and DRABMAN, R.S. 1970. The effects of loud and soft reprimands on the behavior of disruptive students. *Exceptional Children* 37(2):145–155.

O'LEARY, K.D., KENT, R.N., and KANOWITZ, J. 1975. Shaping data collection congruent with experimental hypotheses. *Journal of Applied Behavior Analysis,* 1:92–100.

O'LEARY, K.D., and O'LEARY, S.G. 1977. *Classroom management: The successful use of behavior modification,* 2nd ed. New York: Pergamon Press.

O'LEARY, K.D., POULOS, R., and DEVINE, V.T. 1972. Tangible reinforcers. Bonuses or bribes? *Journal of Consulting and Clinical Psychology* 38:1–8.

O'LEARY, K.D., TURKEWITZ, H., and TAFFEL, S. 1973. Parent and therapist evaluation of behavior therapy in a child psychological clinic. *Journal of Consulting and Clinical Psychology* 41:289–293.

O'LEARY, K.D., and WILSON, G.T. 1975. *Behavior therapy: Application and outcome.* Englewood Cliffs: Prentice-Hall.

O'LEARY, S.G. 1974. Children's avoidance responses to three probabilities of threatened consequences. *Journal of Experimental Child Psychology* 17:507–518.

O'LEARY, S.G. 1976. *The use of punishment with normal children.* Paper presented at the Association for the Advancement of Behavior Therapy, New York, New York, December, 1976.

O'LEARY, S.G., and DUBEY, D.R. 1979. Applications of self-control procedures by children: A review. *Journal of Applied Behavior Analysis,* 12:111–127.

O'LEARY, S.G., and PELHAM, W.E. 1978. Behavior therapy and withdrawal of stimulant medication with hyperactive children. *Pediatrics* 61:211–217.

PATTERSON, G.R. 1974. Interventions for boys with conduct problems: Multiple settings, treatments, and criteria. *Journal of Consulting and Clinical Psychology,* 42:471–481.

PATTERSON, G.R., WEISS, R.L., and HOPPS, H. 1976. Training of marital skills: Some problems and concepts. In *Handbook of behavior modification and behavior therapy,* ed. H. Leitenberg. Englewood Cliffs: Prentice-Hall.

PAUL, G.L. 1966. *Insight versus desensitization in psychotherapy.* Stanford: Stanford University Press.

PAUL, G.P., and LENTZ, R.J. 1977. *Psychosocial treatment of chronic mental patients: (Milieu vs. social learning programs).* Cambridge, Mass.: Harvard University Press.

PAVLOV, I.P. 1927. *Conditioned reflexes: An investigation of the physiological activity of the cerebral cortex.* New York: Oxford University Press.

PETERSON, D.R. 1968. *The clinical study of social behavior.* New York: Appleton-Century-Crofts.

PHILIPS, C. 1977. The modification of tension headache pain using EMG biofeedback. *Behaviour Research and Therapy* 15:119–129.

PHILIPS, C. 1978. Tension headache: Theoretical problems. *Behaviour Research and Therapy* 16:249–261.

PHILLIPS, E.L. 1968. Achievement Place: Token reinforcement procedures in a home-style rehabilitation setting for "pre-delinquent" boys. *Journal of Applied Behavior Analysis* 1:213–223.

PHILLIPS, E.L., PHILLIPS, E.A., FIXSEN, D.L., and WOLF, M.M. 1971. Achievement Place: Modification of the behaviors of pre-delinquent boys within token economy. *Journal of Applied Behavior Analysis* 4:45–59.

PHILLIPS, E.L., PHILLIPS, E.A., WOLF, M.M., and FIXSEN, D.L. 1973. Achievement Place: Development of the elected manager system. *Journal of Applied Behavior Analysis* 6:541–561.

POMERANZ, D. 1975. *Preliminary report on the evaluation of our clinical training program.* Unpublished manuscript, State University of New York at Stony Brook, Long Island, N.Y.

PORTER, L.W., LAWLER, E.E., III, and HACKMAN, J.R. 1975. *Behavior in organizations.* New York: McGraw-Hill.

PORTERFIELD, J.K., HERBERT-JACKSON, E., and RISLEY, T.R. 1976. Contingent observation: An effective and acceptable procedure for reducing disruptive behavior of young children in a group setting. *Journal of Applied Behavior Analysis* 9:55–64.

POWELL, J., and AZRIN, N.H. 1968. The effects of shock as a punisher for cigarette smoking. *Journal of Applied Behavior Analysis* 1:63–71.

PREMACK, D. 1959. Toward empirical behavioral laws: I. Positive reinforcement. *Psychological Review* 66:219–233.

QUAY, H.C. 1979. Classification: Patterns of aggression, anxiety-withdrawal and immaturity. In *Psychopathological Disorders of Childhood,* eds. H.C. Quay and J.S. Werry. 2nd ed. New York: Wiley.

RACHLIN, H. 1976. *Behavior and learning.* San Francisco: W.H. Freeman and Company.

RACHLIN, H. 1976. *Introduction to modern behaviorism* 2nd ed. San Francisco: W.H. Freeman and Company.

RACHLIN, H. 1977. A review of M.J. Mahoney's *Cognition and Behavior Modification. Journal of Applied Behavior Analysis* 10:369–374.

RACHMAN, S. (Ed.) 1977a. *Contributions to medical psychology,* Vol. 1. Oxford: Pergamon Press.

RACHMAN, S. 1977b. The conditioning theory of fear-acquisition: A critical examination. *Behaviour Research and Therapy* 15:375–388.

RACHMAN, S. (Ed.) 1978. Perceived self-efficacy: Analyses of Bandura's theory of behavioural change. *Advances in Behaviour Research and Therapy,* 1:139–269.

RACHMAN, S., COBB, J., GREY, S., MacDONALD, B., MAWSON, D., SARTORY, G., and STERN, R. (in press) The behavioural treatment of obessional-compulsive disorders, with and without clomipramine. *Behaviour Research and Therapy.*

RACHMAN, S., and HODGSON, R. 1968. Experimentally induced "sexual fetishism": Replication and development. *Psychological Record* 18:25–27.

RACHMAN, S., and HODGSON, R. 1980. *Obsessions and compulsions.* Englewood Cliffs: Prentice-Hall.

RACHMAN, S., and WILSON, G.T. *Effects of psychotherapy.* Oxford: Pergamon Press, in press.

RATHUS, S.A. 1973. A 30-item schedule for assessing assertive behavior. *Behavior Therapy* 4:398–406.

REDD, W.H., MORRIS, E.K., and MARTIN, J.A. 1975. Effects of positive and negative adult-child interactions on children's social preference. *Journal of Experimental Child Psychology* 19:153–164.

REDMOND, D.P., GAYLOR, M.S., and McDONALD, R.H. 1974. Blood pressure and heart-rate to verbal instruction and relaxation in hypertension. *Psychosomatic Medicine* 36:285–297.

REISS, M.L., PIOTROWSKI, W.D., and BAILEY, J.S. 1976. Behavioral community psychology: Encouraging low-income parents to seek dental care for their children. *Journal of Applied Behavior Analysis* 9:387–397.

RESCORLA, R.A., and SOLOMON, R.L. 1967. Two-process learning theory: Relationships between Pavlovian conditioning and instrumental learning. *Psychological Review* 74:151–182.

RESCORLA, R., and WAGNER, A. 1972. A theory of Pavlovian conditioning: Variations in the effectiveness of reinforcement and nonreinforcement. In *Classical conditioning II,* eds. A.H. Black and W.F. Prokasy. New York: Appleton-Century-Crofts.

REYNOLDS, G.S. 1968. *A primer of operant conditioning.* Glenview, Illinois: Scott, Foresman and Co.

RINGER, R.J. 1977. *Looking Out for Number One.* New York: Funk & Wagnalls.

RISLEY, T. 1968. The effects and side effects of punishing the autistic behavior of a deviant child. *Journal of Applied Behavior Analysis* 1:21–34.

RISLEY, T.R., CLARK, H.B., and CATALDO, M.F. 1976. Behavior technology for the normal, middle-class family. In *Behavior modification and families,* eds. E.J. Mash, L.A. Hamerlynck, and L.C. Handy. New York: Brunner/Mazel.

RITTER, B. 1968. The group treatment of children's snake phobias, using vicarious and contact desensitization procedures. *Behaviour Research and Therapy* 6:1–6.

ROBERTS, R.R., Jr., and RENZAGLIA, G.A. 1965. The influence of tape recording on counseling. *Journal of Counseling Psychology* 12:10–16.

ROBIN, A., SCHNEIDER, M., and DOLNICK, M. 1976. The Turtle Technique: An extended case study of self-control in the classroom. *Psychology in The Schools* 13:444–453.

ROGERS, C.R. 1951. *Client centered therapy: Its current practice, limitations, and theory.* Boston: Houghton Mifflin.

ROGERS, C.R. 1961. *On becoming a person: A therapist's view of psychotherapy.* Boston: Houghton Mifflin.

ROGERS, T., and CRAIGHEAD, W.E. 1977. Physiological responses to self-statements: The effects of statement valence and discrepancy. *Cognitive Therapy and Research* 1:99–120.

ROMANCZYK, R.G. 1974. Self-monitoring in the treatment of obesity: Parameters of reactivity. *Behavior Therapy* 5:530–540.

ROMANCZYK, R.G., TRACEY, D.A., WILSON, G.T., and THORPE, G.L. 1973. Behavioral techniques in the treatment of obesity: A comparative analysis. *Behaviour Research and Therapy* 11:629–640.

ROMANCZYK, R.G., and GOREN, E.R. 1975. Seven self-injurious behaviors: The problem of clinical control. *Journal of Consulting and Clinical Psychology* 43:730–739.

ROOTH, F.G., and MARKS, I.M. 1974. Persistent exhibitionism: short-term response to self-regulation and relaxation treatment. *Archives of Sexual Behavior* 3:227–248.

ROSEN, G.M., GLASGOW, R.E., and BARRERA, M. 1976. A controlled study to assess the clinical efficacy of totally self-administered systematic desensitization. *Journal of Consulting and Clinical Psychology* 44:208–217.

ROSENBAUM, M.S., and DRABMAN, R.S. in press. Self-control training in the classroom: A review and critique. *Journal of Applied Behavior Analysis.*

ROSENTHAL, R. 1969. Interpersonal expectations: Effects of the experimenter's hypothesis. In *Artifact in behavioral research,* eds. R. Rosenthal and R.L. Rosnow. New York: Academic Press.

ROSENTHAL, T.L., and BANDURA, A. 1978. Psychological modeling: Theory and practice. In *Handbook of psychotherapy and behavior change,* eds. S.L. Garfield and A.E. Bergin. 2d ed. New York: Wiley.

ROSENTHAL, T.L., and ZIMMERMAN, B.J. 1978. *Social learning and cognition.* New York: Academic Press.

RUBINSTEIN, E.A., and SPRAFKIN, J.N. 1978. Television: A channel to social values. In *Education for values,* ed. D.C. McClelland. Report to Cleveland Foundation.

RUSH, A.J., BECK, A.T., KOVACS, M., and HOLLON, S. 1977. Comparative efficacy of cognitive therapy and pharmacotherapy in the treatment of depressed outpatients. *Cognitive Therapy and Research* 1:17–37.

RUSSELL, A., and WINKLER, R. 1977. Effectiveness of assertive training and homosexual guidance service groups designed to improve homosexual functioning. *Journal of Consulting and Clinical Psychology* 45:1–13.

RUTTER, M. Epidemiology. In *Psychopathological disorders of children,* eds. H.C. Quay and J.S. Werry. New York: Wiley, in press.

SAGER, C. 1976. *Marriage contracts and couples' therapy.* New York: Brunner/Mazel.

SAGOTSKY, G., PATTERSON, C.J., and LEPPER, M.R. 1978. Effects of training in self-monitoring and goal-setting techniques on classroom study behavior and academic performance. *Journal of Experimental Child Psychology* 25:242–253.

SANTOGROSSI, D.A., and O'LEARY, K.D. 1978. *External monitoring of self-administered reinforcement for academic task performance.* Unpublished manuscript, Purdue University, West Lafayette, Indiana.

SANTOGROSSI, D.A., O'LEARY, K.D. ROMANCZYK, R.G., and KAUFMAN, K.F 1973. Self-evaluation by adolescents in a psychiatric hospital school token program. *Journal of Applied Behavior Analysis* 6:277–287.

SCHREIBER, F. 1974. *Sybil.* New York: Warner Books.

SCHULMANN, J.L., and REISMAN, J.M. 1959. An objective measurement of hyperactivity. *American Journal of Mental Deficiency* 64:455–456.

SCHWARTZ, G., FAIR, P.L., SALT, P., MANDEL, M., and KLERMAN, G.L. 1976. Facial muscle patterning to affective imagery in depressed and nondepressed subjects. *Science* 192:489–491.

SCHWARTZ, G.E., and WEISS, S.M. 1977. What is behavioral medicine? *Psychosomatic Medicine* 39:377–381.

SCOTT, P.M., BURTON, R.V., and YARROW, M.R. 1967. Social reinforcement under natural conditions. *Child Development* 38:53–63.

SEARS, R.R., MACCOBY, E.E., and LEVIN, H. 1957. *Patterns of child rearing.* Evanston, Ill.: Row Peterson.

SEAVER, W.B., and PATTERSON, A.H. 1976. Decreasing fuel oil consumption through feedback and social commendation. *Journal of Applied Behavior Analysis* 9: 147–152.

SELIGMAN, M.E.P. 1971. Phobias and preparedness. *Behavior Therapy* 2:307–320.

SELIGMAN, M.E.P. 1975. *Helplessness.* San Francisco, CA: Freeman.

SHAPIRO, D. 1973. Role of feedback and instructions in the voluntary control of human blood pressure. *Japanese Journal of Biofeedback Research* 1:2–9.

SHAPIRO, D., SCHWARTZ, G.E., and TURSKY, B. 1972. Control of diastolic blood pressure in man by feedback and reinforcement. *Psychophysiology* 9:256–304.

SHAPIRO, D., and SURWIT, R.S. 1976. Learned control of physiological function and disease. In *Handbook of behavior modification and behavior therapy,* ed. H. Leitenberg. Englewood Cliffs: Prentice-Hall.

SHAW, B.F. 1977. Comparison of cognitive therapy and behavior therapy in the treatment of depression. *Journal of Consulting and Clinical Psychology* 45:543–551.

SHEPPARD, N., Jr. 1977. A lesson in prison life, taught by experts. *N.Y. Times,* Jan. 25, p. 39:3.

SHIMP, C.P. 1976. Short-term memory in the pidgeon: The previously reinforced response. *Journal of the Experimental Analysis of Behavior* 26:487–493.

SKINNER, B.F. 1938. *Behavior of organisms.* New York: Appleton-Century-Crofts.

SKINNER, B.F. 1948. *Walden two.* New York: Macmillan.

SKINNER, B.F. 1953. *Science and human behavior.* New York: Macmillan.

SKINNER, B.F. 1963. Behaviorism at fifty. *Science* 140:951–958.

SKINNER, B.F. 1968. Reflections on a decade of teaching machines. *Teachers College Record* 65:168–177.

SKINNER, B.F. 1971. *Beyond freedom and dignity.* New York: Alfred A. Knopf.

SKINNER, B.F. 1967. B.F. Skinner. In *A history of psychology in autobiography,* eds. E.G. Boring and G. Lindzey. vol. 5. New York: Appleton-Century-Crofts.

SLABY, R.G., QUAFORTH, G.R., and MCCONNACHIE, G.A. 1976. Television violence and its sponsors. *Journal of Communication* 26:88–96.

SLOANE, R.B., STAPLES, F.R., CRISTOL, A.H., YORKSTON, N.H., and WHIPPLE, K. 1975. *Psychotherapy versus behavior therapy.* Cambridge, Mass.: Harvard University Press.

SNYDER, M., TANKE, E.D., and BERSCHEID, E. 1977. Social perception and interpersonal behavior: On the self-fulfilling nature of social stereotypes. *Journal of Personality and Social Psychology,* 35:656–66.

SOLOMON, R.L. 1964. Punishment. *American Psychologist,* 19:239–253.

SOLOMON, R.L., and BRUSH, E.S. 1956. Experimentally derived conceptions of anxiety and aversion. In *Nebraska symposium on motivation, 1956,* ed. M.R. Jones. Lincoln, Nebraska: University of Nebraska Press.

SPERLING, M. 1971. Sleep disturbances in children. In *Modern Perspectives in international child psychiatry,* ed. J.G. Howells. New York Brunner/Mazel.

SPOCK, B. 1940. *Baby and child care.* rev. ed. (1957). New York: Pocket Books.

SPRAFKIN, J.N., LIEBERT, R.M., and POULOS, R.W. 1975. Effects of a prosocial televised example on children's helping. *Journal of Experimental Child Psychology* 20:119–126.

STAMPFL, T.G., and LEVIS, D.J. 1967. Essentials of implosive therapy: A learning-theory-based psychodynamic behavioral therapy. *Journal of Abnormal Psychology,* 72:496–503.

STEIN, A.H., and FRIEDRICH, L.K. 1972. Television content and young children's behavior. In *Television and social behavior, Vol. 2:Television and social learning.* eds. J.P. Murray, E.A. Rubinstein, and G.A. Comstock. Washington, D.C.: GPO.

STEINMAN, W.M. 1977. Generalized imitation and the setting event concept. In *New developments in behavioral research,* eds. B. Etzel, J. LeBlanc, and D.M. Baer. Hillsdale, N.J.: Lawrnece Eilbaum.

STEINMARK, S.W., and BORKOVEC, T.D. 1974. Active and placebo treatment effects on moderate insomnia under counterdemand and positive demand instructions. *Journal of Abnormal Psychology* 83:157–163.

STERN, R., and MARKS, I. 1973. Brief and prolonged flooding. *Archives of General Psychiatry* 28:270–276.

STERNGLANZ, S.H., and SERBIN, L.A. 1974. Sex role stereotyping in children's television programs. *Developmental Psychology* 10:710–715.

STOKES, T.F., and BAER, D.M. 1977. An implicit technology of generalization. *Journal of Applied Behavior Analysis* 10:349–368.

STOLZ, S.B., and others. 1978. *Ethical issues in behavior modification.* San Francisco: Jossey-Bass.

STONE, N., and BORKOVEC, T.D. 1975. The paradoxical effect of brief CS exposure on analogue phobic subjects. *Behaviour Research and Therapy* 13:51–54.

STOYVA, J., ed. 1978. *Biofeedback and self-control.* Chicago, Illinois: Aldine.

STUART, R.B. 1967. Behavioral control of overeating. *Behaviour Research and Therapy* 5:357–365.

STUART, R.B. 1977. *Behavioral self-management: Strategies, techniques, and outcomes.* New York: Brunner/Mazel.

STUMPHAUZER, J.S., AIKEN, T.W., and VELOZ, E.V. 1977. East side story: Behavioral analysis of a high juvenile crime community. *Behavioral Disorders* 2:76–84.

STUNKARD, A.J., and MAHONEY, M.J. 1976. Behavioral treatment of the eating disorders. In *Handbook of behavior modification and behavior therapy,* ed. H. Leitenberg. New York: Appleton-Century-Crofts.

STURGIS, E.T., TOLLISON, C.D., and ADAMS, H.E. 1978. Modification of combined. migraine-muscle contraction headaches using BVP and EMG feedback. *Journal of Applied Behavior Analysis* 11:215–223.

SULLIVAN, H.S. 1954. *The psychiatric interview.* New York: Norton.

SULZER-AZAROFF, B., and MAYER, G.R. 1977. *Applying behavior-analysis procedures with children and youth.* New York: Holt, Rinehart and Winston.

SURWIT, R.S., SHAPIRO, D., and GOOD, M.I. 1978. Comparison of cardiovascular biofeedback, neuromuscular biofeedback, and meditation in the treatment of borderline essential hypertension. *Journal of Consulting and Clinical Psychology* 46:252–263.

SWAN, G.E., and MACDONALD, M.L. 1978. Behavior therapy in practice: A national survey of behavior therapists. *Behavior Therapy,* 9:799–807.

TARLER-BENLOLO, L. 1978. The role of relaxation in biofeedback training: A critical review of the literature. *Psychological Bulletin,* 85:727–755.

TASTO, D.L., HICKSON, R., and RUBIN, S.E. 1971. Scaled profile analysis of fear survey schedule factors *Behavior Therapy* 2:543–549.

TAYLOR, F.G., and MARSHAL W.L. 1977. Experimental analysis of a cognitive behavioral therapy for depression. *Cognitive Therapy and Research* 1:59–72.

THARP, R.G., and WETZEL, R.J. 1969. *Behavior modification in the natural environment.* New York: Academic Press.

THASE, M.E., and MOSS, M.K. 1976. The relative efficacy of covert modeling procedures and guided participant modeling on the reduction of avoidance behavior. *Journal of Behavior Therapy and Experimental Psychiatry* 7:7–12.

THOMAS, D.A., BECKER, W.C., and ARMSTRONG, M. 1968. Production and elimination of disruptive classroom behavior by systematically varying teacher's attention. *Journal of Applied Behavior Analysis* 1:35–45.

THORESEN, C.E., and MAHONEY, M.J. 1974. *Behavioral self-control.* New York: Holt, Rinehart, and Winston.

THORPE, G.L. 1975. Desensitization, behavior rehearsal, self-instructional training and placebo effects on assertive-refusal behavior. *European Journal of Behavioural Analysis and Modification* 1:30–44.

Time. Commoner cancer screen; mutagenic screening test for carcinogenicity. 106, Aug. 11, 1975, pp. 45–50.

Time. Conquering the quiet killer. Medicine Section. Jan. 13, 1975, pp. 60–64.

TIMM, F.H. 1975. *Effects of teacher behavior on student behavior and student report.* Unpublished manuscript. University of Wisconsin, Oskosh, Wisconsin.

TRUAX, C.B. 1966. Reinforcement and nonreinforcement in Rogerian psychotherapy. *Journal of Abnormal and Social Psychology* 71:1–9.

TUCKER, C.M. 1976. *Effects of reasons on children's behavior.* Unpublished manuscript. State University of New York, Stony Brook, New York.

TURKEWITZ, H., O'LEARY, K.D., and IRONSMITH, M. 1975. Generalization and maintenance of appropriate behavior through self-control. *Journal of Consulting and Clinical Psychology* 43:577–583.

TURNER, S.M., HERSEN, M., BELLACK, A.S., and WELLS, K.C. 1979. Behavioral treatment of obsessive-compulsive neurosis. *Behaviour Research and Therapy,* 17:95–106.

TWENTYMAN, C.T., and MCFALL, R.M. 1975. Behavioral training of social skills in shy males. *Journal of Consulting and Clinical Psychology,* 43:384–395.

ULLMANN, L.P., and KRASNER, L. 1965. *Case studies in behavior modification.* New York: Holt, Rinehart and Winston.

ULLMANN, L.P., and KRASNER, L. 1975. *A psychological approach to abnormal behavior.* 2nd ed. Englewood Cliffs: Prentice-Hall.

VERNA, G.B. 1977. Effects of four-hour delay of punishment under two conditions of verbal instruction. *Child Development* 48:621–624.

VERNON, D.T. 1973. Use of modeling to modify children's responses to a natural, potentially stressful situation. *Journal of Applied Psychology* 58:351–356.

VERNON, D.T. 1974. Modeling and birth order in responses to painful stimuli. *Journal of Personality and Social Psychology,* 29:794–799.

VERNON, D.T., and BAILEY, W.C. 1974. The use of motion pictures in the psychological preparation of children for induction of anasthesia. *Anasthesiology,* 40:68–72.

WACHTEL, P.L. 1977. *Psychoanalysis and behavior therapy: Towards an integration.* New York: Basic Books.

WALEN, S., HAUSERMAN, N.M., and LAVIN, P.J. 1977. *Clinical guide to behavior therapy.* Baltimore: Williams and Wilkins Co.

WALKER, S. 1977. *Help for the hyperactive child.* New York: Houghton-Mifflin Co.

WALLACE, I. 1977. Self-control techniques of famous novelists. *Journal of Applied Behavior Analysis* 10:515–525.

WALTERS, R.H., and ANDRES, D. 1967. *Punishment procedures and self-control.* Paper presented at the Annual Meeting of the American Psychological Association, Washington, D.C., 1967.

WALTERS, R.H., PARKE, R.D., and CANE, V.A. 1965. Timing of punishment and the observation of consequences to others as determinants of response inhibition. *Journal of Experimental Child Psychology* 2:10–30.

WARDEN, C.J., and AYLESWORTH, M. 1927. The relative value of reward and punishment in the formation of a visual discrimination habit in the white rat. *Journal of Comparative Psychology,* 7:117–127.

WATSON, D., and FRIEND, R. 1969. Measurement of social-evaluative anxiety. *Journal of Consulting and Clinical Psychology,* 33:448–457.

WATSON, J.B., and RAYNER, R. 1920. Conditioned emotional reactions. *Journal of Experimental Psychology* 3:1–14.

WEINER, H. 1962. Some effects of response cost upon human operant behavior. *Journal of the Experimental Analysis of Behavior* 5:201–208.

WEXLER, D.B. 1973. Token and taboo: Behavior modification, token economies, and the law. *California Law Review* 61:81–109.

WHALEN, C.K., and HENKER, B. 1976. Psychostimulants and children: A review and analysis. *Psychological Bulletin* 83:1113–1130.

WHEELIS, A. 1973. *How People Change.* New York: Harper & Row.

WHITE, G.D. 1977. The effects of observer presence on the activity level of families. *Journal of Applied Behavior Analysis* 10:734.

WHITE, M.A. 1975. Natural rates of teacher approval and disapproval in the classroom. *Journal of Applied Behavior Analysis* 8:367–372.

WHITEHURST, G.J. 1978. Observational learning. In *Handbook of applied behavioral research: Social and instructional processes,* eds. T.A. Brigham and A.C. Catania. New York: Irvington and Halstead.

WIENS, A.N., 1976. Pharmacological aversive counter-conditioning to alcohol in a private hospital: One-year follow-up. *Journal of Studies on Alcohol* 37:1320–1324.

WIGGINS, J.S. 1973. *Personality and prediction: Principles of personality assessment.* Reading, Mass.: Addison-Wesley.

WILEY, R.E. 1977. Family viewing: A balancing of interests. *Journal of Communication* 27:188–192.

WILLIAMS, C.D. 1959. Case report: The elimination of tantrum behavior by extinction procedures. *Journal of Abnormal and Social Psychology* 59:269.

WILSON, G.T. 1973. Innovations in the modification of phobic behaviors in two clinical cases. *Behavior Therapy* 4:426–430.

WILSON, G.T. 1978a. Aversion therapy for alcoholism: Issues, ethics, and evidence. In *Behavioral assessment and treatment of alcoholism,* eds. G.A. Marlatt and P.E. Nathan. New Brunswick, NJ: Center for Alcohol Studies.

WILSON, G.T. 1978b. Booze, beliefs, and behavior: Cognitive processes in alcohol use and abuse. In *Alcoholism: New directions in behavioral research and treatment,* eds. P.E. Nathan and G.A. Marlatt. New York: Plenum Press.

WILSON, G.T. 1978c. Cognitive behavior therapy with sexual disorders. New York: BMA Audio-Cassette Programs.

WILSON, G.T. 1978d. Ethical and professional issues in sex therapy: Comments on Bailey's "Psychotherapy or massage parlor technology?" *Journal of Consulting and Clinical Psychology,* 46:1510–1514.

WILSON, G.T. 1978e. On the much discussed nature of the term "behavior therapy." *Behavior Therapy,* 9:89–98.

WILSON, G.T. 1978f. The importance of being theoretical: Comments on Bandura's "Self-efficacy: Toward a unifying theory of behavioral change." *Advances in Behaviour Research and Therapy,* 1:217–230.

WILSON, G.T. 1979. Cognitive factors in life-style changes: A social learning perspective. In *Behavioral medicine,* ed. P. Davidson. New York: Brunner/Mazel.

WILSON, G.T., and DAVISON, G.C. 1969. Aversion techniques in behavior therapy: Some theoretical and meta-theoretical considerations. *Journal of Consulting and Clinical Psychology,* 33:327–329.

WILSON, G.T., and DAVISON, G.C. 1971. Processes of fear reduction in systematic desensitization: Animal studies. *Psychological Bulletin* 76:1–14.

WILSON, G.T., and DAVISON, G.C. 1974. Behavior therapy and homosexuality: A critical perspective. *Behavior Therapy* 5:16–28.

WILSON, G.T., and EVANS, I.M. 1976. Adult behavior therapy and the therapist-client relationship. In *Annual review of behavior therapy: Theory and Practice,* eds. G.M. Franks and G.T. Wilson. vol. IV. New York: Brunner/Mazel.

WILSON, G.T., and EVANS, I.M. 1977. The therapist-client relationship in behavior therapy. In *The therapist's contribution to effective psychotherapy: An empirical approach,* eds. R.S. Gurman and A.M. Razin New York: Pergamon Press.

WILSON, G.T., and LAWSON, D.M. 1976. The effects of alcohol on sexual arousal in women. *Journal of Abnormal Psychology* 85:489–497.

WINCZE, J.P., and CAIRD, W.K. 1976. The effects of systematic desensitization and video desensitization in the treatment of essential sexual dysfunction in women. *Behavior Therapy,* 7:335–342.

WOLFF, H.G. 1963. *Headache and other head pain.* New York: Oxford University Press.

WOLPE, J. 1958. *Psychotherapy by reciprocal inhibition.* Stanford: Stanford University Press.

WOLPE, J. 1976. Behavior therapy and its malcontents—II. Multimodal eclecticism, cognitive exclusivism and "exposure" empiricism. *Journal of Behavior Therapy and Experimental Psychiatry* 7:109–116.

WOLPE, J., and LANG, P.J. 1964. A fear survey schedule for use in behavior therapy. *Behaviour Research and Therapy* 2:27–30.

WOOD, R., and FLYNN, J.M. 1978. A self-evaluation token system versus an external evaluation token system alone in a residential setting with predelinquent youths. *Journal of Applied Behavior Analysis* 11:503–512.

WOOLFOLK, A.E., WOOLFOLK, R.L., and WILSON, G.T. 1977. A rose by another name . . .: Labeling bias and attitudes toward behavior modification. *Journal of Consulting and Clinical Psychology* 45:184–191.

WOOLFOLK, R.L., and RICHARDSON, F.C. 1978. *Stress, sanity, and survival.* New York: Soverign.

ZEISS, A.M., ROSEN, G.M., and ZEISS, R.A. 1977. Orgasm during intercourse: A treatment strategy for women. *Journal of Consulting and Clinical Psychology* 45:891–895.

ZIMMERMAN, B.J. 1977. Modeling. In H.L. Hom, Jr., & P.A. Robinson (Eds.), *Psychological processes in early education.* New York: Academic Press.

ZLUTNICK, S., MAYVILLE, W.J., and MOFFAT, S. 1975. Modification of seizure disorders: The interruption of behavioral chains. *Journal of Applied Behavior Analysis* 8:1–12.

Author Index